DISCARDED

John Dryden (1631–1700)

His Politics, His Plays, and His Poets

John Dryden (1631–1700)

His Politics, His Plays, and His Poets

A Tercentenary Celebration
Held at Yale University
6–7 October, 2000

Edited by
Claude Rawson and Aaron Santesso

DELAWARE

Newark: University of Delaware Press
London: Associated University Presses

© 2004 by Rosemont Publishing & Printing Corp.

All rights reserved. Authorization to photocopy items for internal or personal use, or the internal or personal use of specific clients, is granted by the copyright owner, provided that a base fee of $10.00, plus eight cents per page, per copy is paid directly to the Copyright Clearance Center, 222 Rosewood Drive, Danvers, Massachusetts 01923. [0-87413-842-6/04 $10.00 + 8¢ pp, pc.]

Other than as indicated in the foregoing, this book may not be reproduced, in whole or in part, in any form except as permitted by Sections 107 and 108 of the U.S. Copyright Law, and except for brief quotes appearing in reviews in the public press.

Associated University Presses
2010 Eastpark Boulevard
Cranbury, NJ 08512

Associated University Presses
Unit 304
The Chandlery
50 Westminster Bridge Road
London SE1 7QY

Associated University Presses
P.O. Box 338, Port Credit
Mississauga, Ontario
Canada L5G 4L8

The paper used in this publication meets the requirements of the American National Standard for Permanence of Paper for Printed Library Materials Z39.48-1984.

Library of Congress Cataloging-in-Publication Data

John Dryden (1631–1700) : his politics, his plays, and his poets / edited by Claude Rawson and Aaron Santesso.
   p. cm.
"A tercentenary celebration held at Yale University, 6–7 October, 2000."
   Includes bibliographical references and index.
   ISBN 0-87413-842-6 (alk. paper)
   1. Dryden, John, 1631–1700—Criticism and interpretation. 2. Dryden, John, 1631–1700—Political and social views. 3. Dryden, John, 1631–1700—Knowledge—Literature. 4. Dryden, John, 1631–1700—Dramatic works. I. Rawson, Claude Julien. II. Santesso, Aaron, 1972–
PR3424 .J635   2003
821'.4—dc21
                                                    2003009220

PRINTED IN THE UNITED STATES OF AMERICA

In Memoriam

Louis L. Martz
1913–2001

Contents

Preface and Acknowledgments   9
  CLAUDE RAWSON

Part I: The Court, the Town, and the Playhouse

Dryden's London   15
  LAWRENCE MANLEY

Dryden, Rochester, and the Invention of the "Town"   36
  HAROLD LOVE

Dryden's Drama: A Revaluation   52
  HOWARD ERSKINE-HILL

Dryden's *The Spanish Fryar:* Modernity and Exclusion   65
  DAVID WOMERSLEY

John Dryden's Politics: The Rabble and Sovereignty   86
  MAXIMILLIAN NOVAK

Part II: Dryden and the Poets

Mastering Virgil   109
  STEVEN ZWICKER

Dryden's Persius   123
  EMRYS JONES

Safe Sex? Dryden's Translation of Juvenal's Sixth Satire   139
  SUSANNA MORTON BRAUND

The Janus Poet: Dryden's Critique of Shakespeare   158
  PAUL HAMMOND

Dryden's Poem of Paradise: *The State Of Innocence, And Fall Of Man*   180
  LOUIS L. MARTZ

Dryden, Marvell, and the Painful Lesson of Laughter   198
  ANNABEL PATTERSON

Dryden and Swift   217
  IAN HIGGINS

Plotting Parallel Lives: Pope's "A Parallel of the
Characters of Mr. Dryden and Mr. Pope" 235
   VALERIE RUMBOLD
Dryden's *Hamlet:* The Unwritten Masterpiece 263
   BARBARA EVERETT

Appendix: The Yale Production of *Marriage A-la-Mode* 279
Contributors 292
Index 295

Preface and Acknowledgments
CLAUDE RAWSON

IN PLANNING THIS TERCENTENARY CELEBRATION, THE ORGANIZERS of this conference, Vincent Giroud and I, were acutely conscious that this was not the only one to mark the anniversary of Dryden's death three hundred years ago. Though we naturally hoped to achieve a broadly representative view of his extraordinary range, we chose also to narrow our focus to two aspects of his works: the politics of his plays, and his relations with some of the poets, ancient and modern, who helped to shape his work, or who, in his own and the next generation, absorbed his influence, or regarded him with hostility. Even in these two areas, systematic coverage, either of his drama or his poetic relationships, would have been impossible. In the case of the poets, we were especially conscious of the omission of Homer, Lucretius, Ovid, and Chaucer. But we trust that this volume's attention to what might be called Dryden's Virgil, Persius, Juvenal, Shakespeare, Milton, Marvell, Rochester, Swift, and Pope will nevertheless provide a generous sampling of the poetic tradition in which Dryden was an unignorable and distinctive presence.

The celebration was one to which Louis Martz contributed one of his last scholarly compositions. It was written specially for the occasion, and delivered with the intellectual energy and grace that all who knew him recognized as the special mark of his long and brilliant career as a teacher and scholar. He was a cherished friend, colleague, or teacher of many of the participants, and none of us escaped the enriching influence of his writings. He died before this volume could appear, and it is dedicated, with the deepest affection and respect, to his memory.

The celebration could not have taken place without the support and encouragement of the Beinecke Rare Book and Manuscript Library at Yale University, and especially of Vincent Giroud, its Curator of Modern Books and Manuscripts. He was in the fullest sense a codirector of this event, a wise counselor, generous host, and administrator of genius. Warm thanks for additional hospitality and support are also due to Maggie Powell, Librarian of the Lewis Walpole Library at Farmington, and to Patrick McCaughey, at the time Director of the Yale Center for British Art, where all the papers were delivered.

Donald Mell was good enough to preside over some of the papers. In his capacity as Director of the University of Delaware Press, he subsequently brought about the publication of these papers. This book owes much to his active interest, and to the diligent collaboration of my coeditor, Aaron Santesso.

John Dryden (1631–1700)

His Politics, His Plays,
and His Poets

Frontispiece to *The Conquest of Granada*, from *The Dramatick Works of John Dryden, Esq.* (Tonson, London, 1735). By permission of the Yale University Libraries.

Part I
The Court, the Town, and the Playhouse

Dryden's London

LAWRENCE MANLEY

DRYDEN FORMALLY ADDRESSED HIMSELF TO THE CITY OF LONDON ON two separate occasions. On the first of these, in the Dedication to *Annus Mirabilis* (1667), it was to laud London for its "true Loyalty" and to anticipate the city's heroic recovery from the devastating fire of September 1666. Under the solicitous rule of Charles II, Dryden prophesies, a new *kind* of city will emerge:

> More great then humane, now, and more *August,*
>   New deifi'd she from her fires does rise:
> Her widening streets on new foundations trust,
>   And, opening, into larger parts she flies.
>   (1177–80)[1]

A new *kind* of city because renovation here takes the form of expansion, a participial widening and opening in which quantity, scale, and scope become the measure of qualitative change, an enlarging of the spirit. When Dryden boasted in his dedication of being "the first who ever presented a work of this nature to the Metropolis of any Nation," he was pointing (I suspect) not simply to the novelty of the poem's kind or decorum, but also to the novelty of addressing London *as* a metropolis. For part of what the poem enacts is a transformation of London itself from a chartered municipality and merchant commune into a metropolis whose economic influence extends the nation's reach beyond its shores to encompass the globe. As the tides of the Thames bear the incoming wealth of East and West, London becomes the center of an *imperium* first predicted in the poem's earlier digression on the Royal Society, where "Instructed ships shall sail to quick Commerce" and make "one City of the Universe" (649–51).

Paul Hammond has observed that Dryden is here invoking the Ovidian formula, *Romanae spatium est urbis & orbis idem.*[2] This allusion is perhaps meant to supplant the Virgilian epigraph on the fall of Troy that heads the poem: *Urbs antiqua ruit, multa dominata per annos*. The fire of London, which Dryden likens to the incendiary mobs of the Puritan revolution, has burned itself out; in doing so, it has purged away the old municipality, which had served, in Milton's terms, as the "mansion house of liberty."[3] Rejoined to the king to form what the Dedication calls "a pair of matchless Lovers," London is espoused to a future in which its local identity and fiercely guarded municipal privileges are exchanged for its new role as metropolis and seat of empire.

Dryden's second formal address to the city is the apostrophe to London in *The Medall*, published in early 1682, just after a Whig-dominated London grand jury had returned a verdict of *ignoramus* on high treason charges against the Earl of Shaftesbury. Like Dryden's earlier address to London, this one is also based on a vision of expanding metropolitan influence, but to far different effect:

> *London*, thou great *Emporium* of our Isle,
> O, thou too bounteous, thou too fruitfull *Nile*!
> How shall I praise or curse to thy desert!
> Or separate thy sound, from thy corrupted part!
> I call'd thee *Nile*; the parallel will stand:
> Thy tydes of Wealth o'rflow the fattend Land;
> Yet Monsters from thy large increase we find;
> Engender'd on the Slyme thou leav'st behind.
>
> (167–74)

Here, as epic prophecy yields to Jeremiad and the bounteous tides of the Thames are transformed into the fecundating floods of the Nile, London is no longer the old Troy, an obstacle to empire, but a fatal and seductive Egypt, the center of a monstrous and terrifying counter-empire.

Just as striking as the obvious differences between these two addresses to the city is the continuity in Dryden's vision of London as a metropolis whose influence transcends its boundaries and whose quantitative expansion transforms the quality of moral and political life. This is in fact a vision that in many ways reflects the actual development of London in the course of the seventeenth century, as it became, by the end of Dryden's lifetime, the second largest metropolis in Europe after Paris. Even as Dryden was writing his greatest satires on the Exclusion Crisis and pondering the political opposition developing in the City, he would have found cold comfort in the spate of publications celebrating the accomplishment of the very developments he had prophesied in *Annus Mirabilis*. In his *Essay in Political Arithmetick, Concerning the Growth of London* (1682), Sir William Petty, in the scientific spirit of the age, gathered statistics from various sources to suggest "that London doubles [its population] in Forty Years, and all England in Three hundred and sixty Years." Petty was drawing on the earlier statistical research of Captain John Graunt, who had concluded, even before the plague of 1665, "Let the mortality be what it will, the City repairs its loss of inhabitants within two years," through immigration from the countryside. Graunt's findings, augmented and frequently republished after 1665, pointed to a disturbing consequence: "that London, the Metropolis of England, is perhaps a Head too big for the Body, and possibly too strong . . . this Head grows three times as fast as the Body to which it belongs." In 1682, Petty came to the staggering conclusion that if growth were to proceed at the current differential rates, then by "1840, the People of the City will be 10718880, and those of the whole Country but 10917389."[4] Urbs become orb, "too bounteous" indeed, a thought that might have been alarming to Tories contemplating the London tumults of the Excursion Crisis years.

The statistics, however cracked, are an index to the way people were thinking about the consequences of metropolitan expansion, the way in which they rightly saw the implications of London's cultural domination of the nation. This domination was the result of many developments, including the growth of national markets and patterns of distribution and migration that doubled carrying services from the capital to the countryside between 1637 and 1715 and made one in nine Englishmen Londoners at some point in their lifetimes.[5] A taste for London goods, fashions, and ideas spread along the coaching thoroughfares to regional centers. To give just one example: by 1675 the newly fashionable coffeehouses had become numerous "not only here in our metropolis"—it is estimated there were perhaps 2000 in greater London by 1700—"but in . . . most cities and eminent towns throughout the nation."[6] During the Exclusion Crisis coffeehouses served as meeting places for political clubs and key distribution points for propaganda from the capital. In one pamphlet of 1682, a country gentleman complained that "Reports, like Bubbling *Circles* in Water, still grow *larger* as they are *further* from the Place where raised . . . Why, Man! we cannot send a Servant-wench to Market but she brings us home *Soap* wrapt up in an *Heraclitus* . . . our Coffee-Houses are stuff'd with 'um; and still, like *Fairy-Gifts*, the *Devil* knows who sends 'um us."[7]

At the center of this extended influence was the vibrant life of the metropolis itself, with a burgeoning variety of communities and cultures that paradoxically enhanced London's cultural domination through the centrifugal effects of greater heterogeneity, mobility, and innovation, and through the diversification and specialization of markets, tastes, and social roles. The effects of this variety were celebrated in a treatise on *The Present State of London,* published in 1681 by the Baptist preacher Thomas DeLaune and dedicated to the Whig mayor of London, Sir Thomas Clayton:

> *London* ... is the mighty *Rendezvous* of *Nobility, Gentry, Courtiers, Divines, Lawyers, Physitians, Merchants, Seamen,* and all kind of Excellent *Artificers,* of the most Refined Wits, and most Excellent Beauties: for it is observed, that in most Families of *England,* if there be any Son or Daughter that Excells the rest in Beauty or Wit, or perhaps Courage or Industry, or any other rare Quality, *London* is their *Pole-Star* ... which vast Confluence ... must needs bring a vast Advantage and Increase to Trade, besides the most Exquisite Ornament and Gallantry that any Place in the World can shew. (298)

De Laune's catalogue points to the way in which the infrastructural and institutional variety of the metropolis contributed to an ethical transformation of the person, an enlargement of capacities and outlook, in "Wit," "Courage," "Industry," and "Gallantry." As Edward Waterhouse explained in *The Gentleman's Monitor* (1665), London was the "best Nursery for Wisdom and Conversation" because it was "a Collection and Digest of all men and things, to all ends and accomplishments of life" (295).

Modern urban sociologists have noted that in the opportunities they create for social interchange and combination, the infrastructural technologies of metropolitan life contribute to *behavioral urbanization,*[8] to what Robert Park describes as "changes in the habits, sentiments, and character of the urban population."[9] As Georg Simmel explains these changes in his classic essay on "The Metropolis and Mental Life," there is a point in urban development when a city ceases to be identical with its environs, where "in transcending this visible expanse ... any given city becomes the seat of cosmopolitanism," and where the "quantitative aspect of life is transformed directly into qualitative traits of character. ... Man does not end with the limits of his body or the area comprising his immediate activity. Rather is the range of the person constituted by the sum of effects emanating from him spatially and temporally."[10] So, might one add, are the ethical resources of the metropolite constituted by the sum of his interactions, at whatever distance spatially and temporally.

If there is one feature that best characterizes "Dryden's London," both the one he experienced and the one he imagined, it is this sense of the enlarged capacity of the metropolite and, with it, both a liberation from the fixed ties of traditional society and a propensity for new modes of freely chosen association. And if there is one moment in Dryden's lifetime that epitomizes the development of these traits it is the years of the Exclusion Crisis, when, in the absence of Parliament and the height of political opposition to the Stuart succession, London became the principal scene for the concerted efforts of a political coalition—the first political party—that drew its membership and support from a variety of groups and interests brought into contact by the metropolitan environment. Recent scholarship on the Exclusion Crisis has challenged the perspectives of older historians who, perhaps relying excessively on Tory satire and propaganda, regarded the period 1678–82 as marked by anti-popish hysteria, paranoid plots, provincialism, xenophobia, and fixation on the issue of succession. Work by Tim Harris, Jonathan Scott, Gary DeKrey, Richard Ashcraft, and others has suggested how these narrower developments were merely symptoms of a broader set of issues involving the emergence of a political opposition, the status of parliaments and the constitution, and perhaps above all a concern for religious liberty and the rights of the subject, causes that, precisely because they lacked a clear institutional focus or solution, have to be called libertarian rather than republican.[11] It was the metropolis as much as any institution that helped to shape and to connect the participants in this alliance, especially the two partners of the alliance as they are represented in the work of Dryden and his Tory contemporaries—the libertine courtly opposition and the substantial body of religious nonconformists who were well established in London's merchant and artisan communities. Dryden's satires ridicule this unholy alliance, but his ridicule stems from his underlying apprehension about the odd affinities of its apparently incompatible members.

In the remainder of this essay I would like to work against the grain of the Tory perspective, to point to some of the common features of the social extremes that Dryden caricatures as courtly libertinism and nonconformist fanaticism, and to locate the common roots of these different modes of deportment in the increasingly metropolitan character of London life. I will then examine

Dryden's efforts to distinguish them as opposites in terms that derive from his more traditional view of London society. And finally I will reflect upon the ways in which Dryden's own point of view meets or fails to meet the criteria of what we might call a metropolitan personality.

The problem of metropolitan life, as Georg Simmel presents it, is "the intensification of nervous stimulation" that comes with the quantum leap from the discrete and enduring impressions of customary communal life, with its fixed social roles, to the rapid crowding of changing images, the sharp discontinuity, and the unexpectedness of unrushing impressions" in the metropolis. According to Simmel, the metropolite's compensatory response to this overwhelming variety of contacts and commitments is the specialization of personality, particularly the hyperdevelopment of intellection and the cultivation of a capacity for instinctive choice and quick, intuitive discrimination. The metropolite's freedom *from* traditional roles is a freedom *for,* a defining of a self that must "somehow be expressed in the working out of a way of life."[12]

One such "way of life"—with many subvarieties—was worked out in the developing culture of the "town," which since the Jacobean and early Caroline periods had become the point of social confluence for country, court, and city. With its patterns of seasonal migration, its exclusive housing, parks, pastimes, pleasures and pursuits, its clubs and social circles, the town brought an urbanizing gentry into contact with a gentrifying city, transforming London into what Thomas Fuller called "the inn-general of the gentry and nobility of this nation."[13] The literary-social dimensions of town life are to be found in the urbane poetry of Ben Jonson and his many imitators, where the search for "ways to be more intimate and informal," set against the mass and complexity of the city, works out a cosmopolitan way of life by moving inwardly toward the exclusive domains of self, friends, distinctive place, occasions, and tastes.[14] Not just a "creation of the period 1595 to 1640," but, as Earl Miner long ago pointed out, a "possession of the period from . . . 1640 to 1680,"[15] the social mode drew heavily on the work of Horace and Stoic-Epicurean sources more generally to link the quality of *autarkeia* (or self-sufficiency) to the quality of *oikeiosis* (or reasonable like-mindedness). The root sense of "conviviality," exemplified in the social intimacies of seventeenth-century epistle, elegy, epigram, and ode, gives a good idea of the ways in which a sense of self was made available through association with others, in the celebration of friendships and social virtues, the good life and its pleasures, the proper uses of leisure, the proprieties of the social occasion in place and time. A circuit of inter-legitimating contacts, associations, and tastes provided a validating social consensus that in turn endowed the individual with mobility, a freedom to circulate widely, to experience and appropriate aspects of the urban environment without breaking the spiritual circumference of a circle that becomes incarnate on social occasions or on the page in verse.

The obverse to such conviviality, of course, is exclusivity. As Pierre Bourdieu notes, "tastes are perhaps first and foremost distastes, disgusts provoked by horror or visceral intolerance of the tastes of others."[16] A sure sign of the ethical transformation wrought by the changing life of London is the modulation of traditional moral complaints about such urban vices as avarice and deception into aesthetic and psychoperceptual responses—expressions of weariness, irritation, malaise, visceral recoil. A good example is John Evelyn's description in his *Character of England* (1659), where London is

> A very ugly Town, pestered with *Hackney-coaches*, and insolent *Carre men*, *Shops* and *Taverns*, *Noyse*, and such a cloud of *Sea-coal* [smoke], as if there be a resemblence of *Hell* upon Earth, it is in this *Vulcano* in a foggy day. (29–30)

For Evelyn, London is significantly a sensory rather than a moral Hell, an assault on the sense and sensibility. Evelyn's treatise on urban air pollution, *Fumifugium*, is one of the period's countless complaints in prose and verse against the smoke, noise, irritations, and inconveniences of metropolitan life. While occasioned by physical realities, such as increasingly heavy use of coaches and coal fuel, these sensitivities also arose from a new cultural receptivity to equivalent responses, in the verse of Horace, Martial, and Juvenal, to the annoyances of the Roman metropolis.

A special mark of such visceral response in the town literature of the Restoration is the new prominence of the sensation of "nausea," a term whose transformation from a medical condition to a metaphor for general loathing dates to just this period (John Spencer's *Discourse Concerning Prodigies* [1665] thus refers to "that nausea which the tedious repetition of things present and familiar creates in the Soul of Man"). Millamant's "I nauseate walking; 'tis a country diversion," is a good example, but so are John Oldham's "Resolve to quit the nauseous Town" in his rendering of Juvenal's third satire, Thomas D'Urfey on "the jilting

Breeding of the nauseous Town," Robert Gould on London's "nauseous Converse, or more nauseous Plays," Mulgrave's attack on "nauseous men" in the *Essay on Satire,* and perhaps most tellingly, in Rochester's *Letter from Artemiza in the Town to Chloe in the Country,* the depiction of love as "That cordial drop heaven in our cup has thrown, / To make the nauseous draft of life go down."[17]

Such visceral distaste or disgust, Simmel points out, is an essential feature of the metropolitan personality, a mode of distancing and detachment that, along with selectivity, helps to "effect the distances" necessary to metropolitan life, for what appears as withdrawal or dissociation, he observes, is "in reality only one of the elementary forms of socialization." Simmel calls the affect associated with such disengagement the blasé attitude. As he decribes it, the blasé attitude is, like the Stoic-Epicurean virtues of *apatheia* (freedom from passion) and *ataxaria* (or imperturbability), a kind of willed insensitivity or condescension toward the sources of displeasure or distaste. As a result of the metropolite's blasé attitude, Simmel explains, "the meaning and differing values of things, and thereby the things themselves, are experienced as insubstantial," so that "the self-preservation of certain personalities is bought at the price of devaluing the whole objective world."[18] Such devaluation is an important dimension of seventeenth-century poetry—in lyric, for example, where Cavalier anacreontic shades off toward the coarser catches and burlesque drinking songs of the commonwealth and Restoration, or where the anti-idealistic eroticism of elegy modulates, in the work of Restoration wits, toward erotic insusceptibility expressed in the form of postcoital drunken carouses.[19] The merging of discourse and demeanor in the works of the court wits, where privilege and disgust expressed themselves in the celebration of snobbery, outrage, and antisocial hijinks (Milton's "Sons / Of *Belial,* flown with insolence and wine," *Paradise Lost,* 1.501–2) exemplifies Simmel's claim that the metropolite, seeking the regard of the social circle, may be "tempted to adopt the most tendentious pecularities . . . the specifically metropolitan extravagances of mannerism, caprice, and capriciousness" (57). In the escapades of the court wits, and in the libertine craze that swept the stage in the 1670s, the flaunting of traditional morals and the violation of traditional social boundaries in illicit interclass rendezvous are not simply ways of repudiating a puritanical past; they also express the enlarged and liberating possibilities of a newly expansive phase in the life of London.

The younger Dryden must be reckoned among the important participants and creators of that life. As early as the prologue to *The Wild Gallant* (1663), Dryden addressed himself to the wits and beauties of the "Town," and Pepys's diary for 1664 places the poet at Will's Coffee House in Covent Garden, surrounded by "all the wits of the town" and "very witty and pleasant in discourse."[20] In *Marriage A-la-Mode* Dryden contributed importantly to the libertine fashion on the stage in the 70s, and his 1673 dedication of the play to Rochester, acknowledging "the favour, of being admitted to your Lordship's Conversation," extolled the Earl as the model of "the Gallantries of Courts, the Delicacy of Expression, and the Decencies of Behaviour"—a compliment whose stress on polite moderation, James Winn suggests, may presume to give advice.[21] In the same year, the dedication of *The Assignation* to the court wit Sedley, invoking the friendships of the Roman poets, makes a bid for patronage by placing Dryden in the intimate circle of London sophisticates: "We have . . . our Genial Nights; where our discourse is neither too serious, nor too light; but always pleasant, and for the most part instructive . . . and the Cups onely such as will raise the Conversation of the Night, without disturbing the business of the Morrow" (*Works*, 11:320–21). Once again commending a much-to-be-desired moderation, Dryden airily dismisses the complaints of anti-libertine moralists, the "ignorant and ridiculous Descriptions which some Pedants have given of the Wits (as they are pleas'd to call them:) which are a Generation of Men as unknown to them, as the People of *Tartary* or the *terra Australis* are to us . . . The Wits they describe, are the Fops we banish" (*Works,* 11:321).

Despite his familiarity with London's most fashionable circles, however, Dryden had also expressed his own discomfort with the more extravagant liberties of town manners, tracing his unfitness for writing comedy, for example, to a want of "that gaiety of humour which is required to it. My conversation is slow and dull; my humour saturnine and reserved; in short, I am none of those who endeavour to break jests in company, or make repartees."[22] Ridiculed for his gaucheries in Buckingham's *Rehearsal*, Dryden later became the victim of one of the Restoration's most accomplished exercises in the display of social and literary snobbery, Rochester's "An Allusion to Horace." While drawing a clear line between the refinement of courtly amateurs and the adulterated work of "poor-led Poets of the Town" (118), Rochester's poem epitomizes the latter in the "Lumpish fancy" and "loose slattern Muse" (91–92) of Dryden, whom the author pointedly excludes from the final alliance of courtiers and professionals who constitute the true elite:

> I loathe the Rabble, 'tis enough for me
> If Sydley, Shadwell, Shepheard, Wicherley,
> Godolphin, Butler, Buckhurst, Buckinghame
> And some few more, whome I omitt to name
> Approve my sence, I count their Censure Fame.
>
> (120–24)

We know from the Preface to *All for Love* (1677) just how much Dryden was stung by the circulation of Rochester's poem. But by 1677 there was probably a further animus, for some of the leading courtly amateurs (Buckingham and Rochester) had gone over to the political opposition (Dorset and Sedley would later become supporters of the Princess Mary). As a result of these defections, Dryden's exclusion from their libertine circles (as well as the corresponding elevation of Shadwell) was becoming fraught with political significance. Having witnessed the decade-long fashion for libertine comedy pass into the hands of Shadwell and then to the farces of D'Urfey, Dryden began to associate the corrupt extravagance of libertine taste with the madness of London's Protestant mobs. "The Plays that take on our Corrupted Stage, / Methinks resemble the distracted Age," he wrote in the Prologue to Tate's *The Loyal General* (1679, published 1680), "Noise, Madness, all unreasonable Things, / That strike at Sense, as Rebels do at Kings!"(14–15). "Whiggs, at their Poets never take offence" (16), Dryden objected in the Epilogue to Southerne's *The Loyal Brother* (1681–82); indeed, it was quite the reverse, as the London triumph of Shadwell in *Mac Flecknoe* had demonstrated and Dryden's Epilogue now insisted: "Tho Nonsense is a nauseous heavy Mass, / The Vehicle call'd Faction makes it pass" (18–19).

The persistent yoking of rakish libertinism and London nonconformity in Dryden's Exclusion Crisis satires is at once the expression of a personal grudge, a literal acknowledgment of the political realities of the hybrid Whig alliance, and an important metaphorical resource; but it is also something more than all of these: a recognition of the ways in which the English polity—with its reliance on traditional status groups, and its deference to the once-glorious mysteries of church and crown—was under threat of being dissolved by the liberating effects of a new metropolitan culture. It is a threat implicit in the period's use of the term "libertine" to designate both rakish immorality and politico-religious deviance (the Ranters had obligingly demonstrated the compatibility of the meanings).[23] And it is a threat that Dryden underlines in the Prologue to *The Duke of Guise,* where he assails the Whig attempt to "Make *London* independant of the Crown: / A Realm apart; the Kingdom of the Town" (41–42).

It is perhaps an uphill battle to make the case for Restoration nonconformists as metropolitan sophisticates, despite their cosmopolitan trading connections and their admiration for the tolerant prosperity of cities like Amsterdam. But Michael Walzer has pointed usefully to the ways in which the separatist and religious independent communities of London, from the 1630s onward, contributed to a crucial process of social reorientation. Appealing not so much to London's traditional elite as to "men newly come to the city, uneasy there, not yet urbane, not yet sharing the sophistication of the town-dweller or the courtier . . . the congregational discipline taught them an urban style, provided new standards of order and a new routine, set them apart from the motley population of the expanding city and eventually produced a new self-confidence."[24] A revolutionary self-confidence, we might add, in its relative freedom from the traditional ties of neighborhood, parish, and fixed locality in general, and in its insistence on the right of religious assembly, the right of worshipers "to choose their own company, place, and time."[25]

In contrast with the fervor and inward light of the independent movement during the mid-century revolution, the call for toleration among Exclusion Crisis dissenters is a pallid thing, but all the more interesting from the standpoint of urban history for its stronger basis in social practicality. Among Dissenters, a disidentification with the defining limits of geographical locale, a denial "that whosoever lives within such a precinct must be a Member of such a Church," went hand in hand with the insistence that congregational membership must be "by the peoples consent," for "people," said Stephen Lobb, "are invested with a right to choose."[26] Such choice was indeed necessitated, in the Dissenting argument, by population growth and by the dilatory rebuilding of parish church fabric after the fire. As Vincent Alsop explained, parish clergy "were so *overlaid with a numerous throng of people*" that they "cannot personally take care of the hundredth part of them." Those searching for truth in the City parishes, he added, would have to spend "our Lords days in an undecent trotting up and down the Town for one scrap here, a snap there."[27] Choosing a congregation was not like choosing a hat, of course;

the inquiring Christian was to "go where he finds the worship to be in a way most agreeable to Scripture."[28] But to a surprising extent, in the new arguments for toleration, the test of scriptural interpretation was being left to the power of conscience, not a new faculty, exactly, but one that was increasingly taking on the character of an affect or almost visceral response. "Delicate and tender," as John Owen and many others described it, its dictates were to be followed, Stephen Lobb said, even "though erroneous."[29] And its promptings were increasingly put in terms of taste and palatability—what conscience could or could not swallow or stomach. Thus the Baptist Thomas DeLaune refuted those who called Dissenters "silly Sectaries, because they hant so wide a Throat" as they, "to swallow what they cannot Digest."[30] William Penn protested that "Men abhor to thrust that Meat and Drink down their Neighbours Throat, which will not agree with their Stomachs. They say commonly, Pray take that which best likes you; and why are they not thus civil in the matter of religion?"[31]

In the course of their conscientious pursuits, Dissenters were counseled to respond to persecution in what looks, in John Howe's description, a lot like a more general adaptation to the complexity of metropolitan life: "[with] an equal temper and composure of mind, not apt to be unduly mov'd, or entertain any thing that occurs with indecent perturbation."[32] Compared with earlier defenses of separatism, which typically denied any separatist intent by insisting on adherence to the one true way from which others had strayed, the apologists for Restoration dissent tended to regard social disaffiliation and religious variety as almost inevitable concomitants of life in human society. There is an astonishing degree of prudence (if not downright skepticism) in Howe's observation that "we ourselves do not know, had we been, by our circumstances, led to associate and converse mostly with men of another judgment, what our own would have been."[33] Because, said Stephen Lobb, "there are almost as many different persuasions of conscience about some lesser things, as there are considering minds, there will be as many different practices where there are different Sentiments about matters of practice."[34]

By the 1680s, there were more than 400 nonconformist meeting houses and congregations in and around the metropolis, as compared with 130 parish churches, and the estimated 15–20 percent of Londoners who were Dissenters made up more than 20 percent of the Dissenting population throughout all of England. Not as easily excluded from civic office-holding as from the church, Dissenters had, by the later 1660s, begun to play a prominent role in London politics. Dissenter membership on the Common Council, elected by all freemen in the wards, steadily increased until, by the mid-'70s, more than a quarter of all councillors were Dissenters. Far more important was the cadre of Dissenters from the liveries and courts of assistants, who eventually formed a voting majority in the city's electoral body, Common Hall. The results of this majority were the Whig mayoralties of Sir Thomas Player and Sir Patience Ward, 1679–81, and the series of Whig sheriffs who, between 1680 and 1682 created the two-thirds majority of Whigs on city juries.[35]

In the absence of parliament, the Whig lords turned for political support to this new London opposition, itself a coalition that brought together leading Dissenting clergy and civic officials with a wide range of political allies, from old commonwealthmen and radical republicans to East End Baptists and Huguenot laborers. It is Dryden's point, and a source for the grotesque humor of his satires, that this was, by the terms of traditional society or traditional ways of assessing social status and moral character, an improbable alliance. But as William Penn told his fellow Dissenters in *England's Great Interest* (1679), "*Prodigal* or *Voluptuous* Persons" were to be preferred as allies to "those, that are *Sober to do mischief*; whose debauchery is of the mind . . . men of . . . *sinister Principles,* who, the soberer they be to themselves, the *worse they are to you*" (3).

Dryden was not the first to object to the illicit social mixtures and alliances of London society. Attempts to close the coffeehouses and curtail their political activities in the mid-'70s were accompanied by a wave of propaganda objecting to the "confusion of qualities and conditions" where the "gentleman, mechanic, lord, and scoundrel mix, and are all of a piece, as if they were resolved into first principles." *The Character of a Coffee-House* (1673) inveighed against the "company" of coffeehouses, where "each man seems a Leveller, and ranks and files himself as he list, without regard to degrees or order; so that oft you may see a silly *Fop,* and a worshipful *Justice,* a griping *Rook,* and a grave *Citizen,* . . . a Reverend *Nonconformist,* and a Canting *Mountebank;* all blended together, to form an *Oglio* of Impertinence" (2–3). This, said the anti-libertine pamphlet *Remarques on the Conversations of the Town* (1672), was "a strange sort of levelling to wish to see in the world"; to participate in such a life was "to abandon particular societies and chop with all in common; the Park, the Playhouse, the eating-house, and the Coffee-house: you will hear an unintelligible buzzing, and a noise of what you understand not."[36]

In the answers to works like these it is just this free intercourse outside of traditional communities that was seen to encourage new kinds of interlegitimation. "Converse and acquaintance" among different groups, said one writer, is to "the general improvement of Knowledge and Manners of his Town."[37] For the author of *Coffee-Houses Vindicated,* a company that was not "*stingy* and reserved . . . but *free* and *communicative,*" among whom "a variety of *Humours*" could express themselves, was "the Minds best *Dyet,* and the great *Whet-stone* and Incentive of Ingenuity." The "*Intelligent Society*" of Town life, its "*Converse . . . Discourses,* and *Deportment,*" would "*civilize* our manners, Inlarge our *understandings,* refine our *Language,* teach us a generous *confidence* and handsome *Mode of Address.*"[38]

It is one of the functions of Dryden's Exclusion Crisis satires to undermine such expansive social possibilities. The "Epistle to the Whigs," prefixed to *The Medall,* makes it clear that Dryden's ultimate concern is with political and institutional principle. The civil question, he notes, is the dubious right of "any man among you, or any Association of men, (to come nearer to you,) *who out of Parliament, cannot be consider'd in a publick Capacity,* to meet, as you daily doe, in Factious Clubs . . . to intermeddle in the management of Affairs; or to arraign *what you do not like"* (italics mine). It is precisely this extraordinary, extra-institutional situation (into what traditional institutional category *could* one possibly put the Whig alliance?) that explains Dryden's primary focus on character as the means of prosecuting his satire. The political opposition, as he sees it, is a new social phenomenon, a function of metropolitan interchange, and its agenda is a function of the affects and social antipathies engendered by the urban environment. And so, while Dryden's focus on the "character" of the opposition is appropriate to the ad hominem function of satiric lampoon, it is just as crucially Dryden's way of registering and defusing a danger that he believes is posed by the changing nature of London social life.

In *Absalom and Achitophel,* Dryden's primary concern is with royal sexual politics; but the poem also includes an effort to discredit the libertarian cause by driving a wedge between the allegedly libertine aristocratic Whig leadership and their dissenting supporters among the Solymaen mob. In this first sketch of the Whig alliance it is not Shaftesbury but Buckingham whose portrait serves to characterize the political danger of libertine morals, and not so much for the obvious reasons of debauchery (Zimri, he writes, was "all for Women, Painting, Rhyming, Drinking; / Besides ten thousand freaks that dy'd in thinking." [551–52]) as for Buckingham's affect, his whimsically violent and unreasoned sympathies and antipathies (*The Rehearsal* was perhaps still rankling in Dryden's mind):

> Rayling and praising were his usual Theams;
> And both (to shew his Judgment) in Extreams:
> So over Violent, or over Civil,
> That every man, with him, was God or Devil.
>
> (555–58)

In Dryden's catalogue of conspirators, Shimei or Slingsby Bethel, the Whig sheriff of London, serves as Zimri's opposite number, linked with him in clubable urbane license:

> During his Office, Treason was no Crime;
> The Sons of *Belial* had a glorious Time:
> For *Shimei,* though not prodigal of pelf,
> Yet lov'd his wicked Neighbour as himself.
>
> (597–600)

The righteous Shimei, Dryden adds, had rather join in cursing the king "than break good Company" (605). Yet the two can never *be* good company, for Shimei, "not prodigal of pelf" in the manner of Zimri and other Whig aristocrats, is painted as self-righteously abstemious—"No *Rechabite* more shund the fumes of Wine"—and avaricious (599, 617). His manner of thriving—"heaping Wealth, by the most ready way / Among the *Jews,* which was to Cheat and Pray"(591–92)—rules out on economic grounds any possible social affinity to the prodigal Zimri:

> In squandring Wealth was his peculiar Art:
> Nothing went unrewarded, but Desert.
> Begger'd by Fools, whom still he found too late:
> He had his Jest, and they had his Estate.
>
> (559–62)

Avarice and prodigality are opposite moral extremes and therefore suitable to extremists like Buckingham and Bethell; but more importantly, they are also socially polarizing markers, the very terms that in traditional social taxonomy had distinguished gentlemen from merchants and defined the boundary between the landholding gentry and the insular community of London's merchant class.

The stuff of city comedy for almost a century, this conservative distinction becomes a primary device in the divisive strategy of *The Medall*. With Buckingham fading from the political scene, it is perhaps inevitable, given Dryden's way of thinking about the nature of the Whig alliance, that this poem should have put Zimri's clothes on Achitophel's body, transforming Shaftesbury into an unlikely rake and hypocrite whose attempt "to cast himself into the Saint-like mould" is betrayed by "His open lewdness" and "Whoring" (33, 37, 40). Invoking the stereotype of libertine disdain for traditional norms is essential to Dryden's conception of Shaftesbury's "Trait'rous Combination" with Dissenters, whose conscientious convictions similarly place them above the same traditional norms, making them "God- a'mighties in their turns" (205, 110). The Whig alliance, on this account, produces a kind of mutual elation or euphoria, but in the worst possible sense, as mercurial (and thus pox-ridden) libertinism and bellowing protestant enthusiasm course through a common circulatory system.

> Religion thou hast none: thy *Mercury*
> Has pass'd through every Sect, or theirs through Thee.
> . . . .
> What else inspires the Tongues, and swells the Breasts
> Of all thy bellowing Renegado Priests,
> That preach up Thee for God; dispence thy Laws;
> And with thy Stumm ferment their fainting Cause;
> (263-64, 267-70)

As in *Absalom and Achitophel,* the strategy is to diffuse the threat of inter-legitimation by insisting on the mutually isolating differences in manners and morals that the Whig alliance cannot hope to bridge. London, the great and too fruitful emporium, after all, breeds monsters in its slime, but they conform to a venerable city comedy stereotype:

> In Gospel phrase their Chapmen they betray:
> Their Shops are Dens, the Buyer is their Prey.
> The Knack of Trades is living on the Spoyl;
> They boast, ev'n when each other they beguile.
> (191-94)

In the terms of those old city comedy plots, Shaftesbury becomes the interloping predatory seducer, a

> Pander of the Peoples hearts,
> (O Crooked Soul, and Serpentine in Arts,)
> Whose blandishments a Loyal Land have whor'd,
> And broke the Bonds she plighted to her Lord.
> (256–58)

Shaftesbury's seduction of the people's hearts hearkens back to the sexual politics of *Annus Mirabilis,* where Charles and London were "a pair of matchless Lovers" united after "the interposition of many rivals, who violently ravish'd and witheld" the City from her king. In some ways Dryden's pandering Shafestbury is not so much a rakish rival as a city comedy fumbler, which is pretty much the way he is portrayed in a number of the plays that appeared with the beginning of the Tory revenge in 1682–83.[39] But for Dryden, it is finally the predatory, rakish libertinism he assigns to Shaftesbury that guarantees a failure of rapprochement with those who must, by more traditional terms, be his social enemies:

> Thy Canting Friends thy Mortal Foes wou'd be;
> Thy God and Theirs will never long agree.
> For thine, (if thou hast any,) must be one
> That lets the World and Humane-kind alone:
> A jolly God, that passes hours too well
> To promise Heav'n, or threaten us with Hell;
> . . . .
> A Tyrant theirs; the Heav'n their Priesthood paints
> A Conventicle of gloomy sullen Saints;
> A Heav'n, like *Bedlam,* slovenly and sad;
> Fore-doom'd for Souls, with false Religion, mad.
> (275–86)

Characterizing Dissenters in this way—as narrow, repressive, and provincial—is a way of imaginatively reducing the city's terrifyingly liberating influence; as Dryden paints them, the Whig dissenters are not so much "above" traditional affiliation, as their own rhetoric would have it, as they are simply "out of it." Dryden's advice to Londoners—to be "content to thrive and to obey" (184)—is a hardbitten piece of traditional advice that enables him to reimagine the city he addresses ("London, thou great *emporium* of our isle") as a reassuringly confining and parochial community—confining in just the way it is in *The Hind and the Panther* when Dryden addresses Dissenters who thought they had

> freed from God and monarchy your town.
> ... though your native kennel still be small
> Bounded betwixt a puddle and a wall.
>
> (203–5)

With the fading of the Whig coalition and the beginnings of the Tory revenge, when the government of Charles II revoked the charter of the City of London and began a renewed wave of persecution against Dissenters, London did indeed for a time become more confining. "The City Air," John Howe wrote in 1685, "was much better and more healthy to me formerly, than since; the Anger and Jealousys of such as I have never had a disposition to offend, have of late times occasioned persons of my Circumstances very seldom to walk the Streets."[40] Milton would have understood, and perhaps called Howe a victim "of Custom, and a World / Offended" (*Paradise Lost*, 11.810–11). But as *The Hind and the Panther* suggests, so eventually, and in his own way, did Dryden. If, as many have suggested, there is a change in the character of the later Dryden—translator of Horace, Juvenal, and Persius—it stems in part from an increasing sense of detachment, an effecting of emotional distance and moral independence, that one might describe as a resocialization, a new kind of urbanity. In his *Discourse Concerning the Original and Progress of Satire* (1693), perhaps the closest thing we have to Dryden's intellectual autobiography, Dryden weighs, in the styles and personae of the Roman satirists, the varied strands of his own career and the kinds of selves he might have affected or become: the Horace "accomplish'd, and knowing in all the Arts of Complacency and good behaviour" (4:58) who, living in the best of ages, could curb his "Splenetick Reflections," serenely "give the Rules of a Happy and Virtuous Life" (4:59), and render us "well bred in relation to those with whom we are oblig'd to live, and to converse" (4:75) (there are significantly few Horatian imitations in Dryden's corpus, the critical prose being perhaps the most Horatian of Dryden's oeuvre); or the "vigorous and masculine" Juvenal, whose moral protest in a wicked time strikes the most immediate chord with Dryden's emotions ("my particular Taste," he says [4:61]). But there is also a striking degree of identification with Persius, a youth of "great acquired knowledge" writing under Neronian tyranny—a man, in Dryden's words, "not good at turning things into pleasant ridicule . . . not a laughable writer," but one whose Stoic detachment and philosophic integrity "raise in us an undaunted Courage, against the assaults of Fortune; to esteem as nothing the things that are without us . . . In short, to be always Happy, while we possess our minds, with a good Conscience . . . Here is nothing propos'd but the quiet and tranquillity of Mind; Virtue lodg'd at home, and afterwards diffus'd in her general Effects, to the improvement, and good of Humane Kind" (4:55–56).

It is perhaps in these phrases that we find the best measure of the influence of the metropolis on Dryden's own character. In them we can see the way in which the metropolitan "effecting of distances"—and with it, the sort of disaffiliation from traditional social structures and values that Dryden earlier deplored—was perhaps for Dryden himself a means of resocialization and personal enlargement.

Notes

1. Dryden's works are cited from original editions, and agree with *The Works of John Dryden,* ed. H. T. Swedenberg et al., 20 vols. (Berkeley and Los Angeles: University of California Press, 1956–).

2. *Dryden and the Traces of Classical Rome* (Oxford: Oxford University Press, 1999), 9.

3. *Areopagitica,* in *The Complete Prose Works of John Milton,* ed. Don M. Wolfe, 8 vols. (New Haven: Yale University Press, 1953–82), 2:553–54.

4. Sir William Petty, *Another Essay in Political Arithmetick. Concerning the Growth of the City of London* (London, 1682), 3, 17; John Graunt, *Natural and Political Observations* (London, 1674), sig. Av, 153.

5. Peter Borsay, *The English Urban Renaissance: Culture and Society in the Provincial Town 1660–1770* (Oxford: Clarendon Press, 1989), 140–41; Roger Finlay, *Population and Metropolis: The Demography of London 1580–1650* (Cambridge: Cambridge University Press, 1981), 9.

6. *Coffee-Houses Vindicated in Answer to the late Published Character of a Coffee-House* (London, 1673), 3.

7. *A Word for the City* (London, 1682), 1; see also Steven Pincus, "Coffee Politicians Does Create: Coffeehouses and Restoration Political Culture," *Journal of Modern History* 67 (1995): 807–34.

8. Jan de Vries, *European Urbanization, 1500–1800* (Cambridge: Harvard University Press, 1984), 10–13.

9. "The City: Suggestions for the Investigation of Human Behavior in the Urban Environment: (1916)," in *Classic Essays on the Culture of Cities,* ed. Richard Sennett (Englewood Cliffs, N.J.: Prentice-Hall, 1969), 110.

10. "The Metropolis and Mental Life," in Sennett, *Classic Essays on the Culture of Cities,* 47–50.

11. Tim Harris, *London Crowds in the Reign of Charles II: Propaganda and Politics from the Restoration until the Exclusion Crisis* (Cambridge: Cambridge University Press, 1987); *Politics under the Later Stuarts: Party Conflict in a Divided Society* (London: Longman, 1993); Jonathan Scott, *Algernon Sidney and the Restoration Crisis, 1677–1683* (Cambridge: Cambridge University Press, 1993); Gary De Krey, *A Fractured Society: The Politics of London in the First Age of Party* (Oxford: Clarendon Press, 1985); DeKrey, "The London Whigs and the Exclusion Crisis Revisited," in *The First Modern Society: Essays in English History in Honour of Lawrence Stone,* ed. A. L. Beier, David Cannadine, and James M. Rosenheim (Cambridge: Cambridge University Press, 1989); De Krey, "London Radicals and Revolutionary Politics 1675–1683," in *The Politics of Religion in Restoration England,* ed. Tim Harris, Paul Seaward, and Mark Goldie (Oxford: Basil Blackwell, 1990); Richard Ashcraft, *Revolutionary Politics and Locke's Two Treatises of Government* (Princeton: Princeton University Press, 1986).

12. "The Metropolis and Mental Life," 48, 50.

13. Lawrence Stone, "The Residential Development of the West End of London in the Seventeenth Century," in *After the Reformation: Essays in Honor of J. H. Hexter,* ed. Barbara C. Malament (Philadelphia: University of Pennsylvania Press, 1980), 388. On the "town" as a new cultural domain, see Martin Butler, *Theatre and Crisis, 1632–1642* (Cambridge: Cambridge University Press, 1984), 141.

14. Alastair Fowler, *Kinds of Literature: An Introduction to the Theory of Genres and Modes* (Cambridge: Harvard University Press, 1982), 202; Katharine Eisaman Maus, *Ben Jonson and the Roman Frame of Mind* (Princeton: Princeton University Press, 1984), 138.

15. Earl Miner, *The Cavalier Mode from Jonson to Cotton* (Princeton: Princeton University Press, 1971), 87.

16. *Distinction: A Social Critique of the Judgement of Taste,* trans. Richard Nice (Cambridge: Harvard University Press, 1984), 56.

17. *The Way of the World,* 4.4; D'Urfey, "On the Ensuing Poems of Mr. John Oldham," in Oldham, *Works* (London, 1684), line 28; Oldham, "A Satyr, in Imitation of the Third of Juvenal," in *The Poems of John Oldham,* ed. Harold F. Brooks (Oxford: Clarendon Press, 1987), 247, line 35; Gould, "To my Lord of Abingdon, at his Country House," in *Works* (London, 1709), 127; Mulgrave, *An Essay upon Satire,* in *The Poetical Works of Dryden,* ed. George R. Noyes (1909; reprint, Boston: Houghton Mifflin, 1950), 914, line 80; Rochester, "A Letter from Artemesia in the Town to Chloe in the Country," in *The Complete Poems of John Wilmot, Earl of Rochester,* ed. David M. Vieth (New Haven: Yale University Press, 1968), 105, lines 44–45.

18. "The Metropolis and Mental Life," 51–53.

19. Good examples would be the verse exchanges between Buckhurst and Sedley, or Alexander Radcliffe's post-Rochesterian *The Ramble: An Anti-Heroick Poem* (London, 1682).

20. Robert W. McHenry, Jr., "Dryden and the 'Metropolis of Great Britain,'" in *The Restoration Mind,* ed. Gerald Marshall (Newark: University of Delaware Press, 1997), 177–92.

21. *The Works of John Dryden,* 11:221; James Anderson Winn, *John Dryden and his World* (New Haven: Yale University Press, 1987), 246–47.

22. "A Defense of an Essay of Dramatic Poesy," in *Of Dramatic Poesy and Other Essays,* ed. George Watson, 2 vols. (New York: Everyman, 1962), 1:116.

23. See James G. Turner, "The Properties of Libertinism," in *'Tis Nature's Fault: Unauthorized Sexuality during the Enlightenment,* ed. Robert Purks Maccubbin (Cambridge: Cambridge University Press, 1985), 75–87.
24. Michael Walzer, *The Revolution of the Saints* (Cambridge: Harvard University Press, 1965), 243.
25. John Cook, *What the Independents Would Have* (1647), 2.
26. Stephen Lobb, *The Harmony between the Old and Present Non-Conformists Principles* (1682), 80.
27. Vincent Alsop, *The Mischief of Impositions* (London, 1680), epistle dedicatory.
28. Lobb, 85.
29. Owen, *A Brief Vindication of the Non-Conformists* (London, 1680), 22; Lobb, *The Harmony Between the Old and Present Non-Conformists Principles* (London, 1682), 85.
30. *Compulsion of Conscience Condemned* (London, 1683), 31.
31. *A Persuasive to Moderation to Dissenting Christians* (London, 1685), 2.
32. *A Letter Written out of the Countrey to a Person of Quality in the City* (London, 1680), 2.
33. Ibid., 44.
34. *The Harmony Between the Old and Present Non-Conformists Principles,* 85.
35. See especially the works of De Krey, cited in note 11, above.
36. *Remarques on the Humours and Conversations of the Town* (London, 1672), 124; see also Maximillian E. Novak, "Margery Pinchwife's 'London Desease': Restoration Comedy and the Libertine Offensive of the 1670's," *Studies in the Literary Imagination* 10 (1977): 1–23.
37. *Remarks upon Remarques: Or, a Vindication of the Conversations of the Town* (London, 1673), 118.
38. *Coffee-Houses Vindicated in Answer to the Late Published Character of a Coffee-House* (London, 1674), 4–5.
39. See K. H. D. Haley, *The first Earl of Shaftesbury* (Oxford: Clarendon Press, 1968), 211–15.
40. Quoted in N. H. Keeble, *The Literary Culture of Nonconformity in Later Seventeenth-Century England* (Leicester: Leicester University Press, 1987), 188.

Dryden, Rochester, and the Invention of the "Town"

Harold Love

In the prologue to *Marriage A-la-Mode*, Dryden speaks through the voice and body of Charles Hart of the willingness of the actresses of the King's Theatre *"T' oblige the Town, the City, and the Court."*[1] At the end of the epilogue, this time through Michael Mohun, he repeats this three-way division:

> *Since therefore Court and Town will take no pity,*
> *I humbly cast my self upon the City.*
>
> (31–32)

This division may, in the first instance, be a theatrical one, referring to the Court in the boxes, the City in the middle gallery, and the Town as represented by the pit; but it also reflects a new or at least newish way of compartmentalizing the inhabitants of the metropolis, which is worked out with some care in a passage from 3.1 to which I will return shortly. Shadwell, Buckingham, Lee, Otway, and Crowne all make the same distinction.[2]

Lawrence Manley in *Literature and Culture in Early Modern London* has described how the "town" as both a cultural entity and a built environment came into existence during the early Stuart period;[3] however, at that time the word itself was normally used with a more general meaning. When one encounters the triad "city, town, and court" before about 1665 it is with reference to cities and towns in the abstract, not to *the* city and *the* court as distinct parts of metropolitan London. Between 1660 and 1700, the notion became much sharper and more stable. There was a sense of the Town as something that could be defined in four ways: by locality, by demography, by characteristic forms of sociability, and as a distinctive mentality. I would like to explore all these usages, but specially the last, and to examine the roles of Dryden and Rochester in articulating the nature of the Town to those who comprised it. This will involve some heavy simplifying, but I hope it will point to a fundamental difference in their attitudes in which Dryden shows as pro-Town and Rochester as anti-Town.

In Shakespeare's time there had been no "Town" in this sense. London was synonymous with the City and its suburbs, while the Court had a completely separate municipal existence at Westminster. In between the two, once one left the river frontage, was mostly open space. St Martin's and St Giles's were still in the fields. The Haymarket was a lane with hedges. Windmill Street was the site of a windmill. Covent Garden was a garden. Royal policy, directed toward keeping the gentry and aristocracy on their estates, performing their traditional functions in local government, restricted building on what is now the West End.[4] By the 1670s all this had changed. As part of a process accelerated by the Great Fire, the parishes of St Martin's, St Paul's, St Anne's, St Giles's, and St James's were covered with streets, many of which bore the names of members of the Restoration nobility. It would be too procrustean to say that these parishes constituted the Town in a geographical sense; but it is perfectly fair to make this claim in a demographical sense, because it was precisely this area that the defining social class of the Town chose as their place of settlement.

This class was the very people whom Elizabeth, James, and Charles I had tried to keep on their estates—the lower aristocracy and the wealthier country gentry now become urban dwellers. The upper aristocracy, those with major roles at court, already had their grand houses along the Strand and around Whitehall. What now took place was an immigration of the next class down, a much larger body. From being occasional visitors to London they became much more frequent ones, establishing permanent residences instead of renting, and generally trying to spend the whole winter in London before returning to their estates in the summer. Sir Charles Sedley, to take one signal example, established himself as a town-dweller in 1657, moving from his estate in Kent to Great Queen Street. He was engaging as early as 1658 in such riotous behavior as traveling by coach at sermon time on Sunday. Sedley was to become an iconic representative of one kind of Town behaviour, as epitomized in the Cock Tavern riot of 1663 where he confessed to "showing himself naked on a balcony, and throwing down bottles (pissed in) *vi et armis* among the people."[5] But in many cases the moving spirits in this migration were the women of the families, to whom the country was far less congenial than it was to their more mobile, fox-hunting husbands, and who valued London as a marriage market for their children. Their view must often have been that of Harriet in *The Man of Mode*, speaking of her imminent return to the country:

> Pitty me, who am going to that sad place. Methinks I hear the hateful noise of Rooks already—Kaw, Kaw, Kaw—There's Musick in the worst Cry in *London!* My Dill and Cowcumbers to pickle. (5.2)

By settling where they did, the migrating gentry drew tradespeople, attendant professionals, and entertainers into the same parishes. As part of this process, the Town, so defined, became the pleasure district of the metropolis. The theaters moved from the old pleasure district on the south bank into the Covent Garden area, and with them came the dramatists. Whereas in Shakespeare's time playwrights had lived and socialized in the red-light district of Southwark or as adjacently as possible on the north bank, they now congregated in the much more salubrious area north of the Strand, making Will's coffeehouse in Russell Street their unofficial headquarters. One of the effects of this was to make literature itself more respectable.

Patterns of Sociability

The movement of the country gentry to town also involved the development of new patterns of sociability that further distinguished the Town from both the City and the Court. City sociability was organized on its grandest scale around the meetings and feasts of the Livery Companies and, at a lesser level, in taverns and coffeehouses, which had become professionally specialized in their clientele, often doubling as places of business. At Court, on the other hand, the ruling pattern of sociability was still that of the levee: in the morning, clients would "wait," in the technical sense, at the houses of the nobility, who might themselves proceed later in the day to wait on members of the royal family or stand as silent spectators of meals taken in state. Melantha describes such a life in *Marriage A-la-Mode*: "you shall be every day at the King's *Levé*, and I at the Queen's; and we will never meet, but in the Drawing-room."[6]

This court pattern of sociability was rigidly hierarchical, and heavily formalized. The town replaced it with a freer pattern which was known simply as "the visit." While much less hierarchical than the levee, the visit still had its rules, and required access to a coach to be performed correctly. In 1675 Hannah Woolley described its governing ethos as one of civility rather than familiarity. One should listen attentively to those of higher rank, without interrupting them, but it was permissible to disagree with them, providing the correct form of words was used. Compliments should never be prolix, nor should one make "a bold entrance without Ceremony" but do it "quietly and civilly" without "bawling noise or obstreperousness." It was never civil to whisper in company "and much less to laugh when you have done."[7] The kind of painting known as a conversation piece reveals the nature of the visit as an assembly of people of roughly equivalent rank conversing semiformally in a large private room. The visit offered a way for extended families moving down from the country to bond with each other and with similar families. Rochester wrote a remarkable poem about visits, "Artemiza to Chloe," to which I shall return shortly, and they are represented in many scenes of Restoration comedy. There is a satire of 1679–80 called "The Visit" which mentions them as an occasion for the exchange of satirical lampoons and speculation over their authorship.[8] Dryden's Melantha is "the most eternal Visiter of the Town."[9] But the best account of them is in Susan E. Whyman's recent study of the Verney family.[10] From the very detailed correspondence that survives between London and country members of the family she is able to track down the process by which the country members were initiated into the culture of visiting. She also makes clear that this culture was guided and regulated by the town-based women of the family. Of course the Town also had its coffee- and chocolate-houses, and some of its members were courtiers who waited at Whitehall, but the visit was its own invention.

What I have been describing is a process by which a newly built-over region of the metropolis attracted a new and highly prestigious body of inhabitants who saw themselves as distinct from both the courtiers and the citizens and who began to work out their own ways of communicating and getting on with each other. Obviously much more could be said about this; but what is most interesting is the development of a *mentality* of the Town—a process by which the new arrivals could become conscious of the nature and potentialities of this new kind of urban living centered on the sociable pursuit of pleasure. "Get you gone to your business together," says Sir Jasper Fidget in *The Country Wife*, "go, go, to your business, I say, pleasure, whilst I go to my pleasure, business."[11] This mentality was articulated by the writers, especially Dryden and the dramatists.

THE THEATER AS TOWN SENATE

The Restoration theater was a particularly important institution for the Town. The questions of behavior addressed in Restoration comedy were frequently questions of how one should behave as a member of the Town, someone whose business was pleasure, in relation to the Court, in its preoccupation with power, and the City in its preoccupation with profit. Insofar as the Town had a central representative body to which communal issues could be referred, it was the theater audience, especially on first days. Horner in *The Country Wife* submits himself to the judgment of this senate by making an appearance at the theater after circulating the bogus story of his emasculation. In 1.1.166–89 the reactions of the ladies are reported as they collectively construct a new identity for him which will govern his future participation in Town sociability.[12] In Southerne's *The Wives' Excuse,* when Mr. Friendall is offered a choice of suitable places for accepting a public apology for an affront, the options are "in full *Mall,* before the Beau's, or the Officers of the Guard; or at *Will*'s Coffee-House before the Witts, or in the Play-House, in the Pitt, before the Vizard Masks, and Orange Wenches; or behind the Scenes, before the Women-Actors; or any where else, but upon the Stage" from which he chooses "in the Side-box, before the Ladies."[13] The theater is preferred because it is the principal site for the assigning of social identities, the place where one could be viewed and communally summed up.

The most interesting theater texts for a study of the invention of the Town are prologues and epilogues, especially Dryden's as the finest examples of the genre. In writing prologues, Dryden could escape from his own inadequacies as a speaker and impromptu wit by having his words delivered by actors. Looking at these marvellously assured and subtle texts, what strikes one above all is the sense they convey of a brilliant rhetorician's authority over an often recalcitrant audience. While the drama that followed or preceded might receive only intermittent attention, the words of a stage oration would be followed eagerly because they were expected to represent wit at its most sublime; indeed, it must often have been true, as Dryden himself conceded, that *"The Wit is ended e'r the* Play's *begun."*[14] They are also, as a rule, strongly interactive, imaging the audience to itself and dividing it against itself, as its various sections were made the target in turn of the laughter of the other sections.[15] If the theater is the senate of the Town, Dryden is its Cicero.[16]

These stage orations also offer positive and valuable lessons about the Town and how to appreciate it, serving both as condensed survival manuals and definitions by negatives of what was to be avoided if the full promise of the life of urban pleasure was to be realized. One insistent theme is that of the superiority of Town life to that of the money-grubbing City and the barbarous Country; but Dryden also gives vivid descriptions of the excesses sometimes witnessed under the theater's own roof:

> But stay: methinks some Vizard Masque I see,
> Cast out her Lure from the mid Gallery:
> About her all the flutt'ring Sparks are rang'd;
> The Noise continues though the Scene is chang'd:
> Now growling, sputtring, wauling, such a clutter,
> 'Tis just like Puss defendant in a Gutter:[17]

These accounts used to confuse theater historians, who thought they were accurate descriptions of everyday behavior; but what they present is not the reality of the audience, but a gallery of violations of accepted Town decorum presented in order to discourage imitation. Dryden's lessons are taught in a style that is itself a manifestation of the new sociability of the Town—witty, ironic, companionable, and unhierarchical (in the sense that no one is beyond judgment). But what I would particularly stress, and will shortly return to, is their welcoming, uncensorious attitude toward the new possibilities for urban living created by the Town, and their insistence that pleasure could be enhanced by the avoidance of overindulgence and excess (which, when one thinks about it, are rather countrified). Behind the sardonic surface there is an appreciation of the merits of an urbane and quintessentially urban hedonism.

Court and Town

Rochester also appreciated the pleasures of the Town—in his strange way—but was never fully part of them or it. He was much too serious and intense, even in his vices. He had no objection at all to excess so long as it was performed with flair: the real crime was to debauch tepidly. His point of vantage was always that of the court, and, as we would expect from a courtier, he was fixated on personal style. For him, the style of the town had always to be an inferior imitation of the style of the court. "Timon," which if it is not by Rochester is by his close friend Sedley, is about a courtier having to dine with unspeakable townies. "Tunbridge Wells" carries the same horror down to a fashionable outpost of the Town. There is a related passage in *Marriage A-la-Mode* (3.1.105–16), which I am inclined, for that reason, to suspect as being one of Rochester's additions made when the play was submitted to him by Dryden for "amendment." If, however, this is genuine Dryden, one needs to ask just where the satire was meant to lie. Melantha has been characterized in 1.1.182 as "a Town-Lady, without any relation to the Court"—that is, a gate-crasher—who nonetheless insists on being "seen there three or four times a day." At 3.1.107 she asserts that "nothing can be so *ridicule*, as a meer Town-Lady," without realizing that she is one herself. Doralice and Artemis gently convey this to her by describing the behavior of town ladies who "crowd and sweat in the Drawing-room" so that they can "write Letters into the Countrey" about what they see, while the true court ladies are laughing at them. Melantha is then advised that she should "live either wholly in the Town; or, . . . in the Countrey," with the second suggestion activating a series of images of the country's desperate hunger for the scraps and leavings of the Town. Doralice concludes by sketching in a hierarchy under which the "little Courtiers wife" lords it over the "Town-Lady," who in turn lords it over the "Merchants Wife," who in her turn "insults over the Countrey Gentlewoman that never comes up."[18]

There are two possible messages to be extracted from this passage. The first is that the court has sunk to being just another place of amusement for the Town, but one that should not be indulged excessively or in a way that provokes the ridicule of the custodians. Melantha, in this view, would be a cautionary example of bad *Town* behavior as well as bad Court behavior. This I suspect would have been Dryden's view. The other reading, which would have been Rochester's, is that style and manners are the creation, if not the monopoly, of the Court, and that they are inevitably and progressively coarsened in being imitated by the Town, the City and the Country in that order. In this case Melantha represents the Town as a whole, not one aberrant figure from it.

This anti-Town perspective also governs Rochester's approach to writing: as a patron and critic he supported the principle that the standard of good dramatic dialogue should be the impromptu wit of courtiers, "An Allusion to Horace" being his clearest exposition of this view.[19] In this poem he concedes that Dryden's plays "embroyder'd up and down / With witt and learning justly pleasd the Town" (5–6), but attacks him for conducting his career like a Town professional rather than a court amateur.[20] That Dryden was no good at impromptu spoken wit is specifically held against him: he becomes "Poet Squab." The satire concludes with a defiant rejection of the judgment of "the poor led Poets of the Town" and their admirers, who are characterized as "the Rabble," in favor of that of a small, individually named group of court cognoscenti—". . . Sydley, Shadwell, Shepheard, Wicherley, / Godolphin, Butler, Buckhurst, Buckinghame" (118–24).[21] The authority that Rochester attempts to reclaim in this remarkable passage is that which Dryden had won for himself in the teeth of court opposition.

Dryden had begun his career by appealing to that very court coterie, or at least to its predecessors of the early 1660s. He made no secret of his ambition to be an English Virgil endowed by a courtly modern Maecenas in order to celebrate the virtues of a new Augustus. But the role of the court, as he saw it, was to support, inspire, and commend, not to impose and direct, and least of all to compete by advancing its own writings as rivals to his own. Despite the bestowal of the laureateship, he was never to secure the kind of Court support he wanted and, instead, earned his living from the Town by writing plays, prologues, and poems, editing miscellanies, and publishing translations. He realized early that he needed to establish a center of critical authority sympathetic to an enlightened professionalism in order to counterpoise the authority of the court amateurs, whose real standing is hinted at in his pointed reference in the argument to his translation of the first satire of Persius to "the Noblemen and their abominable Poetry, who in the Luxury of their Fortune, set up for Wits, and Judges."[22] At the heart of the Dryden-Rochester contestation was the issue of whether literary values were to be defined and enforced from the Wits' Withdrawing Room at Whitehall or the upper chamber at Will's, in the heart of the Town.[23]

"Artemiza to Chloe" and *Marriage A-la-Mode*

In my edition of Rochester I set out to edit and annotate him as a court poet, looking in particular for evidence to relate the occasions of poems to court sociability and court factionalism; but in "Artemiza to Chloe" he is deeply engaged with the Town, and I need to say something about the way in which this happens. Let me repeat that while the poem is *about* the Town it is not *of* the Town—its perspective is emphatically that of the Court, for whom the Town is the scene of vulgar and derivative rather than truly refined pleasures. Dryden's advocacy of a "polite," moderated hedonism has no place in Rochester's scheme. Artemiza's values are those of the Court.

To begin with we might note how often the word "Town" occurs in "Artemiza to Chloe"—nine times, including the title. Artemiza warns herself against becoming "the Fiddle of the Towne" (21); the Town is "lewd" (33); the fine lady notes that in her time there, there was "Hardly a Wench in Towne, but had her Foole" (178); the hours were "wing'd with Joy" when the Town first knew Corinna's early beauties (193); and so on. Next, the poem is constructed around firstly a species of text and secondly a social ceremony native to the town. The species of text is the kind of letter by which town news was circulated to the country, and whose effect is described in *Marriage A-la-Mode:*

> *Mel.* And they tell, for news, such unlikely stories; a letter from one of us is such a present to 'em, that the poor souls wait for the Carriers-day with such devotion, that they cannot sleep the night before. (3.1.126–29)[24]

The ceremony is that of the visit—Artemiza begins the narrative part of the poem, "Where I was visiting the other night. . . ." On this occasion the visit is made memorable by the arrival of her anti-type, the fine lady, an unbelievably vulgar Town figure unwillingly exiled by marriage to her husband's estate in the country, and there forced to play the same game as the Verney women of luring him to London. Once they have arrived all she requires of him is that he should disappear from her presence and get fashionably drunk. Her view of herself is exactly that of Melantha:

> When I have been at grass in the Summer and am new come up again, methinks I'm to be turn'd into *ridicule* by all that see me . . . (3.1.148–50)[25]

or as the fine lady puts it:

> I fynde my selfe ridiculously growne
> Embarassé with being out of Towne . . .
>
> (97–98)

Marianne Thormählen has pointed out that the fine lady breaks all Hannah Woolley's rules of visiting.²⁶ She is someone who carries the Town mentality with her wherever she goes, and with it a stock of Town worldly wisdom, which she immediately unburdens on the others present at the visit. The country for her is as much a place of horror as it was to be for Harriet at the conclusion of *The Man of Mode* or for Doralice, Melantha, and Artemis in 3.1 of *Marriage A-la-Mode*.²⁷ Her monologue leads into the story of Corinna, a typical town siren, who entraps and destroys a country male before he has had time to learn the necessary skills of town survival.

Everything Rochester has to say about the Town in this poem is negative. It has devalued love ("the most gen'rous Passion of the mynde" [40]) by reducing it to an "Arrant Trade" (51); writing does not fare much better; the pursuit of the Town's vaunted pleasures leads to betrayal and death. Yet, there is no condemnation of Corinna: she has simply undone her fool as any Town jilt might be expected to. Even Artemiza does not seem horrified by the story: it is not Corinna's crime that offends her but the brash behavior of the fine lady. Now, this fine lady is an old friend of ours: she is another version of Melantha in *Marriage A-la-Mode*.²⁸ Both of them are shameless, totally self-centered, irrepressibly voluble exhibitionists, who nonetheless exercise a bizarre and irresistible fascination. At line 96, the fine lady picks up "Let me dye," Melantha's primary catchphrase in *Marriage A-la-Mode*, where it is used by her twenty-eight times. At 2.1.16–17 Melantha announces "Oh Count *Rhodophil!* Ah *mon cher!* I could live and die with him." At Rochester's line 145, the fine lady says to the monkey "Oh I could live, and dye with thee," following this a few lines later with *"mon cher"* (169). And so on.²⁹ Undoubtedly Elizabeth Boutell's stage performance as Melantha stands as an intermediary term in this joint portrait—we possess only two elements of what was originally a triptych—but my point here is simply that the two works give us viewpoints on what is essentially the same character, and there is no mystery about how this happened. *Marriage A-la-Mode* was dedicated to Rochester and, as I have already mentioned, "receiv'd amendment" at his hands "e're it was fit to be presented."³⁰ How far Dryden's portrait is borrowed from Rochester or Rochester's from Dryden is not determinable; but the character Melantha/fine lady is common to both of them. What differs is the perspective. Let us quickly make some comparisons.

Although the characters of *Marriage A-la-Mode*, apart from

Melantha, are supposedly courtiers, Dryden knows they are really of the town, and in the epilogue he makes the application:

> *But by examples drawn, I dare to say,*
> *From most of you, who hear, and see the Play.*
> *There are more* Rhodophils *in this Theatre,*
> *More* Palamedes, *and some few Wives, I fear.*
>
> (7–10)

Some "stabbing Wits, to bloudy Satyr bent" (17)—surely this category must include Rochester—would have been less complimentary to the audience, but the "modest Authour" of the epilogue is merciful and has chosen not to expose them to shame because, within broadly drawn parameters, he respects their right to pursue pleasure in their own fashion. The epilogue is a brilliant example of a poet speaking to the Town in its own language and by this act helping to invent it to itself. Dryden recognizes that this new kind of urban existence, for all its excesses and absurdities, represents a valuable relaxing of the claims of hierarchy in personal relationships: there is nothing here of Rochester's disapproval of this life nor of his anxiety over his inability to control it. In the end it comes down to pleasure. Dryden had no problem with the idea that the human being is a pleasure-seeking machine or with the Town as a system for facilitating the functioning of that machine. For Rochester, on the other hand, I believe that pleasure always remained a revolutionary act, performed in moral defiance of the Puritanism that would eventually reclaim him.[31] He despised the Town because it would never allow him to be a martyr to pleasure—only its victim.

To raise the issue in these terms is to move our focus from Rochester's confident enforcement of court hegemony to the nihilism that lies just beneath the assured surface, or may even erupt through it, as in "The Maimed Debauchee" and "Against Reason and Mankind." Each of these poems is an explicit rejection of the Town's urbane hedonism, but in different ways. The first argues, with a backward glance at Sylla's speech at the beginning of Jonson's *Catiline*, that the only truly meaningful pleasure comes from destruction, whether it is of brothels and ancient churches or of one's own body through excess. The second maintains that the uncomplicated animal pleasures of a dog, a monkey, or a bear are superior to those of human society, and much more so than any form of thinking.

But the gap between the court poet and the poet of existential despair is often less marked; indeed, at times it collapses in a way that betrays Rochester's embracing of the extreme as simply another mode of court performance or, if we like, of anti-Townism. In a number of poems he proposes that while gross pleasure, in its more violent forms, might have something to be said for it, there is more real enjoyment to be had from its opposite, suffering:

> Fantastick fancys fondly move
> And in fraile joys believe,
> Taking false pleasure for true love,
> But pain can ne're deceive.[32]

The pain here is that of "sacred Jealousy," which is characterized as "Love rais'd to an extream"; but before we take this claim at its face value, let us see how it relates to an undoubted court poem, "A Pastoral Dialogue between Alexis and Strephon," which was written when Rochester was acting as unofficial Chamberlain to the Duchess of Portsmouth at Bath in 1674, and clearly has her as its suitably remote Petrarchan subject.

> Be dead before thy Passion dies;
>   For if thou should'st survive,
> What Anguish would the Heart surprize,
> To see her Flames begin to rise,
>   And Thine no more Alive.
>
>   (46–50)

In real life, at the time he wrote this, Portsmouth, who was, of course, the king's mistress, was taking Rochester bathing with her in the king's bath, where to the horror of the locals they would throw flowers at each other. The locals got their revenge on Portsmouth by refusing to "wait" at her state dinners, which were conducted as if she was a member of the royal family.[33] Alexis's account of his suffering is no less vivid than that of the speaker of "An age in her embraces pas'd" or "Could I but make my wishes insolent," which I would read as another piece of court Petrarchanism; but the Bath context locates the poem firmly within the hierarchies of the household. If what they describe is indeed a form of pleasure, it is one of so sublimated a kind as to be well beyond the comprehension of the Town. If they are not about pleasure, or pain, at all, but a suavely performed kind of duty, then they are solely and peculiarly of the court in a way that does not even acknowledge the existence of the town except as potential misreaders who would be incapable of penetrating beyond their surface meaning as love poems.

Dryden is certainly interested in such highly refined states of adoration as material for heroic plays but they never enter into his direct addresses to the Town except to be mocked; and context, once more, is one reason for this. Undercutting the humanistic dignity he claims for his work for the theater—especially in his Oxford prologues—is the frank acknowledgment of Nathaniel Lee's epilogue to *Theodosius* (1680) that, by the estimation of the Town, in reducing all things to the meridian of pleasure, a poet is no different from a whore:

> So should wise Poets sooth an awkard Age,
> For they are Prostitutes upon the Stage:
> To stand on points were foolish and ill-bred,
> As for a Lady to be nice in Bed:
> Your wills alone must their performance measure,
> And you may turn 'em ev'ry way for pleasure.
>
> (33–38)

Poetry as much as love has become what Rochester calls "an Arrant Trade."

Dryden's stage orations hold back from any acknowledgment quite as direct as this about the realities of his situation as a paid entertainer to the Town, though they hint at it in some of their many analogies between poetic and sexual performance. But he might have taken heart from the earlier part of Lee's epilogue, which stresses that poet and prostitute alike are not victims of the urban pleasure industry but its masters. The prostitute

> Turns with all winds, and sails with all desires;
> All hearts in City, Town, and Court, she fires,
> Young callow Lords, lean Knights, and driv'ling Squires.
> She in resistless flattery finds her ends,
> Gives thanks for Fools, and makes ye all her Friends.
>
> (28–32)

The Town may have its jest but it is the poet and the whore (let us call her Corinna) who, if they are lucky, will end up with its estate, and who, by creating the Town itself, learn to control it.

Lee repeats Dryden's distinction, with which I began this paper, between City, Town, and Court, this time as part of a chiasmus. The court is represented by "Young callow Lords": the word still had its primary sense of a bird that had not yet grown its feathers and is thus identical with Dryden's nickname "Poet Squab." Rochester, the author of that insult, has already got his comeuppance in the prologue to the same play:

> The Wit and Want of *Timon* point thy mind,
> And for thy Satyr-subject chuse Mankind.[34]

The city, here conflated with the country, is represented by "driv'ling Squires." That speaks for itself: Corinna's victim in "Artemiza to Chloe" is clearly one of this breed. Finally the Town is represented by "lean Knights." Why "lean"?—presumably because they have paid one visit too many to the lady who is never "nice in Bed." Is it possible, though, that drama might itself turn out to be a sexually transmissible disease? The attitudes, and the ironies, set up by Lee's address are as complex as any in Dryden's prologues and epilogues, and like those magnificent pieces they are deeply implicated in the interpersonal dynamics of the auditorium. But what matters to us is the sense of a newly created community, the Restoration Town, reflecting on itself through the voice of its poets, and, in recompense for having made them the instruments of its pleasure, accepting their directions for how it ought to speak and to live.

Notes

1. *The Works of John Dryden*, ed. H. T. Swedenberg Jr. et al., 20 vols. (Berkeley and Los Angeles: University of California Press, 1956–), 11:226, line 39.
2. In the epilogue to *The Sullen Lovers* (1668), line 8; "A Familiar Epistle to Mr Julian, Secretary to the Muses," line 61; the epilogue to *Theodosius* (1680), line 29; 5.1.489–90 of *The Soldier's Fortune* (1681) (*The Works of Thomas Otway*, ed. J. C. Ghosh, 2 vols. [Oxford: Clarendon Press, 1932], 2:186); and 2.3.25 of *The English Frier* (1690) (*The Comedies of John Crowne: A Critical Edition*, ed. B. J. McMullin [New York: Garland, 1984], 522) respectively.
3. *Literature and Culture in Early Modern London* (Cambridge: Cambridge University Press, 1995), 481–97.
4. The most draconian expression of this policy was "A proclamation commanding the gentry to keep their residence in the country, and forbidding them to make their habitations in London and places adjoining" issued on 20 June 1632. See *The Stuart Constitution 1603–1688: Documents and Commentary*, ed. J. P. Kenyon (London: Cambridge University Press, 1966), 502–3.
5. J. Keble, *Reports in the Court of the King's Bench . . . From the 12th to the 30th Years of the Reign of Charles II* (London, 1685), 1:168.
6. 2.1.73–5 (*Works* 11:244).
7. *The Gentlewoman's Companion; or, A Guide to the Female Sex* (London, 1675), 49–50.

8. Reprinted in my *Scribal Publication in Seventeenth-Century England* (Oxford: Oxford University Press, 1993), 257–58, from Lincolnshire Archives Office MS Anc 15/B/4. A second text, Leeds University Library, Brotherton Collection, MS Lt 87, ff. 50r–51r, is discussed in Paul Hammond, "The Miseries of Visits: An Addition to the Literature on Robert Julian, Secretary to the Muses," *The Seventeenth Century* 8 (1993): 161–3. There is a third text in the Beinecke Library at Yale University (MS Osborn b 327, f. 23r–v).

9. *Marriage A-la-Mode*, 1.1.190 (*Works*, 11:234).

10. *Sociability and Power in Late-Stuart England: The Cultural Worlds of the Verneys 1660–1720* (Oxford: Oxford University Press, 1999), esp. 87–109.

11. 2.1.567–8, *The Plays of William Wycherley*, ed. Arthur Friedman (Oxford: Clarendon Press, 1979), 282.

12. Ibid., 254–55.

13. *The Works of Thomas Southerne*, ed. Robert Jordan and Harold Love, 2 vols. (Oxford: Oxford University Press, 1989), 1:304.

14. Prologue to *The Rival Ladies*, line 10 (*Works*, 8:103).

15. The mechanics of this process are considered in my "Who were the Restoration Audience?" *Yearbook of English Studies* 10 (1980): 24–27 and "The Theatrical Geography of *The Country Wife*," *Southern Review* [Adelaide] 16 (1983): 404–15.

16. A relationship made explicit in the "Prologue and Epilogue to the University of Oxford," lines 41–42; but this was another senate which was seen as more supportive of the orator, unlike the "*Prætorian* Bands" of the Town.

17. The epilogue "To the King and Queen, at the Opening of their Theatre . . . in 1682," lines 1–16 (*Works*, 2:198).

18. *Works*, 11:261–62.

19. Text in *The Works of John Wilmot, Earl of Rochester*, ed. Harold Love (Oxford: Oxford University Press, 1999), 71–74.

20. The issues underlying this controversy are explored in my "Shadwell, Rochester and the Crisis of Amateurism," in *Thomas Shadwell Reconsider'd*, ed. Judith Slagle, published as *Restoration* 20 (1996): 119–34.

21. Shadwell's presence in this list is owing to his having been taken up first by Newcastle and then by the Buckingham circle as the chief professional proponent of their Jonsonian program for the comic drama. Dryden's principal model was Fletcher.

22. *Works*, 4:257.

23. The immediate judges were the "Jury of the Wits, who still stay late" described in the epilogue to *Sir Martin Mar-all*, lines 9–12; but, whereas in that case their verdict is delivered to "the Boxes," from where it will be relayed to "all the Town," Dryden worked to have such decisions referred to the professionals.

24. *Works*, 11:261.

25. Ibid., 11:262.

26. *Rochester: The Poems in Context* (Cambridge: Cambridge University Press, 1993), 113.

27. Lines 117–53.

28. The name Artemisia may come from Artemis, another character in *Marriage A-la-Mode*. For the wider resonances of the name see Gillian Manning, "*Artemiza to Chloe*: Rochester's 'Female' Epistle," in *That Second Bottle: Essays on John Wilmot, Earl of Rochester*, ed. Nicholas Fisher (Manchester: Manchester University Press, 2000), 101–18.

29. For the full list of parallels, see my edition, pp. 396–404.
30. *Works*, 11:221.
31. This aspect of Rochester is brilliantly caught in Oldham's "Satyr against Vertue" ("Now curses on you all ye virtuous fools").
32. "Song" ("An age in her embraces pas'd"), lines 29–32 (*Works*, 28).
33. Henry Stubbe to the Earl of Kent, 18 July 1674, British Library Add. MS 35838, f. 276r—v, reprinted in James Jacob, *Henry Stubbe, Radical Protestantism and the Early Enlightenment* (Cambridge: Cambridge University Press, 1983), 135–36. See also Rochester, *Works,* 348 and 414–20.
34. The two previous lines—"Bursting with spleen, abroad thy Pasquils send, / And chuse some Libel-spreader for thy Friend"—begin with a semi-quotation from Rochester's "My Lord All-Pride." In other words three poems attributed to Rochester have been alluded to in the space of three lines.

Dryden's Drama: A Revaluation

Howard Erskine-Hill

The bottom line is that any text may be of interest for its content to some; next to the bottom, perhaps, are texts produced by an author with some measure of fame that cast a light on his or her development or decline. Such texts might not in themselves be of high value. On such grounds, at least, Dryden's earlier plays have a claim on our attention. Some might say (though I would strongly disagree) that the same applies to his post-revolutionary drama of the 1690s.

If we think of Dryden's drama alone—probably a mistake in the longer run—the question arises as to where, if anywhere, a high-water mark may be found. Two answers might be given. First, the most salient of Dryden's theatrical successes, *The Conquest of Granada* (1670) might occur to our mind. If, on the other hand, we consult the wisdom of posterity, oriented largely toward Shakespeare, *All for Love* (1677) will surely be mentioned. "Not one but nods, and talks of *All for Love*," as Pope might have put it. A short paper such as this can only paint with a broad and selective brush. Numerous other cases in Dryden's Restoration record, many subtler suggestions, will, with regret, have to be set aside: in particular his line of comedy seems to call for more attention

The Conquest of Granada is a prominent point in the early Restoration taste for rhyming heroics. The question we have to ask is: is this a drama, or only a text that we know to have been performed? The response of the wife of John Evelyn applies to it the term: "Utopia."[1] Whether we interpret the name as meaning "ideal" or as "no place," it seems clear that Mrs. Evelyn saw in the work little of the confusions and oppositions of the world from which drama must draw its life. Dryden had produced a blueprint for the heroic rather than a drama. But that is not all. We are also confronted with a related problem of language:

> *Almanzor.* No man has more contempt than I, of breath;
> But whence hast thou the right to give me death?

> Obey'd as Soveraign by thy Subjects be,
> But know, that I alone am King of me.
> I am as free as Nature first made man
> 'Ere the base Laws of Servitude began
> When wild in woods the noble Savage ran.
>
> (1.1.203–9)[2]

A notable brief speech, filled with concepts, and containing I believe the first English reference to the noble savage, plunges into a banality entirely linguistic with its attempt at stunning simplification: "... know, that I alone am King of me." Pope would attempt this kind of vertiginous simplification better, though even he got into trouble with "Whatever is, is right." At moments like these we can, in retrospect, see Almanzor becoming Drawcansir. Such a style is deservedly ridiculed by Buckingham:

> I drink, I huff, I strut, look big and stare;
> And all this I can do, because I dare.
>
> (*The Rehearsal*, 4.1.248–49)

"There's a brave fellow for you now, Sirs," as Bayes remarks after another speech of Drawcansir (5.1.353). The second line of this couplet is, of course, an actual quotation from *The Conquest of Granada,* part 2 (2.3.106). In the derisive, down-to-the-boards setting of *The Rehearsal* the line becomes a satire on itself. Yet the original idea in Dryden's mind is inherently heroic: it is that of the sovereignty of the individual. If in Dryden's plays we are to find dramatic justice done to this idea we must turn to *Don Sebastian,* at that point where the deserter Dorax speaks of Sebastian himself:

> *Dorax.* My Master? By what title,
> Because I happen'd to be born where he
> Happen'd to be a King?
>
> (1.1.86–88)

These questions, at once colloquial and structured, mark the distance between apprenticeship and a mature dramatic talent. They set the notion of the sovereign individual in full contingency. We feel also the release from rhyme, though it should be said that it is not rhyme itself that is a problem with the earlier heroic plays. The rhyming alexandrines of Corneille and the earlier Racine, with sense played against line, and with greater attention to diction and tone, show a standard the earlier Dryden cannot match.

Dryden had, however, learned something by the time he wrote *All for Love* (1677). His language is no longer debating and definitional—and it is no longer rhyming, but of that more anon. Dryden is now more interested in expressiveness and sees that familiar language may serve his turn:

> *Antony.* Give, you Gods,
> Give to your Boy, your *Cæsar*,
> This Rattle of a Globe to play withal. . . .
>
> (2.1.443–45)
>
> My Queen and thou have got the start of me,
> And I'm the lag of Honour.
>
> (5.1.337–38)

That language is naturally, not definitionally simple, and learned from Shakespeare no doubt. The play is nevertheless strange. External conflict is slighted despite the presence of Ventidius, and Caesar's formidable part is never expressed (save briefly by Antony himself). The introduction of Octavia turns the play toward domestic rather than military strife, but even in the arena of Antony's mind there seems no psychomachia. He is simply influenced by each situation, each appearance, each ruse: putty in the hands of the plot, while the silent Caesar slowly advances. The play certainly displays a series of versions or phases of Antony as the plot grows more and more involute, but is there conflict here? Is the play a drama or a masque of the different faces of Antony's weakness? Whatever our answer, pragmatism tells us that *All for Love* will never be much admired while *Antony and Cleopatra* is remembered.

Even the drastically selective mode of this paper must acknowledge that there is at least one prerevolutionary drama of Dryden that is truly exceptional, worthy of reading and indeed of performance. This is *Aureng-Zebe* (1675), the last rhyming play if we except the reprises of *Love Triumphant*. It is not just that Dryden's couplet verse has improved (there are still some moments of embarrassment) but because this form, associated now with the attempted heroic and "Nature wrought up to an higher pitch,"[3] has here a dual role. On the one hand it connives at effects of almost operatic extravagance (the recounted battles of 1.1); on the other, it repeatedly encounters and recognizes experience of the most unheroic kind.

Take the Old Emperor's really rather magnificent attempt to reassure the Empress, Nourmahal, of his love:

> Have patience, my first flames can ne'r decay:
> These are but Dreams, and soon will pass away.
> Thou know'st, my Heart, my Empire, all is thine:
> In thy own Heav'n of Love serenely shine:
> Fair as the face of Nature did appear,
> When Flowers first peep'd, and Trees did Blossoms bear,
> And Winter had not yet deform'd th' inverted Year:
> Calm as the Breath which fans our Eastern Groves . . .
> (2.1.221–28)

The dissatisfied and jealous Nourmahal is not appeased, and soon the emperor is constrained to adopt a different mode of address:

> Such virtue is the plague of humane life:
> A virtuous Woman, but a cursed Wife.
> In vain of pompous chastity y' are proud:
> Virtue's adultery of the Tongue, when loud,
> I, with less pain, a Prostitute could bear,
> Than the shrill sound of Virtue, virtue hear.
> (2.1.257–62)

This is more than a turn to domestic tragedy; the heroic world has been allowed to sink into the realistic realm of domestic comedy, and the couplet verse has all the tang of family recrimination.

Not a one-off moment, this exemplifies the larger design of the drama. The amazing victories of Aureng-Zebe, the loyal heir, are rewarded only by the humiliating indecisions of a sexually jealous father and sovereign. This situation leads to that notable speech of Aureng-Zebe, imprisoned and awaiting his death, which is so ethically perceptive and stylistically unheroic:

> When I consider Life, 'tis all a cheat;
> Yet, fool'd with hope, men favour the deceit;
> Trust on, and think to morrow will repay:
> To morrow's falser than the former day;
> Lies worse; and while it says, We shall be blest
> With some new joys, cuts off what we possest. . . .
> (4.1.33–38)

This couplet verse is more syntactically developed; in attitude and style it is moving toward *Religio Laici* and the Lucretius translations. But that opening line is the disillusioned heart of the play, hardly modified by the lines with which the Old Emperor concludes its action. What above all makes *Aureng-Zebe* a drama, and an unusual one at that, is that it does not simply replace one mode for another, heroic by unheroic. Nothing is more "wrought up to an higher pitch" than the two fire speeches of act 5, that of the faithful Melesinda as she goes to perform the act of suttee after the death of her husband, Morat, and that of Nourmahal as she flames through jealousy into a burning madness. I hesitate to invoke the much-invoked term "tension," but I think it applicable to this transitional drama, which both heroicises and satirises a gaudy, disappointing, world.

Dryden's dedications to *Aureng-Zebe* and *Don Sebastian* are, as Paul Hammond has observed,[4] two of the fullest pieces of autobiography we have from the poet's hand. It is no surprise that their mood of deep disaffection should preface two of his finest tragedies. *Aureng-Zebe* marks Dryden's move from the king's to the duke's party (its political allusion suggesting Charles in the Old Emperor, and the Duke of York in Aureng-Zebe himself).[5] Dryden here for the first time abandons his Augustan hopes for Charles and his court, though the Exclusion Crisis will bring him round again. *Don Sebastian* sees Dryden's duke figure, who has finally come to the throne and whose religion the poet has embraced, become an exile—an exile with the will to fight back. In 1675, still more in 1689, Dryden is an internal exile. This position did not produce his best satire, perhaps, but I would argue that it produced his best drama. "Mad England hurt him into tragedy," as W. H. Auden might have written.

The question of political parallels now arises. Both *Aureng-Zebe* and *All for Love,* it has been argued, propose parallels, suggesting Charles II in the Old Emperor, the Duke in Aureng-Zebe; Charles in Antony, Louis XIV in Caesar.[6] One mark of *Don Sebastian*'s greater maturity is Dryden's more complex treatment of parallel and expectation of parallel. If there is a more or less lasting allusion in the exiled Sebastian to the exiled James II, characters in this play are not meant to portray historical figures; rather, they are addressed to contemporary and fundamental issues. Further, apparent parallels are checked and reversed; apparent identifications offered to audiences and readers of different viewpoints turn out to be traps that are later sprung. This manner of allusion is superior to that of any previous drama of Dryden, and the tragedy, less a party piece than *Absalom and*

Achitophel with its straightforward parallel, is more complex and exploratory.

Over and above the ambiguities and intricacies of the public realm, this drama explores the limits of human heroism. Sebastian, impetuous but defeated in battle, is ready to die almost, he seems to feel, in redemption of his loyal subjects who lost their lives for him. Death has no fears for Sebastian, but he gives orthodox counsel against suicide to his love, the Queen Almeyda, not appreciating fully the vision of a Christian death which she expresses:

> *Almeyda.* If shunning ill be good, then Death is good
> To those who cannot shun it but by Death:
> Divines but peep on undiscover'd Worlds,
> And draw the distant Landshape as they please:
> But who has e'er return'd from those bright Regions,
> To tell their Manners, and relate their Laws?
> I'll venture landing on that happy shoar
> With an unsully'd Body, and white Mind;
> If I have err'd, some kind Inhabitant
> Will pity a stray'd Soul, and take me home.
>
> (2.1.530–39)

Full of Renaissance and indeed heroic resonance, Almeyda's speech ends on a note of simple and unforced humility. It sketches (to use one of his own words) a "landshape" against which we have to consider Sebastian. As the theme of unknowing incest inexorably emerges from the plotted past, Sebastian once again contemplates death, this time by his own hand. It is, he now says, all he can do in reparation for his sin. The returned renegade, Dorax, now interposes:

> *Dorax.*   Your pardon, Sir;
> You may do more, and ought.
> *Sebastian.*   What, more than death?
> *Dorax.* Death? Why that's Childrens sport: a Stage-Play, Death.
> We Act it every Night we go to bed.
> Death to a Man in misery is sleep.
> Wou'd you, who perpetrated such a Crime
> As frighten'd nature, made the Saints above
> Shake Heav'ns Eternal pavement with their trembling,
> To view that act, wou'd you but barely dye? . . .
> *Sebastian.* To expiate this, can I do more then dye?
> *Dorax.* O yes: you must do more; you must be damn'd:
> You must be damn'd to all Eternity.

> And, sure, self-Murder is the readiest way.
> *Sebastian.* How, damn'd?
> *Dorax.*   Why, is that News?
>
> (5.1.502–18)

This exchange sets the physical courage of Sebastian in a metaphysical perspective (expressed already by Almeyda) and turns Sebastian from suicide to being a hermit. There is more, it seems, to the scheme of things than heroism. The lost king will neither prematurely die, nor return to his kingdom. The well-schooled English commentator who wrote of *Don Sebastian*, "Which abdicated Laureate brings / In praise of abdicated kings" saw the public side of the play: the numerous, shifting, allusions all in the end ask what the exiled James II is, and what he may become. The commentator also detects Dryden's outcast voice: the voice of one living, with all his wits about him, with defeat.

Dryden's five post-revolutionary dramas are all different from one another and, with the partial exception of the collaborative *Cleomenes* (1692), each is a striking success. We have a classical comedy, *Amphitryon* (1690), a musical drama of enchantment, *King Arthur* (1691), and the tragicomedy *Love Triumphant* (1694), the deliberatively prepared farewell play that, like Shakespeare's *Tempest,* recapitulates in briefer form the major themes and styles of much of the author's former drama. The psychological, political, and religious landscape of these three plays is treacherous and hardly possible to control. Where are we? Who are we? To whom do we owe faith? In *Amphitryon* the double-identity device of Plautine tradition adapts perfectly to a new public situation in which you no longer know who your master or servant is. The derisively skeptical dialogue of Phoebus and Mercury give the contemporary political signals we require, but the potentially tragic heart of this agnostic comedy is the experience of Alcmena, tricked by "the impostour God" in the shape of her husband.

> *Alcmena.* I know not what to hope, nor what to fear.
> A simple Errour, is a real Crime;
> And unconsenting Innocence is lost.
>
> (5.1.390–92)

Ambiguity of public situation reaches into personal life, and we can see from these lines of Alcmena how the unknowing incest of *Don Sebastian* is expressive of some fear in the Jacobite dilemma.

The secular and skeptical *Amphitryon* comes from the side of Dryden's mind that responded to Lucretius, as *Don Sebastian* had from the side that created the Anne Killigrew ode or *The Hind and the Panther*. Each side, one may think, is active in creating the perilous romance world of *King Arthur* in which a blind heroine is vulnerable to two contending warlords, Oswald and Arthur, of whom it is at first hard to decide which is invader and which defender. Further, the seemingly ambiguous spirit Philidell, the double agent who eventually adheres to the Christian cause of Arthur and Merlin, and restores the sight of Emmeline, gives the audience a line of faith, at least, though no sure prospect of happiness. James Winn must be right to see something of the autobiographical in Dryden's Philidell, who then casts an interesting light on the role of the poet in the new era.

That fear, that initial failure to interpret the signs, conveyed in *Amphitryon* by the double-identity device, and in *King Arthur* by a dark and dangerous physical landscape and by blindness, is expressed in *Love Triumphant* by the repeatedly surprising turns of the plot, a tour de force of late Renaissance intricacy, in which our surprise is on each occasion attended by realization of the moral inadequacy of our previous assessment of the situation. In particular, the loyalty and understanding of the two princesses, Victoria and Celidea, models for the judgment of those two less admirable princesses, Mary and Anne Stuart, each to be queen, have to be accommodated in any lasting prosperous conclusion. A tragicomedy that once again explores rightful warfare and wrongful conquest, duty to the wronged but equally duty to the wrongdoer, love as instinct, love as duty, faith as duty, and faith as instinct, Dryden's last play is no doubt the subtlest study of loyalty he ever wrote. Its perceptiveness and its unashamed ceremony and formalism come together most memorably, perhaps, in that prophet-like speech of the Princess Celidea in act 5, which is at once the moral of the play and the lever that finally produces the long-deferred prosperous outcome. Seeming to accuse while she moves steadily to defend, she here addresses her brother Alphonso, originally played by the great Betterton:

> *Celidea.* Yes, Proud *Alphonso,* you were banish't hence;
> Your Father was confin'd; and doomed to Death;
> The Beauty you Ador'd was made another's.
> How durst you, then, attempt t'avenge your wrongs,
> And force your Mistress from your Rival's Arms,
> Rather than Dye contented, as you ought?

> *Alphonso.* Even for those very Reasons you alledge,
> *Ximena.* (*aside*) At last I find her drift.
> *Veramond.* Thou justifiest, and not Accusest him.
> *Celidea.* Patience, good Father, and hear out the rest.
> (To Alphonso.) Thought you, because you bravely
>   Fought, and Conquer'd
> For Royal Veramond, nay sav'd his Life,
> And set him free, when you had Conquer'd him,
> Only because he was Victoria's Father,
> Thought you for such slight Services as these,
> That he shou'd spare you now? O Generous Madman,
> To give your Head to one, who ne're forgave.
>   (5.2.176–92)

That this speech should melt into reconciliation the pride of Veramond, the William figure in the drama as Ramirez is the James figure, is consistent with the play's steady emphasis on emotion and instinct, as well as on reason and advantage: *Love Triumphant; Or, Nature Will Prevail* is the longer title of the play. After seeming to write Jacobite protagonists out of history in *Don Sebastian* and *Cleomenes,* Dryden in his last drama comes round to write a parable of reconciliation, applicable to William and James, in the vision of which the poet's Jacobite faith finds the conclusion it deserves.

In recommending the imaginative achievement of Dryden's later plays I must admit to a measure of disappointment and a measure of frustration. I have of course written about these plays at more length. What they need now is a fuller, not a more compressed defense. I am disappointed that, through what Dryden might have called "the blind contingence of events," my book *Poetry of Opposition and Revolution* came out in the same year as volume 16 of the California Dryden, containing *King Arthur, Cleomenes,* and *Love Triumphant.* The editor declares that the only sustained consideration of *Love Triumphant* appeared in 1905.[7] I did not have the advantage of the edition when I wrote about these plays, while the editor was apparently unaware that they had a critical advocate on the other side of the Atlantic.

In recommending the later plays I have also here made a basic assumption, open to challenge. This is that while plays may be written at any time, whether they amount to drama depends on social and ideological rifts implicit or explicit in the body politic. I find it credible that when, in the early Restoration, English society seemed to Dryden to be united, he failed to produce good drama. In 1675, on the other hand, when even in the eyes of loyalists and royalists Charles II appeared such a hedonistic and evasive figure, that painful paradox for Dryden produced, in *Aureng-Zebe,* his first genuine drama outside the comedies. Though Dryden converted to Catholicism during James II's short period on the throne he was, we know, uneasy at the impetuous religious policies of the new king.[8] *The Hind and the Panther* shows that he had no confident golden visions of the historical future. The expulsion of the king and the change of dynasty in 1688 left Dryden an alien in his own country. He remained loyal to James, refusing the oaths to William, but the exiled monarch was the object of a double awareness: had there been some curse, was there some secret sin, which had brought about the failure of political right and true religion? Would the exiled monarch now become a hermit and hidden king? Or would he become a returning conqueror? These questions, this troubled and dual awareness, is the major factor in the dramatic importance of Dryden's later plays.

It has sometimes been suggested that Dryden's plays cannot be much good because in the later twentieth century so few of them have been revived in the theater.[9] Of the works discussed here, I have seen in the theater *All for Love* and *King Arthur.* The effect was in each case extremely unusual: theatrical in a strange way. This seemed especially so with *King Arthur,* enhanced by music and lavish stage effects, which did not in the end feel extraneous in performance. More recently I have seen Murray Biggs's fine amateur production of *Marriage A-la-Mode* and have no doubt about the viability of that play in the theater. There is no doubt great difficulty for modern directors and actors in addressing themselves to many of Dryden's tragic or tragicomic plays. They are part of a courtly, late Baroque, mode, not without its theatrical energies and rituals, but alien to modern theatrical practice. To stage *Don Sebastian,* probably Dryden's greatest play, would take courage and imagination indeed, but I am confident that to do so would be a positive revelation. Literary criticism should have the courage of its convictions, and we should remember for how long a period in the opinion of actor-managers and players Shakespeare's *Lear* with Shakespeare's ending would have seemed quite unactable. The judgments of the theater are not always right.

Other problems in the reception of Dryden confront the twenty-first–century reader. These bear upon his plays as upon his most famous poetry. A dual approach to Dryden, which would have been par for the course to Walter Scott or James Kinsley, seems to have been pulling apart. It used not to be a matter of dismay that Dryden should have been deeply involved in the political and religious affairs of his own time. To accept as much was not, of course, to deny the great importance of earlier literary sources, the classics and the earlier Renaissance, in the shaping of his major works. Associated, however, with the distinguished new Longman's Edition of the *Poems of Dryden*, edited by Paul Hammond and David Hopkins, of which four fine volumes have so far appeared, seems to be the view that while Dryden's classical derivations are always a matter for congratulation, his contemporary concerns (though it may be the dull duty of an editor to explain them) are mainly a matter for regret. The great mark of this edition and this approach is their recognition of the extraordinary quality of Dryden's own translations from the classics, though attention has so far had to be paid to Lucretius, Ovid, and Horace, rather than Virgil who, in Dryden's time, was so often seen as author of a narrative that could be used for the better understanding of one's own age—like the Bible.

This trend applies as much to the drama as to the poetry. Even the California editors of Dryden are inclined sometimes to play down contemporary allusion while sturdily affirming his insistence on "universal truths." For the Longman editors such allusions tend either to be a series of barbed allusions, which may thus be recognized as a marginal feature; or, if a contemporary allusion appears unavoidably major, a totalizing allegory has to be accepted, with the implicit or explicit consequence that the work concerned is critically degraded. These are not, however, the only critical categories available.

Dryden, as James Winn remarked at the Tercentenary Conference on Dryden at Bristol in July 2000, is greater than all of us and our academic programs. He could draw on the great classics, allude to major contemporary affairs without lapsing into bald parallel or allegory, and at one and the same time plumb the depths of moral and religious psychology through dramatic expression. Let us turn, for one final time, to the dialogue between Sebastian and Almeyda on suicide and death in act 2, scene 1, where the latter has given the impression that she might take her own life. Sebastian rejoins:

>Death may be call'd in vain, and cannot come;
>Tyrants can tye him up from your relief:
>Nor has a Christian privilege to dye.
>Alas thou art too young in thy new Faith;

> *Brutus* and *Cato* might discharge their Souls,
> And give 'em Furlo's for another World:
> But we, like Centry's, are oblig'd to stand
> In starless Nights, and wait the 'pointed hour.
>
> (2.1.522–29)

Brutus and Cato, kinsmen and defenders of a legitimate Roman Republic against a Caesar who sought to subvert it into a kind of monarchy, took their own lives when faced by military defeat, Brutus in Macedonia, Cato in Utica. Each expresses a way in which defeated legitimacy and exile became heroic. Each reminds us of, without being a parallel to, the exiled King James, especially in this play, though the California editors do not point this out. But James and Sebastian are Christian; furthermore, Dryden seems to echo Cicero, colleague of Brutus and Cato Uticensis, when in three places he writes against suicide, as Earl Miner and George R. Guffey do point out in a particularly rich note.[10] In one of these places, *Tusculan Disputations* 1.30.74, Cato and Socrates are mentioned, and much that Cicero says derives from Plato's *Phaedo,* which Cato was supposed to have been reading on the last night of his life. When Miner's commentary demonstrates that the image of life as sentry duty is also to be found in Montaigne and Spenser, famous refashioners of ancient wisdom, we can see that Sebastian's speech is almost a paradigm of humanist indebtedness to the classics. Yet Brutus and Cato, named in the speech and natural examples to occur to the mind of Sebastian as he is situated at this moment of the action, are political figures at the matrix of the classical sources. It is Cato who takes us to the *Tusculan Disputations* and thence to Plato: what unwinds the thread of classical influence is a political allusion and one with an obvious bearing on Dryden's situation after 1688. Furthermore, Dryden's own apparent addition, his "starless Nights," only underlines the bewilderment of the dutiful after the withdrawal of authority. It is evident from the example of this speech that classical awareness and political awareness are not mutually exclusive and are not at odds with one another. If it were not demeaning for Cicero to praise Cato of Utica, which he apparently did in a work now lost, why should it be demeaning for Dryden to explore the situation of his exiled king? Sometimes contemporary issues and affairs are as important as ancient issues and affairs. In this case the two are inseparable, and it is a matter of life and death.

NOTES

1. *The Diary of John Evelyn,* ed. E. S. de Beer, 6 vols. (Oxford: Oxford University Press, 1955), 3:570. See Annabel Patterson's essay in this collection, page 202, for Mary Evelyn's comments.

2. Quotations from Dryden's plays are drawn from original editions, and agree with the California Edition of *The Works of John Dryden,* general ed. H. T. Swedenberg, Jr. et al., 20 vols. (Berkeley and Los Angeles: University of California Press, 1956–). Buckingham's *The Rehearsal* is quoted from *George Villiers, Duke of Buckingham: The Rehearsal,* ed. D. E. L. Crane (Durham: University of Durham, 1976).

3. *Works,* 17:74.

4. Paul Hammond, "Is Dryden a Classic?" *John Dryden: Tercentenary Essays,* ed. Paul Hammond and David Hopkins (Oxford: Oxford University Press, 2000), 9.

5. George McFadden, *Dryden the Public Writer, 1660–1685* (Princeton: Princeton University Press, 1978), ch. 6.

6. John Dryden, *All for Love,* ed. David M. Vieth (Lincoln: University of Nebraska Press, 1973), xxxiii. Generally speaking the notion of political parallels in Dryden's works should be treated with caution and delicacy. It should be appreciated that *Absalom and Achitophel* is not typical Dryden. Sometimes a parallel can be a broad ground plan for a drama, not the be-all-and-end-all of the work, but one layer of its meaning. Sometimes parallels seem to be offered, but are then found to run only for a short time, or to run in reverse. Political allusion in Dryden is more subtle than used to be thought. In its general approaches Phillip Harth's *Pen for a Party: Dryden's Tory Propaganda in its Contexts* (Princeton: Princeton University Press, 1993) is a valuable example though it does not cover the post-revolutionary period with which the present essay is chiefly concerned. Harth is probably right when he suggests that Dryden's political allusion after the death of Charles II is less programmatic and more exploratory than before (271). David Bywaters, in *Dryden in Revolutionary England* (Berkeley and Los Angeles: University of California Press, 1991) offered an effective discussion of Dryden's later period. In *Poetry and the Realm of Politics: Shakespeare to Dryden* and *Poetry of Opposition and Revolution: Dryden to Wordsworth* (both Oxford: Clarendon Press, 1996) I attempted to give an adequately complex account of political allusion in the late Dryden.

7. *The Works of Dryden,* 16:393 n. 17.

8. *The Letters of John Dryden,* ed. C. E. Ward (Durham, N.C.: Duke University Press, 1942), 27 (Dryden to Etherege, 16 Feb. 1687).

9. See, for instance, Barbara Everett's essay in this collection.

10. *The Works of Dryden,* 15:434–35, note to lines 526–29. The editors acknowledge James Russell Lowell, who indeed stands behind the note.

Dryden's *The Spanish Fryar:* Modernity and Exclusion

DAVID WOMERSLEY

What do you take me to be and what do you take yourselves to be?

Charles II, January 1680

SCOTT COINED A STRIKING PHRASE WHEN HE SUGGESTED THAT, IN writing *Absalom and Achitophel,* Dryden was addressing a subject "the issue of whose contention was yet in the womb of fate."[1] The metaphor of the "womb of fate" encourages us to think afresh about the position of the writer who chooses to address public issues and events while the character of those events and issues is as yet undecided: while, that is—to pursue the implications of Scott's obstetric metaphor—they are still in the gristle, and have not yet hardened into the bone. To know that a development is imminent, that a political birth will take place, without yet knowing what the character of that development will be, and to be in doubt therefore as to what precisely will be born: a position so equally compounded of knowledge and ignorance makes the task of the would-be writer on public affairs an unusually delicate one. Such was Dryden's position when he wrote *The Spanish Fryar: or, The Double Discovery*. Written and performed, so far as we can judge,[2] while events were still in the womb of fate, but with the mother experiencing strong contractions, it allows us to see Dryden addressing public life while the posture of affairs is still doubtful. At the same time, as what its most recent editor has roundly called "one more piece of official propaganda for the royal program," it comes to us with unimpeachable loyalist credentials. What does it tell us about how the king's adherents perceived those agitating for exclusion and against popery and arbitrary government?

Temple said of Shaftesbury that he "would try every door to

get in"³—a remark I shall take as offering at least some precedent for my own outlandish way in to this subject, which will be by means of a poem by Wallace Stevens, "Of Modern Poetry" (1942):

> The poem of the mind in the act of finding
> What will suffice. It has not always had
> To find: the scene was set; it repeated what
> Was in the script.
>   Then the theatre was changed
> To something else. Its past was a souvenir.
> It has to be living, to learn the speech of the place.
> It has to face the men of the time and to meet
> The women of the time. It has to think about war
> And it has to find what will suffice. It has
> To construct a new stage. It has to be on that stage
> And, like an insatiable actor, slowly and
> With meditation, speak words that in the ear,
> In the delicatest ear of the mind, repeat,
> Exactly, that which it wants to hear, at the sound
> Of which, an invisible audience listens,
> Not to the play, but to itself, expressed
> In an emotion as of two people, as of two
> Emotions becoming one. The actor is
> A metaphysician in the dark, twanging
> An instrument, twanging a wiry string that gives
> Sounds passing through sudden rightnesses, wholly
> Containing the mind, below which it cannot descend,
> Beyond which it has no will to rise.⁴

I take it that Stevens's subject in this poem is not in any narrow or contracted sense simply the poetry being written in the late thirties and early forties—that is to say, it is not about "modern poetry" construed in a leveling, Warholian, sense whereby all literary art at the moment of its promulgation enjoys fifteen minutes of modernity before subsiding into the past. Rather, he is concerned about the condition of modernity in literary art, a condition he invites us to understand as arising from a particular kind of self-consciousness on the part of the writer which in its turn produces a certain kind of formal disarray in the literary work. That self-consciousness is an awareness of being surrounded by the unprecedented. In Stevens's conveniently theatrical metaphors, the theater has been "changed," the "script" is no longer available, and the past is no sustaining tradition, but has dwindled into "a souvenir," the memento of a foreign place.

This produces the need to improvise, "To construct a new stage." The result is that modern poetry has a double aspect. One of those aspects is public and engaged:

> It has to be living, to learn the speech of the place.
> It has to face the men of the time and to meet
> The women of the time. It has to think about war . . .

But the other is private and reflective:

> It has to be on that stage
> And, like an insatiable actor, slowly and
> With meditation, speak words that in the ear,
> In the delicatest ear of the mind, repeat,
> Exactly, that which it wants to hear, at the sound
> Of which, an invisible audience listens,
> Not to the play, but to itself, expressed
> In an emotion as of two people, as of two
> Emotions becoming one.

In finding "what will suffice," then, modern poetry is both bare and exact. It also has a dynamic and uneven aesthetic, in which dissonance yields abruptly to "sudden rightnesses," and in which spareness is accompanied by strength. For modern poetry is "wiry" in both senses.

It is this kind of modernity which I wish to claim for *The Spanish Fryar*.[5] That is to say, I wish to discuss it as a play emerging from a particular kind of self-consciousness on Dryden's part concerning the unformed and indeterminate nature of the times through which he was living—times in which the new was imminent but as yet unknowable, and even (as we shall see) if not precisely unnamed then at least *between* names. And I shall wish to suggest that this self-consciousness on the part of the playwright results in a play with formal properties that closely resemble the disrupted aesthetic for modern poetry imagined by Wallace Stevens. By attending to the way in which "twanging" yields to "sudden rightnesses" in *The Spanish Fryar*, we can focus on the private and reflective aspect of the play, can understand how and why in this play "two / Emotions" are united, and can see that, if Dryden was committed wholly to Charles during these years (and I can see little reason to doubt it), his commitment was no blinkered bigotry. His intelligence was larger than his loyalty; as indeed it must be, if loyalty is not to descend into mere partisanship.

We do not lack for scholarly and persuasive accounts of the public aspect of *The Spanish Fryar*. In *The Laureate,* his poem of 1687, Robert Gould had attributed the anti–Roman Catholic satire of the play to resentment on Dryden's part at the stopping of his pension. The result, he alleged, was a petulant and shallow Whiggism:

> The Fryar now was writ: and some will say
> They smell a Male-content through all the Play.
> The Papist too was damn'd, unfit for Trust,
> Call'd Treacherous, Shameless, Profligate, Unjust,
> And Kingly Power thought Arbitrary Lust.[6]

This was first questioned by Malone, and then on several further occasions discredited in the nineteenth century, before being finally dispatched by Louis Bredvold in 1932.[7] But its removal raised the question of quite how the play's satirical presentation of Friar Dominic was to be construed. If there seemed no longer to be grounds for believing that Dryden had temporarily become a resentful Whig, what was his reason for apparently mocking the religion of the Duke of York in a play that was given its premiere by the Duke of York's own company?[8] On closer inspection, the play's anti-Catholic satire seemed comparatively genial, falling some way short of damnation, and surely mild in comparison with some of the vituperation to be encountered when the rumors of the Popish Plot were at their height in 1679.[9] The subplot, to which Friar Dominic is confined, therefore invited interpretation as only a ruse or feint—a tub thrown out to amuse the whiggish leviathan—but not at all a distraction for the more intelligent members of the audience, who would have easily extracted from the more elevated, serious plot a message of unimpeachable loyalism. This is a view associated with Robert Hume and Judith Milhous, and also James Winn, who are united in their admiration of what their accounts present as a drama of astute political footwork on Dryden's part.[10]

However, there is no greater provocation to academics than even an incipient consensus, and it was not long before this view of *The Spanish Fryar,* which commanded the mid-1980s, came under critical pressure. As part of his broader argument that Dryden signed up as a Tory partisan only with *Absalom and Achitophel,* in 1993 Phillip Harth proposed that we should see Dryden in this play "deliberately avoiding controversial topics that could have alienated any part of his audience, and of choosing to represent in his play those very aspects of both politics and religion that were least likely to give offense to the spectators." Thus the play "takes for granted a system of values that all members of the audience can be expected to share in despising Dominic, sympathizing with Torrismond's moral dilemma, and welcoming the rightful king's restoration."[11] This account possesses two notable strengths, one textual, the other contextual. In the first place, it allows Harth to make sense of those elements in the play that blur or undermine the clear commitment argued for by Milhous, Hume, and Winn. If Harth is right that Dryden's "primary interest" in late 1680 was that of a "professional man of the theatre" who wished to ensure the "success of his plays by appealing to all members of his prospective audience and by avoiding overt political partisanship that would have alienated any considerable segment,"[12] then those features of the play that are incommensurable with a purely partisan interpretation fall into place as strokes in a deliberate policy of confusing the play's political signals in order to maximize its popularity.[13] And in respect of context, Harth's argument is attractive because it can accommodate the fact that in the autumn of 1680 (but not only then) there was considerable common ground between many of those who were seeking Exclusion, and many of those who were opposed to it.[14] The fact that at this time there was no clear water between the two parties makes it possible that a trimming play such as he describes *The Spanish Fryar* to have been could indeed have found a plentiful and appreciative audience.

Susan Owen, in an article published the year after Harth's *Pen for a Party*, acknowledged on the one hand the reality and significance of the complicating textual features of the play on which Harth relied, but was reluctant to relinquish the belief that *The Spanish Fryar* was a play of decided political engagement.[15] The circle was squared by means of a more exact appeal to the political circumstances of the play's moment. Noting that the later months of 1680 were an "uncertain period of apparent Whig ascendancy," Owen construed the play's mixed political signals, not as the strategy of a playwright eager to maximize his profits,[16] but rather as a celebration of the broadly appealing values of "compromise, forgiveness, marriage, moderation and good humour."[17] This is also substantially the view of Vinton Dearing, who in his introduction to the play in the California *Dryden* draws a distinction between the position of Charles II and that of the Tories, and holds that "at the time of its writing, its premiere, and its first publication . . . the play accurately reflected the king's official position during the prosecution of the Popish Plot and the ensuing succession crisis."[18] According to Dearing, the manner in which the play fosters "moderation and harmony" demands that we see it as an instrument of Charles's known desire at this time for an abatement of inflammatory writings.[19] It therefore becomes "one more piece of official propaganda for the royal program."[20]

Although, therefore, there is clearly a spread of scholarly opinion concerning precisely what position it is that Dryden is writing in support of in *The Spanish Fryar*—the king, the Tories, or simply his own financial well-being—all these accounts of the play share the premise that it is to be considered as the instrument of a clear and sufficient authorial intention, and that we are to infer that intention from the play's likely reception in the theater. This approach does, I think, capture much that is central to the play. However, it may not capture everything worth pondering, as Dryden himself seems to warn us when in the dedication he dwells on how the "false Beauties of the Stage" can distort a play: "In a Play-house every thing contributes to impose upon the Judgment; the Lights, the Scenes, the Habits, and, above all, the Grace of Action . . . surprize the Audience, and cast a mist upon their Understandings. . . ."[21] Moreover, even when students of *The Spanish Fryar* such as Susan Owen have adduced in argument the uncertainty of the play's political circumstances, they have not perhaps taken the full measure of both the extent and the depth of the inchoateness of the time. The uncertainty in the light of which she reads Dryden's play is rather like the uncertainty of a football match at halftime: the outcome is as yet unknown, but you do nevertheless know the names of the teams, the players the teams contain, and the goal toward which each team is playing. Yet this, as the most recent historical research on the politics of the years 1678–83 admonishes us, is a far greater degree of certainty than the first audiences of *The Spanish Fryar* could have enjoyed when they turned their gaze toward the drama of contemporary politics—what William Marshal at his trial had called "a mournful theater, upon which such a tragedy is acted, as turns the eyes of all Europe toward it."[22] On all those three, crucial, points—nomenclature, personnel, and objectives— they would have had well-founded reasons to feel unsure. If we wish to persist in viewing the Exclusion Crisis under the metaphor of sport, we will have to accept that it was a fixture in which the names of the teams were changing as the match went on, some of the players swapped shirts during the game, and both teams were trying to score in the same goal.

Firstly, the question of nomenclature. The Exclusion Crisis is always presented as a match played between the Whigs and the Tories, but it is worth reminding ourselves that these labels for, respectively, those who advocated and those who opposed Exclusion, were used to describe the divisions of English politics only during the course of the crisis. In particular, there seems to have been no use of the word "Whig" to refer to Englishmen before the middle of February 1681, after which it was not used again for some five months.[23] Dryden himself did not use either term before he composed the prefatory letter to *Absalom and Achitophel*, when he expected that *"he who draws his Pen for one Party, must expect to make Enemies of the other. For,* Wit *and* Fool *are Consequents of* Whig *and* Tory: *And every man is a Knave or an Ass to the contrary side."*[24] Therefore it is important to bear in mind that *The Spanish Fryar* was composed and staged some months before these labels were even available for use, let alone current. Indeed, when in the Prologue to *The Spanish Fryar* Dryden mocks the weak and variable judgment of the pit—*"what e'er base metal come, / You coin as fast as Groats at* Bromingam:"[25]— he glances at one of the earlier labels that had been applied to the petitioners for Exclusion, namely "Birmingham Protestants," so called because Birmingham was then infamous for counterfeiting.[26] I am not here arguing for an extreme form of historical nominalism, the kind that would charge with anachronism any identification in the past of whiggism before the term "Whig" had been applied to that particular political grouping. In this particular case, where there are evident continuities underlying the developments in language, such a stance would be perverse. But I do contend that evolutions in political language such as the emergence of the label "Whig" in the early months of 1681 should not be dismissed as merely epiphenomenal. Such volatility in language often accompanies an underlying volatility of situation. If therefore we present *The Spanish Fryar* in a context—no matter how moderate or nuanced—formed by a definite opposition between Whigs and Tories, we have already made the moment of the play slightly more defined, a shade more clear cut, than in fact it was.

When Dryden, probably in the spring of 1681, wrote that "Wit *and* Fool *are Consequents of* Whig *and* Tory: *And every man is a Knave or an Ass to the contrary side,"* he not only used those party labels for the first time, but also referred to a condition of polarization and extremity that had not obtained during the previous winter.[27] The question of the substantial overlap between the "petitioners" (those who favored Exclusion) and the "abhorrers" or "Yorkists" (those who opposed it) needs to be considered under two headings: policy and personnel. In respect of policy, we need in the first place to appreciate that only a small proportion of the advocates of Exclusion were republicans, or commonwealthsmen, and that the doctrines of popular sovereignty and the original contract played hardly any part in the pamphlet war created by this crisis. There were only very few who, like Algernon Sidney, viewed the issue of Exclusion as a stalking horse, and who were at bottom only lukewarm about a measure that would merely replace one monarch with another.[28] So when Charles and his supporters decried those seeking Exclusion for reviving the spirit of '41, this was either a shrewd and knowing attempt to besmirch them with a political extremity they did not deserve,[29] or (on the part of those who offered the parallel in good faith) an understandable but substantially erroneous instance of political memory. On the contrary: it is arguable that most of the supporters of Exclusion engaged on that side of the question because they wished to strengthen the monarchy, not do away with it. They desired Exclusion because they feared the political damage that might be inflicted on the institution of monarchy by a highhanded, popish sovereign.[30] As the Earl of Huntingdon said in the Lords on 15 November 1680: "there is not a man in this House, I am confident, who is for the passing of this bill [the second Exclusion Bill] who is not most zealous for the support of this monarchy and the King in his royal prerogatives."[31] So the political grouping that later became known as the Whigs was from the very first an ideological hybrid.[32] As Sunderland's mother noted with satisfaction of the men with whom her son was having to contend, "they are not all of a mind."[33] Moreover, Whiggism was a hybrid that shared much genetic material with those on the other side of the question.

That this should be so will seem less surprising when we note that those on the other side of the question might not always have occupied opposing ground. Almost one hundred years after this crisis, Burke would extol political parties as "a body of men united, for promoting by their joint endeavors the national interest, upon some particular principle in which they are all agreed."[34] Such discipline (which he nevertheless was careful to separate from blinkered servitude) was the price of practical politics, and the unpredictability in voting of the so-called "independents" who stood aloof from party made them, in Burke's eyes, ridiculous and lightweight.[35] But parties in this sense seem not to have existed in the reign of Charles II. When in the spring of 1791 Burke crossed the floor of the House, abandoning Fox and joining Pitt, it was a tearful and self-lacerating remedy of last resort.[36] The 1670s and '80s were, however, a less sentimental time. And when a substantial tract of policy is held in common between different groupings, movement between them may naturally be less scandalous, because it need not imply any full-blown political apostasy. So we find that political actors such as Winnington and Capel, who were initially opposed to Exclusion, ultimately supported it. And there were also flows of support in the other direction. William Sacheverel, an enthusiastic supporter of Exclusion at the outset, passed through moderation until in the Oxford parliament he remained silent. Lionel Duckett went even further, and from being a committed petitioner, ultimately refused election to the Oxford parliament.[37] Hardy spirits such as Sidney might therefore understandably wring their hands, and bemoan the fact that they were mired in "the strangest confusion that I ever remember to have seene."[38] Their demoralization flowed inevitably from the consideration that their views were both more pure and more extreme than the views of the majority, who, staunch in their opposition to Roman Catholicism and arbitrary government, nevertheless might at different moments vary greatly in the particular measures by which they sought to fend off those dire possibilities. For these men, trimming was not so much cynical calculation as an attempt, when surrounded by political turbulence, to retain their balance while not losing sight of such lights as they had. The moment of *The Spanish Fryar*, falling as it did between the introduction of the second Exclusion Bill and the Oxford Parliament, coincided with the period when this fluidity was running high.[39]

There was therefore a double aspect to the political crisis in the midst of which this play was put on. It was a crisis that was represented increasingly as a contest between opposed camps, and a new political vocabulary of "Whigs" and "Tories" was coined during the crisis to capture that experience of sharpening polarity. But these parties were more ideological abstractions than organizations with well-defined and stable memberships. The political reality of the time was extremely volatile, and this in two senses: it was volatile in that the outcome was uncertain, and it was volatile in that political groupings were friable. In circumstances such as these, identity itself might come to seem freshly dubious. When in January 1680 Charles II responded to a group of petitioners by asking "What do you take me to be and what do you take yourselves to be?," it is easy to take this as simply a lofty reproof, and thereby not to catch the unrhetorical undertone to the question. This particular crisis had at its heart questions of what monarchs and subjects were and would be in the future, and it moved forward in a series of reverses and discoveries—the most dramatic of which was Charles's theatrical coup of the dissolution of the Oxford parliament—in which individuals were revealed as possessing surprising characteristics. Suddenly, they stood forth endowed with previously unsuspected potencies, virtues, and failings.

It is this circumstantial volatility of plot and character that I wish particularly to take over from the political context into *The Spanish Fryar*, a play in which we see the characters repeatedly wondering what kind of action they are part of, and trying to grasp the essential identities of the other characters with whom they share the stage. Moreover, if the times were double, and concealed political equivocation and ambiguity under the vehement, simplifying labels of "Whig" and "Tory," then Dryden's dedication of *The Spanish Fryar* to Lord Haughton reveals a similar doubleness in his play. The dominant theme of this dedication (which, as Dryden acknowledges toward the end, is in fact more of a critical preface than a dedication) is the way in which theatrical performance is a kind of confidence trick in which literary art is coarsened and the understanding of the audience imposed upon to accept the false for the true:

> I ... am as much asham'd to put a loose indigested Play upon the Publick, as I should be to offer brass money in a Payment: For though it shou'd be taken, (as it is too often on the Stage,) yet it will be found in the second telling: And a judicious Reader will discover in his Closset that trashy stuffe, whose glittering deceiv'd him in the action ... In a Play-house every thing contributes to impose upon the Judgment; the Lights, the Scenes, the Habits, and, above all, the Grace of Action, which is commonly the best where there is the most need of it, surprize the Audience, and cast a mist upon their Understandings; not unlike the cunning of a Juggler, who is always staring us in the face, and overwhelming us with gibberish, onely that he may gain the opportunity of making the cleaner conveyance of his Trick. But these false Beauties of the Stage are no more lasting than a Rainbow; ... But as 'tis my Interest to please my Audience, so 'tis my Ambition to be read; that I am sure is the more lasting and the nobler Design: for the propriety of thoughts and words, which are the hidden beauties of a Play, are but confus'dly judg'd in the vehemence of Action: All things are there beheld, as in a hasty motion, where the objects onely

glide before the Eye and disappear. The most discerning Critick can judge no more of these silent graces in the Action, than he who rides Post through an unknown Countrey can distinguish the scituation of places, and the nature of the soyle.[40]

Dryden here gives us a series of oppositions: acting versus reading, the authentic versus the spurious, the theater versus the closet, interest versus ambition, "false Beauties" versus "hidden beauties" and "silent graces," the fragmentary knowledge yielded by fleeting acquaintance versus that deeper and more exact knowledge produced by a more patient and reflective engagement. It would be odd, then, if in respect of this play we were to allow our sense of its meaning to be fully confined within what has come to be called "producible interpretation," and were thus to agree with Vinton Dearing that "the meaning of the play is to be found in audience reaction," since Dryden seems here explicitly to tell us that *The Spanish Fryar* was not exhausted, was not fully represented, by what happened in the theater.[41] The experience of the audience, Dryden warns us, needs to be supplemented by the understanding of the reader. If the "producible interpretation" of the play reveals the carefully-nuanced Toryism noticed by many of the play's most recent critics, we may expect careful reading to disclose other facets of the play, facets that perhaps will not engage with the time in quite the direct and instrumental manner of the "producible interpretation." So we should not expect the "hidden beauties" and "silent graces" uncovered by reading to be interventions in a public crisis in the manner of "producible interpretation." In reading, we should expect to encounter on Dryden's part a more tentative, less tendentious engagement with the time, in which the imperative lies more with the effort to understand for oneself than with the need to persuade others. In fact, we may expect to encounter something akin to that ruminative self-overhearing—at once staged but also untheatrical—that Wallace Stevens found to be at the heart of modern poetry:

> It has to be on that stage
> And, like an insatiable actor, slowly and
> With meditation, speak words that in the ear,
> In the delicatest ear of the mind, repeat,
> Exactly, that which it wants to hear, at the sound
> Of which, an invisible audience listens,
> Not to the play, but to itself, expressed
> In an emotion as of two people, as of two
> Emotions becoming one.

When we consider *The Spanish Fryar* in this way, what do we find? In the first place, we notice that we have, not so much a paralleling of contemporary circumstance, as the creation of an expectation of parallelism that yet does not settle into any stable form.⁴² This is particularly evident when we consider how the characters reflect, but always in an incomplete and even contradictory manner, the actual personalities then on the stage of English politics. For instance, Torrismond, the "successfull Warriour," who considers himself to be "base," but who in a "wondrous Secret" is revealed by the plot to be legitimate⁴³: at the moment when rumors were flying of a "black box" containing evidence that Charles was actually married to Lucy Walters, it would be hard not to see in him at least some glance toward the Duke of Monmouth, the recent victor over the rebellious Scots at Bothwell Bridge the previous year.⁴⁴ Yet Torrismond also disdains popular support:

> I have no taste
> Of popular Applause; the noisie Praise
> Of giddy Crowds, as changeable as Winds;
> Still vehement, and still without a cause:
> Servants to Chance; . . .⁴⁵

This seems rather unlike the character of the man who would shortly be touring the countryside in a series of quasi-royal progresses and stirring up wild popular enthusiasm. There is a similar dispersal, rather than focusing, of attributes in the character of Bertran, whom for most of the play we take to be Torrismond's jealous and unprincipled rival. Yet when he reproves Torrismond as a "Fond young Man!" whose "Ambition must be clipt," for a moment he plays Charles to Torrismond's Monmouth.⁴⁶ However, when, later in the play, Leonora explains her inability to punish Bertran by reminding Raymond that "You saw he came surrounded with his Friends," the kaleidoscope of parallelism has been given a further turn, since this was precisely how Shaftesbury arrived in Oxford to attend parliament.⁴⁷ Leonora herself is no more constant than either Bertran or Torrismond. Her "Guards"—an innovation of some importance in preserving Charles's authority as well as his person during the crisis—and her being the focus of city discontent, as Pedro reports, makes her almost an amalgam of the royal brothers.⁴⁸ However, in the discussion she has in 4.2 with Bertran on the highly topical question of the relationship between a monarch and his ministers,

Dryden puts into her mouth the sentiments that, at the time, dropped most commonly from the lips of those who sought to exclude the Duke of York.[49] And there is a similar political ambivalence in Raymond. On the one hand Raymond will fiercely attack Torrismond when he advances the doctrine that the passage of time can ripen a usurped title into legitimacy, and thus commit himself to the ultra-Yorkist position that the royal title cannot be varied.[50] But only a few moments later he seems to play Shaftesbury to Torrismond's Monmouth, when he entices the younger man to join a "brave Conspiracy . . . to punish Tyrants and redeem the Land": a Whiggish feature that is reinforced by the terms in which he harangues the mob in 5.2, and by Torrismond's description of him as a "Tribune of the People."[51]

This persistent confusion of political qualities amongst the leading characters of the play needs to be considered in the light of Dryden's preoccupation in this work with the changeableness of identity. In the subplot, Lorenzo, ignorant for the time being of the identity of his mistress, finds it "unconscionable" not to "know whose livery" he wears.[52] But this is a prevalent condition in a play where characters are frequently "in Metamorphosis," and where Leonora is not the only one who finds herself inwardly transformed by "a change so swift" that "rush'd upon me, like a mighty Stream, / And bore me in a moment far from Shore."[53] The dominant form of interaction between the characters is that of the probing and tentative assessment of "shrewd signs" and enigmatic tokens, captured in a language of sounding and fathoming.[54] As Alphonso says of Leonora:

> Who knows which way she points?
> Doubling and turning, like an hunted Hare.
> Find out the Meaning of her mind who can.[55]

The political ambivalence of the play's main characters is one aspect of this broader volatility of character: a volatility to be found, too, as we have noted, in the political circumstances of late 1680 and early 1681. It is accompanied in *The Spanish Fryar* by a volatility of plot. Repeatedly in this play we find that characters mistake, not only who the other characters are and even who they themselves are (most notably Torrismond and Lorenzo), but also, if one can put it like this, what kind of play they are in. Gomez thinks he is in a libertine comedy in which the wealthy old cit with the beautiful young wife is cuckolded by the youthful cavalier: but as it turns out, he is not. Torrismond thinks he is bound to experience a version of Oedipus's fate, and has been led by natural passion into a polluted marriage: but in fact, he has not.[56] The play begins on the bitter note of providence denied or questioned, as Pedro, recalling that Leonora's usurper father "dy'd in peace," exclaims: "Unriddle that ye Pow'rs."[57] But the imperfect knowledge of the characters as they construe their experience has the result that what they encounter as impediments often prove in the end to be providences. Were it not for Gomez's apparently inconvenient habit of surprising them, Elvira and Lorenzo would have committed incest. (In this view even Dominic achieves a kind of justification, since it was his malignity in having Gomez falsely charged with treason that produces the ensemble scene in which the fact that Elvira and Lorenzo are siblings comes to light.) And the main plot is rescued from tragedy and bloodshed by the surprising fact that, contrary to appearances, Bertran is not a second Edmund, and Sancho not a second Lear and Cordelia rolled into one.

To put the matter like that by recalling *King Lear* encourages us to think about the way in which *The Spanish Fryar* is almost a cento, a mosaic composed of fragments of earlier dramas. Reviewing the extent to which Dryden had employed elements of the plot of *The Spanish Fryar* in earlier plays, Dearing hardly exaggerates when he says that "Dryden could have written *The Spanish Fryar* without borrowing from anyone but himself."[58] But the pointlessness of this self-borrowing is almost as remarkable as its extensiveness. For instance, at a number of moments Torrismond challenges comparison with Almanzor, even at one point using the notorious phrase "Lethargy of Love."[59] But no rich hinterland of implication opens up once the connection has been made, beyond the simple observation that both men experience conflicts of love and duty. And we find the same end-stopped quality in some of the play's frequent Shakespearean echoes.[60] For instance, when Pedro deplores Torrismond's enthrallment to Leonora—"O, wou'd the General / Shake off his Dotage to th' usurping Queen"[61]—is this a conscious and deliberate allusion to Philo's condemnation of Antony, in the play of Shakespeare's which Dryden had remodeled three years earlier?[62] If so, what should we make of it? In what way is Torrismond like Antony? And if it is not a conscious allusion, what are the implications for our evaluation of Dryden's art in this play if its language can wander, unwittingly, so close to Shakespeare's? The same difficult questions are raised by an even more startling echo. Leonora assures Raymond of her repentance for the murder of Sancho, which she believes she has commissioned, in these words:

> My future days shall be one whole Contrition;
> A Chapel will I build with large Endowment,
> Where every day an hundred aged men
> Shall all hold up their wither'd hands to Heaven,
> To pardon *Sancho*'s Death.[63]

It was of course in very similar language that Henry V had on the eve of Agincourt tried to assure God of the depth of his own contrition:

> Five hundred poor have I in yearly pay
> Who twice a day their withered hands hold up
> Toward heaven to pardon blood. And I have built
> Two chantries, where the sad and solemn priests
> Sing still for Richard's soul.[64]

But once one has noted the obvious fact that they are both the children of usurpers, surely Leonora is even less like Henry V than Torrismond is like Antony?

Are these simply culpable thefts on Dryden's part? It is possible that they are, but I am tempted by a more charitable construction, which will lead us back to the question of how the "hidden beauties" of this play, which might not be noticed in the theater, relate to the political climate of its composition and production. When Alphonso urges that Torrismond deserves "such Triumphs as were giv'n by Ancient *Rome*," and asks Lorenzo if he agrees, Lorenzo, surprised in inattention and thinking about harlots, replies that "As you say, Sir, . . . *Rome* was very ancient."[65] It is a throwaway line, another gag in the immemorial double-act played out between uncomprehending age and heedless youth, but it also encapsulates something close to the center of this play, in which the continuity of past with present is sometimes hard to see. Rome *is* very ancient in a world in which new almanacs, such as Gomez's, reshape the calendar and replace feasts with lents and ember-days,[66] or in which the traditional is turned inside out, as Pedro remarks of Torrismond:

> So, here's fine work!
> He has supply'd his onely foe with arms
> For his destruction. Old *Penelope*'s tale
> Inverted: h' has unravell'd all by day
> That he has done by night.[67]

It is not the past that haunts this play, but the future; its characters are gripped, not by the memory of precedents, but by their own attempts at prescience. It is an anxious, scanning disposition evoked in Leonora's dream, of being "on a wide River's Bank, / Which I must needs o'erpass, but knew not how."[68] And it generates in the main plot a sense of acute crisis, of feeling the future in the instant. As Raymond admonishes Leonora:

> This hour's the very Crisis of your Fate,
> Your Good or Ill, your Infamy or Fame;
> And all the colour of your Life depends
> On this important Now.[69]

This sense that the present is laboring with an imminent but unknown future is perhaps shared between the playwright and his characters. In the words of Stevens's poem, in modern times, when the theater is "changed / To something else," the script of the past is torn up, and persists only as the fragments that Dryden has distributed amongst his characters.

In 1716 *The Spanish Fryar* was performed, and drew the applause of the Whigs, and catcalls from the Tories.[70] It is a detail of reception that reminds us how misleading it can be to look for the politics of the early eighteenth century in the seventeenth. It also suggests that, although Dryden's play was versatile enough to be made to live again in the midst of crises quite different from the one in which it was composed, such resurrections were distorting.[71] But neither would it be right to see *The Spanish Fryar* as imprisoned within its moment. Its "silent graces" show Dryden dispassionately taking the temperature of his time, and finding an imaginative shape within which to catch, not some tendentious party slogan, but a more deeply perceptive response to the fluid and baffling political structure then being born. He ends the play with a double discovery: two "sudden rightnesses," to recall Stevens again, which fend off calamity, as King Sancho is discovered alive, and Elvira and Lorenzo are revealed to be sister and brother. Dryden must have hoped that something similar might happen in the world of real politics, and perhaps the dissolution of the Oxford parliament was such an event. But to the end he resists the easy consolations of wishful thinking. The play's last lines—"But let the bold Conspirator beware, / For Heaven makes Princes its peculiar Care."[72]—have been found by some to be emphatically Tory, and thus to clinch the play's political character. Certainly the direction of the warning to the "bold Conspirator" makes that the dominant meaning. But if Heaven indeed makes princes its "peculiar"—that is, exclusive—care, then this may hold some monitory force for the officious loyalist, too. Moreover, after the mid seventeenth century "peculiar" possessed its more common, current meaning of "unusual."[73] "Unusual" is perhaps a mild word for the way in which Heaven chose, in *The Spanish Fryar,* to evince its care for the deposed, imprisoned, and nearly murdered King Sancho. Providence may be affirmed in the play, but that affirmation exists alongside the awareness that providence does not preclude suffering, and rarely takes the shortest route. It is hard to imagine how the full spectrum of meaning in the line could be conveyed in the theater. But in the quiet of the closet, perhaps even in the different quiet of the lecture room, the silent grace beneath what an audience might take for a tub-thumping conclusion can be uncovered, and the undoctrinaire humanity of Dryden's political intelligence be restored to view.

Notes

1. Sir Walter Scott, "The Life of John Dryden," in *The Works of John Dryden,* ed. Sir Walter Scott, rev. and corr. George Saintsbury, 16 vols. (Edinburgh: William Paterson, 1882–92), 1:207–8.

2. The chronology of composition, performance, and publication is summarized by Dearing as follows: "We do not . . . know when he [Dryden] wrote it, nor do we know the date of the premiere. Perhaps he had finished most of it by the summer of 1680. In any event, it was new on the stage in October 1680 and was drawing crowds. The first edition was advertised in the second week of March 1681" (*The Works of John Dryden,* [Berkeley and Los Angeles: University of California Press, 1956–], 14:427; hereafter cited as *Works*). Phillip Harth locates the premiere to November 1680 (Harth, *Pen for a Party: Dryden's Tory Propaganda in Its Contexts* [Princeton: Princeton University Press, 1993], 277). In this he follows Robert Hume and Judith Milhous, *Producible Interpretation: Eight English Plays, 1675–1707* (Carbondale: Southern Illinois University Press, 1985), 147, who place the premiere around 1 November 1680.

3. Quoted in F. S. Ronalds, *The Attempted Whig Revolution of 1678–1681* (Totowa, N.J.: Rowman and Littlefield, 1974), 74.

4. *The Collected Poems of Wallace Stevens* (New York: Alfred A. Knopf, 1978), 239–40.

5. Dryden refers to it as a poem as well as a play (*Works,* 14:99), and of course Stevens figures poetry as drama.

6. Quoted in Harth, *Pen for a Party,* 53.

7. Harth, *Pen for a Party,* 295 n. 93. The payments due to Dryden as Poet Laureate and Historiographer Royal were not interrupted (*Works,* 14:432 and n. 32). Louis I. Bredvold, "Political Aspects of Dryden's *Amboyna* and *The Spanish*

Fryar," University of Michigan Publications in Language and Literature 8 (1932): 123–27.

8. *Works,* 14:429.

9. Consider, for instance, the language of Jeffreys when sentencing the five Jesuits to death on 14 June 1679: "Murder, and the blackest of crimes here, are the best means among you to get a man to be canonized a saint hereafter. Is it not strange that men professed in religion, that use all endeavours to gain proselytes for heaven, should so pervert the scripture . . . and make that justify your impious designs of assassinating kings and murdering their subjects? What can be said to such a sort of people, the very foundation of whose religion is laid in blood?" (quoted in John Kenyon, *The Popish Plot* [London: Heinemann, 1972], 165).

10. Milhous and Hume, *Producible Interpretation,* 141–71. James Winn, *John Dryden and his World* (New Haven: Yale University Press, 1987), 332–37.

11. Harth, *Pen for a Party,* 54.

12. Ibid., 54–55.

13. The play's popularity was confirmed by Johnson (*Works,* 14:427 n.6).

14. Harth, *Pen for a Party,* 54 (where he quotes with approval Susan Staves, *Players' Scepters: Fictions of Authority in the Restoration* [Lincoln: University of Nebraska Press, 1979], 77). More recently, the substantial overlap between Whig and Tory positions in the long eighteenth century has been explored by Jonathan Clark, who writes of the particular moment of *The Spanish Fryar*: "Despite the powerful arguments of Filmer, Sidney and Locke, the supporters of sole monarchical rule on one side and the Rye House conspirators on the other, neither group spoke for the broad middle ground, in Parliament or outside. Most even of the parliamentary Whigs sought to preserve the ancient constitution as they saw it. Even in the Exclusion Crisis they tried desperately not to invoke ideas of popular sovereignty or the original contract, and constantly invoked history and constitutional precedent for the right of Kings, Lords and Commons together to vary the succession" (*English Society 1660–1832: Religion, Ideology and Politics during the Ancien Regime,* second edition [Cambridge: Cambridge University Press, 2000], 71–72). The recent work of Jonathan Scott is crucial here: see in particular *England's Troubles: Seventeenth-Century English Political Instability in European Context* (Cambridge: Cambridge University Press, 2000). The dynamics of the recent historiographic debate on the nature of the Exclusion Crisis are reflected and captured in the various contributions to *Albion,* 25.4 (1993).

15. Susan J. Owen, "The Politics of John Dryden's *The Spanish Fryar; or, the Double Discovery,*" *English* 43 (1994): 97–113.

16. Although Dryden was not indifferent to that consideration, as he made clear in the "Dedication": "What Credit it has gain'd upon the Stage, I value no farther than in reference to my Profit . . . 'tis my Interest to please my Audience" (*Works,* 14:102).

17. Owen, "Politics": 99.

18. *Works,* 14:428.

19. As Robert Willman explained in 1974, "Royalist spokesmen, whatever their private utterances, had to be studiously moderate in print" (Robert Willman, "The Origin of "Whig" and "Tory" in English Political Language," *Historical Journal* 17 [1974]: 254). This was because Charles's policy throughout the crisis was to "rally opposition to the Whigs by exposing their intransigence and unreasonableness" (J. R. Jones, *The First Whigs: The Politics of the Exclu-*

sion Crisis 1678–1683 [Oxford: Oxford University Press, 1961], 140). Therefore in August 1680 Charles had commanded his spin doctor, Roger L'Estrange, to "forbear writing such papers as tend to division" (Willman, "Origin": 254). Given that *The Spanish Fryar* received its premiere in November 1680, this period of royal restraint is either the same as, or very close to, the period of the play's composition.

20. *Works,* 14:429.
21. *Works,* 14:100.
22. Quoted in Ronalds, *Attempted Whig Revolution,* 41. For the third edition of the play Dryden made some changes to the text that seem to restore the readings of a state of the play earlier than the first edition. One of these revisions gives to Lorenzo the following lines, on the moral elasticity of Friar Dominick, which capture something of the uncertainty that the metaphor of sport only occludes: "'Tis but giving a man his price, and Principles of Church are bought off as easily as they are in State; no man will be a Rogue for nothing, but Compensation must be made, so much Gold for so much honesty; and then a Churchman will break the Rules of Chess; for the black Bishop will skip into the white, and the white into the black, without considering whether the remove be lawfull" (*Works,* 14:584. For the significance of the revisions for the third edition, see p. 580).
23. Willman, "Origin": 260.
24. *Works,* 2:3.
25. Ibid., 14:105. This label is also alluded to in the prefatory letter to *Absalom and Achitophel* (*Works,* 2:3).
26. According to North, "Whig" was preferred to "Birmingham Protestant" because the latter was "not fluent enough for hasty Repartee" (Willman, "Origin," 249).
27. Robert Willman offers 2 July 1681 as the moment when "English politics were first envisaged as a dialogue between Whig and Tory" (Willman, "Origin," 262).
28. Jonathan Scott, *Algernon Sidney and the Restoration Crisis, 1677–1683* (Cambridge: Cambridge University Press, 1991): 12 and n.32. This is a point on which J. R. Jones and Jonathan Scott do not differ: Jones, *First Whigs,* 214.
29. Note Shaftesbury's anxiety not to have extremists succeed in the shrieval elections of 1680 (Scott, *England's Troubles,* 192–93).
30. Charles saw the agitation for exclusion as an attack on monarchy: but that only shows how far his idea of what a healthy monarchy was differed from that of many of his subjects.
31. Quoted in Tim Harris, *Politics Under the Later Stuarts: Party Conflict in a Divided Society 1660–1715* (London and New York: Longman, 1993), 86.
32. See Jones, *First Whigs,* 10–18 for a review of the spectrum of support on which the advocates of Exclusion drew. He identifies five main groupings: 1. presbyterians; 2. country opposition; 3. adventurers; 4. Monmouth and his adherents; 5. radicals. Of the last, he says: "The radicals were generally republicans, which in itself marked them off very sharply from most Whigs . . . They shared in the common insistence upon Exclusion, but they had no hope of being able to gain support for the further political, social, and legal reforms which they alone advocated" (15–16).
33. Quoted in Scott, *Restoration Crisis,* 22.
34. Edmund Burke, *Thoughts on the Cause of the Present Discontents* (1770), in *Edmund Burke, A Philosophical Enquiry into the Sublime and Beautiful and*

Other Writings, ed. David Womersley (Harmondsworth: Penguin Books, 1998), 271.

35. For Burke's mockery of the specious rectitude of the "disconnected," see especially the coda in defense of parties to his *Thoughts on the Cause of the Present Discontents* (1770), in Burke, *Philosophical Enquiry,* 268–76.

36. For the high emotional tone of this episode, see Conor Cruise O'Brien, *The Great Melody: A Thematic Biography and Commented Anthology of Edmund Burke* (London: Sinclair-Stevenson, 1992), 425–31.

37. Jones, *First Whigs,* 138–39 and 158–59. See also Scott, *Restoration Crisis*: 21–25.

38. Quoted in Scott, *Restoration Crisis,* 22.

39. Premiere of *Spanish Fryar,* 1 November 1680: introduction of second Exclusion Bill, 4 November 1680: publication of *Spanish Fryar,* March 1681, at the same time as the opening of the Oxford parliament.

40. *Works,* 14:99–102.

41. Ibid., 14:441.

42. Consider here the account of the play offered by Richard McCabe in his *Incest, Drama and Nature's Law, 1550–1700* (Cambridge: Cambridge University Press, 1993), especially 278–79.

43. 1.1.36; 2.2.104; 3.3.200.

44. Rumors about the "black box" abounded during the second half of 1680 (Jones, *First Whigs*: 124). Scott, *Restoration Crisis,* 149–53.

45. 1.1.191–95.

46. 1.1.246–47.

47. 4.2.153. *The Spanish Fryar* was published on the day the Oxford parliament opened, and there are reasons for believing that the text was revised for publication (see above n.22). Therefore, Dryden had the opportunity to incorporate an allusion to very recent events, subsequent to the play's premiere.

48. 5.2.198; 4.2.52ff.

49. 4.2.80–116.

50. 4.2.307–10.

51. 4.2.336–37; 5.2.194.

52. 1.1.377–78.

53. 3.1.5; 2.2.64–66.

54. 4.2.81; "sounding and fathoming"—e.g., 1.1.208.

55. 2.2.54–56.

56. On the point of comparison with Oedipus, see also Winn, *John Dryden and his World,* 334.

57. 1.1.21–22.

58. *Works,* 14:434

59. 4.2.327; cf. 1 *Conquest of Granada,* 3.1.339. The repetition of the phrase is not noted in *Works*.

60. For some of the most obvious, see *Works,* 14:434.

61. 2.1.23–24.

62. "Nay, but this dotage of our General's / O'erflows the measure" (*Antony and Cleopatra,* 1.1.1–2).

63. 5.2.119–23.

64. *Henry V,* 4.1.295–99. Again, not noted in *Works*.

65. 1.1.156–58.

66. 1.1.478–81.

67. 1.1.274–78.

68. 3.3.36–37.
69. 4.2.272–75.
70. *Works,* 14:433.
71. It was popular in the theater in 1715, 1745, and 1778–83 (when Spain interfered in Britain's war with her American colonies).
72. 5.2.431–32.
73. For the meaning of "peculiar" that implies a special or exclusive possession, see *OED* A 1 a (illustrative usages from 1460, 1548, 1652, 1668, and 1724); for the word's more recent meaning of "unusual," see *OED* A 4 a (illustrative usages from 1608, 1726, 1811, 1837, and 1888).

John Dryden's Politics: The Rabble and Sovereignty

MAXIMILLIAN NOVAK

DRYDEN'S POLITICS AND OURS

IN APPROACHING A GENERAL OVERVIEW OF DRYDEN'S POLITICS, I soon realized that it would be necessary to limit my subject to one of the major theoretical concerns that seemed to drive Dryden's involvement in the issues of his time. My first thought was to treat his very conscious effort to create a literature that celebrated the monarchy and the state. In the exchange between Thomas Hobbes and William Davenant, written at the time of the Interregnum, both authors agreed that it was the duty of the writer to glorify the sovereign by creating images of heroism and greatness that would make him or her appear to belong to a sphere beyond the reach of ordinary mortals. Such an aura of magnificence would serve the purpose of avoiding any future disturbance in the state by creating the illusion that the sovereign existed on a plane entirely different from that of his subjects.[1] Certainly Dryden followed such a program in his serious plays through to the last of them, *Love Triumphant* (1694). But I decided, instead, to examine the other side—poetry and drama as a mode of staving off anarchy by which Davenant's advice about "taming this wilde monster, the People," is even more vividly demonstrated.[2] I have deliberately attempted to mediate between a variety of angles of vision, from those of Dryden and his contemporaries to modern judgments and attitudes. In so doing, I have not failed to acknowledge how uncomfortable his attitudes may sometimes appear to modern political sensibilities.

My bland title is intended to echo the first serious treatment of Dryden's politics by Alexandre Beljame in 1881. Unlike Edmond Malone, Beljame was skeptical of the motives behind Dryden's politics. He disapproved of the immorality of his plays and thought he pandered to a corrupt court. Hence his image of Dryden as doting on his "mistress," the Court, which scorned him:

> There he is, for ever thrusting himself on her, and when she wants him she is sure to find him waiting, as submissive as ever, as eager as ever to do her bidding. She may fling him now and then a careless smile, but so little fear has she of losing his devotion that she has no mind to make any sacrifices for his benefit. It is a vicious circle: the more he needs the Court, the more he humbles himself to woo her; the more he abases himself, the less his graceless mistress does for him."[3]

In his view, the changes in Dryden's beliefs, from supporter of Cromwell to out-of-power defender of James II are to be ascribed entirely to "worldly motives" and to his quest after "personal advantage."[4]

I want to begin by trying to think of Dryden's politics in broad historical terms with particular relation to our own times. Writing at the end of the nineteenth century, Beljame appeared certain of his values. He was charting the rise of the author to independence—his freedom from pandering to patrons or to a corrupt audience. On the other hand he did have opinions that he did not hesitate to express, including a faith in the progress of society and institutions. If such a faith may appear somewhat naïve to a modern reader, it has the benefit of being entirely understandable within the context of Beljame's era. Although I believe that one can create an imaginative and sympathetic understanding of Dryden in his age, such a view can never be without influence from our own time. We are almost all believers in a degree of democracy. Dryden flaunted his contempt for democracy, what he called "Popularity, and Majority of Voices," in his Dedication to *The Duke of Guise*,[5] and in *Albion and Albanius*, Democracy, an allegorical character, appears as a fiend from hell. We have to acknowledge this and deal with it even as we appreciate the power of his mind and his talent as a writer.

When a volume I edited for the California Dryden was reviewed in the *Times Literary Supplement* some years ago, the reviewer implied that my treatment of Dryden's approach to sex indicated that I had lived too long in Southern California. His suggestion was that sex ought to be treated from the perspective of a more "normative" time—that of Sir Walter Scott. The absurdity of such an attempt should be obvious to everyone. The same is true of politics. To an age of modern democracy, Dryden's choices were clearly on the wrong side.⁶ It is particularly on Dryden's attitude toward the people and the mob upon which I want to concentrate in this essay. For at a time when the evil rabble, the traditional object of satire, became the carnivalesque crowd, sometimes benevolent and enjoyable, a divide opened on the way society might be viewed—not that urban riots fail to inspire mixed feelings for most of us, but few would suggest executing all of the participants.⁷

Treating Dryden's politics is not an easy matter for a modern critic. He was eminently politically incorrect. His remarks on women can, on occasions, be remarkably generous, but for the most part, he is also the master of misogynistic put-downs that are breathtaking in their contempt. He can praise his cousin, Mr. Driden, for not marrying, in terms that suggest that lengthy relationships with women are simply stupid. His picture of the daughter of Sycorax in *The Tempest* (Queen "Slobber Chops," Queen "Blobber-lips," "Queen Blouze the first") is both misogynistic and, allowing that she is closer to an African native or an American Indian than a fish, racist.⁸ And his contempt for the mob stands somewhere between that of Coriolanus and Gustave Le Bon. He saw in the popular discontent that government propagandists believed to be part of the Rye House Plot a return to the Parliament's war against Charles I. Shaftesbury he regarded as the leader of the forces of anarchy.

It was not as if there were not choices. Writers such as Henry Care and Andrew Marvell set down an ideal of civil rights in a balanced system. They supported a monarchy, but they believed in a degree of tolerance and in a representative system. On the other hand, some of the attitudes of those championing absolute monarchy appear superficial or shallow. Never mind the bluster of Bishop Parker, whom Marvell attacked with so much wit and intelligence. What of Roger North, who exulted in how being a king was a "brave thing," the corollary to which must be that being poor was a contemptible thing!⁹ Apprehending the notion that the king was more important than the multitudes over which he ruled is not easy for a modern reader, yet that was the moral of Henry Nevil Payne's play, *The Siege of Constantinople* (1674/1675), in which it is the people who are sentenced to slavery while their emperor is freed by the victorious Turkish emperor. Those attached to the court, particularly the courtiers surrounding the Duke of York, would have had no difficulty grasping the moral of such a work. This political philosophy is also at the heart of Louis Maimbourg's *History of the League,* a work that Dryden translated at the behest of Charles II in 1684 and defended at some length in a postscript. What is perhaps surprising about this work is that Maimbourg views the monarch as superior to the people, the nobles, the Pope, and Catholicism in general.[10] Although Maimbourg's position concerning the sovereign may be seen as traditional—that connected with the usual acknowledgment of government as divine and the monarch as God's regent upon earth—the metaphysics of some essential power emanating from the monarch seems to go beyond traditional religious doctrine. Indeed, a critic of Dryden's defense of the political ideas in his and Nathaniel Lee's *The Duke of Guise* was right in suggesting that Dryden had omitted from his "Parallel," the love that is supposed to be felt by a monarch for his people.[11] Although the system of absolutism embodied in the image of Louis XIV exerted a powerful attraction for the age, and for many appeared to represent the wave of the future, theoretical arguments for arbitrary government within an English context must have been extremely difficult to make.

Dryden's defense of a single source of sovereignty was Hobbesian. The people had made a final contract of complete obedience—a contract that could not be annulled.[12] Dryden affirms God's role far less than Maimbourg did. His emphasis is upon a fear of the mob and of anarchy, and of all that this entailed. Phillip Harth has taught us to look at Dryden's arguments in the context of the most immediate events, and certainly many of Dryden's stated positions shifted from the idealism of the heroic plays to the anti-Williamite positions of the 1690s. But his attitude toward the mob and the threat of anarchy is a consistent element in his thought.

While writing this paper, I happened to watch a somewhat odd but interesting movie called *Fight Club*—a movie with a modern sociopolitical message but which bears a strange resemblance to Dryden's heroic plays and terminal tragedies.[13] While retaining myths of sensibility that had their origin in the middle of the seventeenth century, this piece of cinema is relatively innocent of some of the political ideology that has dominated the politics of the twentieth century. Compared to D. H. Lawrence's *The Plumed Serpent*, with its interplay of ideologies, it may be regarded as "post-political," to use the term of Slavoj Žižek.[14] The true enemy to individual happiness is the desensitized world of global capitalism. Older reviewers hated it, suspecting a fascist message, but it has a cult following among the young. Toward the end of the film, an attractive villain named Tyler Durden gathers about him a group of men who distinguish themselves by indulging in displays of sadism and masochism. If they are not exactly the mob, in the traditional sense, they certainly resemble a *Lumpen Proletariat,* functioning outside the mainstream of capitalist accumulation. They subject their will entirely to their leader, whose aim is to destroy the present state with its soulless enslavement to greed and materialism. Tyler turns out to be the alter ego of the hero, who regains his soul from Tyler by a heroic attempt at suicide. The movie concludes with the wounded hero holding the hand of the heroine as they watch the destruction of the corporate world through the window of a high-rise. This ending is similar in many respects to those heroic plays and tragedies of Dryden in which a new type of civilization triumphs over an older one—the Spanish over the Aztecs, Christian Spain over the Moors, Rome over Egypt.

Was there anything in this work that Dryden would have failed to understand were we able to imagine him transported to modern times as a member of the audience? He would not have appreciated the literal splitting of the ego of the hero, but he would certainly have comprehended the difference between the totalitarian figure of Tyler and the virtuous hero. And he would have had no difficulty understanding the ease with which the mob surrenders its will to a leader. The contemporary interest in the writings of Carl Schmitt shows that seventeenth-century political ideas have not died, since, for the most part, Schmitt, with his decisionist theory of a government that may suspend all laws under a state of emergency is clearly a second coming of Thomas Hobbes.[15] A believer in power and control, Schmitt assigns the sovereign complete authority over the lives of the citizens within the state; small wonder that such notions, as a model for political behavior, are almost universally excoriated today.[16]

And again, what of sexual politics? What would he have made of the modern heroine who experiences violent sex with the hero throughout the movie? Would he have seen it as the ultimate development of the kind of sexuality he portrayed in his comedies? As I have mentioned previously, his comments on marriage in his poem "To my Honour'd Kinsman, John Driden" suggest the libertine position on sex as momentary pleasure and marriage as a honeyed trap for foolish people. Though he creates vivid women characters in comedies such as *Marriage A-la-Mode,* they are all as sexually alive as his Cleopatra. We can hardly believe in his idealized feminine heroines—his Almahides, his Porphyria, and Saint Catharine—as real figures, and surely neither did he.[17]

Dryden, Hobbes, and the Mob

All of this may seem far afield, but if Mildred Hartsock was exaggerating somewhat when she said that Dryden wrote as if he had a copy of Hobbes in his hand when he composed his plays, it is certainly true that he absorbed much of Hobbesian philosophy.[18] William Winterbottom may have assured us years ago that it was for the most part the villains, both male and female, in Dryden's plays who fully advance Hobbesian doctrines, but this does not remove their power and excitement.[19] Dryden wrote dramas, not morality plays, and, whether defeated or not, his villains are often his most memorable characters. And their arguments about self-interest, if lacking in the daring honor and *gloire* that accompanies his heroic figures, are clearly the material of everyday life. In his comedies, such as *Amphytrion,* everyone, with the possible exception of Alcmena, is motivated by self-interest.[20]

What I want to concentrate on here is a consistent line in Dryden's thinking—not his real enough "Royalist" sympathies or even his Hobbesian beliefs in sovereignty, but rather his fear of chaos and the mob. On the matter of his being exclusively committed to the Stuarts, I do not see this as an intellectual position. He remained a supporter of James II until his death, but what he really wanted was clear sovereignty and firm control of the "rabble." In the writings of his enemies, as in Beljame, Dryden was depicted as a person without political principles, an opportunist who changed his opinions as self-interest directed. In one such work, Cromwell's mad Porter in Bedlam considers Dryden's political tergiversations a sign of mental instability:

> Such frequent Turns should you to *Bedlam* bring
> From *Rump* to *Cromwel, Cromwel* to the King;
> Then to your Idol Church, next to the Pope,
> Which may one day prefer you to the Rope.
> I among Madmen am confin'd, 'tis true,
> But I have more Solidity than you.[21]

Dryden did make abrupt political shifts in his lifetime, but when, at his most extreme, he was advocating more hangings of the followers of Shaftesbury and the Rye House Plotters, he appears to have been consistent enough in believing the Hobbesian doctrine that there was one sovereign power in the state and that the purpose of the state was to keep order and preserve the citizen from harm. For Dryden, rebellion was associated not with some greater good that might be achieved but with political and aesthetic chaos, disorder, and death.

In Thomas Killigrew's *Thomaso the Wanderer,* Angellica, the beautiful courtesan, contemplates the revolutions of the mid-seventeenth century and wonders which are worse, "*Frondeur,* Round-head, [or] a Massaniellian," concluding that all are "devils."[22] Of these, none called up greater anxiety than the prospect of Masaniello, or Tommaso Aniello (1623–47), the Amalfi fisherman who led a revolt of the impoverished that succeeded in intimidating the Spanish viceroy out of Naples. He and his followers were protesting at the imposition of a tax upon fruit, after a series of heavy burdens upon the populace. They hearkened back to an original constitution, made in the days of Charles V, that made the imposition of such taxes illegal. Masaniello's body, like that of the Republican De Witt, was mutilated by a mob composed of the people he had led, but for a time, he seemed to be the symbol of a new social order. Nor was Angellica the only person to see connections between the revolutionary forces of the period. Several medals were struck with a figure of Cromwell on one side and Masaniello on the other. The fisherman's cap that appears on the head of Masaniello in the engraving before the popular history of the rebellion in Naples by Alessandro Giraffi was metamorphosed into a cap of liberty. He became a mythic and sometimes even a heroic figure throughout Europe for leading a temporarily successful revolt against the nobles, the viceroy, and the Spaniards.[23]

The pictorial rendering of the scenes of revolt by Micco Spaddo (Domenico Gargiulo) showed a scene of general chaos. Influenced by the scenes of warfare and marketplaces engraved by Jacques Callot, Spaddo's vivid paintings seems to be anarchy itself. In the most famous of the group, the heads of criminals adorn a central structure while the mob mills around. Masaniello, dressed in white, is a dim, small figure in the background. There appears to be little arrangement or order in this painting, as if Spaddo had decided to imitate the chaotic events by an equally chaotic composition. In another of the paintings that Spaddo did on this theme, the execution of Giuseppe Carafa, a nobleman responsible for inflicting taxes upon the people may be seen in the foreground, while the heads of others who have already been executed are carried on pikes in a manner predictive of the French Revolution.[24] This is not the organized army led by Cromwell. This is the mob incarnate. Small wonder that Masaniello was linked to Captain Tom, the mythical leader of the English mob.[25]

When I edited the Dryden-Davenant *Tempest* for the *California Edition of the Works of John Dryden* many years ago, it never occurred to me that one needed to go beyond the images of anarchy that had occurred when Somers and his crew were shipwrecked in the Bermudas. Several members of the crew proclaimed themselves free from the hierarchical divisions of European society, arguing that they were ruled by the laws of nature on the island and need obey none of the traditional laws of society. This anarchic moment was enough to inspire Shakespeare's picture of the revolt of Stefano, Trinculo, and Caliban against Prospero. Shakespeare may have known something about the revolt in Naples in 1585, which showed considerable organization among the lower strata of the people.[26] But it was George Guffey, my colleague and the textual editor for the volume containing the Dryden-Davenant *Tempest* who suggested Masaniello as a possible model for Dryden's character. When he mentioned it to me, I was astonished because I instantly knew that he was right.

By 1667, an English audience would be likely to associate a revolt conducted by Italian sailors, not with the long forgotten Somers voyage, but with the revolt led by the Neapolitan fisherman, Masaniello. James Howell's translation of Giraffi's history of the revolt of 1647 was extremely popular and a new edition had appeared in 1664. It was retold in popular historical accounts and had already been the subject of a play before Thomas D'Urfey came out with his two-part drama in 1699. Although Davenant frequently doubled up characters as a device, the addition of two more sailors, Mustacho and Ventoso, along with Caliban's sister, Sycorax, gave much more of the appearance of a mob. Shakespeare already had a Viceroy as the leading statesman, but the mention of a Viceroy in 1667 would have reminded knowledgable members of the audience of the Duke of Arcos, Viceroy of Naples, whose rule over his city was so thoroughly shaken by the complete control of Masaniello and his forces. The absurd scene at the end of act 4, scene 2, of the Dryden-Davenant version, when Mustapho and Ventoso fight over the status of Viceroy, is a reenactment of the scenes of 1647. Giraffi depicted Masaniello as becoming drunk at various times, both on liquor and a sense of power, and Dryden did expand the drunken scenes involving the sailors. That he changed Alonzo from the King of Naples into the Duke of Savoy had to be a method of avoiding too obvious a political reference.

Of course, it was always more convenient to mention Jack of Leyden as the best example of anarchy because it threw discredit on the Nonconformists, who became a particular subject of the government's wrath after 1681. It is they whom Dryden accused of turning the world upside down and of wishing to bring the "Anarchy of the times" to Oxford where they would willingly introduce their tub for more effective preaching.[27] On the other hand, it is interesting that in *The History of the League,* Dryden accused Shaftesbury of trying to encourage the fishermen to revolt against Charles II. Aside from the fact that seamen were notoriously independent, it has the ring of an old conspiracy—of the sailors of Naples rising against their masters.[28] But what is important here is the threat of the mob taking over. For Dryden's politics, Masaniello is the absent signifier that is ever present—the possibility of a heroic rebel drawn from the rabble, and of a just revolt. Its opposite is the very visible, ever to be scorned, image of the unheroic, unaristocratic, and materialistic Dutchman.

For all the dynamic between Monmouth and Shaftesbury in his most successful political poem, *Absalom and Achitophel* (1681), then, the real threat in Dryden's mind appears to have been pure anarchy. For where the surrender of all sovereignty to the king appeared to be the final and irrevocable act in the state of nature, there was nothing preventing a people in fear of their lives from appealing to the first law of nature—self-preservation—to overthrow the monarchy.[29] Such a view is offered in *The Spanish Fryar* (1680/1681), for despite all the contempt addressed to the mob in that play, the right of self-defense is seen as working for both monarch and people. Although the speech is put in the mouth of the somewhat Machiavellian Bertran in that play, it seems to sum up the ambiguous politics of that work:

> Self-preservation is the first of Laws:
> And if, when Subjects are oppress'd by Kings,
> They justifie Rebellion by that Law,
> As well may Monarchs turn the edge of right
> To cut for them, when self-defence requires it.[30]

Dryden makes his contempt for the mob clear enough, but the main question raised by this "*Whig* Play" is: who has more power?[31]

Hence Achitophel or Shaftesbury in *Absalom and Achitophel* is "born a shapeless Lump, like Anarchy."[32] But the best description of Shaftesbury the anarchist is in *The Medall* (1682). After describing the relativism that seems to be sweeping the nation's religious and political attitudes—a relativism that would overturn the permanence of the Hobbesian surrender of rights to the monarch—Dryden turns to Shaftesbury as the leader of the mob. Shaftesbury is seen as encouraging the mob to realize its power:

> But this new *Jehu* spurs the hot-mouth'd horse;
> Instructs the Beast to know his native force;
> To take the Bit between his teeth and fly
> To the next headlong Steep of Anarchy.

Dryden points to the experiment of the Interregnum, which he sees as a period in which the quest for freedom led to slavery.[33] Whatever movement toward authority one may wish to find in Dryden's religious attitudes, it seems clear that it was always present in his politics.

The works that I have just been discussing fall roughly within the period of the Exclusion Crisis when Dryden's attack upon the mob was most vehement. I do not want to spend too much time on these years, which Phillip Harth has so well treated, except to say that from a theoretical standpoint, it is then that Dryden's Hobbesian approach became ever more pronounced. Quoting from *The Medall* the passage, "Almighty Crowd, thou shorten'st all dispute; / Pow'r is they Essence; Wit thy Attribute!" (91–92), Alan Roper remarks that Dryden was making the mob into a "voluntarist god impatient of reason," adding that Dryden "stiffened the orthodox directives of divine right with the coercive terms of Hobbism"—that is, of the Hobbes who maintained, in an often quoted passage, that "covenants without the sword, are but words, and of no strength to secure a man at all."[34]

After the Revolution: Art, Order, and the Mob

For us, at least, it is far less unpleasant to read Dryden when he was no longer the defender of those in power. At least he was not threatening his enemies with the notion that *"hanging is a fine dry kind of death."*[35] Nevertheless, his attitudes toward the mob never varied. I do not intend to discuss at any length *Don Sebastian* (1689/90), that politically complex play, but there is no doubt about the intent of Dorax's speech dismissing the crowd:

> For Justice cannot stoop so low, to reach
> The groveling sin of Crowds: but curst be they
> Who trust revenge with such mad Instruments,

> Whose blindfold bus'ness is but to destroy:
> And like the fire Commission'd by the Winds,
> Begins on sheds, but rouling in a round,
> On Pallaces returns. Away ye skum,
> That still rise upmost when the Nation boyls:
> Ye mungrill work of Heaven, with humane shapes,
> Not to be damn'd, or sav'd, but breath, and perish,
> That have but just enough of sence, to know
> The masters voice, when rated, to depart.[36]

The mobs in this play are seen as entirely fickle and no match for the true soldiers who handle them with ease. Dorax dismisses them at the very beginning as "No part of Government, but Lords of Anarchy, / Chaos of Power, and priviledg'd destruction."[37] In short, Dorax represents the royalist view as we have already seen it presented by Henry Neville Payne and in Dryden's translation of Maimbourg. So far is government from being by the people and for the people; they, in fact, have nothing to do with it. The action of *Don Sebastian* seems like one of Dryden's final daydreams, in which the mobbish governments of Whigs will eventually be replaced by the order and authority of a true monarchy.

To a certain extent, Dryden's fear of anarchy connects to his aesthetic vision. He looked upon the disorder of Renaissance literature as embarrassing. In his remaking of Shakespeare's *Troilus and Cressida* (1678/1679) from a satire on love and war into a tragedy, Dryden tried to demonstrate what was wrong with the Shakespearean concept of the drama, and, enlisting Rapin and Boileau on his side, attempted to recreate a Shakespeare who was more artful. In clearing out the "Rubbish" that cluttered Shakespeare's play, he was trying to show what a true artist might do with such intractable material.[38] Though he came to write more fondly of Shakespeare in his later writings, there is no sign that he gave up this position. What he called the "Anarchy of wit" was not to be tolerated in a work of art.[39] Similarly, in politics as in music, the rule of the rabble was discord, while a powerful monarchy was harmony.[40]

For writers such as John Dryden, the dislike of the mob or the people seems a consistent trend throughout his writing, though, as Phillip Harth has suggested, consistency is not easy to discover in Dryden's politics. Harth's argument to the effect that from 1680 until 1685, Dryden was essentially part of the propaganda branch of the government seems irrefutable.[41] And until 1688, it is difficult to find a time when Dryden was not writing as a representative of state politics or as a poet seeking to impress those in power with his abilities as a propagandist. It may be thought that he was principled when he refused to accept the new regime's legitimacy, and continued on as a convert to Catholicism. But like most Jacobites, he hoped and believed that James would return to England with all of the power of France—a return that would have restored him to his former eminence as Poet Laureate and Historiographer Royal. To deny him a degree of integrity—to follow Beljame into complete skepticism about Dryden's motives—would be to take too harsh a view. As with his religious faith, so with his politics. He had committed himself to an unqualified acceptance of the ultra-royalist position of the court after 1680, and while there was not much room to express such views during the reign of William and Mary, and then William III, there is no reason to believe he ever abandoned it.

Dryden's Politics and His Audience

How did the theatrical audience of the time respond to Dryden's allusions? Robert Hume, attempting to arrive at a formula for audience reaction, has recently questioned the degree to which any large part of the contemporary audience would have responded to seemingly political comments.[42] Such an argument fails to take into account the nature of the audience over the decades. In the 1660s, many, but hardly a majority, would have responded to the sailors in the *Tempest* with a knowledge of Masaniello, but by the 1680s and 1690s even the slightest suggestion of a political or social allusion would produce a reaction. It was an audience educated to grasp and react to allusions and innuendoes. In a preface to one of his plays, Thomas D'Urfey had to deny any possible personal allusions—allusions upon which the audience had seized. He complained bitterly about listeners who seemed to take every word and every character as reflecting upon some contemporary event or real personality.[43] This was not a matter of exact parallels that might easily be picked up. At one point in his "Vindication" of *The Duke of Guise* (1683), Dryden answered a critic by saying "whoever told him, that I intended this *Parallel* so far?"[44] But as Laurence Sterne was to remind his readers, once a system of relationships is established, it is difficult to prevent an endless expansion. By the 1690s, Dryden's reference in *Don Sebastian* to the protagonist's "Man Mistress," Enriquez, was sufficient to establish an allusion to the supposed male lovers of William III—the William III of Tory propaganda that everyone would have recognized. No other parallel need apply.[45]

I can certainly understand the heated expectations of contemporary audiences. I went to a recent performance of *King Arthur* on a moment's notice. I had no chance to reexamine the play, and my memory of it was not very acute. Yet I sat in the audience wondering why the names of the two villains began with an O. Was it a reflection on William of Orange? After all, the play is about an invasion of England from Germanic forces. What kind of reaction, I wondered, was I supposed to have? Dryden's "parallel" was somewhat obscure but could anyone have doubted that some kind of political statement was being made? It was a time in which the failure to take up innuendoes was regarded as a sign of naïvete. That the modern use of the term "innuendo" began at just this time is no accident,[46] and that the Whigs in the audience drove Dryden from the stage after *Love Triumphant,* with its scarcely veiled allusions to illegitimacy, incest, and false sources of authority, is hardly surprising.[47]

I take the preface to *King Arthur* as offering a scarcely veiled wish for French victory over the combined forces of England and Holland—a wish that must have dimmed without disappearing with the victory of the Dutch and English at La Hogue in 1692. And after 1695, when William's victory at Namur made the Treaty of Ryswick inevitable, he could simply join with the Tories and the Country Party in complaining about William's army and in idealizing parliament. No doubt, like Sir Roger North, he thought the glory of the monarchy a wonderful thing, but beyond that, it is not always easy to find a core of conviction in Drdyen's writings. From that standpoint, the Porter of Bedlam and another antagonist, Tom Brown, were entirely correct.

Dryden's role, then, as the propagandist for Charles II and James II was, and was regarded as, frenzied in its partisanship, and it is hardly surprising that in both *Albion and Albanius* (1685) and *The Duke of Guise* (1682/1683) as later in *King Arthur* (1691), he cast the struggle in terms of demonic forces. He was attempting to counter the entire doctrine of popular rights, which seemed to have had a strong hold on the English imagination from the time of the civil wars. The question is: how did Dryden get to the point of seeming to offer Dorax's point of view in *Don Sebastian,* to the effect that the people are "no part of government," but merely "lords of Anarchy."[48]

Dryden's explanation, as John Wallace argued, seemed to have been based upon the ideal of benefits developed by the Stoics, particularly Cicero and Seneca.[49] The most glorious kind of gesture of obedience was due to those whose benefits were essentially beyond payment, and the leader of the nation, the monarch who could confer the most benefits, deserved the highest loyalty. It was a standard sociopolitical system of the time, and there is no reason to doubt that Dryden did not believe in this system of hierarchy and patronage with all his heart. Meanwell, the typical and somewhat dense defender of Tory politics, who tries to counter the sensible arguments of Freeman in James Tyrrell's compendious treatise on contemporary political theory, *Anthologica Politicus,* might serve as a stand-in for the Poet Laureate.[50] But it was a system under attack by new forces—a belief in personal liberty and individualism.[51]

Dryden could find excitement in the new epistemology of Locke's *Essay concerning Human Understanding.*[52] But Locke's *Two Treatises,* which set out concepts of liberty and property that were to have a permanent influence on political thinking, apparently had nothing to offer him.[53] The ideal world of the superior beings, the consummate leaders who populate his heroic plays and operas, cast those who spoke of liberty and freedom as the enemy. What was important in this ideal world was a natural superiority that showed itself in a contempt for self-interest, commercial matters, and the lives of those who composed the mob. Like Carl Schmitt, who conceived of politics in terms of the friend-enemy duality, Dryden, in *Religio Laici* and *The Medall,* treated the Dissenters and the followers of Shaftesbury as subhuman vermin who posed a threat to the state and who, therefore, deserved no pity.

Insofar as he staged this contemporary political conflict as a battle between conflicting forces, using allegory and parallel historical plots, however much he may have loaded the dice in favor of the old system of benefits and hierarchy, we can still admire his artistry. The wit and imagination of *Absalom and Achitophel* was obvious even to those who hated its political message. The struggles of the magicians, Merlin and Osmond and the spirits, Philidel and Grimbald, in *King Arthur* function perfectly well on the level of fantasy, whatever political meaning we may want to attach to them. And he did maintain one bit of independence. When the government was proclaiming the providential nature of Charles II's salvation at the time of the Rye House Plot (1683) in simplistic terms, Dryden seemed somewhat reluctant to utilize a line of argument that might easily be turned against those in power. His own use of providential history, drawing upon the complex nature of the way events operated in the natural world, was filled with ambiguity.⁵⁴ Under these circumstances, he was one of the few critics of the reign of William and Mary who could, with some sense of consistency, sneer at notions such as the "Providential Wind" that blew William's fleet to Torbay.

Frankly, I prefer Dryden when he is expressing a sense of loss—a feeling that the system he was defending and to which he adhered, whether in politics or in art, was doomed and already in a state of decline. It is one of his great poetic effects, partly because it is at once complex and ambiguous. He could lament the failure of his age compared to the "strength" of what was called the "Last Age," yet in his mind, the artistic achievement of the Restoration more than suggested its superiority. He could state that "The second Temple was not like the First," while arguing that a Congreve or a Southerne could add the genius that was lacking in the mix.⁵⁵ Dryden's fascination with this subject makes *All for Love: or the World Well Lost* (1677/1678) his best play, for surely he saw the world of Charles II and his beloved Portsmouth in the doomed Antony and Cleopatra. During the triumph of James II, he was fairly insufferable. As for his opposition politics during the time of William III, it amounted to little more than sniping at William as a sodomite and longing for the triumph of Louis XIV over English forces on the Continent. Under these circumstances, it is hard to see much conviction in the "Old England" chorus in *King Arthur* or much principle in his critique of William's reign as a "stupid Military State."⁵⁶ He had been happy enough to hymn the military prowess of James. And while his championing of Englishness may point to the Dutchness of William, he would have been happy enough with French troops on English soil—the troops that the Jacobites hoped Louis would give to James for his promised invasions.⁵⁷

Somehow I feel that the real Dryden emerges best in *Amphytrion* (1690), in which power and self-interest prevail over everything. Amphytrion must accept his fate. The "Impostour God," Jupiter, has taken his place in his bed, cuckolded him, but the "Disgrace and Infamy" that might attach to such a situation may be turned into something valuable.⁵⁸ This is Dryden speaking no longer as the poet laureate defending his masters, but willy-nilly as the ordinary citizen, feeling victimized by a government he cannot control. And since William III's governments allowed a wide latitude to political dissent, he could complain at leisure.

Despite the effectiveness of his artistic treatment of loss and decline, I do not think Dryden's Jacobitism ever sank into mere nostalgia. Certainly the victory of William III at Namur and the Treaty of Ryswick in 1697 had to be discouraging, but Dryden never abandoned his attacks upon what he considered an illegitimate monarchy. During 1698 and 1699, when political discontent was everywhere, when Thomas D'Urfey produced his *Massaniello* as a satire on the mob and when Richard Newman's *The Complaint of English Subjects* stressed the poverty suffered by the English people, Dryden seems to have continued in his belief that the nation would eventually turn to James or to his son as a solution. If the *Fables* show little of the early glorification of monarchy and of heroic power that appeared in his youthful works, it is because he was so intent upon attempting to destabilize the reign of William III through his poetry that he had little space for restoring an heroic ideal. It is difficult to see much political principle in the gestures of his final years beyond a few simple principles. He was now Catholic; he longed for the return of a James II who would keep the mob in check and restore a proper system of patronage that would see him as poet laureate once more. But he certainly seems more understandable and attractive to us in these final years. Having to couch his attacks upon William in ironic disguise produced works such as *Alexander's Feast* (1697) and *Fables* (1700), in which that poem was reprinted. As a master of indirection, he was far better in such a mode than he was in propaganda pieces such as *The Medall*. He still had his poetic gifts, and fortunately, he was no longer in a position to threaten those he considered the enemies of a truly authentic monarch with hanging.

Notes

1. See Sir William Davenant, "Preface to *Gondibert, An Heroick Poem*," and Thomas Hobbes, "Answer to Davenant's Preface," in *Critical Essays of the Seventeenth Century*, ed. J. E. Spingarn, 3 vols. (Bloomington: Indiana University Press, 1963), 2:1–67. See especially page 45 where Davenant speaks of the ability of the "Heroick" to transform and purify society.
2. Ibid., 2:35.
3. *Men of Letters and the English Public in the Eighteenth Century*, ed. Bonamy Dobrée, trans. E. O. Lorimer (London: Kegan Paul, 1948), 211.
4. Beljame, 206.
5. *The California Edition of the Works of John Dryden*, ed. H. T. Swedenberg et al., 20 vols. (Berkeley and Los Angeles: University of California Press, 1956–), 14:207.
6. I am using the criteria set forth by John Rawls in his *A Theory of Justice* (Cambridge: Harvard University Press, Belknap Press, 1977), 111–14, 142–350.

For Rawls as offering an almost universally accepted view, see Annabel Patterson, *Early Modern Liberalism* (Cambridge: Cambridge University Press, 1997), 19.

7. John Rawls argues that a just society must accommodate civil disobedience, a position similar to that held by a number of writers during the Interregnum. See Rawls, *A Theory of Justice*, 363–91; and Antony Ascham, *Genesis kai telos exousias, The Original & End of Civil Power* (London, 1649), 27.

8. *Works*, 10:53, 56. "Queen Blouze" associates Sycorax with the lower orders, since the word signified an ugly, or red-faced female worker or beggar. Blowzabella is the wife of Masaniello in D'Urfey's satirical presentation of the Neapolitan fisherman turned revolutionary.

9. *Autobiography*, in *The Lives of the Norths*, ed. Augustus Jessopp, 3 vols. (London: George Bell, 1890), 3:19. North believed that "the people left to themselves never did right, and never failed to destroy each other" (3:116), viewing the mob, in Cartesian fashion, as a mere "engine."

10. Alan Roper refers to this work as "squinting history," because it deliberately distorted well-known facts to bolster his political argument. See *Works*, 18:446.

11. "*Some Reflections upon the Pretended Parallel in the Play called The Duke of Guise, In a Letter to a Friend*," *Works*, 14:618–20. The importance of this relationship between the sovereign and the people is discussed in Victoria Kahn's "'The Duty to Love'; Passion and Obligation in Early Modern Political Theory," *Representations* 68 (1999): 84–107.

12. "The Postscript of the Translator," in *The History of the League*, in *Works*, 18:393–94.

13. *Fight Club* (1999) was directed by David Fincher and starred Brad Pitt, Edward Norton, and Helena Bonham Carter.

14. "Carl Schmitt in the Age of Post-Politics," in *The Challenge of Carl Schmitt*, ed. Chantal Mouffe (London: Verso, 1999), 18–37.

15. Schmitt argued that Hobbes's notion of sovereignty was correct and that it had been corrupted by Benedict Spinoza, who had revised Hobbes's arguments by stressing the private freedoms allowed to the citizen. See *The Leviathan in the State Theory of Thomas Hobbes*, trans. George Schwab and Erna Hilfstein (Westport, Connecticut: Greenwood Press, 1996), 57–59.

16. Chantal Mouffe uses Schmitt as a "challenge" to the consensus of writers on liberal democracy, but she and the contributors in her volume reject the direct arguments of Schmitt, particularly those that argue for a homogeneous society from which the "enemy" has been expelled. See Mouffe, *The Challenge of Carl Schmitt*, 1–6, 38–53.

17. Mrs. Evelyn's response to the figures in Dryden's *Conquest of Granada* was appropriate. She regarded them as idealized characters. Dryden's aim, following Corneille, was to produce a sense of admiration for the extremities of their "glory." See Paul Benichou, *Morales du grand siècle* (Paris: Gallimard, 1948), 15–120. Both Corneille and Dryden were influenced by the idealized figures in the romances of Scudéry and others. For Mrs. Evelyn's comments, see John Evelyn, *Diary and Correspondence*, ed. William Bray, 4 vols. (London: Bohn, 1859), 4:25–26. (See also Annabel Patterson's essay in this collection, p. 202).

18. *Dryden's Plays: A Study in Ideas*, in *Seventeenth Century Studies*, 2d series, ed. Robert Shafer (Princeton: Princeton University Press, 1937), 89.

19. John Winterbottom, "The Place of Hobbesian Ideas in Dryden's Tragedies," *Journal of English and Germanic Philology* 57 (1958): 665–83.

20. Alcmena is certainly an innocent victim, but her preference for Zeus is based on her feeling that he is more loving than her real husband. Her sexuality, re-enforced by the most notoriously sexually promiscuous actress of her day, Mrs. Barry, is put in play at the end, despite her argument that she admires the "Mind" of Zeus. See *Works,* 15:309 (act 5, scene 1).

21. "Enter Oliver's Porter, Fidler, and Poet in Bedlam," in *Poems on Affairs of State* (London, 1707), 3:242.

22. *Comedies and Tragedies* (London, 1664), 328 (act 2, scene 1).

23. For English retellings of the Masaniello's brief revolt in popular histories, see Samuel Clarke, *A Mirrour of Looking Glass for Both Saints and Sinners* (London, 1657); and Nathaniel Crouch, *Extraordinary Adventures, Discoveries and Events* (London, 1683). Crouch's account is particularly favorable, viewing him as someone who righted injustices.

24. For a discussion of the paintings associated with Masaniello and the revolt, see Wendy Wassyng Roworth, "The Evolution of History Painting: Masaniello's Revolt and Other Disasters in Seventeenth-Century Naples, *Art Bulletin* 75 (1993): 219–34.

25. See "Mr. Richardson," *Providence and Precept: or, The Case of Doing Evil that Good May Come of It,* 2d ed. (London, 1691), 20.

26. See Rosario Villari, *The Revolt of Naples,* trans. James Newell and John Marino (Cambridge, Mass.: Polity Press, 1993).

27. *Works,* 1:160–61.

28. *Works,* 18:540. Ironically, James II was treated poorly by English seamen when he tried to escape from England after the invasion of William of Orange.

29. David Haley has argued that Dryden was reacting to what he perceived as the anarchic conditions of 1659, when, following the collapse of the army leaders in London, individuals formed groups of armed men under no central control. Although Haley quotes Ronald Hutton on the collapse of order during this period, Hutton, in fact, is careful to indicate that, for the most part, the functioning of government went on as usual. See *Dryden and the Problem of Freedom: The Republican Aftermath* (New Haven: Yale University Press, 1997), 107–23; and Hutton, *The Restoration* (Oxford: Clarendon Press, 1985), 71–84.

30. *Works,* 14:169 (act 4, scene 2).

31. See "Enter Oliver's Porter, Fidler and Poet in Bedlam" 3:243. Dryden is speaking here as "Johnny." I agree with Phillip Harth and disagree with Robert Hume on the politics of the play. The anti-Catholic bias would have positioned the work on the side of those who believed firmly in the Popish Plot, despite Dryden's expressed contempt for the mob.

32. *Absalom and Achitophel,* line 172 (*Works,* 2:10).

33. I am not suggesting that Dryden's attitude toward civil wars was unique in any way. The fear of civil war was the basis of the arguments of Edward Bohun in his preface and conclusion to his edition of Sir Robert Filmer's *Patriarcha* in 1685. He wrote of attempts to right the injustices of a tyrannical prince: "This can onely serve to fill the World with Rebellions, Wars, and Confusions, in which more thousands of Men and Estates must of necessity be ruined, and Wives Ravished and murthered in the space of a few days, than can be destroyed by the worst Tyrant that ever trod upon the Earth amongst his own Subjects in the space of many years, or of a whole life" (London, 1685), sig. A4v. For Bohun's other comments on this matter in this work, see 165–78.

34. See *Works,* 18:26–527.

35. Epilogue to *The Duke of Guise,* in *Works,* 14:213.

36. *Works,* 15:181
37. Ibid., 15:85.
38. Ibid., 13:226.
39. Prologue to *Albumazar Revived,* line 17.
40. See the "Prologue to the Duchess on her return from Scotland," *Works,* 2:195–96, especially lines 39–46.
41. Harth, *Pen for a Party* (Princeton: Princeton University Press, 1993).
42. "The Politics of Opera in Late Seventeenth-Century London," *Cambridge Opera Journal* 10 (1998): 15–43.
43. Thomas D'Urfey, *The Marriage-Hater Match'd* (London, 1692), sig. A2v. D'Urfey complained that "Modest Reproof is taken for absurd Abuse, and honest Satyr for Dogmatick Slaunder."
44. *Works,* 14:346.
45. Ibid., 15:184 (act 3, scene 3).
46. For a discussion of the development of the term during the Restoration, see Alan Roper, "*Innudendo* in the Restoration," *Journal of English and Germanic Philology* 100 (2001): 22–39.
47. See Montagu Summers, ed., *Dryden: The Dramatic Works,* 6 vols. (London: Nonesuch, 1930), 6:401–2.
48. *Don Sebastian,* in *Works,* 15:85 (act 1, scene 1).
49. Wallace, John, "John Dryden's Plays and the Conception of a Heroic Society," in *Culture and Politics from Puritanism to the Enlightenment,* ed. Perez Zagorin (Berkeley and Los Angeles: University of California Press, 1980), 113–34.
50. Meanwell appears throughout Tyrrell's *Bibliotheca Politica: or an Enquiry into the Antient Constitution of the English Government* (London, 1718), stubbornly maintaining his argument for loyalty against the compelling arguments of Freeman. The first edition appeared in 1692.
51. In his *Households of the Soul* ([Baltimore: The Johns Hopkins University Press, 1997], 22–24, 171–76), Vincent Pecora contrasts the ideals of the "noble household" with its system of benefits, conspicuous consumption, and magnanimity with the development of a world dominated by the market economy and its origins in notions of individualism. Although Pecora centers his discussion on Xenophon and Aristotle in dealing with the ancient world, he concentrates on the ways in which this ideal influenced the attitudes of later thinkers seeking ways of avoiding a world dominated by individualism and economic forces.
52. In addition to his direct comments (*Works,* 16:27–28) on what was known as "Molyneux's Question"—the exchange between William Molyneux and John Locke on the matter of the way a blind man might perceive the world were he to regain his sight—in *King Arthur,* the theme of the entire play is related to concepts of perception. Dryden raises similar notions in *Don Sebastian* (15:90 [act 1, scene 1]).
53. Dryden would probably have associated Locke's *Two Treatises* with Shaftesbury and the defense of the "Ancient Constitution," which had been under severe attack during the 1680s by professional historians favorable to James II. See J. G. A. Pocock, *The Ancient Constitution and the Feudal Law, A Study of English Historical Thought in the Seventeenth Century* (Cambridge: Cambridge University Press, 1957).
54. The complexities of Dryden's approach to Providence and history have been explored by David Haley, who shows the way Dryden's concept of Providence contained all sorts of "ironies," including the frequent inability of human

beings to grasp the workings of God in the world. Despite Dryden's overt use of Providential patterns, I see far more of Hobbes and secular politics in Dryden than Haley, but see his discussion of *Annus Mirabilis,* in *Dryden and the Problem of Freedom,* 129–39.

55. "To My Dear Friend Mr. Congreve," line 14, *Works,* 4:432. For a discussion of Dryden's attitudes toward the poetry of his time in relation to the past, see M. E. Novak, "Shaping the Augustan Myth," in *Greene Centennial Studies* ed. Paul Korshin and Robert Allen (Charlottesville: University Press of Virginia, 1984), 1–21.

56. See his "To Sir Godfrey Kneller," line 51 (*Works,* 4:463). See also "Palamon and Arcite," *Fables,* book 3, line 672, where he comments upon the Standing Army controversy.

57. The Englishness of James and his Stuart descendants was championed even after they had lived on the Continent for half a century. A mid-century edition of Defoe's *The True-Born Englishman* was published with a frontispiece of Bonny Prince Charlie.

58. *Amphytrion,* in *Works,* 15:315.

Frontispiece to the second volume of *Poems and Fables* (A. Reilly, Dublin, 1753). By permission of the Yale University Libraries.

Part II
Dryden and the Poets

Mastering Virgil

Steven Zwicker

Dryden spent more than forty years mastering Virgil. The Roman poet was the central figure in his writing life. He more often alludes to, borrows from, and adapts Virgil than any other writer in a career of continuous borrowing and adaptation. Dryden translated all of Virgil's works, passages from some of them more than once; he wrote one of the longest of his many long essays as a preface to the *Æneis;* and he sought from Virgil's poetry epigraphs for his plays, miscellanies, and poems including *Astræa Redux, Annus Mirabilis, The Medall, Threnodia Augustalis, The Hind and the Panther, Britannia Rediviva, Eleonora, Fables,* and, of course, *The Works of Virgil.* But what appears to us so likely and so obvious an accommodation, an acceptance of Virgil at the center of his writing life, does not in fact seem to have been easily made. In these remarks I want to consider some of the moments in Dryden's career at which we can see him coping with Virgil. My aim is not so much to document a literary kinship—that has been well done, and more than once[1]—as to explore its rhythms, the dynamics of this ambivalent relationship, the productivity of that ambivalence, and how the addiction to Virgil allowed Dryden to discover, indeed to produce, his own voice, to gain the authority and style of Latin antiquity, to master a set of covers and fronts, and, late in his career, to express the costs and compromises of imperium.

At the beginning Dryden was full of dodges and feints; near the end, he accepted Virgil by swallowing him whole, remaking Virgil as Dryden, occupying the Roman poet to such an extent that he could virtually speak through his master at any point in Virgil's text. But even then, the act of consuming and digesting Virgil did not prove altogether easy or agreeable, and when Dryden returned to Virgil one last time, in the Preface to *Fables* (1700), we can see again the old maneuvering, Dryden moving away from Virgil, picking out another ancient with whom he might claim greater intimacy and affinity. At the beginning of the career it was Ovid whom Dryden took as a shield against Virgil, at the end it was Homer; but it was the relation to Virgil that was crucial, and it was the continuous rewriting of Virgil that allowed Dryden to discover, and to formulate, more and more of himself at Virgil's center, and, we should add, sometimes at Virgil's expense. No writer was more keenly aware than Dryden of the story of literary indebtedness figured through relations between fathers and sons, and few literary relations express the rhythms of that indebtedness, its powers and ambiguities, more exactly than Dryden's ties to Virgil, and not only struggle and rivalry but also intimacy, kinship, and the propriety of descent and inheritance.

The contradictory rhythms of Dryden's relation with Virgil are beautifully and almost artlessly set out in the Preface to *Annus Mirabilis* where Virgil is acknowledged in his full importance, but where, in uncovering his debts to the literary past, Dryden awards the laurels so conspicuously and so repeatedly to Ovid that we might wonder what Virgil is doing in the preface altogether. Ovid moves the heart, Ovid touches the "tender strokes" of the passions; "quickness of the Imagination" and "fertility" of fancy are Ovid's crowning glory.[2] On Virgil, Dryden seems grudging, first allowing him preeminence only in "accuracy" of expression; later, Dryden warms to Virgil; finally, he acknowledges that Virgil "has been my Master in this Poem: I have followed him every where" (1:55). And, indeed, what else could he say of a set of texts shot through with Virgilian references and allusions, a fabric woven out of the *Aeneid* and the *Georgics* with dozens of Virgilian echoes, a poem underscoring the Augustan destiny of the nation, the piety of its prince, and the struggle of its people with the unforgiving fates.

What the Preface to *Annus Mirabilis* expresses is Dryden's awareness of his obvious, indeed overwhelming, indebtedness to Virgil, and his efforts to shield himself from the extent of that debt by claiming Ovid as the inspiration for a poem that seems in fact to have hardly anything whatsoever to do with Ovidian forms and imagination, with generic subversions and transformations, with Ovid's fascination for the psyche and feelings for heterogeneity. It is Virgil who provides the inspiration and the idioms for this poem's work as epic and history, and Dryden's strategic covering of one influential poet by another is virtually a map to his later work with models and precedents, with the poetry of classical antiquity and with the theatrical exemplars of England and France.[3] Not that Dryden aims wholly to hide his debts either in the Preface to *Annus Mirabilis* or elsewhere, but rather that he would display them in sufficiently complex and variegated a manner as both to suggest the complicity of his work with other literatures and literary models and to obscure the exact patterns of indebtedness, partially to cover, as it were, the tracks that he has elsewhere laid down.

Ovid's invention and fancy are a foil for Dryden; he uses Ovid to cast Virgil into the shadows, to deflect attention from what he owes to Virgil in the historical, national, and epic dimensions of *Annus Mirabilis,* and in those moments of eloquence and gravity to which Dryden aspires in his little epic. By the time Dryden addressed his relations to Virgil in the 1685 Preface to *Sylvæ,* he had come so much into his own, especially in his masterpieces of satiric writing, that he was capable of a much freer expression of his indebtedness to and various admiration of Virgil: his compression, variety, and expressiveness, especially Virgil's ability "to crowd his sence into as narrow a compass as possibly he cou'd" (3:6). Expressiveness and depth of allusion are exactly what Dryden had achieved in the elegy to Oldham; and in the opening lines of *Absalom and Achitophel,* or its gallery of wicked portraits, or in the passage on Presbyterian scribbling in the Preface to *Religio Laici,* he produces a superb sense of compression and variety. By the 1680s Dryden's self-confidence allowed him both to broaden his appreciation of Virgil and to remark, as he announces the beginning of his formal career as translator of Virgil, the extraordinary difficulty of translating a poet who

> weigh'd not only every thought, but every Word and Syllable; who was still aiming to crowd his sence into as narrow a compass as possibly he cou'd; for which reason he is so very Figurative, that he requires, (I may almost say) a Grammar apart to construe him.... This exact propriety of *Virgil,* I particularly regarded, as a great part of his Character; but must confess to my shame, that I have not been able to Translate any part of him so well, as to make him appear wholly like himself... *Virgil* ... can never be translated as he ought, in any modern Tongue: To make him Copious is to alter his Character; and to Translate him Line for Line is impossible; ... In short they who have call'd him the torture of Grammarians, might also have call'd him the plague of Translatours; for he seems to have studied not to be Translated. (3:6–8)

Yet out of this paradox, prefacing translations of Virgil with a confession of their near impossibility, comes a new assertion of intimacy with Virgil and the trope of particular literary privilege and understanding:

> I encourag'd my self to renew my old acquaintance with *Lucretius* and *Virgil;* and immediately fix'd upon some parts of them which had most affected me in the reading . . . I have both added and omitted, and even sometimes very boldly made such expositions of my Authors, as no *Dutch* Commentator will forgive me. Perhaps, in such particular passages, I have thought that I discover'd some beauty yet undiscover'd by those Pedants, which none but a Poet cou'd have found. . . . I desire the false Criticks wou'd not always think that those thoughts are wholly mine, but that either they are secretly in the Poet, or may be fairly deduc'd from him: or at least, if both those considerations should fail, that my own is of a piece with his, and that if [Virgil] were living, and an *Englishman,* they are such, as he wou'd probably have written. (3:3–4)

The passage foreshadows Dryden's disquisition on kinship with Virgil spun out in the Dedication of the *Æneis;* here, it cools off a bit when Dryden gets busy with the idea of Virgil as an Englishman. In the middle of this passage, however, just after he thrusts together the Dutch commentators, false critics, and pedants (the fools against whom he and Virgil are arrayed), Dryden touches on that secret kinship that so marks his work on Virgil in the 1690s when he possesses an understanding of Virgil that flies in the teeth of the commentators and that allows him to bend and shade his translations of Virgil to reveal particular topical and political urgencies, and then to shape the whole of Virgil in ways that express his own broad ideological concerns. So is it with this seed planted in the Preface to *Sylvæ;* so, much more freely, it became in the adaptation of Virgil that occurs in *The Hind and the Panther.*

Prior to the 1697 Virgil the most remarkable example of Dryden's Virgilian experiments and importations occurs in a passage set deeply and intricately within part 3 of Dryden's religious allegory (lines 766–80), where he reaches into book 7 of the *Aeneis* (7.290 ff.) to find material for an exchange between his fabling beasts. Never mind that the Panther is made to seem a fluent student of the Latin master's epic poem—this is probably no stranger than the beasts' theological erudition. What is truly striking about Dryden's address to the *Æneis* is his decision to deploy Virgil not on behalf of a triumphant traditionalism, an application we might well have expected from the new convert's schooling in the themes of Latin antiquity and eternity, but rather as a site of resistance to invasion, conquest, and the interpolation of alien gods. In the midst of this poem's fabling energies and enigmas, we hear Virgil narrated and applied as part of a complex program of Anglican apologetics. Meditating on Virgil, and on the efforts of James II's court to compromise Anglican hegemony, the Panther argues:

> Methinks such terms of proffer'd peace you bring
> As once *Æneas* to th' *Italian* King:
> By long possession all the land is mine,
> You strangers come with your intruding line,
> To share my sceptre, which you call to join.
> You plead like him an ancient Pedigree,
> And claim a peacefull seat by fates decree.
> In ready pomp your Sacrificer stands,
> T' unite the *Trojan* and the *Latin* bands,
> And that the League more firmly may be ty'd,
> Demand the fair *Lavinia* for your bride.
> Thus plausibly you veil th' intended wrong,
> But still you bring your exil'd gods along;
> And will endeavour in succeeding space,
> Those houshold Poppits on our hearths to place.
> (3:184, lines 766–80)

Of course, Dryden could not have known in the winter of 1686/87 that he would return to the Virgilian themes of invasion and conquest to complain against the injustice of the revolutionary settlement, that he would cast a melancholy interpretive spell over the whole, and that he would see the story of Roman triumph, when applied to the Glorious Revolution, not so much as imperial destiny but as a brooding and unsettled narrative of the costs and compromises of empire. Yet here in 1687 he, or perhaps we should say the Panther, is doing exactly that, spinning out an interpretation of Aeneas's entry into Latium from the point of view Dryden would hence apply to the whole of the imperial destiny of Rome. In the Panther's scheme, the invading and intruding Aeneas is the Catholic Church, the good Latinus suffering Anglicanism, marriage with fair Lavinia the union of Rome and Canterbury, and those exiled gods and household poppits the long-scorned idols of Roman Catholic spirituality.

Part of the puzzle is Dryden's all too apparent pleasure in the fluency and wit of the Panther's reading of Virgil, both its intricate and clever interpretive moves and the familiar satiric edge in the rendering of Roman Catholic ritual. Nothing in *The Hind and the Panther* reminds us more of *Absalom and Achitophel* than these lines; yet, of course, they are invested in the "wrong" point of view. Perhaps the satiric edge is best explained by the deep ambivalence Dryden felt about his own circumstances in the winter and spring of 1686/87. He faced problems surely of his own devising, but his dilemmas were compounded by obligations in which he felt trapped as laureate of a regime that had devised a sudden and embarrassing courtship of dissent and now seemed bent on a program of certain self-destruction. On that topic Dryden issues what are at once bold and enigmatic prophecies of doom through the whole of the third part of his poem.

What the Panther's narration of Virgil reveals is Dryden's ability to think outside and against his own circumstance. What the passage also reveals is Dryden's freedom in his handling of Virgil. He has reached a stage of literary mastery at which he can occupy Virgil from any point of view whatsoever. In the Preface to *Annus Mirabilis* Dryden had to arm himself against Virgil by explaining his supposed debts to Ovid; here, he seems to be completely open, capable of turning Virgil sharply against what his audience would have perceived as his own interest. But the story turns out to be more complicated than they might first have thought.

No one reading *The Hind and the Panther* in the spring of 1687 could have forgotten that its fables were acts of intricate ventriloquism, that in this poem Dryden was speaking not only through the spotless Hind, and occasionally through his own excited person in outbursts of self-display, but also through the Panther. And if Dryden were doing all the voices and at the same time reminding his readers of that fact by allowing them to hear in these lines the familiar rhythms and satiric thrust of *Absalom and Achitophel* where those same gods, those "houshold Poppits," were "recommended by their taste," what could his Virgilian intentions here have been? Perhaps to suggest that the Panther is too clever by half, that she unwittingly narrates not only a deceptive—and, we might add, self-deceived—arrogation of Virgil to her partial and polemical interests, but as well the final triumph of Rome. After all, Dryden's readers knew how this story would end: with Aeneas's triumph and, for Dryden and his fellow Catholics, with Roman destiny fulfilled not through the edifice of secular empire but in the eternity of the mother church. The Panther overlooks this element of the narrative in her application, but Dryden knew how history fulfilled Virgil's prophetic mood. Nor could his readers have been in any doubt about that end, or that Dryden was ventriloquizing in a particularly brilliant manner, conceding the momentary triumph of interpretive wit to the Panther, but holding the winning cards in his own hand. Dryden exhibits his mastery of Virgil in this superb and seemingly offhand application of the *Æneis,* and it is a display of remarkable freedom. This is not so much an exercise that prepares him for the Dedication of the *Æneis* or the translation itself but rather a signal that he has arrived at a place where he can make Virgil completely his own.

And that is exactly Dryden's work in the Dedication of the *Æneis,* where he writes intimately and protectively of Virgil but where he also participates in, even (we might add) seems to take pleasure in, the exposure of a certain moral weakness, a discomforting collaboration between Virgil and the tainted authority of imperial Rome. Virgil has been attacked, Dryden tells us, "by many Enemies: He has a whole Confederacy against him" (5:277). The length of the poem has been criticized as have the manners of its hero and its many faults of grammar. And Dryden concedes not only the "inconsiderable faults" (5:277); he also allows larger, more fundamental flaws. Virgil had to compromise his poem because of the circumstances in which he wrote; he was resigned to the task of pleasing his patron, of caressing and flattering Augustus, because he had been "enrich'd, esteem'd and cherish'd" (5:281) by the emperor. Perhaps, Dryden allows, it was more than self-interest that drove Virgil to shadow Augustus "in the Person of *Æneas*" (5:283), and "dext'rously" manage "both the Prince and People" (5:283) with flattering images, genealogies, and narratives [Dryden's text is: "But as *Augustus* is still shadow'd in the Person of *Æneas,* of which I shall say more, when I come to the Manners which the Poet gives his Hero: I must prepare that Subject by shewing how dext'rously he mannag'd both the Prince and People, so as to displease neither"]. Perhaps it was an appreciation of the public welfare that Virgil might advance in so flattering and managing, so shaping his epic to the interests of the "common good," even if that meant servicing a compromised civic ideal. All this, Dryden tells us, "proves that it is possible for a Courtier not to be a Knave" (5:283).

Rather a blunt conclusion; and we might suspect that the Virgil here rehearsed, here placed under hostile scrutiny and direct attack, might just be not only (should we say) comforting—fitted with surprising exactness to the translator's sense of his own circumstances, past and present—but also convenient. Dryden displays the problems that critics and pedants have discovered, he fans the fire and perhaps adds an ember or two of his own, and then works to extinguish its flames. Only a poet, only this poet, can both defend and appreciate, at once conjure the pressures and sorrows under which Virgil worked, write so knowingly of the difficulties of a courtier fixed in the compromises of aristocratic patronage, and register the private aims and desires that animate the work of poetry. The story that runs like a colored thread through the whole of the dedication is ambivalence and admiration. Swift detected exactly those braided strands in Dryden's appropriation of Virgil, and he thus imagined their encounter on the field of literary battle:

> On the left Wing of the Horse, *Virgil* appeared in shining Armor, compleatly fitted to his Body; He was mounted on a dapple grey Steed, the slowness of whose Pace, was an Effect of the highest Mettle and Vigour. He cast his Eye on the adverse Wing, with a desire to find an Object worthy of his valour, when behold, upon a sorrel Gelding of a monstrous Size, appear'd a Foe, issuing from among the thickest of the Enemy's Squadrons; But his Speed was less than his Noise; for his Horse, old and lean, spent the Dregs of his Strength in a high Trot, which tho' it made slow advances, yet caused a loud Clashing of his Armor, terrible to hear. The two Cavaliers had now approached within the Throw of a Lance, when the Stranger desired a Parley, and lifting up the Vizard of his Helmet, a Face hardly appeared from within, which after a pause, was known for that of the renowned *Dryden*. The brave *Antient* suddenly started, as one possess'd with Surprize and Disappointment together: For, the Helmet was nine times too large for the Head, which appeared Situate far in the hinder Part, even like the Lady in a Lobster, or like a Mouse under a Canopy of State, or like a shrivled Beau from within the Pent-house of a modern Perewig: And the voice was suited to the Visage, sounding weak and remote. *Dryden* in a long Harangue soothed up the good *Antient,* called him *Father,* and by a large deduction of Genealogies, made it plainly appear, that they were nearly related. Then he humbly proposed an Exchange of Armor, as a lasting Mark of Hospitality between them. *Virgil* consented (for the Goddess *Diffidence* came unseen, and cast a Mist before his Eyes) tho' his was of Gold, and cost a hundred Beeves, the others but of rusty Iron. However, this glittering Armor became the *Modern* yet worse than his Own. Then, they agreed to exchange Horses; but when it came to the Trial, *Dryden* was afraid, and utterly unable to mount.[4]

Who better than Swift to understand mixed motives? No one, save Pope, was a keener student of Dryden's mockery and irony than Swift, and no one was shrewder in his feigned indifference to that literary debt than Swift, who summed up his appreciation for *The Hind and the Panther* by calling it ". . . the Master-piece of a famous Writer now living, intended for a compleat Abstract of sixteen thousand Schoolmen from *Scotus* to *Bellarmin.*"[5]

But Dryden's willingness to display Virgil's problems was driven not only by his understanding of the convenience of that display—that it would be all the easier to mount Virgil's defense once he had thoroughly aired the opinions of pedants and critics—he also understood, or intuited, the ways that this image of Virgil might reveal the deep kinship of poet and translator. Dryden allowed Virgil's distance; he acknowledged the disparity between their circumstances—what "*Virgil* wrote in the vigour of his Age, in Plenty and at Ease, I have undertaken to Translate in my Declining Years: struggling with Wants, oppress'd with Sickness, curb'd in my Genius, lyable to be misconstrued in all I write" (6:807)—but Dryden aimed steadily to discover himself at Virgil's center, especially at moments when the *Æneis* seemed most to reveal the Roman poet:

> I could not but take notice, when I Translated [the Fifth Book], of some Favourite Families to which he gives the Victory, and awards the Prizes, in the Person of his Heroe, at the Funeral Games which were Celebrated in Honour of *Anchises.* I insist not on their Names: But am pleas'd to find the *Memmii* amongst them, deriv'd from *Mnestheus,* because *Lucretius* Dedicates to one of that Family, a Branch of which destroy'd *Corinth.* I likewise either found or form'd an Image to my self of the contrary kind; that those who lost the Prizes, were such as had disoblig'd the Poet, or were in disgrace with *Augustus,* or Enemies to *Mæcenas*: And this was the Poetical Revenge he took. For *genus irritabile Vatum,* as *Horace* says. When a Poet is throughly provok'd, he will do himself Justice, however dear it cost him. . . . I think these are not bare Imaginations of my own, though I find no trace of them in the Commentatours: But one Poet may judge of another by himself. The Vengeance we defer, is not forgotten. (5:282-83).

The merging of impulses and identities seems complete: Virgil's have become Dryden's own, and Dryden has assumed Virgil's sensibility and literary authority. Having achieved this interiority we might suppose that Dryden had reached a resting point—and the translation itself is full of such moments of merged identity when Dryden speaks with utter freedom through Virgil. Near the end of his career Dryden is so much at ease with, so much at one with Virgil, that he allows himself to extend and appropriate, to construe Virgil's impulses and motives as his own and to interpolate his own work into the midst of Virgil's epic, because "one Poet may judge of another by himself." Competition and admiration have reached the point of perfect and productive equilibrium; and nothing short of equilibrium would have allowed Dryden's fluent mastery as he worked steadily to produce some 16,000 lines of translated Virgil. Dryden understood exactly what he was carrying over in this translation; in his hands the monument of Latin antiquity would become a contribution to the English language and to English letters, an act of literary and linguistic patriotism, but it would also address the sorrows of imperium. Dryden's *Æneis* is a beautifully sustained meditation on the costs of empire at a moment when William III was ploughing his way through Europe with English arms.[6] Though Dryden complained that he had come to the Virgil too late in his own life, the middle years of the 1690s were exactly the right moment for this translation.

Yet the collaboration between Dryden and Virgil did not rest here. Dryden wandered from this intimacy and interiority, and when he next had occasion to reflect on his work with Virgil we can feel him sliding away from the Latin poet:

> If it shall please God to give me longer Life, and moderate Health, my Intentions are to translate the whole *Ilias* . . . and this I dare assure the World before-hand, that I have found by Trial, *Homer* a more pleasing Task than *Virgil* . . . For the *Grecian* is more according to my Genius, than the *Latin* Poet. . . . *Virgil* was of a quiet, sedate Temper; *Homer* was violent, impetuous, and full of Fire. The chief Talent of *Virgil* was Propriety of Thoughts, and Ornament of Words: *Homer* was rapid in his Thoughts, and took all the Liberties both of Numbers, and of Expressions, which his Language, and the Age in which he liv'd allow'd him . . . if *Homer* had not led the Way, it was not in *Virgil* to have begun Heroick Poetry . . . I say not this in derogation to *Virgil*, neither do I contradict any thing which I have formerly said in his just Praise. . . . But to return: Our two Great Poets, being so different in their Tempers, one Cholerick and Sanguin, the other Phlegmatick and Melancholick; that which makes them excel in their several Ways, is, that each of them has follow'd his own natural Inclination. . . . You never cool while you read *Homer*, not even in the Second Book, . . . From thence he hurries on his Action with Variety of Events, and ends it in less Compass than Two Months. This Vehemence of his, I confess, is more suitable to my Temper: and therefore I have translated his First Book with greater Pleasure than any Part of *Virgil*.[7]

Whatever complex piece of self-presentation and, might we say, self-deception Dryden has here entered into—and Homer's violence and vehemence as mirror of Dryden's temper seems particularly implausible—it is clear that part of Dryden's work with himself and with his readers is to prepare for an English Homer. But I think that Dryden is not only feeling his way forward but also feeling his way back and away from the position Virgil had assumed for him in the years of the great translation. Perhaps we can feel a slight nervousness in this move as Dryden seems to acknowledge the coolness of his appraisal: "it was not in *Virgil* to have begun Heroick Poetry. . . . I say not this in derogation to *Virgil,* neither do I contradict any thing which I have formerly said in his just Praise." The sentence is revealing not only in the way it acknowledges a change of allegiance but also in its slightly awkward and defensive formality: the appraisal is too careful, too judicious. Or perhaps Dryden's awkwardness simply registers his awareness that injury has been done. To say that "it was not in *Virgil* to have begun Heroick Poetry" is of course to write in derogation; but it is the language of "just praise" closing the sentence that most distances and diminishes. Who has asked Dryden to rationalize what he had formerly said of Virgil, especially in that long and intimate appraisal of the relations between poet and translator that prefaces the *Æneis*?

At first it is disappointing to see this relationship close with Dryden coolly pushing Virgil away. He would have known that these were likely his last words on Virgil, but there is little here to indicate farewell, little that is elegiac, intimate, summative, even reflective. He had, after all, made peace even with Milton; after the years of partisan and literary rivalry, he had allowed the old Republican into the family of poets:

> *Milton* was the Poetical Son of *Spencer,* and Mr. *Waller* of *Fairfax;* for we have our Lineal Descents and Clans, as well as other Families. . . . *Milton* has acknowledg'd to me, that *Spencer* was his Original; and many besides my self have heard our famous *Waller* own, that he deriv'd the Harmony of his Numbers from the *Godfrey of Bulloign,* which was turn'd into *English* by Mr. *Fairfax.*[8]

It took Dryden a long time to arrive at this sentence, but such remarks seem to have about them an air of both resolution and intimacy, they are summative and appreciative, as if the Preface to *Fables* were a place where Dryden wanted to set personal relations and literary records straight. But if this were so, what are we to think of this last accounting of his relations with Virgil?

Why, at the end, is he willing to allow even Milton more intimacy than Virgil when nothing could be clearer than the continuity and power of Dryden's relations with Virgil, when Virgil had been more important than any other poet, ancient or modern, when out of that overwhelming indebtedness Dryden had invented himself? And of course, no sooner do we formulate the question than an answer begins to appear. Could it be that Dryden allowed poets like Milton proximity because they were not at the center of invention, because, in the final accounting, it cost little to stage this reconciliation? But with Virgil, the story was different. The shadow of the Virgil translation, and of the forty years during which Dryden went to school at Virgil's poetry, fell over this last text, and the cool diminishing of Virgil, though it seems to us the wrong note, is in fact the only one he could truly have sounded. We might like these great stories of literary relations to end with a proper narrative gesture, but the best tribute to Virgil's significance is sounded here where the register of literary relations—with its marks of indifference, distance, and deferral—allows us to hear all the complicating anxieties that stir relations among writers, even those in literary "clans," even (or should we say especially) those between "poetical" fathers and sons.

The language of fathers and sons, of affiliation and inheritance, seems the right place to close these remarks about Dryden and Virgil because the enduring force of their encounter helps us to understand all the ways in which Dryden fashioned a career from literary materials borrowed from his elders. It is tempting, however, to take one additional step; the final encounter with Virgil points not only back over a whole career, but also forward to the place from which Dryden was attempting to avert his gaze.

The contest staged between Homer and Virgil in the Preface to *Fables,* like that between Horace and Juvenal eight years earlier, served as a way for Dryden to distance from himself those aspects of his own personality that he associates with melancholy and vulnerability. Once he had gone through Virgil to the end, once he had fully absorbed Virgil and deeply associated him with his own feelings of weakness and passivity, the most powerful impulse in relation to Virgil became not the acknowledging of indebtedness, but the longing for separation. The rupture in relations with Virgil and the choice of Homer offered Dryden a way to deny, and to attempt to master, what he most feared.

Everywhere in *Fables* Dryden struggles against closure and finality. The book is a collection of fragments and digressions;

more than in any other of Dryden's texts, digression here served as a structural and psychological principle, a way of forestalling inevitabilities.[9] In 1693 Dryden had written of digression as a "sweet way" to hold off the end of a story; now in 1700 he hinted at a different kind of imaginative space that digression allowed and of a different end that might be delayed by fragmentary and digressive forms of writing. Virgil is the poet Dryden associates with melancholy and mourning, and the *Aeneid* is the text through which he speaks most often in that mode. It is from Virgil that Dryden fashioned his most poignant elegiac moments; it is from Virgil that Dryden learned a way of writing inflected by loss and restraint. The poem to Oldham is spun out of stories from the *Æneid*, it is flooded by memories of Virgil; the tributes to Ossory and Ormonde are shot through with Virgilian echoes; and it is Virgil who gave Dryden a way to honor the absence and longing that everywhere underwrote his celebration of the Duchess of Ormonde.[10]

Homer is all vigor, vehemence, and heat; these are the qualities that now, near the end of his life, Dryden claims to have discovered most deeply within himself. But *Fables* has only one selection from Homer. The book is a collection of texts that narrate flux and uncertainty; here are thousands of lines of Ovid and Chaucer, eight hundred from Homer. In the Dedication of *Fables*, Dryden made a particular and, given the career and character of his dedicatee, daring show of contempt for the heroic; but in the Preface he is overcome by a sudden taste for violence and warfare. It is no longer the merciful and submissive Aeneis who is Dryden's model but the "hot, impatient, revengeful" Achilles—a hero, Dryden would have us think, after his own heart. But the change of heart has little to do either with aesthetics or ethics. The embrace of Homer and the turning away from Virgil comes from another place and one partly hidden from Dryden's own view; it suggests not, I think, the formation of new tastes, but the continuing force of old ones. Dryden averts his gaze from Virgil because he is overwhelmed by the identification with Virgil and because Virgil and his hero represented a bowing to the fates and a submission to the elements. He had spent a long time mastering Virgil, but at the end it was Dryden who had been mastered by Virgil; turning away after a lifetime of translation was in fact the deepest and most touching acknowledgment of Virgil that Dryden could have made.

Notes

1. See, for example, Reuben A. Brower, "An Allusion to Europe: Dryden and Poetic Tradition," in *Alexander Pope: The Poetry of Allusion* (Oxford: Clarendon Press, 1959), 1–14; R. G. Peterson, "Larger Manners and Events: Sallust and Virgil in *Absalom and Achitophel,*" *PMLA* 82 (1967): 236–44; Thomas H. Fujimura, "Dryden's Virgil: Translation as Autobiography," *Studies in Philology* 80, no. 1 (1983): 67–83; and, most recently, Paul Hammond, *Dryden and the Traces of Classical Rome* (Oxford: Oxford University Press, 1999).

2. "So then, the first happiness of the Poet's imagination is properly Invention, or finding of the thought; the second is Fancy, or the variation, deriving or moulding of that thought, as the judgment represents it proper to the subject; the third is Elocution, or the Art of clothing and adorning that thought so found and varied, in apt, significant and sounding words: the quickness of the Imagination is seen in the Invention, the fertility in the Fancy, and the accuracy in the Expression. For the two first of these *Ovid* is famous amongst the Poets, for the latter *Virgil.*" From the Preface to *Annus Mirabilis,* in *Works of John Dryden,* ed. H. T. Swedenberg et al., 20 vols. (Berkeley and Los Angeles: University of California Press, 1956—), 1:53; all further citations, unless otherwise indicated, agree with this edition.

3. See David Bruce Kramer, *The Imperial Dryden: The Poetics of Appropriation in Seventeenth-Century England* (Athens: University of Georgia Press, 1993).

4. Jonathan Swift, "The Battle of the Books," in *A Tale of a Tub with Other Early Works, 1696–1707,* ed. Herbert Davis (Oxford: Basil Blackwell, 1965), 157–58.

5. Swift, "A Tale of a Tub," sect. 1, "The Introduction," in *A Tale of a Tub with Other Early Works, 1696–1707,* ed. Davis, 41.

6. On the relationship of Dryden's *Virgil* and the military campaigns of William III, see the notes in *Works,* 6:843–89; Steven Zwicker, *Politics and Language in Dryden's Poetry, The Arts of Disguise* (Princeton: Princeton University Press, 1984), 177–205; David Bywaters, *Dryden in Revolutionary England* (Berkeley and Los Angeles: University of California Press, 1991), esp. chap. 4; Hammond, 225–28; and Tanya Caldwell, *Time to Begin Anew: Dryden's Georgics and Aeneas* (Lewisburg, Pa.: Bucknell University Press, 2000), chap. 4.

7. Preface to *Fables,* in *Poems of John Dryden,* ed. James Kinsley, 4 vols. (Oxford: Clarendon Press, 1958), 4:1448–449.

8. Preface to *Fables, Poems of John Dryden,* 4:1445.

9. On Dryden's digressiveness, see, for example, Anne Cotterill, "The Politics and Aesthetics of Digression: Dryden's *Discourse Concerning the Original and Progress of Satire,*" *Studies in Philology* 91, no. 4 (1994): 464–95; and "Parenthesis at the Center: The Complex Embrace of *The Hind and the Panther,*" *Eighteenth-Century Studies* 30 (1997): 139–58.

10. See Steven Zwicker, "Dryden and the Dissolution of Things: The Decay of Structures in Dryden's Later Writing," in *Tercentenary Essays,* ed. Paul Hammond and David Hopkins (Oxford: Oxford University Press, 2000), 308–29.

Dryden's Persius

EMRYS JONES

"IF I HAD TO GIVE MY VOTE TO OUR GREATEST TRANSLATOR, IT would go to Dryden." So says Charles Tomlinson, introducing his *Oxford Book of Verse in English Translation* (1980). The judgment sounds right; it may even be true. Dryden's achievements as a verse translator are now fully recognized among the scholarly community, even if this splendid corpus of translated verse is not as widely known outside the universities as one could wish. His versions of Lucretius and Juvenal and his paraphrase of Horace's ode 2.29 are now recognized as being among his finest poems, and no selection of his poetry is likely to leave them out. Much the same could be said of the best things in his versions of Virgil and Ovid and of the first book of the *Iliad*. Dryden's translation of Persius, however, does not belong in this company; it has not been rediscovered and reclaimed in the way that these other translations have been. In fact scarcely anyone since the early eighteenth century has had much good to say about Dryden's Persius. Recent opinion can be summed up in the words of two classical scholars. R. G. M. Nisbet, former Professor of Latin at Oxford and the esteemed editor of Horace's odes, glances at Dryden in his essay on Persius only to say "his translation is for once unsuccessful"; while J. P. Sullivan states more forcefully that Dryden translated Persius "with indifferent success due to his incomprehension of Persius' aims."[1]

I shall not be attempting to reverse these judgments on Dryden's Persius, nor shall I be claiming that what we have here is a shamefully neglected masterpiece. A large part of what I have to say will concur with these adverse views. I propose to take Dryden's encounter with Persius as an instructive minor episode in his poetic career, and I want to do so by looking as closely at Persius as at Dryden. Persius is of course a difficult poet, and in my attempts to read him I have been greatly helped and enlightened by a number of classical scholars who have published essays or books on Persius over the past thirty or so years. These scholars are not a group, or, if a group, only in the sense that their work, however different in emphasis, is similar in direction; otherwise they are independent of each other. What they have in common is a sense of excited discovery. They have discovered that Persius is not, as one might have gathered from a lot of earlier criticism, just a weakish follower and close imitator of Horace, but a powerfully original poet in his own right. How original is still being discovered, since the story is not finished. It is hardly too much to say that a small revolution has taken place in Persius studies, not as big as the revolution in Lucan studies but of a similar kind and equally exciting in its transformative effect. Of course Lucan's astounding and thrilling epic is far greater in bulk than Persius's small collection of six short satires and a prologue: Persius's entire output, as we have it, is hardly as long as one of the books of Lucan's ten-book epic. Still, there is an appropriateness in the fact that the two poets should have been fundamentally reappraised—and appraised upward—at much the same time. They were acquaintances of each other, perhaps friends (Lucan certainly approved of Persius's poems); they lived under Nero, and both died under Nero while still in their twenties. Despite the obvious generic differences in their work, the two poets have important qualities in common.[2]

Persius's notorious obscurity has often been put down to youthful affectation. In Ben Jonson's comedy *Epicoene,* the foolish Sir John Daw dismisses Persius as "a crabbed coxcomb not to be endured"—a sure sign that Daw's creator Jonson had a high opinion of Persius. But the "crabbed" charge persisted for centuries—the notion that Persius's poems were written in an ugly, cramped, clotted form simply because he was either foolish enough to like such barbarities or incompetent to do any better. What emerges from the recent critical work is that it would be an absurd mistake to patronize Persius in this way, to assume that excuses have to be made for him. Persius is one of those poets who reach early whatever maturity they have it in them to realize. He is not a tyro; he's a young master. It has always been noticed that he in some sense "took over" a very great deal from Horace: a large number of Persius's words and phrases, ideas and themes, are derived from Horace's satires, epistles, and odes. This feature of his writing has given rise to the view that his poetry as a whole is no more than the work of a beginner who never freed himself from Horace's influence. Recent scholars, however, like J. G. Henderson and D. M. Hooley, have read this literary relationship differently. In their view Persius is not simply imitating Horace; he is deconstructing him, reshaping him, subjecting him to a skeptical rereading. Sometimes, for example, he destabilizes what in Horace may seem in retrospect some slightly complacently held fixed points. In some satires Horace sets his own authorial persona—an attractively tolerant person, principled yet easygoing, eminently civilized—against an aggressively dogmatic antagonist (say, a boorishly sanctimonious Stoic). Persius adapts this Horatian arrangement yet refuses to privilege the authorial persona, introducing instead an unsettling current of feeling that results in a radical diffidence and indeterminacy and inconclusiveness on the part of the poem. He does this not in the interests of a helpless nihilism but so as to enforce a sense of the obstacles to self-awareness and self-improvement.

The pervasive difficulty of Persius's poetry can be broken down into more or less three categories: difficult diction and vocabulary; difficult syntax; and difficult structure. Since I am far from being a classical scholar and can make no claim to read Persius with anything like a proper inwardness with his Latin language, I shall pass over the first two categories (diction and syntax) but say something brief about the third (structure or form), since this bears directly on Dryden's translation. Persius's satires often take the form of a mixture of authorial discourse and dialogue of a kind that derives from "diatribe" (a form of vehement popular preaching which, for instance, Lucretius also drew on). Yet, as one can see from the history of Persius scholarship, editors of his text, who must punctuate the poems, have faced almost insoluble problems in determining who is speaking to whom, since the apparent speakers seem to change with bewildering rapidity (if they do change). Nor sometimes is it clear whether a dialogue has not ceased altogether, in order to give place to the author's own primary discourse. Reading through some of Persius's satires is like overhearing snatches of several conversations going on at once—we jump from one to another with disconcerting abruptness and never stay long with any one of them. These poems are also dense with difficult or unusual metaphors, sudden changes of register, and bold effects of parody, pastiche, and other forms of sardonic mimicry or allusion. English readers may well be reminded of parts of Eliot's *The Waste Land,* or Skelton's *Speak Parrot* (which mentions Persius by name), or certain moments in Pope's *Dunciad*. Persius's poems are, in short, fluidly and perpetually metaphorical, at times phantasmagoric, always demandingly figurative. When he describes the repulsive symptoms of bodily disease or decay, he has also in view spiritual or moral deterioration; the effect, though, is not of a simple mind-body allegory but rather of an acute insight into a unified psychosomatic degenerative process. When he attacks bad writers and the effete artistic circles that abet and encourage them—as he does in his programmatic first satire—he is also saying something larger. The attack on corrupt style is an attack on corrupt morality. The method is always synecdochic, the part for the whole. The speakers in his dialogues who suddenly loom out and as suddenly disappear may not in fact be distinct autonomous individuals "out there" so much as opposing voices or impulses within the poet himself, the "you" another aspect of the "I." And similarly the sage-teacher may abruptly change places with or merge into the wiser-because-humbler pupil-disciple. As D. M. Hooley says, discussing the third satire, the poem is an ironically self-interrogating work that refuses to allow any single voice a privileged authority. Doing this, it enacts the truth-seeking, self-examining Stoic's continuing efforts to live well. It evokes, only to reject, Horace's limited ironies, which favor the poet-speaker's own modest and attractive common sense.[3]

Much more could be said about some of these recent ways of reading Persius. But before returning to Dryden, I will simply quote two of Persius's scholarly exponents, who focus entirely on his language. J. P. Sullivan insists on Persius's quite exceptional feeling for words. He does this by invoking the example of literary modernism and by appropriating Ezra Pound's theory of *logopoeia*—"a refined mode of irony which shows itself . . . in a sensitivity to how language is used in other contexts, and in a deployment of those other uses for its own humorous and satiric aims, to produce an effect directly contrary to their effect in the usual contexts. So magniloquence can be made to criticise magniloquence, vulgarity to criticise vulgarity, and poeticisms to criticise poeticizing." "Despite its sporadic appearance in other periods this poetic mode strikes us," he says, "as an extremely 'modern' style of writing and requiring so much 'inwardness' with the relevant language, that if I am correct about Persius' style and aims, then it is small wonder that it was not until the last decade that critics have shown much insight into his work." Sullivan concludes: "Once we can feel our way into some such reading of Persius' satires, into an appreciation of his mastery, not only of the genre, but also of the Latin language, then we shall be able to put to one side the misleading conventional pictures of the earnest young poet or the Stoic moralist." J. G. Henderson makes the point more tersely: "Persius' convoluted acrimony skips the millennia, piercing the reader with wordage as palpable and spare as any poetry from modernity. . . . My pupils have taught me how intimately Persius means."[4]

The Persius who was inherited by the young John Dryden at Westminster School under Dr. Busby was, we can assume, very much according to the image that J. P. Sullivan deplores and rejects: "the earnest young poet," "the Stoic moralist"—for this is precisely how Persius was to be described in Dryden's "Discourse concerning the Original and Progress of Satire." In the course of his splendidly adroit and assured comparison between the three great Roman satirists, Dryden places Persius first for one feature only—for being passionately serious, sincere, and consistent in what he aimed to teach: namely, the Stoic philosophy. (Modern scholars, at least the most recent, play down the Stoicism: they maintain that there is relatively little doctrine in Persius's poems). It is the religious and moral Persius whom Dryden commends, as he could hardly fail to do: Persius had been welcomed into the Christian tradition for centuries—St. Jerome had imitated him, and St. Augustine had actually praised this pagan poet for some of his excellent moral teachings. But simply as poets—that is to say, in every other literary respect—Dryden enormously prefers Horace and Juvenal. He reads Horace and Juvenal, especially Juvenal, with unaffected delight. Indeed Juvenal, says Dryden, in a characteristically outrageous phrase, "gives me as much Pleasure as I can bear" (4:63). Persius, on the other hand, has a style that it would not be too much to call execrable: "his Verse is scabrous ["harsh, unmusical, unpolished," *OED*], and hobbling, and his Words not every where well chosen . . . his diction is hard; his Figures are generally too bold and daring; and his Tropes, particularly his Metaphors, insufferably strain'd." "After all," says Dryden, "he was a Young Man, like his Friend and Contemporary *Lucan*: Both of them Men of extraordinary Parts, and great acquir'd Knowledge, considering their Youth. But neither of them had arriv'd to that Maturity of Judgment, which is necessary to the accomplishing of a form'd Poet." And finally: "He is manifestly below *Horace*; because he borrows most of his greatest Beauties from him. . . ."[5]

The wonder is that, thinking so poorly of Persius in strictly poetic and literary terms, Dryden chose him for translation in the first place and then, having chosen him, performed as masterfully as he did. But Dryden was by this time nothing if not an absolute monarch in his own style, which he proceeded to impose on Persius with a boundless confidence. He decided, that is to say, not just to translate Persius but to transform him—giving him the literary finish which, in Dryden's view, Persius was unable to achieve himself. No doubt, in the early 1690s, Dryden felt attracted to Persius because he saw him as a fellow sufferer, someone who had to endure life under the tyrant Nero just as he had to put up with things under William and Mary. Dryden followed Casaubon in believing that Persius constantly had Nero in his satiric sights (he "aims particularly at him in most of his Satires"). Modern classical scholars won't have any of this either: the consensus seems to be that there is no dangerous topical allusion anywhere in Persius. But Dryden likely felt sympathy for what he saw as Persius's difficult political position. Nevertheless, his translation provides abundant evidence for the *literary* antipathy Persius aroused in him. Persius's spiky, rebarbative, endlessly provocative style must have been a constant irritant. Besides, Dryden persisted in thinking that Persius simply had not had time to learn poetic mastery. Dryden has a revealing note on the sixth satire concerning a brief description of a shipwreck: "this is the most Poetical Description of any in our Author: And since he and *Lucan* were so great Friends, I know not but *Lucan* might help him, in two or three of these Verses, which seem to be written in his stile; certain it is, that besides this Description of a Shipwreck, and two Lines more, which are at the End of the Second Satyr, our Poet has written nothing Elegantly" (4:360). This suggestion seems to be Dryden's own idea; and it has been accepted by no one. It's an instance of what J. P. Sullivan called Dryden's "incomprehension of Persius' aims." And this "incomprehension" goes along with what we must surely acknowledge as a massive underestimation of Persius's poetic powers. Persius did not need to be helped by Lucan to write his own poem. Again one may appeal to a modern classical scholar. Professor Nisbet is a cautious, sober, level-headed and philologically-inclined scholar-critic. He brings to his work an expert and refined knowledge of classical Latin poetic diction. Nisbet says of Persius's one-line imitation of Pacuvius: "The description of Antiopa is perhaps the best parody in Latin"—the best parody anywhere in the Latin language. Dryden refers disapprovingly in his prefatory essay to Persius's "boisterous metaphors" (meaning "violently harsh"). Nisbet quotes one of them and remarks: "Only Persius among Latin poets could have contrived so magnificent a mixture of metaphors." Nisbet finds much to criticize in Persius; he thinks the poems are distinctly uneven. But he finds a great deal also to enjoy and admire; and he puts the stress not on his supposed Stoic doctrines or his value as a teacher of morals but on his capacity as a writer: "Above all he can write." Persius repeatedly used words in an original way. And Nisbet ends with a reproof to those scholars in the recent past who should have known better: "If you, reader, can do as well when you are twenty-seven, you will deserve more than the clumsy misapprehensions and patronizing rebukes which have been the fate of Persius."[6]

Persius scholars disagree among themselves over the structure of his satires—whether they are each carefully arranged in a meaningful sequence or whether they are more haphazardly put together, with relatively little thought given to which passage follows which. Nisbet inclines to the older view, which saw Persius focusing on individual sections and using a somewhat piecemeal method of composition, whereas younger critics like D. M. Hooley find a more thorough-going artistry involving long-term planning throughout each poem. Whichever view one favors, there can be no doubt that Persius is a poet of often piercingly vivid set pieces and unforgettable single lines. As the late nineteenth-century Persius scholar B. L. Gildersleeve put it: "single verses ring in the ear for months and years."[7] Persius undoubtedly lends himself to publication in the form of extracts. Many readers—in the sixteenth and seventeenth centuries, for instance—must have come across passages of Persius in just this way: in collections of extracts thematically arranged. I want to single out one such set piece which may well have been selected for circulation in this form. This passage suddenly erupts at a point not far into the third satire (3.35–43). It does not very noticeably develop out of or follow on from what went before—I have not found a wholly convincing explanation of why it is there—but it forms an impressive poetic unit, virtually a poem complete in itself.[8] It concerns the punishment of tyrants, and as such it might easily have found its way into sixteenth-century anthologies. Modern commentators say that its declamatory style shows it to be a deliberate pastiche of "those rhetorical school exercises that involved the *saeuus tyrannus.*"[9] The theme was a hackneyed one; but Persius's treatment has a forcefulness and a characteristic specificity that make it memorable. I quote it first in a modern translation by Guy Lee:

> Great Father of Gods, be it Thy will no otherwise
> To punish cruel tyrants when malignant lust
> Dipped in fiery venom has disturbed their mind:

Let them have sight of Virtue and pine at having left her.
Did brazen bull of Sicily more bellow in pain
Or sword, hung from gilt fretted ceiling, strike more fear
Into the purple necks beneath, than if one said
To himself "We're sunk, sunk headfirst!" and turned pale inside
(Poor devil) at what the closest wife must never know?[10]

Lee's translation is a line-for-line version and comes close to reproducing something of Persius's conciseness and compression. Here is Dryden's version:

> Great Father of the Gods, when, for our Crimes,
> Thou send'st some heavy Judgment on the Times;
> Some Tyrant-King, the Terrour of his Age,
> The Type, and true Vicegerent of thy Rage;
> Thus punish him: Set Virtue in his Sight,
> With all her Charms adorn'd; with all her Graces bright:
> But set her distant; make him pale to see
> His Gains out-weigh'd by lost Felicity!
>
> *Sicilian* Tortures, and the Brazen Bull,
> Are Emblems, rather than express the Full
> Of what he feels: Yet what he fears, is more:
> The Wretch, who sitting at his plenteous Board,
> Look'd up, and view'd on high the pointed Sword
> Hang o'er his Head, and hanging by a Twine,
> Did with less Dread, and more securely Dine.
> Ev'n in his Sleep he starts, and fears the Knife;
> And, trembling, in his Arms, takes his Accomplice Wife:
> Down, down he goes; and from his Darling-Friend
> Conceals the Woes his guilty Dreams portend.
> (3.65–83)

In Dryden's version, Persius's seven lines have become nineteen lines (the odd number is reached not by the use of a triplet but by the introduction of a single unrhyming line). With the increase in number of words, the feeling expressed by Persius undergoes a marked change. There is more rhetorical afflatus, and with the increased wordage comes a loss of precision: for example, the entire couplet "Some Tyrant-King, the Terrour of his Age, / The Type, and true Vicegerent of thy Rage," has nothing corresponding to it in Persius. Dryden has tilted the sense of Persius's Latin away from the plural "cruel tyrants" ("saeuos ... tyrannos") to a sharply singular individual: "some Tyrant-King." As James

Winn notes: "The plural 'tyrants' of Persius, whose collective crime is *'dira libido,'* have become a single 'Tyrant-King,' imposed on a people in punishment for their own political 'Crimes.'"[11] In short, Dryden's "Tyrant-King" glances at King William. In the second part of this passage, Dryden takes the Williamite allusion further:

> Ev'n in his Sleep he starts, and fears the Knife;
> And, trembling, in his Arms, takes his Accomplice Wife:
> Down, down he goes; and from his Darling-Friend
> Conceals the Woes his guilty Dreams portend.

Unlike Persius, Dryden makes the tyrant's wife an "Accomplice"—clearly because he is now getting at not only William but Mary as well: Queen Mary was of course assumed to be complicit in her husband's usurpation. Dryden's allusions here to contemporary politics have a distinctly unfortunate effect: by making the tyrant's wife an accomplice, he sacrifices Persius's exquisitely focused stroke of imagination. For Persius, the woman is kept ignorant of what her husband is planning, although she is "proxima," closer to him than anyone else. So in Persius's sequence, we move from the public themes of the earlier lines (the "malignant lust" of "cruel tyrants") to an intimately private marital setting, finally focusing on the husband's agonizing nightly pangs of conscience. The "cruel tyrant" is even seen as "infelix" ("poor devil," as Guy Lee puts it).

These two or three last lines have, in Persius, an extraordinary intensity and human complexity. From them, or so I myself believe, Shakespeare developed the great scene in which Macbeth, planning a second murder, keeps it from his wife: "O, full of Scorpions is my Minde, deare Wife . . . Be innocent of the knowledge, dearest Chuck" (3.2.1194, 1204). Persius's language here anticipates Shakespeare's density of connotation; in comparison with Persius, Dryden's is thinner and coarser, more abstract and imprecise: "and from his Darling-Friend / Conceals the Woes his guilty Dreams portend." That last line resonates with a metallic oratorical hollowness.

The most famous single line in this passage—Hooley calls it "the poem's most famous line"—comes earlier: "Let them have sight of Virtue and pine at having left her" ("uirtutem uideant intabescantque relicta"). Persius here is swift and precise; here, at least, he is simple, wasting no words, allowing them to expand in the reader's mind. Dryden has this:

> Thus punish him: Set Virtue in his Sight,
> With all her Charms adorn'd; with all her Graces bright:
> But set her distant; make him pale to see
> His Gains out-weigh'd by lost Felicity!

Persius's single line becomes four lines, and in place of the two Latin words "uirtutem uideant" ("let them see Virtue"), Dryden elaborates:

> Set Virtue in his Sight,
> With all her Charms adorn'd; with all her Graces bright:

Dryden personifies the abstraction Virtue, but as soon as Virtue begins coming into view as a woman, something tired and commonplace seeps into the language. As a comparison, and contrast, this is how Wyatt incorporated these same lines of Persius into his first Satire:

> None othre pain pray I for theim to be
> > But when the rage doeth led them from the right
> > That lowking backward vertue they may se
> Evyn as she is so goodly fayre and bright;
> > And whilst they claspe their lustes in armes-a-crosse,
> > Graunt theim, goode lorde, as thou maist of thy myght,
> To frete inward for losing suche a losse.[12]

Wyatt has much more of Persius's intimate sharpness of feeling. Wyatt is certainly much less efficient, less lexically practiced, than Dryden—how homely "losing suche a losse" sounds in comparison—but even when, like Dryden, he expands on Persius ("That lowking backward, Vertue they may se / Evyn as she is, so goodly fayre and bright") he does so in a way that does not intrude irrelevantly erotic notions ("With all her Charms adorn'd"). Wyatt is not at all "elegant" in Dryden's understanding of the term, but this gives him an advantage as a translator of Persius.

Dryden's expansive treatment of this passage of Persius leads me to a related, though more general, consideration. Persius's extraordinary economy of expression, his ability to adumbrate a complex human situation in astonishingly few words, will strike even the most perfunctory of readers. An easygoing, garrulous Persius is almost unthinkable; to make him someone of that sort would deprive him of his essential poetic personality. And yet that is what Dryden does to Persius—not by any means always but all too frequently. I must refer here to an essay by William S. Anderson called "Persius and the Rejection of Society." Anderson presents Persius as a passionately devout, uncompromising Stoic whose principles made him feel nothing but hostility to, and alienation from, what Anderson calls "normal Roman society." But this devout Stoic was also a gifted poet. What is more relevant from the literary point of view is that Persius forged a unique poetic style to express his embattled Stoic outlook. Anderson is in no doubt that "we are face to face with a highly original poetic talent." He goes on to analyze a characteristic passage, and continues: "There is nothing pretty about these lines, nothing that I would even call enjoyable, but the abruptness, the ellipsis, the deliberate effort to shatter the line's unity, the catachresis, the abuse of "proper" grammar, the chiasmus, rhetorical questions and carefully placed vulgarity, all manifest the *callidus poeta* [the clever, skilful poet] as Persius seems to have intended him. For my part," he continues, "I believe that this unique style, the product of his poetic rather than his Stoic purposes, provides a surprisingly successful diction for the Stoic speaker."[13]

Anderson makes the essential point by focusing on Persius's style with its rejection of "elegance." The notorious "difficulties," the refusal to ingratiate and meet "normal" expectations are what make Persius what he is. But Dryden's translation normalizes and regularizes Persius. In turning him into English he works hard to socialize the antisocial Roman poet: *un*doing what Persius so pointedly does. Dryden fills him out by lavishly multiplying the number of words Persius uses. Moreover, he keeps on "explaining" Persius, or makes him "explain" himself, so as to make him not too demanding for the polite English reader. The *Critical Heritage* volume includes an anonymous poem called "To Mr. *Dryden*, on his Excellent Translation of *VIRGIL*" (1697). It contains the couplet:

> We saw new gall imbitter *Juvenal*'s Pen,
> And crabbed *Persius* made politely plain: ....[14]

Dryden is praised for making "crabbed Persius" "politely plain." He has made Persius socially presentable: he gives him fluency and ease, supplies clearly signposted transitions, eliminates metaphors and other figures that might perplex ("Yet, for once, I will venture to be so vain, as to affirm, that none of his hard metaphors, or forced expressions, are in my translation"), and patiently removes that unique compression of utterance that is

Persius's hallmark. But it is Persius's refusal to socialize—to be easily affable and entertainingly fluent—that gives him his poetic authority. Dryden's heroic-coupleteering society-speak offers a continuous affront to what Persius is and does.

Of course, that's not the whole story. To his credit, Dryden was enough of a literary artist to go some way to meet Persius and attempt to convey something of his literary temperament. The two or three strikingly indecent passages are, needless to say, rendered with gusto and a full-blooded masculine gutsiness:

> Thy strutting Belly swells; thy Paunch is high;
> Thou Writ'st not, but thou Pissest Poetry.
>
> (Satyr 1:108–9)

Some other passages are endowed by Dryden with a kind of scrupulous meanness, an almost drab bareness that he no doubt felt was appropriate to the Stoic's deportment. He describes or lists things as baldly as possible, as if to say "This is intentionally without 'elegance'"—without an artful niceness in the choice of words. At such times Dryden seems deliberately to sink below his usual stylistic level as a gesture toward Persius's spurning of "elegance." Is it possible that this may in part account for Dr. Johnson's slightly unjust remarks on Dryden's translation? "This work," says Johnson, "though like all the other productions of Dryden it may have shining parts, seems to have been written merely for wages in an uniform mediocrity, without any eager endeavour after excellence or laborious effort of the mind." But Dryden claimed that "it cost me more labour and time than *Juvenal*." It was not perhaps a lack of "laborious effort" that led to his failure so much as his lack of real sympathy with the poet—but, as I have just suggested, it may also sometimes have been due to a decision to withhold "elegance" from his writing.

There are, as Johnson concedes, "shining parts," moments when Dryden lets Persius come through. One of his famously quotable lines occurs in the second satire: "o curuae in terris animae et caelestium inanis" (61) ("O souls bent earthward, empty of things heavenly" [Guy Lee]). Dryden turns this into a good couplet—"O Souls, in whom no heav'nly Fire is found, / Fat Minds, and ever groveling on the ground! (2:110–11)—except for the weak fill-in phrase "is found." But the phrase "Fat Minds" is a more than adequate invention in the Persean style, even though Persius did not here write anything corresponding to it. The conclusion to the fourth satire is another place that shows Dryden briefly at his best:

> Reject the nauseous Praises of the Times:
> Give thy base Poets back their cobbled Rhymes:
> Survey thy Soul, not what thou do'st appear,
> But what thou art; and find the Beggar there.
>
> (4:126–29)

Again, Persius is very freely translated, but the unsparingly bleak tone is close to one of Persius's voices. Dryden is happiest of all in the exuberant snapshots of men destroying themselves through their greedy lusts—like the sensualist who alternately guzzles and takes hot baths "Till, with his Meat, he vomits out his Soul (3:205)." These brief fables anticipate the deathbed vignettes in Pope's *Epistle to Bathurst*. Dryden, though, gives them a slight geniality that is more Horatian than Persean.

There is also a larger anticipation of Pope's satirical manner. At the beginning of the first satire, Dryden invents what is for him a new heroic-couplet style. The impetuous rush of Lucretius's "perpetual torrent," as Dryden recreated it, for instance, is quite different in movement from the long-pent-up outburst that comes at the beginning of the Persius:

> *Persius*   How anxious are our Cares; and yet how vain
> The bent of our desires!
> *Friend*   Thy Spleen contain:
> For none will read thy Satyrs.
> *Persius*   This to Me?
> *Friend*   None; or what's next to none; but two or three.
> 'Tis hard, I grant.
> *Persius*   'Tis nothing; I can bear
> That paltry Scriblers have the Publick Ear:
> That this vast universal Fool, the Town,
> Shou'd cry up *Labeo*'s Stuff, and cry me down.
> They damn themselves; nor will my Muse descend
> To clap with such, who Fools and Knaves commend:
> Their Smiles and Censures are to me the same:
> I care not what they praise, or what they blame.
> In full Assemblies let the Crowd prevail:
> I weigh no Merit by the common Scale.
> The Conscience is the Test of ev'ry Mind;
> *Seek not thy self, without thy self, to find*
> But where's that *Roman?*—Somewhat I wou'd say,
> But Fear;—Let Fear, for once, to Truth give way.

> Truth lends the Stoick Courage: when I look
> On Humane Acts, and Read in Nature's Book,
> From the first Pastimes of our Infant Age,
> To elder Cares, and Man's severer Page;
> When stern as Tutors, and as Uncles hard,
> We lash the Pupil, and defraud the Ward:
> Then, then I say—or wou'd say, if I durst—
> But thus provok'd, I must speak out, or burst.
>   (1:1–26)

This seems to me a new Drydenian style (and one that is *not* sustained through the rest of the Persius translations). The features of this style are a clipped economy, a rushing speed of movement, and an implacable resort to emphasis, often shaped in cleaving antitheses and parallel constructions. Lines in which words or phrases are repeated mimic the insistent Stoic curtness, the uncompromising adherence to doctrine: "Shou'd cry up *Labeo's* Stuff, and cry me down"; "I care not what they praise, or what they blame"; "*Seek not thy self, without thy self, to find.*" Compared with Persius's Latin, Dryden's version has, as usual, greatly increased the number of words used—and not simply because of the differences between the two languages. When, for instance, Dryden has him say "Truth lends the Stoick Courage," he is not translating Persius (who says nothing of the sort): he is expanding Persius so as to explain him to his English reader. Nonetheless, despite the un-Persean volubility, Dryden is inventing a fast and agile style, packed yet light, which is extraordinarily close to Pope's later Horatian manner. Indeed—though there is no time to go further into the comparison—Pope is much closer to Persius in temperament than Dryden is (as more than one critic has noticed); and just as Dryden here makes Persius more like Horace, so Pope was to make Horace more like Persius. It's hardly too much to say that Dryden has here invented the style of Pope's Horatian *Imitations*.

How should Persius be translated? Charles Martindale has written an article "in praise of metaphrase" that I find very persuasive.[15] He refers to Dryden's theory of translation, with its categories of metaphrase (word-for-word translation), paraphrase, and imitation, and argues that the merits of metaphrase have been neglected and should be reinstated. In 1987 Guy Lee brought out his line-for-line verse translation of Persius, which John Henderson, the impassioned advocate of Persius's poetry has called "brilliant." Lee is in agreement with Martindale on the merits of metaphrase, conceding that his translation cannot "give the reader any idea of Persius' allusive style"—such as his innumerable adaptations of Horace. Nor can it reproduce the movement of Persius's "racy but elegant variety of the dactylic hexameter." But, he says, "this English version . . . strives to retain not only his compression but his substance too, as faithfully as possible; in other words it strives to be a metaphrase, avoiding paraphrase. . . . Every effort is made to represent every metaphor and every peculiarity of diction and to reproduce the Latin syntax as far as that is possible in English. This translation is meant to read like a translation and does not pretend to be a factitious original."[16] I find that reading Lee's version, referring constantly to the Latin text on the facing pages, is at the very least a helpful way of coming closer to Persius's poetry.

Over thirty years ago the late William Frost wrote a richly informative essay called "English Persius: the Golden Age."[17] He located this "Golden Age" in the "long" eighteenth century, from Dryden to Gifford. The best of these paraphrasing Augustan translators certainly produced elegantly assured English poems. Persius is made to wear his English costume with style and dash. But, for the reasons given earlier, I do not myself believe it was a true "Golden Age" for Persius. A "Golden Age" for Persius I find very difficult to imagine.

Notes

1. R. G. M. Nisbet, "Persius," in *Critical Essays on Roman Literature: Satire,* ed. J. P. Sullivan (London: Routledge & Kegan Paul, 1963), 40; J. P. Sullivan, "In Defence of Persius," *Ramus* 1 (1972): 50.

2. The scholars to whom I have referred to include Nisbet and Sullivan as well as the following: R. G. Peterson, "The Unknown Self in the Fourth Satire of Persius," *Classical Journal* 68 (1972–73); J. C. Bramble, *Persius and the Programmatic Satire: A Study in Form and Imagery* (Cambridge: Cambridge University Press, 1974); William S. Anderson, "Persius and the Rejection of Society," in *Essays on Roman Satire* (Princeton: Princeton University Press, 1982); J. G. Henderson, *Writing down Rome: Satire, Comedy, and other offences in Latin Poetry* (Oxford: Clarendon, 1999). I have benefited especially from D. M. Hooley's book *The Knotted Thong: Structures of Mimesis in Persius* (Ann Arbor: University of Michigan Press, 1997).

3. Hooley, 229.

4. Sullivan, 60–62; Henderson, 229.

5. *The Works of John Dryden,* ed. H. T. Swedenbery et al., (Berkeley and Los Angeles: University of California Press, 1956–), 4:51–52.

6. Nisbet, 46, 44, 70.

7. Quoted in Hooley, 10.

8. Sarah Grimes has a helpful comment on this passage in "Structure in the Satire of Persius" in *Neronians and Flavians,* ed. D. R. Dudley (London: Routledge & Kegan Paul, 1972), 141–42.

9. *The Satires of Persius,* trans. Guy Lee, with introduction and notes by William Barr (Liverpool: F. Cairns, 1987), 106.

10. Lee and Barr, 27–29.

11. James Winn, "'Complying with the Times': Dryden's *Satires of Juvenal and Persius,*" in *Eighteenth-Century Life* 12 (1988): 84.

12. *Collected Poems of Sir Thomas Wyatt,* ed. Kenneth Muir and Patricia Thomson (Liverpool: Liverpool University Press, 1969), 94–95, lines 106–12.

13. Anderson, 189–90.

14. *Dryden: The Critical Heritage,* ed. James Kinsley and Helen Kinsley (London: Routledge, 1971), 219.

15. Charles Martindale, "Unlocking the Word-Hoard: In Praise of Metaphrase," *Comparative Criticism* 6 (1984): 47–72.

16. Lee and Barr, 8–9.

17. William Frost, "English Persius: The Golden Age," *Eighteenth Century Studies* 2 (1968); reprinted in *John Dryden, Dramatist, Satirist, Translator* (New York: AMS Press, 1988).

Safe Sex? Dryden's Translation of Juvenal's Sixth Satire

SUSANNA MORTON BRAUND

DRYDEN IS NOT SHY WHEN IT COMES TO DESCRIPTIONS OF COPULAtion. Evidence for this is provided amply by his translation of Lucretius's tirade against sex in the finale to book 4 of his *De Rerum Natura*, published in 1685 as part of his *Second Miscellany*. But when we turn to his translation of Juvenal's notorious sixth satire, an epic-scale rant against Roman wives, first published in 1693 as part of a collective project to translate all the poems of Juvenal, we miss the directness and explicitness of his Lucretius translation. How can we account for this?

In this essay I propose to examine Dryden's engagement with Juvenal by study of his prefatory remarks alongside his actual practice in handling the most explicitly sexual material in the poem. I shall argue that Dryden's distaste for what he sees as Juvenal's unfair criticisms of women leads him to sanitize his published translation of the poem in a way that does not do full justice to the Roman satirist. The fact that Dryden has no such qualms in his translations of racy passages in other Latin texts—I shall introduce this essay with an examination of passages from his translation from Lucretius to demonstrate this—suggests that this is not a case of incapacity but rather of disinclination. Safe sex is his preferred mode of dealing with Juvenal.

The situation is complicated by the recent emergence of sixteen lines of the most racy material, virtually certainly by Dryden but never included by him or his publisher in the published editions.[1] These lines pose a problem for modern editors. Keith Walker includes them in his 1987 Oxford edition, while Paul Hammond and David Hopkins in their 2000 Longman edition print them in the notes, on the grounds that their circulation was "strictly limited." Here I propose to discuss them in the appropriate places on the assumption that they were excised at a relatively late stage in the process of publication, since they mostly show comparable polish and flair to the rest of Dryden's translation and since their removal leaves the translation harder to understand at times.[2] I shall proceed to draw attention to the ways in which their excision contributes to a sanitization of Dryden's translation of the sixth satire.

༄

First, I suggest that Dryden is well capable of handling sexually explicit material from his translation of Lucretius. In fact, he embraces the raunchy dimension of Lucretius's Latin so vigorously as to intensify it. Lucretius's disquisition on sex, love, and procreation occupies the final 250 lines of book 4 of his poetic exposition of the Epicurean philosophy, *De Rerum Natura* (4.1037–287). Dryden selected this passage as one of just five excerpts to translate in his *Second Miscellany* (1685), three of which are very brief (the opening of books 1 and 2 and a few lines from the account of the rise of civilization in book 5); the only other substantial passage he selects is the dissuasion from fear of death toward the end of book 3. In other words, I see it as significant that Dryden is attracted to this particular passage from a poem of nearly 7500 lines of Latin.

His translation starts at line 1052 of the Latin and carries through to the end of the book, with 296 lines for 236 lines of Latin, a typical but slightly restrained degree of expansion for Dryden's translations from Latin.[3] There are two passages in which Lucretius describes the act of sex. The first is at 4.1076–83, with Cyril Bailey's 1947 translation:

> etenim potiundi tempore in ipso
> fluctuat incertis erroribus ardor amantum
> nec constat quid primum oculis manibusque fruantur.
> quod petiere, premunt arte faciuntque dolorem
> corporis et dentis inlidunt saepe labellis
> osculaque adfligunt, quia non est pura voluptas
> et stimuli subsunt qui instigant laedere id ipsum
> quodcumque est, rabies unde illaec germina surgunt.

[for in the very moment of possession the passion of lovers ebbs and flows with undetermined current, nor are they sure what first to enjoy with eyes or hands. What they have grasped, they closely press and cause pain to the body, and often fasten their teeth in the lips, and dash mouth against mouth in kissing, because their pleasure is not unalloyed, and there are secret stings that spur them to hurt even the very thing, be it what it may, whence arise those germs of madness.]

This corresponds to lines 35–44 in Dryden's translation:

> When Love its utmost vigour does imploy,
> Ev'n then, 'tis but a restless wandering joy:
> Nor knows the Lover, in that wild excess,
> With hands or eyes, what first he wou'd possess:
> But strains at all; and fast'ning where he strains,
> Too closely presses with his frantique pains:
> With biteing kisses hurts the twining fair,
> Which shews his joyes imperfect, unsincere;
> For stung with inward rage, he flings around,
> And strives t' avenge the smart on that which gave the wound.[4]

Dryden's intensification here resides in a few telling details that go beyond the Latin original: "Too closely presses" for *premunt arte* where the Latin adverb is simple and not comparative; "his frantique pains" for unembellished *dolorem;* and "stung with inward rage," which seems to represent *stimuli subsunt,* where the Latin emphasises not the violence but the surreptitious surprise of the "goads" of lust.

More telling still is Dryden's version of Lucretius's most explicit description of sex, following the evocation of foreplay. First, Lucretius (4.1105–120), then Bailey, then Dryden (71–92).

> denique cum membris conlatis flore fruuntur   1105
> aetatis, iam cum praesagit gaudia corpus
> atque in eost Venus ut muliebria conserat arva,
> adfigunt avide corpus iunguntque salivas
> oris et inspirant pressantes dentibus ora,
> nequiquam, quoniam nil inde abradere possunt   1110
> nec penetrare et abire in corpus corpore toto;
> nam facere interdum velle et certare videntur:
> usque adeo cupide in Veneris compagibus haerent,
> membra voluptatis dum vi labefacta liquescunt.
> tandem ubi se erupit nervis conlecta cupido,   1115
> parva fit ardoris violenti pausa parumper.
> inde redit rabies eadem et furor ille revisit,
> cum sibi quid cupiant ipsi contingere quaerunt,
> nec reperire malum id possunt quae machina vincat:
> usque adeo incerti tabescunt volnere caeco.   1120

[Even at last when the lovers embrace and taste the flower of their years, when the body has a foretaste of its joy and passion is on the point of sowing the woman's furrows, eagerly they clasp and mingle the moisture of their mouths, and pressing lip on lip breathe deeply; yet all for nought, since they cannot tear off ought thence, nor enter in and pass away, merging the whole body in the other's body; for at times they seem to strive and struggle to do it; so eagerly are they locked in the fetters of love, while their limbs are loose and slackened by the force of their delight. And at length when the gathering desire has burst from their limbs, then for a while comes a little respite in their furious passion. Then the same madness returns, the old frenzy is back upon them, when they yearn to find out what in truth they desire to attain, nor can they discover what device may conquer their disease; in such deep doubt they waste beneath their secret wound.]

>   Nor when the Youthful pair more clossely joyn,
>   When hands in hands they lock, and thighs in thighs they twine,
>   Just in the raging foam of full desire,
>   When both press on, both murmur, both expire,
>   They gripe, they squeeze, their humid tongues they dart,   75
>   As each wou'd force their way to t' others heart:
>   In vain: they only cruize about the coast,
>   For bodies cannot pierce, nor be in bodies lost:
>   As sure they strive to be, when both engage,
>   In that tumultuous momentany rage;   80
>   So 'tangled in the Nets of Love they lie,
>   Till Man dissolves in that excess of joy.
>   Then, when the gather'd bag has burst its way,
>   And ebbing tydes the slacken'd nerves betray,
>   A pause ensues; and Nature nods a while,   85
>   Till with recruited rage new Spirits boil;
>   And then the same vain violence returns,
>   With flames renew'd th' erected furnace burns.
>   Agen they in each other wou'd be lost,
>   But still by adamantine bars are crost;   90
>   All wayes they try, successeless all they prove,
>   To cure the secret sore of lingering love.

Dryden captures closely Lucretius's strategy of a long and breathlessly mounting period, which is punctured by *nequiquam*—his "In vain," similarly enjambed—just at the climactic moment. But in the details he conjures much more vividly than does Lucretius the physicality of the act of sex. He develops the hint of *membris conlatis* (1105) into the much more explicit and visually evocative "hands in hands they lock, and thighs in thighs they twine" (72). His phrase "the raging foam of full desire" (73) is not at all close to the Latin; I assume it is his version of Lucretius's agricultural euphemism for the approach to ejaculation in *ir eost Venus ut muliebria conserat arva* (1107). Particularly striking is the way in which Dryden represents the mutual striving of the copulating couple in an undeniable intensification of the Latin, in his repetitions of "both" and "they" and his accumulation of verbs in "both press on, both murmur, both expire, / They gripe, they squeeze, their humid tongues they dart" (74–75). This is continued in the in itself unremarkable but here felicitous elision ("t' others") in the final words of the following line: "As each would force their way to t' others heart."

Dryden proceeds by representing with great accuracy Lucretius's *nequiquam* in initial position and syntactic separation. He then improves upon the Latin in his wonderful phrases "that tumultuous momentany rage" (80) and "the same vain violence" (87). The former is generated by nothing at all in the Latin while the latter is inspired by *rabies eadem et furor ille* (1117) while reusing *nequiquam* from 1110. With these vivid and memorable phrases Dryden conjures the frenzy of sex.

Before we turn to his rendering of sex in Juvenal, it is salutary and useful to take a look at the assertive tone of Dryden's remarks about his choice of this passage to translate and about his handling of this passage in his translation. In the preface to the *Second Miscellany* he articulates his great admiration for Lucretius and writes of his decision to lay aside his "natural diffidence and scepticism for a while, to take up that dogmatical way of his, which, as I said, is so much his character, as to make him that individual poet." He thus makes clear his decision to surrender to his author. Dryden then turns to his selection of the close to book 4:

> 'Tis true, there is something, and that of some moment, to be objected against my *Englishing* the *Nature of Love,* from the Fourth Book of *Lucretius*: And I can less easily answer why I Translated it, than why I thus Translated it. The Objection arises from the Obscenity of the Subject; which is aggravated by the too lively, and alluring delicacy of the Verses. In the first place, without the least Formality of an excuse, I own it pleas'd me: and let my Enemies make the worst they can of this Confession; I am not yet so secure from that passion, but that I want my Authors Antidotes against it. He has given the truest and most Philosophical account both of the Disease and Remedy, which I ever found in any Author: For which reasons I Translated him. But it will be ask'd why I turn'd him into this luscious *English,* (for I will not give it a worse word:) instead of an answer, I wou'd ask again of my Supercilious Adversaries, whether I am not bound when I Translate an Author, to do him all the right I can, and to Translate him to

the best advantage? If to mince his meaning, which I am satisfi'd was honest and instructive, I had either omitted some part of what he said, or taken from the strength of his expression, I certainly had wrong'd him; and that freeness of thought and words, being thus cashier'd in my hands, he had no longer been *Lucretius*. (3:12)

This is a wonderful vindication both of Dryden's selection of the passage and of his vigorous and intense handling of the passage. There is a moral purpose alleged here.[5] As he goes on to say, "the intention qualifies the act; and both mine and my Authors were to instruct, as well as please" (3:13). I suggest that the central difference between his handling of Lucretius and of Juvenal lies precisely here—in his perception of the moral purpose of the works. Let us now turn our attention to Dryden's reading of Juvenal.

In the *Argument of the Sixth Satyr* Dryden states his position on the topic of the poem and demonstrates a reading that is a good deal more subtle than those offered by many critics and readers since then, although he fails to take one final step, which would have made his task as translator that much easier, as I shall suggest at the end of this paper. He starts with the following astute observations: (1) that the poem is double the length of any other satire; (2) that it takes as its theme a commonplace; (3) that while other poems make men their target, "this he reserv'd wholly for the Ladies." All three remarks are well made and provide the essential framework for interpretation of this poem. It is indeed a treatment of a rhetorical topos, on an unprecedented scale, balancing the focus upon men in the preceding satires.[6] Moreover, after these preliminary remarks, once Dryden embarks upon his account of the poem, he sees correctly that lust is its central theme: it is "the most Heroick of their Vices: The rest are in a manner but digression." This too is on target and contrasts markedly with many interpretations of Juvenal's poem that prattle on about Roman women in general. The poem is not about Roman women in general but about Roman wives—about the ways in which they deceive, humiliate and, finally, dispose of their husbands.[7]

After this astute overview of the poem Dryden next proceeds to criticize Juvenal's unfairness in this "bitter Invective." He first makes two points: that "he is not to be excus'd for imputing to all, the Vices of some few amongst them" and that it was not "generously done . . . to attack the weakest as well as the fairest part of the Creation." It is at this point, then, that we start to see Dryden's reservations emerge. The implication of these remarks is that Dryden constructs for himself a personality that values fairness and chivalry more highly than does Juvenal. As he goes on, he seems puzzled about the "Moral" of the poem, asserting that it cannot be to avoid women entirely, which, after all, would spell the end of humankind. He interprets Juvenal's warning about female "Artifices" as "a kind of silent acknowledgment, that they have more wit than Men: which turns the Satyr upon us, and particularly upon the Poet; who thereby makes a Complement, where he meant a Libel" (4:145). This far from obvious reading of the poem demonstrates Dryden's need to salvage women from Juvenal's savagery. In a further puzzled rumination he seems convinced that Juvenal has guaranteed the alienation of more than half of the audience—the female sex and "all the happy Lovers" among the men.

After voicing these criticisms of Juvenal, Dryden proceeds to make his own position absolutely explicit: he states that he is only prepared to translate this poem because he is convinced that "so unjust a Charge" will not convert many of his readers. The fact that he in no way shares Juvenal's opinion is articulated in the form of gallant resistance: "Whatever his *Roman* Ladies were, the *English* are free from all his Imputations."[8] In fact, it is tempting to suggest that one reason that he took on the task of translating this satire himself was to exercise control over the apparent savagery of its content.

It is crucial to bear in mind these preliminary remarks as we examine the translation itself. The central question to pose is how a translator who is overtly resistant to the message he finds in his text handles the most difficult material in the original. In this case, the most difficult material is without a doubt the raunchy sexual material that surfaces at several points. For that reason, I propose to focus particularly upon the most lurid sexual descriptions in the Latin and to examine Dryden's strategies for rendering them into English.[9]

༄

Let me therefore turn directly to the lines in which Juvenal describes how Messalina, the wife of the emperor Claudius, liked to slip away to a brothel at night to attempt to satiate her unbridled lust. This occupies lines 114–32 of the Latin and lines 161–89 of Dryden's translation. First, I observe Dryden's most felicitous rendition of Juvenal's oxymoron *meretrix Augusta* (118) as "th' Imperial Whore" (164).[10] But while he can turn a rhetorical phrase like that brilliantly, I find that in the detailed descriptions of the empress Dryden shrinks from rendering the graphic details designed by Juvenal to appeal to the senses. The fine visual touch of her "blonde wig hiding her black hair" (*nigrum flauo crinem abscondente galero*, 120) is omitted entirely and "the brothel which was steaming with ancient blankets" (*calidum veteri centone lupanar*, 121) is watered down to "That Room in which the rankest Harlot lay" (175).[11] For sure, the word "rank" is highly apposite, but the evocation of the sweaty customers and what they have done on or underneath the ancient blankets is essential to the seediness of the scene—yet Dryden ignores this. Another telling detail he appears to omit is one emphasized by Juvenal—that Messalina proceeds to "an empty cubicle—her very own" (*cellam uacuam, atque suam*, 122), unless this is supposed to be represented by Dryden's weak phrase "the known Brothel-house" (173). Juvenal reserves for the end of the clause the detail that Messalina is such a regular whore that she has her very own cubicle, thus endowing it with shock value. This is missing from Dryden.

The picture of Messalina awaiting her clients turns out rather differently in the translation from the original. Juvenal has two-and-a-half lines embellished with the brilliant details of her gilded nipples and her assumed name Lycisca (itself a calque on the story of the foundation myth of Rome, the suckling of Romulus and Remus by a she-wolf), culminating in outrage at her display of the womb that bore Britannicus. This is pointed by the use of apostrophe, with the effect of summoning up the presence of the young prince in the stinking brothel:

> tunc nuda papillis
> prostitit auratis, titulum mentita Lyciscae,
> Ostenditque tuum, generose Britannice, ventrem
>
> (122–24)

[Then she stood there, naked and for sale, with her nipples gilded, under the trade name of "she-Wolf," putting on display the belly you came from, noble-born Britannicus.]

By contrast, the published version of Dryden is disappointing. The lack of specificity makes for a lack-lustre generic description of any whore, miles away from the Roman empress:

> Prepar'd for fight, expectingly she lies,
> With heaving Breasts, and with desiring Eyes.
>
> (176–77)

At this point we meet the first unpublished addition. Its first two lines seem a fairly feeble rendition of the Latin:

> The fair unbroaken belly lay displayd
> Where once the brave Britannicus was layd.

Dryden obscures Juvenal's outrage to the imperial family perpetrated by Messalina's naked display of the imperial breasts and belly to her clients. That, I take it, is the point of the apostrophe of Britannicus along with the vocative *generose* ("noble-born"), an adjective that in this context becomes heavily ironic. His mother with the gilded nipples is behaving anything but nobly. But perhaps his imagination was already working on what follows.

The unpublished passage has two further lines:

> Bare was her bosome, bare ye field of Lust
> Eagre to Swallow Evry sturdy Thrust.

Here Dryden is translating a line now generally regarded as spurious: *et resupina iacens multorum absorbuit ictus* ("and lying on her back receives the thrusts of many men"), preserved in a few MSS after line 125, a line that Dryden does not translate at all. He elaborates the single word *ictus* ("thrusts") into a repeated representation of sex as a form of combat. In the unpublished text this emerges in "ye field of Lust" as well as "Evry sturdy Thrust," but he also projects backward a few lines and prepares for this image with his "Prepar'd for Fight" in the published text. Moreover, he happily envisages Messalina in a supine position, in contrast to her standing position in the Latin (*prostitit*), again projecting backward by having her lie "expectingly," with heaving breasts and desiring eyes in the preceding lines. Whatever this picture of the supine whore tussling with her many clients reveals about the fantasies or actualities of experience in brothels in the late seventeenth century, it was evidently felt to be too risqué for publication. The "safe" version that was actually published both misses Juvenal's sharp irony and lacks the vigour of Dryden's imaginary brothel.

After the evening's session is over and the pimp has dismissed his girls, Messalina's state of unsatiated lust is represented by Juvenal with startling graphic physicality: *adhuc ardens rigidae tentigine volvae* (129, "still burning with her clitoris inflamed and stiff"). This detail is evidently too much for Dryden who omits it entirely. Admittedly, his turning of line 130 of Juvenal is brilliant, *lassata viris necdum satiata recessit* ("exhausted by the men but not yet satisfied") with his line 185 "Tir'd with the Toyl, unsated with the Sin," thanks to the force of the alliteration. But the intrusion of moralizing here in the notion of "sin" is compounded and seems to blot out the power of the sensual detail in Juvenal's next words: *obscuris . . . genis turpis fumoque lucernae / foeda* (131–32, "with her cheeks filthy, dirty from the smoke of the lamp"), which Dryden renders as "All Filth without and all a Fire within" (184). Where Juvenal allows the details to convey the moral charge, Dryden feels it necessary to spell it out for his readers. Finally, however, Dryden does respond to the physical details here and he proceeds to rework these phrases in his lines 187–89 where he has Messalina returning to the emperor's bed:

> The steam of Lamps still hanging on her Cheeks
> In Ropy Smut; thus foul, and thus bedight,
> She brings him back the Product of the Night.

Yet even here, his fastidiousness substitutes the vague phrase "the Product of the Night" for the much more specific *lupanaris . . . odorem* ("the stench of the brothel"). Finally, I draw attention to Dryden's sarcastic phrase "the modest Matron" (186), which is unwarranted by anything in the Latin.

Examination of Dryden's published translation of this passage reveals him choosing not to respond to the lurid details with which Juvenal laces his depiction of Messalina in the brothel and, moreover, explicitly pointing the moral of the incident. The second pair of unpublished lines demonstrates graphically that he had the capacity to respond to the vigor of the Latin when he wished. But the published version restrains and contains the illicit lust that Juvenal unleashes and so evidently relishes.

৯

The same tendency to restraint and containment applies to Dryden's rendition of the most sustained treatment of lust in the poem.[12] This commences at line 286 in the Latin, where Juvenal provides a kind of second prologue by asking: *unde haec monstra tamen vel quo de fonte requiris?* ("But where do these monstrosities come from, you're asking, what's their source?") and sketching a picture of the virtuous Roman women of ancient times. The arrival of *Luxuria* ("Luxury") is blamed for the decline in morals—and of this Juvenal obligingly provides a graphic scene:

> prima peregrinos obscena pecunia mores
> intulit, et turpi fregerunt saecula luxu
> divitiae molles. quid enim Venus ebria curat?   300
> inguinis et capitis quae sint discrimina nescit,
> grandia quae mediis iam noctibus ostrea mordet,
> cum perfusa mero spumant unguenta Falerno,
> cum bibitur concha, cum iam vertigine tectum
> ambulat et geminis exsurgit mensa lucernis.   305
> i nunc et dubita qua sorbeat aera sanna
> Tullia, quid dicat notae collactea Maurae,   307
> Maura Pudicitiae veterem cum praeterit aram,   308
> noctibus hic ponunt lecticas, micturiunt hic
> effigiemque deae longis siphonibus implent   310
> inque vices equitant ac Luna teste moventur.
> inde domos abeunt: tu calcas luce reversa
> coniugis urinam magnos visurus amicos.
>
> (298–313)

[It was filthy money that first imported foreign ways and effete wealth that corrupted our era with its disgusting decadence. After all, when she's drunk does your Venus care about anything? She doesn't know the difference between head and crotch, the woman who chomps giant oysters when it's already midnight, when the perfumes are foaming after being mixed with undiluted Falernian, when drinking is from perfume-jars, when the ceiling's started going round and round and the table's dancing about with its lamps duplicated. Go on, ask yourself why Tullia sneers as she sniffs the air, and what notorious Maura's "foster-sister" says to her when Maura passes the ancient altar of Chastity. It's here that they halt their litters at night, it's here that they piss and fill the goddess's image with their powerful streams and take it in turns to ride one another and thrash around while the moon looks on.[13] Then they go off home. When the daylight has returned, *you* tread in your wife's urine on your way to call on your important friends.]

Dryden renders Juvenal's sixteen lines in a restrained fourteen (or eighteen including the unpublished lines after 427)—a striking figure when one considers the degree of expansion usually found in Dryden, which runs at a little more than 150 percent[14]:

> What care our Drunken Dames to whom they spread?
> Wine, no distinction makes of Tail or Head.

> Who lewdly dancing at a Midnight-Ball,
> For hot Eringoes, and Fat Oysters call:
> Full Brimmers to their Fuddled Noses thrust; 420
> Brimmers the last Provocatives of Lust.
> When Vapours to their swimming Brains advance,
> And double Tapers on the Tables Dance.
>   Now think what Bawdy Dialogues they have,
> What *Tullia* talks to her confiding Slave, 425
> At Modesty's old Statue; when by Night,
> They make a stand, and from their Litters light;
> [They straighten wth their hands ye nameless place
> And Spouting thence bepiss her venerable face:
> Before the Conscious Moon they get astride;
> By Turns are ridden & by Turns they ride.]
> The Good Man early to the Levee goes,
> And treads the Nasty Paddle of his Spouse.
>
> (416–29)

Dryden certainly produces a wonderful phrase, hardly generated by the Latin, when he pictures the women with their noses thrust into full "Brimmers" at 421: "Brimmers the last Provocatives of Lust." But the published version coyly suppresses the consequence of drunkenness—the women's halting at the altar of Chastity to piss there and to indulge in sexual frolics. In Juvenal the details are lavishly explicit—*micturiunt, longis siphonibus, in ... uices equitant* and *urinam*. Dryden has a fine response in the unpublished lines to this with his "spouting" and "bepiss" and especially with his brilliant "By Turns are ridden & by Turns they ride." But since ladies should not behave like this, even in ancient Rome, we are left, in the published version, with the husband simply splashing through "the Nasty Paddle of his Spouse." Again, the published version deliberately censors the lubricious details that Dryden responds to in the Latin.

The same phenomenon is still more visible in the very next topic, the perversion of the rites of the Good Goddess, which can provide rich fodder for male fantasy. Juvenal provides a highly explicit description in lines 314–45. The fact that Dryden's version, in lines 430–63, is virtually equivalent in length is just the first indication of a reluctance to engage with graphic descriptions of sex, in the published version at any rate. As I shall now demonstrate, he casts a cowl of modesty over the proceedings, which leaves the reader of his translation shortchanged:

Let's start with Juvenal, lines 314–17:

> nota Bonae secreta Deae, cum tibia lumbos
> incitat et cornu pariter vinoque feruntur

> attonitae crinemque rotant ululantque Priapi
> maenades.

[Everyone knows the secret rites of the Good Goddess, when the pipe excites the loins and, crazed by horn and wine alike, the female revellers of Priapus are carried away, whirling their hair and howling.]

With an expansion typical of his approach elsewhere, Dryden provides an entirely unnecessary elaboration of the word *nota* (literally "well-known") with:

> The Secrets of the Goddess nam'd the Good,
> Are even by Boys and Barbers understood.
>
> (430–31)

His next lines present the ingredients of Juvenal's text in a different sequence and with significant weakening of expression:

> Where the Rank Matrons, Dancing to the Pipe,
> Gig with their Bums, and are for Action ripe;
> With Musick rais'd, they spread abroad their Hair;
> And toss their Heads like an enamour'd Mare.
>
> (432–35)

Gone altogether is Juvenal's striking designation of these sex-crazed women as *Priapi maenades*. Dryden substitutes the entirely different image of the sex-crazed mare. In so doing he misses the point that this is a perversion of a religious rite. That accounts for Juvenal's notion that these women are religious devotees (*maenades*) who have refocused their attention from Dionysus, and the deity of revelry, to Priapus, the deity of the erection.

The following lines are omitted from the published version of Dryden. Here is Juvenal:

> o quantus tunc illis mentibus ardor
> concubitus, quae vox saltante libidine, quantus
> ille meri veteris per crura madentia torrens!
>
> (317–19)

[It's then that their minds are all on fire to get laid, that they squeal to the dance of their desire, that an abundant torrent of vintage wine[15] runs over their dripping thighs!]

Here is Dryden:

> Confess their itching in their ardent Eyes
> While teares of wine run trickling down their thighs.

Though the vividness of Juvenal's *ardor concubitus* ("on fire to get laid") and *saltante libidine* ("to the dance of their desire") is heavily tamed in "their itching in their ardent Eyes," Dryden well evokes his sexy picture of fluids on the women's thighs. But evidently the graphic detail of female arousal was felt to be too much for Dryden's public and this passage was suppressed.

Juvenal's next lines again offer a graphic visualisation, which is suppressed in the published version of Dryden. First Juvenal:

> lenonum ancillas posita Saufeia corona
> provocat et tollit pendentis praemia coxae,
> ipsa Medullinae fluctum crisantis adorat:
> palma inter dominas, virtus natalibus aequa.
>
> (320–23)

[Saufeia takes off her garland and issues a challenge to the brothel-keepers' slave-girls. She wins the prize for swinging her arse, then she in turn worships Medullina's undulating surges. The contest is between the ladies: their expertise matches their birth.]

Now the Dryden, with two unpublished lines here incorporated:

> *Laufella*[16] lays her Garland by, and proves
> The mimick Leachery of Manly Loves,
> [Provokes to Flats some batterd household whore
> And heaving up the rubster does adore.]
> Rank'd with the Lady, the cheap Sinner lies;
> For here not Blood, but Virtue gives the prize.
>
> (436–39)

By now the tensions involved in handling this kind of Juvenalian material are becoming familiar: nowhere do we find any "arse-swinging" or "undulating surges." The unpublished lines do provide sexually explicit material with the references to the "Flats," namely lesbian genital stimulation,[17] and to "the rubster," evidently the whore with whom the aristocrat Laufella engages sexually. But the published version is left with the obscure and mealy-mouthed (though nicely alliterative) "mimick Leachery of Manly Loves," with a "cheap Sinner" adding the moralizing ingredient. To give Dryden the benefit of the doubt, it is very likely that his "Manly Loves" are inspired by an awareness of the playfully gendered irony of *virtus* (literally "manliness"), but the effect is bleached into Christian overtones by the pallid word "Virtue."

Then in the next lines, Dryden's published version is actually more vigorous and more explicit than Juvenal, excepting one physical detail:

> Nothing is feign'd, in this Venereal Strife;
> 'Tis downright Lust, and Acted to the Life.
> So full, so fierce, so vigorous, and so strong;
> That, looking on, wou'd make old *Nestor* Young.
>
> (440–43)

The rhythmic thrusts of the line "so full, so fierce, so vigorous, and so strong" seem almost onomatopoeic. Juvenal by contrast takes a moment's break from his porno pic with recourse to epic-style mythology, referring to the aged Homeric figures of Priam and Nestor:

> nil ibi per ludum simulabitur, omnia fient
> ad verum, quibus incendi iam frigidus aevo
> Laomedontiades et Nestoris hirnea possit.
>
> (324–26)

[Nothing there will be pretend or imitation. It'll all be done for real. It could create a spark in the son of Laomedon, already chill with age, or in Nestor's swollen scrotum.]

Dryden eschews the complexity of the double epic reference and he also eschews the physicality of Nestor's scrotum—too revolting a thought to impose upon his readers, we must suppose.

The climax to the episode in the following lines replays differences already familiar to us (Juvenal lines 327–34 and Dryden lines 444–50, with two additional lines at the end):

> tunc prurigo morae inpatiens, tum femina simplex,
> ac pariter toto repetitus clamor ab antro
> "iam fas est, admitte viros." dormitat adulter,
> illa iubet sumpto iuvenem properare cucullo; 330
> si nihil est, servis incurritur; abstuleris spem
> servorum, veniet et conductus aquarius; hic si
> quaeritur et desunt homines, mora nulla per ipsam
> quo minus inposito clunem summittat asello.

[That's the itch of impatience, that's the moment of pure Woman. The shout's repeated in unison from the entire grotto: "Now's the time! Send in the men!" If her lover's asleep, she'll tell his son to put on his hood and hurry along. If that's no good, there's an assault on the slaves. If there's no prospect of slaves available, they'll pay the water delivery-man to come in. If they can't find *him* and there's a deficit of *humans*, not a moment passes before she voluntarily offers her arse to be mounted by a donkey.]

> Impatient of delay, a general sound,
> An universal Groan of Lust goes round;   445
> For then, and only then, the Sex sincere is found.
> Now is the time of Action; now begin,
> They cry, and let the lusty Lovers in.
> The Whoresons are asleep; Then bring the Slaves
> And Watermen, a Race of strong-back'd Knaves.   450
> [Bring any thing that's man: if none be nigh
> Asses have better parts their places to supply.]

First, Dryden spells out the role of passion explicitly in his version in his "universal Groan of Lust," perhaps an overreading of *pariter toto repetitus clamor ab antro.* He nicely captures *tum femina simplex* with "the Sex sincere is found" but misses the significance of *iam fas est,* a continuing allusion to the perversion of religious ritual perpetrated by the women. Finally and most notably, the progression set up by Juvenal is derailed and suppressed in the published version, though the unpublished lines show that Dryden sensed what was required. In a fine feed to male fantasy, Juvenal imagines the women first calling for their lovers (*adulter* and *iuuenem*), then slaves (*seruis*), then watermen (*aquarius*), and finally a donkey (*asello*). Dryden's version of the catalogue is effectively emasculated by the suppression of the climax, the donkey to which the desperate woman offers her arse. The succinct sequence of "Whoresons," "slaves," and "Watermen" gives only the slightest hint of the progressive desperation of the women. But even when we include the unpublished lines in the reckoning, we may still find them lacking. Not only does Dryden give no sign that he was aware that *summittere* is the technical term for putting a male animal to a female animal[18] but the euphemisms of "parts" and "places" fall flat and he omits entirely the woman's eagerness to receive the animal's penis in *per ipsam* ("voluntarily").

Juvenal rounds off this section with an evocation of the profanation of the mysteries of the Good Goddess in 62 B.C.E. when Publius Clodius Pulcher infiltrated the ceremony dressed as a female musician (335–45, in my translation):

> If only our ancient rites or at least our state ceremonies were conducted unsullied by such taints. But all the Moors and the Indians

know about the "lute-girl" who brought a penis larger than both of Caesar's "Anti-Cato" speeches into that place which is avoided even by a male mouse, all too conscious of his balls, the place where any picture portraying the shape of the other sex has to be covered up. And in those old days, what human being ever scorned divine power? What human being had ever dared to laugh at Numa's earthenware ladles or the black bowls or the brittle dishes from the Vatican hill? But *these* days, is there any altar *without* a Clodius?

The Latin is not shy, with its *penem* (337) and *testiculi* (339). Not so Dryden (452–63). His mouse simply retires "guilty of his Sex" (458). What a letdown. (Or, rather, what a coverup.) It looks as if Dryden has overly identified with his mouse. In the presence of the powerful female sexuality depicted with gusto by Juvenal, Dryden has simply "retired" from the scene.

It seems that his unease with the "message" of the satire and his anxiety to distance himself from the personality presented here by Juvenal have driven him to have recourse to what I here call safe sex. Dryden's prefatory remarks to his translation reveal his distaste for what he sees as Juvenal's unfair criticisms of women. This distaste led him, and perhaps his publisher too, to sanitize his translation. In the published version especially, he declines to engage with the raw sexuality of Juvenal's women such as Messalina and the "revellers of Priapus" and instead tones down their activities and demands. Dryden needed to take one more step to see that the personality created by Juvenal is outrageous and offensive—and then maybe he could have embraced the bawdy aspect of the sixth satire more fully than he does.[19] Safe sex may not have been an issue for him in his translation of Lucretius, but it certainly is when he tackles Juvenal's sixth satire.

Notes

1. These lines are preserved in the endpaper of the 1693 edition held in the Huntington Library (RB 428736) and first published by W. B. Carnochan in *The Times Literary Supplement,* 21 January 1972, 73–74. Another copy of the 1693 edition, held in the Beinecke Library at Yale, has the same sixteen lines plus one further line inscribed in the margins. For further details see the Longman annotated edition by Paul Hammond & David Hopkins, *The Poems of John Dryden, Volume 4, 1693–1696* (New York: Longman, 2000) 43–44. It seems impossible to reach any conclusion about whether Dryden himself or his publisher Tonson was responsible for their exclusion.

2. I am delighted to see that Martin Winkler has included these sixteen lines

in his collection *Juvenal in English* (London: Penguin Classics, 2001), 154–55. It might have been still better had he included them *in situ* rather than lopped from their contexts.

3. See below, note 14.

4. *Works of John Dryden,* ed. H. T. Swedenberg et al., 20 vols. (Berkeley and Los Angeles, University of California Press, 1956—), 3:58.

5. For a discussion of the tensions created in Dryden by dealing with Lucretius's "dangerous" poem see W. R. Johnson, *Lucretius and the Modern World* (London: Duckworth, 2000), 81–88.

6. See S. H. Braund, *Beyond Anger: A Study of Juvenal's Third Book of Satires* (Cambridge: Cambridge University Press, 1988), 18.

7. As I argue in "Juvenal—misogynist or misogamist?" *Journal of Roman Studies* 82 (1992): 71–86, where I suggest that adultery is the poem's dominant theme. See too Warren Smith, "Husband vs. Wife in Juvenal's Sixth Satire," *Classical World* 73 (1980): 323–32.

8. For another articulation of Dryden's generous attitude toward women see his preface to Walsh's *A Dialogue Concerning Women* (1691, sig. A4v): "For my own part, who have always been their Servant, and have never drawn my Pen against them, I had rather see some of them prais'd extraordinarily, than any of them suffer by detraction: And that in this Age, and at this time particularly, wherein I find more Heroines than Heroes." James Winn sees this statement as a possible reference to support for King James among aristocratic ladies (*John Dryden and His World* [New Haven: Yale University Press, 1987], 447–48).

9. I may use the word "raunchy" but I should like to make it clear that in terms of the resources available in the Latin language, Juvenal's satires are at the decorous rather than the lurid end of the scale. This emerges clearly from J. N. Adams's thorough investigation, *The Latin Sexual Vocabulary* (London: Duckworth, 1982), 221: "Juvenal did not use the basic obscenities, but neither did he entirely avoid the coarser elements of the Latin sexual language . . . For the most part Juvenal favoured bland euphemisms . . . In Juvenal's hands the sexual language of satire became similar to that of polite prose."

10. Dryden's translation of Juvenal is taken from the California edition; the excised lines appear as footnotes, as well as in the textual notes, 4:791–92.

11. The prose translations of Juvenal are from my draft for a new, revised edition of Juvenal and Persius for the Loeb Classical Library.

12. In the interests of space, I omit discussion of the additional line preserved after Dryden's line 285 only in the edition held in the Beinecke and of the two lines preserved after line 335, lines rightly regarded as superior to the published version.

13. In my edition for the Loeb Classical Library I shall probably adopt the emendation of *Luna* to *nullo,* making a pun on the word *testis*: "with no witness present" and "with no testicle present"; my preferred translation of *nullo teste* would be "with no man present." There may be the same pun at Juvenal 2.76.

14. I derive this figure from the following statistics: Dryden renders the 171 lines of Juvenal satire 1 in 258; the 322 lines of satire 3 in 503; the 366 lines of satire 10 in 561 and the 60 lines of satire 16 in 95. These proportions are very consistent. By contrast, the 661 lines of satire 6 generate only 863 in Dryden.

15. In my Loeb edition I propose to print *veneris* here, my emendation of *veteris*. *Meri veteris* has to mean "vintage wine" and I suppose the point is that the women waste good wine by drenching themselves in it in their sexual frenzy.

On my emendation, *meri veneris* will mean "undiluted lust"; I intend *veneris* to evoke the liquidity produced by the women's sexual antics. Support for this emendation is afforded by Juvenal 11.167–70, especially *inritamentum veneris languenti*, "the provocation of jaded desire."

16. The text(s) used by Dryden preserve names transmitted in the inferior part of the transmission; some modern editors here prefer the name "Saufeia." This is immaterial to the topic under discussion.

17. See note 437a in Hammond, 4:73.

18. See *Oxford Latin Dictionary, submitto* 8.

19. In short, Dryden identified Juvenal the satirist too closely with the voice that he created. The pioneer of reading Juvenal's misanthropic voice as a literary creation was W. S. Anderson (*Essays on Roman Satire* [Princeton: Princeton University Press, 1982]), developing an approach of A. Kernan (*The Cankered Muse: Satire of the English Renaissance* [New Haven: Yale University Press, 1959]). Anderson's work was the chief inspiration behind my thorough application of it to all the satires of Juvenal in *Beyond Anger* (see note 6 above), esp. 1–23, and to satire 6 particularly in "Juvenal—misogynist or misogamist?" (see note 7 above), esp. 82–85: the speaker is utterly unreliable.

The Janus Poet: Dryden's Critique of Shakespeare

PAUL HAMMOND

> To begin then with *Shakespeare;* he was the man who of all Modern, and perhaps Ancient Poets, had the largest and most comprehensive soul. All the Images of Nature were still present to him, and he drew them not laboriously, but luckily: when he describes any thing, you more than see it, you feel it too. Those who accuse him to have wanted learning, give him the greater commendation: he was naturally learn'd; he needed not the spectacles of Books to read Nature; he look'd inwards, and found her there. I cannot say he is every where alike; were he so, I should do him injury to compare him with the greatest of Mankind. He is many times flat, insipid; his Comick wit degenerating into clenches, his serious swelling into Bombast. But he is alwayes great, when some great occasion is presented to him: no man can say he ever had a fit subject for his wit, and did not then raise himself as high above the rest of Poets,
> *Quantum lenta solent, inter viburna cupressi.*

THIS PASSAGE IN DRYDEN'S *ESSAY OF DRAMATICK POESIE* (PUBLISHED in the autumn of 1667, dated 1668), is spoken by Neander, "the new man," representing Dryden himself, and is Dryden's first sustained account of Shakespeare's characteristics, his "genius," to use a seventeenth-century term. The *Essay* is a complex text, a fictitious conversation between four interlocutors who are thinly disguised versions of contemporary men of letters. It is part of Dryden's concerted effort in 1667 to establish himself on the literary scene, the other key text in this project being *Annus Mirabilis* (published in the same year), his poetic account, at once both classical and stylishly modern, of recent English history. The reward of the Laureateship would follow in April 1668. In the *Essay* the description of Shakespeare is part of a self-definition—of Dryden himself, but also of Englishness, and of Restoration modernity.[1] For the discussion of Shakespeare and his contemporary dramatists Jonson and Fletcher is implicated in a complex triangulation: moderns tested against ancients, Restoration writers against their Jacobean and Caroline predecessors, English against French. And this is the text in which Dryden—through these very maneuvers—finds his own voice as a critic, establishing his authority to define and to judge.[2]

Dryden's reference to "those who accuse him to have wanted learning," alludes to the body of commentary on Shakespeare that had built up since the publication of the First Folio in 1623.[3] The antithesis between art and nature runs through these early critiques—as it does through Dryden's own—but those words "art" and "nature" are notoriously complex and fluid concepts, and I would like to explore the usage of them in these early appraisals of Shakespeare before returning to Dryden's passage.[4]

In their preface addressed "To the great Variety of Readers" in the First Folio, John Heminge and Henry Condell remarked that Shakespeare, "as he was a happie imitator of Nature, was a most gentle expresser of it. His mind and hand went together: And what he thought, he vttered with that easinesse, that wee haue scarce receiued from him a blot in his papers."[5] For these colleagues of Shakespeare, his work showed a felicitous union of imitation and nature, and of thought with expression. The observation seems straightforward, but the terms used by Heminge and Condell deserve a closer reading. "Nature" here probably means "the general inherent character or disposition of mankind" (*OED* 2b). "Happie" means "successful in performing what the circumstances require; apt, dextrous; felicitous" (*OED* 5). So his imitations are successful. But the word could also mean "lucky, fortunate" (*OED* 2), or even "happening by chance, fortuitous" (*OED* 1), depending on how much attention one pays to the root "hap," chance (*OED sb.*¹ 1). So the word is poised between being an evaluation of the success of the work, and being an explanation of the origin of the work. I suspect that Heminge and Condell intended it as a compliment to the felicitous truth-to-nature of Shakespeare's plays, but the word leaves open the possibility that the work was the result of, or assisted by, luck. Another curious word is "gentle." It might mean "noble, excellent" (*OED* 1d), or "courteous, polite" (*OED* 3c), or "not violent or severe" (*OED* 6): all these glosses point toward a view of Shakespeare's expression as civilized, not rough or excessive—quite the opposite of the Restoration and eighteenth-century view of Shakespeare's language as often extravagant, rebarbative, and coarse. But there is another connotation of "gentle," which is "cultivated" as opposed to wild (*OED* 4), and this we can gloss from Shakespeare himself. Polixenes is speaking:

> Nature is made better by no meane,
> But Nature makes that Meane: so ouer that Art,
> (Which you say addes to Nature) is an Art
> That Nature makes: you see (sweet Maid) we marry
> A gentler Sien, to the wildest Stocke,
> And make conceyue a barke of baser kinde
> By bud of Nobler race. This is an Art
> Which do's mend Nature: change it rather, but
> The Art it selfe, is Nature.[6]

Here, "gentler" fuses the notions of social superiority and cultivation. For Heminge and Condell, Shakespeare is the noble, cultivated writer.[7]

Shakespeare's rapport with Nature, and his facility in writing, are seen from a different perspective in Ben Jonson's poem "To the memory of my beloued, The AVTHOR Mr. WILLIAM SHAKESPEARE: And what he hath left vs," also prefixed to the First Folio.[8] Shakespeare had "small *Latine,* and lesse *Greeke,*" says Jonson, in a notorious judgment that seems to have been rapidly construed as meaning "he had no learning at all." Jonson's poem has been read as the decisive text in establishing the image of Shakespeare as one who wrote by nature rather than art.[9] But I think that this is a misreading of the poem. His reference to Shakespeare's limited command of the classical languages comes in the context of a passage in which Jonson says, in effect: "Because you transcend your age, and despite your limited Latin and Greek, the only appropriate figures whom I could summon up to provide a fit audience for you would be the Greek and Roman poets." When he introduces the idea of Nature, she is a figure who enjoys wearing the clothes in which Shakespeare has dressed her:

> Nature her selfe was proud of his designes,
>   And ioy'd to weare the dressing of his lines!
> Which were so richly spun, and wouen so fit,
>   As, since, she will vouchsafe no other Wit.
>
> (47–50)

It is explicitly Shakespeare's expertly woven artifacts which Jonson praises. And it is because Shakespeare's art is "so fit" to nature that lesser writers now seem unnatural:

> The merry *Greeke,* tart *Aristophanes,*
>   Neat *Terence,* witty *Plautus,* now not please;
> But antiquated, and deserted lye
>   As they were not of Natures family.
>
> (51–54)

But, says Jonson, what pleases in Shakespeare's work is not just attributable to nature—in other words, to the human nature that they show us so clearly: their success is due to the poet's artistry:

> Yet must I not giue Nature all: Thy Art,
>   My gentle *Shakespeare,* must enioy a part.
> For though the *Poets* matter, Nature be,
>   His Art doth giue the fashion. And, that he
> Who casts[10] to write a liuing line, must sweat,
>   (such as thine are) and strike the second heat
> Vpon the *Muses* anuile:
> . . . .
>   For a good *Poet*'s made, as well as borne.
> And such wert thou.
>
> (55–65)

There is, in fact, nothing in Jonson's poem that presents Shakespeare as a natural, untutored genius: "nature" here is simply "human nature, the world as it really is," the subject matter that Shakespeare's plays imitate so successfully. It is interesting, too, that the epithet "gentle" is used by Jonson at the point where he introduces the subject of Shakespeare's art. This is not "soft, sweet-tempered Shakespeare," but "noble, cultivated Shakespeare."[11] Nevertheless, Jonson's insistence on the need for polish and revision sits awkwardly with the claim by Heminge and Condell on the previous page of the First Folio "that wee haue scarce receiued from him a blot in his papers," and in this context looks suspiciously like a covert rebuke—even like implicit self-praise for his own more laborious methods. Jonson says that the writer who would produce a "living line" such as Shakespeare's are must sweat and strike the second heat; but he does not say that Shakespeare himself did that: "such as thine are," not "such as thou didst." There is an ambiguity here about Jonson's praise, which, coupled with the condescending epigrammatic jibe about "small *Latine,* and lesse *Greeke,*" understandably led Dryden to describe these verses as "An Insolent, Sparing, and Invidious Panegyrick."[12]

The idea of Shakespeare's lack of learning actually predates Jonson's poem. It occurs in the verse letter that Francis Beaumont had written to Jonson a year or so before Shakespeare's death, in which he said:

> heere I would let slippe
> (If I had any in mee) schollershippe,
> And from all Learninge keepe these lines as [cl]eere
> as Shakespeares best are, which our heires shall heare
> Preachers apte to their auditors to showe
> how farr sometimes a mortall man may goe
> by the dimme light of Nature.[13]

Here Beaumont praises Shakespeare for keeping his verse free from the display of learning (would the prickly Jonson have read that as a criticism of himself?); and "the dimme light of Nature" refers to the innate capacity of man without the illumination of divine grace. (Is this also a comment on Shakespeare's religion?) Perhaps Jonson's poem was shaped in part as a response to Beaumont's verses.

Jonson's comment, as part of his praise of Shakespeare's artistry, that "a good *Poet*'s made, as well as borne" is taken up—but contradicted—by Leonard Digges in a prefatory poem to Benson's edition of Shakespeare's *Poems* in 1640, and made to introduce praise of Shakespeare's natural genius:

> Poets are borne not made; when I would prove
> This truth, the glad rememberance I must love
> Of never dying *Shakespeare,*
> . . . .
>   the patterne of all wit,
> Art without Art unparaleld as yet.
> Next Nature onely helpt him, for looke thorow
> This whole Booke, thou shalt find he doth not borrow,
> One phrase from Greekes, nor Latines imitate,
> Nor once from vulgar Languages Translate.[14]

That paradoxical phrase "Art without Art" probably means "works of art without attention to the formal rules." But John Warren, in the same volume, insisted that there was genuine artistry and learning to be found in the poems:

> These learned Poems
> . . . .
> Will make the learned still admire to see,
> The Muses gifts so fully infus'd on thee.
> Let Carping *Momus* barke and bite his fill,
> And ignorant *Davus* slight thy learned skill:
> Yet those who know the worth of thy desert,
> And with true judgement can discerne thy Art,
> Will be admirers of thy high tun'd straine.[15]

Yet despite such insistence that Shakespeare's work did result from artistry (even though it did not make ostentation of its classical learning), the myth of the untutored, natural genius was taking hold. Thus Milton, in "L' Allegro," writes of hearing

> sweetest *Shakespear* fancies childe,
> Warble his native Wood-notes wilde.[16]

In these lines, "native" primarily means "free from art" (*OED* 2)—contrasting with "*Jonsons* learned Sock" (1.132)—and "wild" means "in a state of nature, uncultivated" (*OED* 2). But we might note other possible meanings of "native" that may be significant: not only "free from art, unadorned" (*OED* 2) but also "belonging to the country of one's birth" (*OED* 4), and so characteristically English; and then "forming the source or origin" (*OED* 3b), as when Adam in *Paradise Lost* laments that he may have to "return to native dust" (11.463). I am not sure that Milton would have intended such a meaning in "L' Allegro," but in view of the later construction of Shakespeare as the point of origin for English drama, it is striking that the idea of nature and the idea of origin could be held together in this way. Dryden echoed Milton's lines in 1660, in what reads like a double-edged compliment to his future brother-in-law, Sir Robert Howard:

> As there is Musick uninform'd by Art
> In those wild Notes, which with a merry heart
> The Birds in unfrequented shades expresse,
> Who better taught at home, yet please us lesse:
> So in your Verse, a native sweetnesse dwells,
> Which shames Composure, and its Art excells.[17]

Whether Howard appreciated this implicit comparison of himself with Shakespeare, or was offended by the suggestion of naïveté, history fails to record.

By the Restoration, the notion that Shakespeare was an untutored writer had become a commonplace, so we find Thomas Fuller saying:

> He was an eminent instance of the truth of that Rule, *Poeta non fit, sed nascitur;* one is not *made,* but *born* a Poet. Indeed his Learning was very little, so that, as *Cornish diamonds* are not polished by any Lapidary, but are pointed and smoothed even as they are taken out of the Earth, so *nature* it self was all the *art* which was used upon him.[18]

And the cliché is given epigrammatic formulation by Richard Flecknoe, that would-be Son of Ben, who pronounces this verdict:[19]

> To compare our English Dramatick Poets together (without taxing them) *Shakespeare* excelled in a natural Vein, *Fletcher* in Wit, and *Jonson* in Gravity and ponderousness of Style; whose onely fault was he was too elaborate[20]; and had he mixt less erudition with his Playes, they had been more pleasant and delightful than they are. Comparing him with *Shakespeare,* you shall see the difference betwixt Nature and Art.[21]

So by 1664, just a couple of years before the composition of Dryden's *Essay,* Shakespeare could be simply associated with nature, and Jonson with art. Yet for subtler minds than Flecknoe's the two terms in this antithesis were complex. "Nature" and its cognates had been used in descriptions of Shakespeare to mean "human nature, the world as it really is," or "innate skills unimproved by learning," or "innate skills unimproved by divine grace," or perhaps, in Milton's lines, "innate skills without any artistry at all"; while "art" has meant variously "skill in dramatic composition," or "knowledge of the classics," or "adherence to neo-classical principles," or "ostentatious display of learning." And while Jonson might have said grumpily to Drummond "that Shaksperr wanted Arte" *tout court,* others like Warren relished the artistry that they found in Shakespeare's work.[22]

To return, then, to Dryden: his critique of Shakespeare in the *Essay* takes up some of these ideas that I have just been tracing, but rethinks them in the light of what turns out to be a new aesthetic—one that begins by highlighting certain faults in Shakespeare's style, but gradually comes to admit that these are also the marks of a great and original genius, one whose distinctive rapport with nature is his understanding of the passions. To begin with, Shakespeare is identified in the *Essay* as an outstanding—perhaps *the* outstanding—poet amongst the moderns, thus contributing to the definition of modernity vis-à-vis the ancients. (He is, we note, being appraised as a poet, not simply as a dramatist, and thus he is implicitly comparable with the classical epic poets.) One implication of this is that if Shakespeare becomes the exemplary modern, then the tyranny of the Italian and French neoclassical rules can be escaped. This is important for Dryden's own mode of composition, for his plays often mix prose and poetry, comedy and tragedy; and in his critical debate with Shadwell, Dryden seems to be promoting a freer (perhaps implicitly Shakespearean) dramaturgy in contrast to Shadwell's dogged Jonsonianism.[23] Shakespeare is regarded as the preeminent modern in having "the largest and most comprehensive soul."[24] What does Dryden mean by "comprehensive soul"? Francis Meres had written that "the sweete wittie soule of *Ovid* lives in mellifluous & hony-tongued *Shakespeare*," but that metempsychotic conceit is not what Dryden has in mind here, addicted though he is to the idea of poetic genealogies.[25] He will tell us later on that "*Milton* was the Poetical Son of *Spencer*, and Mr. *Waller* of *Fairfax*; for we have our Lineal Descents and Clans, as well as other Families: *Spencer* more than once insinuates, that the Soul of *Chaucer* was transfus'd into his Body; and that he was begotten by him Two hundred years after his Decease."[26] By contrast, Shakespeare is for Dryden a unique, original genius, as we shall see. Indeed, Dryden's son would say that Shakespeare "may stand by himself as a Phoenix, the first and last of his Order."[27] In the Dedication to *The Rival Ladies* (1664) Dryden had remarked parenthetically that Shakespeare "had undoubtedly a larger Soul of Pœsie than ever any of our Nation,"[28] and that observation is developed more thoughtfully in the *Essay,* as Dryden makes the word do much more precise critical work in describing the faculties that give the poet special insight into human nature: so "soul" here means "seat of the emotions and feelings" (*OED* 3) or "intellectual or spiritual power; high development of the mental faculties" (*OED* 3b). Implicitly, such a developed intellectual and emotional insight generates work that rouses the same faculties in the responsive reader. As for "comprehensive," this means "large in scope" (*OED* 1), and "including much in small compass" (*OED* 1c), as when Roscommon in his *Essay on Translated Verse* speaks of "the Comprehensive, *English energy*" that he thought characterized our verse compared with the diffusiveness of the French.[29] It also means "grasping or understanding a thing fully" (*OED* 2), and "embracing many things, broad in mental grasp or sympathies" (*OED* 2b).[30] Margaret Cavendish, Duchess of Newcastle, had perceived just these qualities in Shakespeare when she enthused that "*Shakespeare* did not want Wit, to Express to the Life all Sorts of Persons, of what Quality, Profession, Degree, Breeding, or Birth soever; nor did he want Wit to Express the Divers, and Different Humours, or Natures, or Several Passions in Mankind; and so Well he hath Express'd in his Playes all Sorts of Persons, as one would think he had been Transform'd into every one of those Persons he hath Described."[31] Newcastle is, I think, the first person in the written record to try to say precisely what is so distinctive about Shakespeare, instead of simply writing variations upon a limited number of panegyrical commonplaces about art and nature: she sees that he has managed to enter into the soul of his various characters, as recognizable types and as distinct individuals.

Whether or not Dryden had read Mad Meg's *CCXI Sociable Letters, written by the Thrice Noble, Illustrious, and Excellent Princess the Lady Marchioness of Newcastle*, it is this insight that seems encapsulated in Dryden's comment about Shakespeare's "comprehensive soul." For, he says, "All the Images of Nature were still present to him, and he drew them not laboriously, but luckily." This observation is modeled closely on Heminge and Condell's description: "as he was a happie imitator of Nature, [he] was a most gentle expresser of it . . . And what he thought, he vttered with . . . easinesse." But Dryden has rethought their terms. What does he mean by "Images of Nature"? James Jensen distinguishes four senses in which the word "image" is used in Dryden's critical thought, two of which seem in play here: (1) an idea or picture of something as it is conceived in the mind, or imprinted on the mind by an external sensation (equivalent to *OED* 5); (2) a model ideal, or perfect idea of what something should be like, approximating to the Platonic sense.[32] And so we come to the question, what does Dryden mean here by "Nature"?[33] He seems to mean both "human beings as they really are" and "the physical world as it really is." But for Dryden, Nature was a powerful force, sometimes personified, most memorably in his "Translation of the Latter Part of the Third Book of Lucretius; Against the Fear of Death," where she urges acceptance of the transitoriness of life. So to associate Shakespeare with nature is to link him with the power of Nature, with what he himself called "great creating-Nature."[34] In using the word in this way, closer to Jonson than to Digges, Dryden has shifted and deepened the critical understanding of Shakespeare, from being a natural, untutored writer, to being a writer who was "naturally learn'd": that is to say, both naturally intelligent about the world, and an accomplished student of human nature.[35]

But even as Dryden fashions this version of Shakespeare, he separates him from us. Running through the *Essay* is a sense that Shakespeare and his contemporaries occupy a remote period and culture that is alienated from the present by the radical discontinuity of the Civil War and Interregnum, and this feeling of separation inflects the vocabulary of Dryden's paragraph on Shakespeare.[36] "All the Images of Nature were still present to him," he says: "present to" means "in the mind of, directly imagined" (*OED* 3), and also "ready at hand, immediately accessible" (*OED* 5). We need not necessarily be guided by Derrida in reading that word "present," or by Heidegger in construing the notion of "ready at hand"; though if we do recall those philosophers we can see more readily that Dryden's phrasing is shaping a point of origin that is always already lost, an authentic enjoyment of the unmediated presence of nature, at once internal and external, which is now distanced and inaccessible; an original that is held away from our grasp even as it is introduced to us. For much depends on that word "still." Jonson had said that "all the *Muses* still were in their prime" when Shakespeare wrote.[37] Looking back in 1623, it had seemed to Jonson that Shakespeare had been writing when the arts of the English stage were at their height; since then there had, implicitly, been a decay. Perhaps Dryden's eye was caught by Jonson's word "still" because he felt the same about the decay of the arts since Jonson's day (a feeling that haunts the *Essay*), but also because it resonated with a profounder thought. "All the Images of Nature were still present to him" runs deeper than Jonson's nostalgia. "Still" might mean "continually, on every occasion, invariably" (*OED* 3), but more potently it may mean "then as formerly" (*OED* 4a) and "then in contrast to the future" (*OED* 4b): the images of nature were present to Shakespeare, as they had been to his predecessors (implicitly, the ancients), but as they are no longer to us, the readers and writers of Restoration England. His was the world before the fall—before a fall from presence and primacy into the condition of lateness and separation.[38]

Shakespeare, we are told, drew these images of nature "not laboriously, but luckily," and here Dryden is revisiting the distinction between Shakespeare's ease and Jonson's laboriousness which several previous commentators had noted.[39] "Luckily" may primarily mean "successfully, with a happy outcome" (*OED* 1, citing this example), approximating to Heminge and Condell's "happie imitator." But, as with "happie," is there a secondary sense, "by chance"?[40] The possibility of writers achieving effects with the help of chance or Fortune clearly interested Dryden. In "To My Honored Friend, Sir Robert Howard," a poem that (as we have seen) is already using ideas from the Shakespearean critical tradition, Dryden toys with (and eventually rejects) the idea that Howard's verse may be the product of random chance:

> Either your Art hides Art,
> . . . .
> Or 'tis some happinesse that still pursues
> Each act and motion of your gracefull muse.
> Or is it Fortune's work, that in your head
> The curious Net that is for fancies spread,
> Let's through its Meshes every meaner thought,
> While rich Idea's there are onely caught?
> Sure that's not all; this is a piece too fair
> To be the child of Chance, and not of Care.
> No Atoms casually together hurl'd
> Could e're produce so beautifull a world.[41]

Three possible explanations of Howard's poems are entertained here: careful art that conceals its labour; a special facility that makes composition successful; and chance—though it is interesting that Dryden the future Fellow of the Royal Society should define this third possibility, the work of Fortune, in physiological terms: the reticulated structure of the brain just happens to let through the rich ideas and filters out the cruder ones. This threefold account of creativity probably has its origins in Plato, who says in the *Laws*:

Λέγουσί πού τινες ὡς πάντα ἐστὶ τὰ πράγματα γιγνόμενα καὶ γενόμενα καὶ γενησόμενα τὰ μὲν φύσει, τὰ δὲ τύχῃ, τὰ δὲ διὰ τέχνην.[42]

(For Plato, of course, the finest works were the product of nature or chance, art being the inferior power.) Evidently, Dryden was intrigued by the possibility that poetry might be the outcome of chance rather than skill, and that the work of art might be the result of a random collocation of atoms, in the way that the physical universe was said to have been formed according to the Epicurean philosophy. The image of the poetic mind as chaos is reworked in the Dedication to *The Rival Ladies* (1664), where Dryden says that his own work had at first been "only a confus'd Mass of Thoughts, tumbling over one another in the Dark: When the Fancy was yet in its first Work, moving the Sleeping Images of things towards the Light, there to be Distinguish'd, and then either chosen or rejected by the Judgment."[43] Here chaos is but a first stage in the creative process, with Fancy marshalling the images, and Judgment eventually selecting them. In his play with various explanations of poetic creativity, Dryden is experimenting with different vocabularies and models for a more inspirational alternative to the neoclassical rules-based criticism that was flourishing in France, and that may have looked like the only respectable version of cultural modernity for England in the 1660s.

Once Shakespeare's work has been created, by whatever means, "when he describes any thing, you more than see it, you feel it too," says Dryden. This remark seems to owe nothing to the tradition of critical commentary on Shakespeare, but instead to be a modification of what had been said about Virgil. For at the same time as he was composing this account of Shakespeare, Dryden was writing this comment on Virgil: "when any such Image is to be set before us . . . we see the objects he represents us with in their native figures, their proper motions."[44] But what is special about Shakespeare is not that he makes us *see* more clearly, as Virgil does, but that he goes beyond that and makes us *feel*. Shakespeare's language has the power to appeal to the passions, even though it often deviates into clenches (puns) or bombast; both of these being forms of expression that are condemned, presumably, because they are liable to strike a reader as being the product of the writer's ingenuity rather than the speaker's feeling, so impeding the representation of nature and our emotional response to it. The essential thrust of Dryden's critique of Shakespeare here is to make him the poet of emotional perception: the words "nature" and "soul" have been lifted out of the clichéd mode of panegyric and made the terminology of a new literary criticism.

From these beginnings, Dryden's critique of Shakespeare develops three principal motifs: Shakespeare as an original genius; Shakespeare as the master in presenting the passions; and Shakespeare's language as both apt and absurd. The idea that

Shakespeare was an untaught, natural genius, and had a unique rapport with nature, soon develops in Dryden's hands into the idea that Shakespeare *is* nature, and that he stands at the origin of English drama. The two points are closely linked, for the idea of Shakespeare as the point of origin is at once a historical and a mythological notion. He "began Dramatique Poetry amongst us,"[45] says Dryden, and is like Aeschylus in being the founding father of the national dramatic tradition.[46] In the prologue to the adaptation of *The Tempest* which he made with Davenant, Dryden moves from saying that Shakespeare was "taught by none" (5) to saying that he gave "labouring *Johnson* Art" (6)—in other words, that he taught Jonson how to write plays. This is a startling reversal of the critical commonplaces about the two writers, and can hardly be defended in terms of the history of English dramaturgy: it is, rather, a mythological claim, for if Shakespeare is at the origin of English drama, then all others must learn from him. Moreover, Shakespeare himself "is that Nature which they paint and draw" (8): he is the source of both art and nature for all his contemporaries and successors.[47] And yet, those who seek to imitate this point of origin find that it cannot be matched: "Within that Circle none durst walk but he";[48] "he has left no praise for any who come after him."[49] His would-be sons cannot approach the founding father, cannot actually assume his mantle.[50] But if that is a problem for Dryden, wishing to emulate Shakespeare, he makes it even more of a problem for Shadwell, wishing to emulate Jonson. In *Mac Flecknoe,* the abdicating poet Richard Flecknoe—he who had made the contrast between Shakespeare and Jonson into a crude antithesis between nature and art—urges his protégé to be a Shakespearean rather than a Jonsonian poet, and rely on his native genius: "Trust Nature, do not labour to be dull." And he exclaims to Shadwell in a moment of sublime mutual congratulation: "What share have we in Nature or in Art?"[51]

Dryden's admiration for Shakespeare as a dramatist of the passions is set out most fully in the Preface to *Troilus and Cressida.* The "end, or scope of Tragedy," says Dryden, "is to rectify or purge our passions, fear and pity."[52] Dryden is of course drawing on Aristotle here, but Aristotle had only said that tragedy accomplishes the catharsis of the audience's passions, not that this is its primary purpose.[53] Dryden, following Horace and the neoclassical insistence that poetry should instruct as well as please, reformulates Aristotle by proposing that as "to instruct delightfully is the general end of all Poetry ... To purge the passions by Example, is therefore the particular instruction which belongs to Tragedy."[54] And drawing on Longinus, he stresses the importance of the poet being able to imitate the passions. We do not know when Dryden encountered Longinus, but he first appears in Dryden's criticism in 1677, in "The Authors Apology for Heroique Poetry; and Poetique Licence" prefixed to *The State of Innocence,* his adaptation of *Paradise Lost.*[55] So it is apropos of Milton that Dryden recalls that Longinus "has judiciously preferr'd the sublime Genius that sometimes erres, to the midling or indifferent one which makes few faults, but seldome or never rises to any Excellence."[56] The grounds on which Dryden bases his appreciation of Milton in 1677 are similar to those on which he appraises Shakespeare in 1679. It is, says Dryden, the task of the poet to depict the passions:

> To describe these naturally, and to move them artfully, is one of the greatest commendations which can be given to a Poet: to write pathetically, says *Longinus,* cannot proceed but from a lofty Genius. A Poet must be born with this quality; yet, unless he help himself by an acquir'd knowledg of the Passions, what they are in their own nature, and by what springs they are to be mov'd, he will be subject either to raise them where they ought not to be rais'd, or not to raise them by the just degrees of Nature, or to amplify them beyond the natural bounds, or not to observe the crisis and turns of them, in their cooling and decay.[57]

In this passage the true poet is both born and made, learning how to describe the passions as they are in nature, and how to deploy his art so as to move the audience with their representation. Once again, Dryden is developing the sketch that he had offered in the *Essay of Dramatick Poesie,* deepening his critique with a more detailed analysis of how the poet understands and represents human nature. And for Dryden, one of the prime examples of this combination of insight and management is the quarrel between Brutus and Cassius in *Julius Caesar,* which he takes as the model for the scene between Troilus and Hector that he adds to Shakespeare's play (act 3 scene 2). Here not only are the passions "extreamly natural," but "the expression of 'em [is] not viciously figurative."[58]

For while Shakespeare understood the nature of the passions, his expression is often extravagant and even unintelligible. Metaphor, as Longinus insists, should not be excluded from the expression of the passions, but it should not be excessive—because then it becomes unnatural. Longinus said that Aeschylus had "a noble boldnesse of expression," whereas Quintilian thought him "daring to extravagance." Just as Aeschylus "affected pompous words, and . . . his sence too often was obscur'd by Figures," so too Shakespeare's style is "so pester'd with Figurative expressions, that it is as affected as it is obscure."[59] Dryden learned from Longinus that this was a defect that is intrinsic to genius, and inextricable from the boldness of the sublime style. Even so, Shakespeare's language does not always manage to be truly sublime: "I will not say of so great a Poet, that he distinguish'd not the blown puffy stile, from true sublimity; but I may venture to maintain that the fury of his fancy often transported him, beyond the bounds of Judgment, either in coyning of new words and phrases, or racking words which were in use, into the violence of a Catachresis."[60] The ideas that were first sketched out in the *Essay of Dramatick Poesie* have now been more fully developed as a result of Dryden's engagement with Longinus. Shakespeare the poet of nature, endowed with a "comprehensive soul" to understand the passions, turns out to be a prime example of the sublime and fiery poet extolled by Longinus. But the sublimity of Shakespeare is often achieved at the cost of linguistic faults that—even as a student of Longinus—Dryden cannot wholly excuse.

I suggested earlier that the *Essay of Dramatick Poesie* was in part an exercise in self-definition, and that continues to be true of Dryden's critique of Shakespeare here. For when he criticizes the use of "pointed Wit, and Sentences affected out of season," which are "nothing of kin to the violence of passion," since "no man is at leisure to make sentences and similes, when his soul is in an Agony," Dryden cites his own earlier work, *The Indian Emperour,* as an example.[61] In his development toward the more Shakespearean style of *Aureng-Zebe* and *All for Love,* Dryden was learning to abandon his delight in witty turns and extravagant images.[62] *All for Love* (1679) is not only based on the Antony and Cleopatra story, but proclaims on its title page that it is "Written in Imitation of *Shakespeare's* Stile."[63] And in his strong, passionate scenes between Antony and Ventidius, and Antony and Dolabella, Dryden seems to be striving not only to emulate Shakespeare's scene between Brutus and Cassius, but also to demonstrate that like Shakespeare, he "writ better betwixt man and man" than between man and woman.[64]

Dryden's criticism of individual writers characteristically proceeds by means of contrast and genealogy: Fletcher is contrasted with Jonson, Milton is seen as the poetical son of Spenser. Given

Shakespeare's addiction to wit and pithy sentences, it is perhaps surprising that Dryden never follows Meres and develops a comparison of him with Ovid. But it is implicit: the comment on Shakespeare's "Wit, and Sentences affected out of season" is echoed just a year later in the Preface to *Ovid's Epistles* (1680) when Dryden says that Ovid often "made his persons speak more Eloquently than the violence of their Passion would admit: so that he is frequently witty out of season: leaving the Imitation of Nature."[65] Perhaps the shift in Dryden's view of Ovid that David Hopkins has identified here (away from his earlier argument that, since Ovid is describing the heights of disordered passion, careful choice of words would be inconsistent) is attributable in part to the turn in Dryden's critical thought brought about by his Longinian engagement with the Miltonic and Shakespearean sublime. Shakespeare's wit is not, it seems, an Ovidian wit—elegant, pointed, playing on words—but rather an Aeschylean or Homeric audacity. For, notwithstanding his adaptation of that description of Virgil to characterize Shakespeare, Dryden sees Shakespeare as Homeric, and Jonson as Virgilian. (Indeed, it is precisely the direction in which the praise of Virgil is adapted by the addition of that emphasis on directness of feeling that shows why Dryden thought Shakespeare Homeric.) "*Shakespeare* was the *Homer*, or Father of our Dramatick Poets; *Johnson* was the *Virgil*, the pattern of elaborate writing; I admire him, but I love *Shakespeare*."[66] The parallel is multiple. Homer, in seventeenth-century critical thought, was the original genius of Greek (indeed, of European) culture.[67] Dryden's choice of "The Last Parting of Hector and Andromache" as the first passage that he translated from Homer shows how he valued the Greek poet for his handling of the passions.[68] And at the end of Dryden's career, when he turned from his complete Virgil to contemplate a complete translation of Homer, he thought of him as better suited to his own genius than the Roman poet, and admired the Greek's energy and pathos: "*Homer* was violent, impetuous, and full of Fire . . . and took all the Liberties both of Numbers, and of Expressions."[69] Deeply attracted to Virgil as Dryden was, there was nevertheless something in his sense of his own distinctive poetic genius that made him feel that he was more nearly allied to Homer and Shakespeare than to Virgil and Jonson.[70]

Some of the qualities that Dryden learned to appreciate in Shakespeare he also found in Homer; others he found in Chaucer. In the Preface to *Fables* we find him reflecting that Chaucer must have been a Man of a most wonderful comprehensive Nature, because . . . he has taken into the Compass of his *Canterbury Tales* the various Manners and Humours (as we now call them) of the whole *English* Nation, in his Age. Not a single Character has escap'd him. All his Pilgrims are severally distinguish'd from each other; and not only in their Inclinations, but in their very Phisiognomies and Persons. . . . The Matter and Manner of their Tales, and of their Telling, are so suited to their different Educations, Humours, and Callings, that each of them would be improper in any other Mouth. . . . Their Discourses are such as belong to their Age, their Calling, and their Breeding.[71]

Those are very much the terms in which Dryden (and Cavendish) had spoken of Shakespeare: this is what it means to be the poet of nature; this is what we expect from the father of English drama and the father of English poetry.

❧

Dryden described Shakespeare as "the very *Janus* of Poets; he wears, almost every where two faces: and you have scarce begun to admire the one, e're you despise the other." For "never did any Author precipitate himself from such heights of thought to so low expressions."[72] That was said before Dryden grew more appreciative of Shakespeare's language, but it introduces a telling image. Janus was two-faced; the god of doorways, one of his faces looked inward, the other outward, like Shakespeare himself in the passage from which I began. His two faces were even interpreted allegorically to represent the human progression from savagery to civilization.[73] Shakespeare stands at the threshold of modernity. And as Janus (says Ovid)[74] controlled the comings and goings even of Jove himself, so Shakespeare keeps a protective but disconcerting watch over Dryden, as Dryden himself admits to Sir Godfrey Kneller:

> *Shakespear* thy Gift, I place before my sight;
> With awe, I ask his Blessing e're I write;
> With Reverence look on his Majestick Face;
> Proud to be less; but of his Godlike Race.
> His Soul Inspires me, while thy Praise I write,
> And I like *Teucer,* under *Ajax* Fight;[75]

Genealogy returns: Dryden is of Shakespeare's race, and is inspired by his soul. Dryden's criticism had helped to establish Shakespeare as a classic, and helped Dryden discover the classic in himself.

Notes

1. It is interesting that what appears to be the first written reference to Shakespeare in German is by someone who has read Dryden's *Essay* admiringly, but has not read Shakespeare himself: see C. M. Ingleby et al., *The Shakspere Allusion Book*, 2 vols. (Oxford: Oxford University Press, 1932), 2:142. For the epigraph, see *The Works of John Dryden* (Berkeley: University of California Press, 1956–), 17:55–56. "As cypresses do among bending osiers" is from Virgil, *Eclogues* 1:25.

2. For the rhetoric of authority and authentication in Dryden's critical essays see Paul Hammond, *Dryden and the Traces of Classical Rome* (Oxford: Oxford University Press, 1999), 25–68.

3. For seventeenth-century comments on Shakespeare see *The Shakspere Allusion Book*; G. E. Bentley, *Shakespeare and Jonson: Their Reputations in the Seventeenth Century Compared*, 2 vols. (Chicago: University of Chicago Press, 1945); and the first two volumes of *Shakespeare: The Critical Heritage*, ed. Brian Vickers, 6 vols. (London: Routledge and Kegan Paul, 1974–81). For contemporary attitudes to Shakespeare's learning, or lack of it, see T. W. Baldwin, *William Shakspere's Small Latine & Lesse Greeke*, 2 vols. (Urbana: University of Illinois Press, 1944), 1:1–52.

4. For the semantic field of "art" and "nature" see the *OED*, and Raymond Williams, *Keywords* (London: Fontana, 1976; second edition, 1983); for Renaissance discussions of art and nature from a Shakespearean perspective see *The Winter's Tale*, ed. Stephen Orgel (Oxford: Clarendon Press, 1996), 42–47, 172; on Shakespeare's own concept of art, see Leo Salingar, "Shakespeare and the Italian concept of 'art'," in *Dramatic Form in Shakespeare and the Jacobeans* (Cambridge: Cambridge University Press, 1986), 1–18; and on meanings of "nature" see Arthur O. Lovejoy, "'Nature' as aesthetic norm," in *Essays in the History of Ideas* (Baltimore: Johns Hopkins University Press, 1948), 69–77, and C. S. Lewis, *Studies in Words*, 2d ed. (Cambridge: Cambridge University Press, 1967), 24–74. For a summary of the use of "art" and "nature" in Restoration criticism of Shakespeare, see *The Critical Works of John Dennis*, ed. Edward Niles Hooker, 2 vols. (Baltimore: Johns Hopkins University Press, 1943), 2:428–31. See also Michael Dobson, *The Making of the National Poet: Shakespeare, Adaptation and Authorship, 1660–1769* (Oxford: Clarendon Press, 1992), 28–31.

5. *Mr. William Shakespeares Comedies, Histories, & Tragedies* (London: Isaac Iaggard and Ed. Blount, 1623), sig. A3r.

6. *The Winters Tale*, 4.4.89–97, from *Mr. William Shakespeares Comedies, Histories, & Tragedies*, 292.

7. Denham also uses the word: see note 40 below.

8. *Mr. William Shakespeares Comedies, Histories, & Tragedies*, sig. A4r-v; *Shakespeare: The Critical Heritage*, 1:23–25.

9. Brian Vickers in *Shakespeare: The Critical Heritage*, 1:23, Michael Dobson, *The Making of the National Poet*, 29.

10. cast: "set oneself with resolution to" (*OED* 34).

11. By contrast, John Tatham cites "the *Plebean* Driller" as a contemporary epithet for Shakespeare in 1652 (*The Shakspere Allusion Book*, 2:23).

12. *Works*, 4:6. The words "Invidious" (i.e., "exciting ill-feeling" [*OED* 1])

and "Sparing" clearly allude to Jonson's claim in the poem's opening lines to "draw no envy" and to be "ample" in his praise.

13. *The Shakspere Allusion Book*, 1:xi.

14. *Shakespeare: The Critical Heritage*, 1:27.

15. *The Shakspere Allusion Book*, 1:459.

16. "L' Allegro," lines 133–34; from *The Poems of John Milton*, ed. Helen Darbishire (Oxford: Oxford University Press, 1961).

17. "To My Honored Friend, Sir Robert Howard," lines 1–6 (prefixed to Howard's *Poems* [1660]; *Works*, 1:17). The editors of *Works* note the borrowing.

18. From *The History of the Worthies of England* (1662); in *The Shakspere Allusion Book*, 1:483.

19. For Flecknoe's ambition to be regarded as Jonson's heir see Paul Hammond, "Flecknoe and *Mac Flecknoe*," *Essays in Criticism* 35 (1985): 315–29.

20. elaborate: "produced or accomplished by labour" (*OED* 1). John Tatham quotes "His Works were too elaborate" as a contemporary criticism of Jonson in 1652 (*The Shakspere Allusion Book*, 2:23).

21. From "A Short Discourse of the English Stage" (1664); in *Shakespeare: The Critical Heritage*, 1:46.

22. From his conversations with William Drummond of Hawthornden, 1619, in *Ben Jonson*, ed. C. H. Herford, Percy and Evelyn Simpson, 11 vols. (Oxford: Clarendon Press, 1925–52), 1:133. Of course, the brusque form in which this comment is recorded may be attributable to Drummond rather than Jonson.

23. The documents in this debate are reprinted in *Dryden and Shadwell*, ed. Richard L. Oden (Delmar, N.Y.: Scholars' Facsimiles and Reprints, 1977).

24. Nahum Tate quotes this comment approvingly in the preface to his play *The Loyal General* (1680), but replaces Dryden's careful "of all Modern, and perhaps Ancient Poets" with the sweeping "of all Men": *Shakespeare: The Critical Heritage*, 1:341.

25. From *Palladis Tamia* (1598); in *Shakespeare: The Critical Heritage*, 1:2. "Soul" had also been used by Jonson when calling Shakespeare "Soule of the Age," perhaps meaning "epitome" or "leading light" ("To the memory of my beloued . . . ," in *Shakespeare: The Critical Heritage*, 1:24).

26. John Dryden, *Fables Ancient and Modern* (London: Jacob Tonson, 1700), sig. *A^r.

27. From John Dryden Jr, Dedication to *The Husband his own Cuckold* (1696); in *Shakespeare: The Critical Heritage*, 1:13.

28. *Works*, 8:99.

29. Wentworth Dillon, Earl of Roscommon, *An Essay on Translated Verse*, 2d ed. (London: Jacob Tonson, 1685 [first ed. 1684]), 4.

30. So in "The Grounds of Criticism in Tragedy" prefixed to *Troilus and Cressida* (1679), Dryden will say that "*Shakespear* had an Universal mind, which comprehended all Characters and Passions" (*Works*, 13:247).

31. From *CCXI Sociable Letters, written by the Thrice Noble, Illustrious, and Excellent Princess the Lady Marchioness of Newcastle* (1664); in *Shakespeare: The Critical Heritage*, 1:43.

32. H. James Jensen, *A Glossary of John Dryden's Critical Terms* (Minneapolis: University of Minnesota Press, 1969), 62–63.

33. Jensen offers two definitions: (1) The world as it usually appears; that which is probable. Thus a play imitates human nature or individuals as they probably are. (2) Quoting Robert Wolseley's Preface to *Valentinian* (1685): "By *Nature* I do not only mean all sorts of material Objects and every species of Sub

stance whatsoever, but also general Notions and abstracted Truths, such as exist only in the Minds of men and in the property and relation of things one to another" (Jensen, *Glossary*, 79–80. Wolseley is quoted from *Critical Essays of the Seventeenth Century*, ed. J. E. Spingarn, 3 vols. [Oxford: Oxford University Press, 1908], 3:21).

34. *The Winters Tale*, 4.4.88.

35. In "To my Dear Friend Mr. Congreve" (1694), Dryden says: "Genius must be born; and never can be taught. / This is Your Portion; this Your Native Store; / Heav'n that but once was Prodigal before, / To *Shakespeare* gave as much; she cou'd not give him more" (lines 60–63; *Works*, 4:433). David Nichol Smith suggested that Dryden had originally written "Nature" for "Heav'n," but changed it to avoid the repetition with "native," leaving the unusual feminine pronoun for heaven: see *The Poems of John Dryden: Volume IV: 1693–1696*, ed. Paul Hammond and David Hopkins (London: Longman, 2000), 334.

36. This is also expressed in "To my Dear Friend Mr. Congreve." See my *Dryden and the Traces of Classical Rome*, 9–16, 57–58.

37. From "To the memory of my beloued . . ."; in *Shakespeare: The Critical Heritage*, 1:24.

38. I have explored these issues in *Dryden and the Traces of Classical Rome*.

39. Thus John Webster, as early as 1612, in the Dedication to *The White Devil*, had written of "The labor'd and understanding workes of maister *Johnson* . . . the right happy and copious industry of M. *Shake-speare*." In 1647 Sir John Denham, writing in the Beaumont and Fletcher folio, contrasted "JOHNSONS oyle and sweat" with "what more easie nature did bestow / On SHAKESPEARES gentler Muse": *The Shakspere Allusion Book*, 1:233, 504.

40. The *OED*'s definition of "lucky," *a.* 1, says: "In early use often, Fortunate, successful, prosperous. Now with narrower meaning: Favoured by chance; successful through causes other than one's own action or merit." There is a gap in the citations between 1641 (clearly the first sense) and 1827 (clearly the second), so one cannot deduce from this evidence when the second meaning came to prevail. The "Prologue to *Julius Caesar*" (*Shakespeare: The Critical Heritage*, 1:141–42), sometimes attributed to Dryden, presents an exaggerated version of the idea, an artless Shakespeare whose work was the result solely of chance. For an argument against the attribution of the poem to Dryden see my "Did Dryden write the 'Prologue to *Julius Caesar*'?" *English Studies* 65 (October 1984): 409–19.

41. "To My Honored Friend, Sir Robert Howard," lines 19–32 (*Works*, 1:17–18).

42. *Laws*, 888e: "We are told that everything which comes, and has come, and will come into existence is by nature, or by art, or through chance." Dryden may have encountered Plato's dictum in Montaigne's essay "Des Cannibales" (*Oeuvres complètes*, edited by Albert Thibaudet and Maurice Rat (Paris: Gallimard, 1962), 204), which he echoes in the Prologue to *The Indian Queen* (performed 1664): see *Poems of John Dryden, Volume I: 1649–1681*, ed. Paul Hammond (London: Longman, 1995), 88.

43. *Works*, 8:95.

44. "An account of the ensuing Poem" prefixed to *Annus Mirabilis* (1667) (*Works*, 1:54). The idea was a commonplace: cp. Poussin, writing to Chantelou on 24 November 1647: "Virgile . . . accommode le propre son du vers avec tel artifice que proprement il semble qu'il mette devant les yeux avec le son des paroles les choses desquelles il traite" (Nicolas Poussin, *Lettres et propos sur l'*

art, ed. Anthony Blunt [Paris: Hermann, 1989], 137). Blunt notes that Poussin's source is Giuseppe Zarlino's *Istituzioni Harmoniche* (1558). I take this point from my essay "Is Dryden a Classic?" in *John Dryden: Tercentenary Essays,* ed. Paul Hammond and David Hopkins (Oxford: Clarendon Press, 2000), 7–8.

45. Preface to *All for Love* (1678) (*Works,* 13:18).

46. Preface to *Troilus and Cressida* (1679) (*Works,* 13:225).

47. "Prologue to *The Tempest*" (1670), lines 5, 6, 8 (*Works,* 10:6). Pope echoed this notion, saying of Virgil: *"Nature* and *Homer* were, he found, the same" (An Essay on Criticism, line 135 [The Twickenham Edition of the Poems of Alexander Pope, ed. John Butt et al., 11 vols. (London: Methuen, 1939–62), 1:255]). The Twickenham editors note the borrowing, and point out that lines 141–80 of the *Essay* are heavily influenced by Longinus, as I argue that Dryden's critique of Shakespeare is.

48. "Prologue to *The Tempest,*" line 20 (*Works,* 10:6).

49. Preface to *All for Love* (*Works,* 13:18).

50. For Dryden's interest in poetic inheritance see *Dryden and the Traces of Classical Rome,* 43–52; Christopher Ricks, "Allusion: The Poet as Heir," in *Studies in the Eighteenth Century III,* ed. R. F. Brissenden and J. C. Eade (Toronto: University of Toronto Press, 1976), 209–40.

51. *Mac Flecknoe,* lines 166, 176 (*Works,* 2:58–59).

52. *Works,* 13:231.

53. περαίνουσα τὴν τῶν τοιούτων παθημάτων κάθαρσιν (*Poetics,* 1449b).

54. *Works,* 13:231.

55. The appearance of Boileau's translation of Longinus in 1674 may well have been the catalyst that prompted Dryden to read or reread Longinus.

56. *Works,* 12:87.

57. *Works,* 13:240–41.

58. *Works,* 13:227, 246. Nahum Tate and Robert Gould also admired the handling of the passions in *Julius Caesar.* See *Shakespeare: The Critical Heritage,* 1:342, 415. Gould's line "Or when I hear his Godlike *Romans* rage" is lifted almost verbatim from Dryden's Prologue to *Aureng-Zebe,* line 15.

59. Preface to *Troilus and Cressida* (*Works,* 13:225).

60. *Works,* 13:244. Catachresis: the unreasonable or extravagant stretching of the meaning of a word beyond normal usage.

61. *Works,* 13:243–44.

62. While *Aureng-Zebe* (1676) is written in rhyming couplets, the prologue confesses a desire to emulate Shakespeare (*Works,* 12:159).

63. *Works,* 13:2.

64. Ibid., 13:247.

65. *Works,* 1:112. For a discussion of Dryden's critique of Ovid, see David Hopkins, "Dryden and Ovid's 'Wit out of Season,'" in *Ovid Renewed: Ovidian Influences on Literature and Art from the Middle Ages to the Twentieth Century,* ed. Charles Martindale (Cambridge: Cambridge University Press, 1988), 167–90.

66. *Essay of Dramatick Poesie* (*Works,* 17:58).

67. See Kirsti Simonsuuri, *Homer's Original Genius* (Cambridge: Cambridge University Press, 1979); *The Poems of John Dryden. Volume IV: 1693–1696,* ed. Paul Hammond and David Hopkins (London: Longman, 2000), 313–14.

68. See Robin Sowerby, "The Last Parting of Hector and Andromache," in *John Dryden: Tercentenary Essays,* 240–63.

69. *Fables Ancient and Modern,* sig. *A2ᵛ; James Winn, "'According to my

Genius': Dryden's Translation of the First Book of Homer's *Ilias,*" in *John Dryden: Tercentenary Essays,* 264–81.

70. Some contemporaries also thought that Dryden and Shakespeare belonged together: Charles Gildon said that only Dryden excels Shakespeare; Colley Cibber said that Dryden only "writ Great and Masterly" in his imitation of Shakespeare's style; and Bevill Higgons had the ghosts of Shakespeare and Dryden introduce George Granville's adaptation of *The Merchant of Venice* (*Shakespeare: The Critical Heritage,* 2:67, 2:102, 2:150). Pope too associates Dryden and Shakespeare as powerful but unrefined writers: "fluent Shakespear scarce effac'd a line. / Ev'n copious Dryden, wanted, or forgot,/ The last and greatest Art, the Art to blot" ("The First Epistle of the Second Book of Horace," lines 279–81).

71. *Fables Ancient and Modern,* sig. *C^v.

72. "Defence of the Epilogue," appended to *The Conquest of Granada* (1672) (*Works,* 11:213).

73. H. David Brumble, *Classical Myths and Legends in the Middle Ages and Renaissance: A Dictionary of Allegorical Meanings* (London: Fitzroy Dearborn, 1998), 185. The idea is found in Dryden's "To my Dear Friend Mr. Congreve" (lines 6–8 [*Works,* 4:432]), where Charles II in 1660 is seen as Janus, bringing the arts of civilization at the Restoration.

74. *Fasti,* 1.117–26.

75. "To Sir Godfrey Kneller" (1694), lines 73–78 (*Works,* 4:463).

Dryden's Poem of Paradise: *The State Of Innocence, And Fall Of Man*

Louis L. Martz

From Dryden's acknowledgment in his prefatory essay it is clear that he did not wish his own poem of Paradise to be regarded as competing in any way with Milton's epic:

> I cannot without injury to the deceas'd Author of *Paradice Lost*, but acknowledge that this POEM has receiv'd its entire Foundation, part of the Design, and many of the Ornaments, from him. What I have borrow'd, will be so easily discern'd from my mean Productions, that I shall not need to point the Reader to the places: And, truly, I should be sorry, for my own sake, that any one should take the pains to compare them together: The Original being undoubtedly, one of the greatest, most noble, and most sublime POEMS, which either this Age or Nation has produc'd.[1]

Nevertheless, with the help of the admirable notes provided by Vinton Dearing in the California edition, I should like to offer such a comparison, from which it will appear that Dryden has taken the utmost pains to avoid tagging Milton's verses, despite Milton's famous permission to do so.[2] I can find no more than half a dozen lines in Dryden's poem that echo a full line of Milton's— and even here a word or two is changed. For the most part Dryden echoes only words, phrases, or short clauses from *Paradise Lost*, weaving them as "Ornaments" into the fabric of his own colloquial diction. The echoes of Milton are not at all confined to the particular episode in *Paradise Lost* that underlies the scene in Dryden. Thus in the play's second scene the conversation between Adam and Raphael is based on Adam's conversation with God in book 8 of *Paradise Lost,* but the scene is studded with ornaments taken from other books of Milton's epic: from books 9, 2, 11, 6, and 10.

It appears, from the range of the poem's Miltonic echoes, that Dryden has virtually memorized Milton's poem. We should not make too much of Dryden's statement that the work was "wholly written" in a month.³ The actual writing seems to have been preceded by many hours of reading and rereading Milton's epic, with the result that the materials were fully stored in Dryden's mind and could readily be called forth in a month of writing his own poem. The work does not appear to be hastily done; the couplets display Dryden's characteristic skill, with their tactful deployment of alliteration, their balancing of half-lines, and their emphatic rhymes. Dryden himself seems to have stressed his particular kind of craftsmanship by writing one scene early in the play (2.2) in blank verse. Why only one such scene? It is enough to show, in Dryden's view, the superiority of rhyme—a sort of answer, perhaps, to Milton's scorn of rhyme in his note on the verse of *Paradise Lost*.

The poem displays the confluence of two styles: the epic and the colloquial, which here blend easily to produce the peculiar hybrid style of this new version of the Paradise story. Such a collocation of styles is of course later used by Dryden and Pope to produce the satirical mock-epic; indeed, the opening scene of Dryden's poem is mock-epic. The vast difference between these two poems of Paradise is immediately displayed in this scene, where Dryden's central figure bears the name Lucifer, not Satan, while he addresses a quite different companion on the burning lake:

> Is this the Seat our Conqueror has given?
> And this the Climate we must change for Heaven?
> These Regions and this Realm my Wars have got;
> This Mournful Empire is the Loser's Lot:
> In Liquid Burnings or on Dry to dwell,
> Is all the sad Variety of Hell.
>
> (1.1.1–6)

The last line, so greatly admired by T. S. Eliot,⁴ seems to echo *Paradise Lost* (6.640): "Earth hath this variety from Heav'n." And so, we might say, Hell has yet another sort of variety. This passage of course echoes Satan's speech to Beelzebub after he has risen from the lake and surveyed that sad variety:

> Is this the Region, this the Soil, the Clime,
> Said then the lost Arch Angel, this the seat
> That we must change for Heav'n, this mournful gloom
> For that celestial light?
>
> (*PL*, 1.242–45)⁵

Dryden picks up the words "Region," "Clime" (modernized to "Climate"), "seat," and "mournful," and takes over the entire clause "we must change for Heav'n." And Milton's reference to "the lost Arch Angel" seems to lie behind Lucifer's phrase, "the Loser's Lot." The line "In Liquid Burnings or on Dry to Dwell," is based on Milton's description of the scene as "Land that ever burn'd / With solid, as the Lake with liquid fire" (*PL*, 1.228–29).

Now Dryden goes backward to pick up words from Satan's earlier speech, delivered while he is lying on the burning lake. Thus Milton:

> But see the angry Victor hath recall'd
> His Ministers of vengeance and pursuit
> Back to the Gates of Heav'n: The Sulphurous Hail
> Shot after us in storm, oreblown hath laid
> The fiery Surge, that from the Precipice
> Of Heav'n receiv'd us falling, and the Thunder,
> Wing'd with red Lightning and impetuous rage,
> Perhaps hath spent his shafts, and ceases now
> To bellow through the vast and boundless Deep.
>
> (*PL*, 1.169–77)

Dryden condenses all this into two couplets, almost, but not quite tagging Milton's last line here:

> But see, the Victor has recall'd, from far,
> Th' Avenging Storms, his Ministers of War:
> His Shafts are spent, and his tir'd Thunders sleep;
> Nor longer bellow through the Boundless Deep.
>
> (1.1.7–10)

Now comes a major surprise, for these words, spoken by Satan to the heroic Beelzebub, are here addressed to quite another devil: "Ho, *Asmoday*, awake." Milton has replaced Beelzebub with the most lustful, murderous, and cowardly of devils—the demon whose jealousy of Sara (in the book of Tobit) has led him to murder seven of her husbands in sequence as they approached the bridal chamber. Tobias escapes this fate by following the advice of Raphael: he burns the heart and liver of a fish in the bridal chamber and the smell so frightens the demon that he flees to the farthest parts of Egypt, where he is bound by Raphael. Milton tells the story in a brilliant passage of the fourth book of *Paradise Lost*:

> So entertaind those odorous sweets the Fiend
> Who came thir bane, though with them better pleas'd
> Then *Asmodeus* with the fishie fume,
> That drove him, though enamourd, from the Spouse
> Of *Tobits* Son, and with a vengeance sent
> From *Media* post to *Ægypt*, there fast bound.
>
> (*PL*, 4.166–71)

Thus Milton manages to evoke the smell of evil even amidst the perfumes of Paradise. Throughout the opening scene, then, this vicious demon replaces the figure that Milton in book 2 has described in the most heroic terms:

> with grave
> Aspect he rose, and in his rising seem'd
> A Pillar of State; deep on his Front engraven
> Deliberation sat and publick care;
> And Princely counsel in his face yet shon,
> Majestick though in ruin . . .
>
> (*PL*, 2.300–305)

This impressive figure is by Dryden reduced to seconding the cowardly advice of Belial, that they do nothing further to provoke the Deity (1.1.129–29).

The opening speech of Lucifer continues thus:

> Ho, *Asmoday*, awake,
> If thou art he: but Ah! how chang'd from him,
> Companion of my Arms! how wan! how dim!
> How faded all thy Glories are! I see
> My self too well, and my own change, in thee.
>
> (1.1.12–16)

These lines adapt the first words of Satan to Beelzebub: "If thou beest he; But O how fall'n! how chang'd . . ." (*PL*, 1.84). Dryden then goes on to describe Asmodeus in terms that Milton applies to Satan: "wan," "dim," "faded" (*PL*, 4.870; 1.597, 602). To see himself in Asmodeus destroys any vestige of heroic stature.

A similar degradation is accomplished a little later (1.1.66), when Dryden gives to Moloch a version of Satan's famous line of defiance in Milton: "Better to reign in Hell, then serve in Heav'n" (*PL*, 1.262). Dryden has changed "reign" to "Rule"—"Better to Rule in Hell"—apparently to make a political distinction. At this point Lucifer remarks in a stage whisper: "There spoke the better half of *Lucifer!*" (1.1.67), thus hinting at the origin of the line and lowering the style with a commonplace phrase.

Meanwhile, to our surprise, a minor character named "Sathan" seconds Moloch's words of violence, arguing from his own character that the heavenly host is relaxed and open to attack:

> Seraph and Cherub, careless of their charge,
> And wanton, in full ease now live at large,
> Ungarded leave the passes of the Skie,
> And all dissolv'd in Hallelujahs lie.
>
> (1.1.106–9)

This is the passage that Dryden in his prefatory essay defends against the ridicule of one of his "Censors" who has said "I have heard . . . of Anchove's dissolv'd in Sauce; but never of an Angel in Hallelujahs." Dryden offers his lines as poetry that "comes nearest" to being an "example of excellent imaging."[6] And so it surely is: the passage expresses exactly the sort of scorn that one would expect from a dissolute character.

Dryden uses other devices to deflate the apparent heroism of Milton's Satan and his host. He compares what Milton calls "the great consult" (*PL,* 1.798) of the fallen angels to the political sessions of the democratic Dutch in the war then raging; thus Lucifer addresses his chiefs:

> Most high and mighty Lords, who better fell
> From Heav'n, to rise States-General of Hell,
> Nor yet repent, though ruin'd and undone,
> Our upper Provinces already won,
> (Such pride there is in Souls created free,
> Such hate of Universal Monarchy;)
>
> (1.1.85–90)

Finally, Dryden will not accept the silence that follows the decision to make the dangerous voyage to earth, as in Milton none of all the fallen angels has the courage to volunteer; thus Milton enhances the heroic stature of his Satan. Dryden is more realistic: he allows Moloch, in accord with his violent character, to attempt to volunteer in a phrase ("This Glorious Enterprise") that echoes Satan's reference to the rebellion in Heaven (*PL,* 1.89), but the offer is at once declined by Lucifer, saying, "Hot Braves, like thee, may fight; but know not well / To manage this, the last great Stake of Hell" (1.1.170, 173–74). Lucifer is a desperate gambler, not an epic hero.

What is the purpose of this parodic deflation? One can see several effects. First, it serves to distinguish Dryden's poem from Milton's. Secondly, it brings the poem down to the contemporary earth on which the play must be acted. And thirdly, more subtly, by implying that the Devil and his host are not so powerful as Milton has presented them, Dryden avoids what he seems to have regarded as major flaws in *Paradise Lost*: that the Devil is the hero, instead of Adam, and that there are "more Machining Persons than Humane, in his Poem"[7]—that is, Milton has allowed the supernatural agents to overwhelm the human factor. Dryden, as dramatist, cannot allow attention to move away from the human scene.

The sense of the present created by the allusion to the States General is continued in the next scene, our introduction to Paradise, as Adam in his opening words alludes to Descartes: "What am I? or from whence? For that I am / I know, because I think" (2.1.1–2). Raphael then introduces Adam to a central principle of seventeenth-century thought: "Right Reason's Law to every humane heart / Th' Eternal, as his Image, will impart" (2.1.29–30). But it soon appears that this power of Reason is not in fact so strong in all created beings, as Raphael describes the soon-to-be-created woman:

> An equal, yet thy subject, is design'd,
> For thy soft hours, and to unbend thy mind.
> Thy stronger soul shall her weak reason sway;
> And thou, through love, her beauty shalt obey
>
> (2.1.64–67)

"An equal, yet thy subject": the rest of the play explores, but never resolves, this paradox by displaying the conflict between Reason and Love—here treated as romantic love in the Renaissance tradition, as Jean Gagen has shown in a perceptive essay.[8] Adam's reason, as Lucifer predicts after Eve's fall, cannot prevail over the power of this love: "He, whose firm faith no reason could remove, / Will melt before that soft seducer, love" (4.2.145–46). This is quite in line with the central theme of Renaissance love poetry, as explained by Kerrigan and Braden in their witty essay on "Milton's Coy Eve": "Male worth remains secondary as the game was usually played in Renaissance poetry, determined primarily by the poet-lover's willing consent to his mistress's demand ... The rule ... is submission to the female's assessment of her value."[9]

In line with this essential contest, Dryden far more openly than Milton (and we must admit, more crudely) stresses the vanity and self-love of his Eve. As we first see her she enters the scene with words that echo Milton's Adam: "Tell me ye Hills and Dales, and thou fair Sun / Who shin'st above, what am I? whence begun?" (2.3.8–9; *PL,* 8.273–77). Adam's thoughts in Milton then lead to his conviction that he must have been created "By some great Maker . . . In goodness and in power præeminent" (8.273–80). But with Dryden's Eve her thoughts soon turn to echo the flattery that Satan has cast upon her in Milton's temptation scene, as Satan says:

> Thee all things living gaze on, all things thine
> By gift, and thy Celestial Beautie adore
> With ravishment beheld . . .
>
> (*PL,* 9.539–41)

Picking up the word "gaze," Dryden activates "all things" into signs of Eve's dominance:

> from each Tree
> The feather'd kind peep down, to look on me;
> And Beasts, with up-cast eyes, forsake their shade,
> And gaze, as if I were to be obey'd.
>
> (2.3.10–13)

"I my self am proud of me," she concludes, as prelude to Dryden's version of the narcissan episode where Eve admires her reflection in the water: "Streams drown the voice, or it would say it loves" (2.3.23). Milton ends this episode by having the mysterious voice of God lead Eve away from admiring her own image toward her first view of Adam, by which she learns, after some hesitation, "How beauty is excelld by manly grace / And wisdom, which alone is truly fair" (*PL,* 4.490–91). In Dryden the concluding voice is all Eve's own, as she berates the disappearing image in terms that suggest her own future actions:

> Ah, fair, yet false; ah Being, form'd to cheat,
> By seeming kindness, mixt with deep deceit.
>
> (2.3.26–27)

Adam at once foretells the defeat of Reason by his entering speech here, which echoes words spoken by Milton's Adam as he is about to choose his Fall, along with words that echo Satan's flattery in Eve's Temptation:

> O Virgin, Heav'n begot, and born of Man,
> Thou fairest of thy great Creator's Works;
> Thee, Goddess, thee th' Eternal did ordain
> His softer Substitute on Earth to Reign . . .[10]

Then Adam, as he contemplates their first sexual union, shows himself to be a callow youth, considerably less than commanding:

> Made to command, thus freely I obey,
> And at thy feet the whole Creation lay.
> Pity that love thy beauty does beget:
> What more I shall desire, I know not yet.
> First let us lock'd in close embraces be;
> Thence I, perhaps, may teach my self, and thee.
> (2.3.46–51)

Eve responds with a four-line variation upon Milton's theme of "sweet reluctant amorous delay" (*Paradise Lost*, 4.311):

> Somewhat forbids me, which I cannot name;
> For ignorant of guilt, I fear not shame:[11]
> But some restraining thought, I know not why,
> Tells me, you long should beg, I long deny.
> (2.3.52–55)

Milton's Adam, in narrating this episode, is fully confident: "To the Nuptial Bowre / I led her blushing like the Morn," while nature discreetly celebrates the event:

> Joyous the Birds; fresh Gales and gentle Aires
> Whisper'd it to the Woods, and from thir wings
> Flung Rose, flung Odours from the spicie Shrub . . .
> (*PL*, 8.510–17)

Dryden's Adam, when he next appears, has so thoroughly recovered his confidence that, in his state of exuberance, he expands Milton's imagery in hyperbolical terms:

> Roses unbid, and ev'ry fragrant Flow'r,
> Flew from their stalks, to strow thy Nuptial Bower:
> The furr'd and feather'd kind, the triumph did pursue,

> And Fishes leapt above the streams, the passing Pomp to view.
>
> (3.1.35–38)

Quite a group of voyeurs! Eve then responds with an eight-line description of the whole sexual process, ending with "sweet tumult" (3.1.39–46). Clearly we are here living in the world of Restoration comedy.

But the most notorious example of language directed toward the contemporary stage still awaits us: in the speech of Eve after she has eaten the forbidden fruit, as she ponders how to proceed with Adam:

> I walk in Ayr, and scorn this Earthly seat;
> Heav'n is my palace; this my base retreat.
> Take me not Heav'n, too soon; 'twill be unkind
> To leave the partner of my bed behind.
> I love the wretch . . .
>
> (5.1.3–7)

The parallel here is not with Milton, but with Shakespeare, as Othello says of Desdemona:

> Excellent wretch! Perdition catch my soul
> But I do love thee! and when I love thee not,
> Chaos is come again.
>
> (3.3.91–93)

An ominous parallel. Editors cite Samuel Johnson's note upon this usage of "wretch": "a term of the softest and fondest tenderness. It expresses the utmost degree of amiableness, joined with an idea . . . of feebleness, softness, and want of protection."[12] This applies well to Othello, but not exactly to Dryden's Eve, whose attitude here is condescending and possessive: "my bed."

Dryden, we see, has taken great pains to make his poem attractive to his presumed audience. Why, then, as Dryden tells us, was the work "never acted"?[13] Older commentators have suggested that the problem lay in presenting the original nakedness of Adam and Eve—a problem now happily overcome in the modern theater. But Dryden apparently had a solution for the problem. In the stage directions for Eve's dream "an Angel enters, with a Woman, habited like *Eve*" (3.3). What kind of filmy costume this indicates we can only conjecture; and for Adam's "habit" we have no hint.

Later scholars have argued that the main difficulty lay in the expense involved in the operatic elements, which Dryden's impoverished company could ill afford.[14] But Dearing's notes make it clear that Dryden's company already possessed, or was in the process of possessing, most of the machinery needed to carry out Dryden's directions;[15] and musicians were not expensive to hire. Indeed, Dryden's company could ill afford *not* to present some sort of operatic spectacle, considering the remarkable success that the rival company was then having with this sort of production.

Some deeper cause, I think, must underlie the work's rejection for the stage; and perhaps we find it in the theme evoked in the long, hundred-line discussion of the problem of determinism versus free will presented in the fourth act (4.1.11–112). Adam there brings up every possible objection to the possession of free will; and the angels are hard put to answer his objections. Milton has been content to have only one angel as Adam's instructor, but Dryden has provided both Raphael and Gabriel to deal with this difficult issue. K. W. Gransden has shown how Adam never gives way in this debate but rather drives the two angels to signs of impatience, as Gabriel charges Adam with "impious fancies" and Raphael cries out, "O chain, which fools, to catch themselves, project."[16] Then Raphael ends the debate with the worst of all arguments: instead of presenting the Creation as the result of God's outflowing goodness, as Milton does, Raphael pictures a Deity who has created human beings with free will in order to have somebody to punish or reward! As if feeling the weakness of this argument, Raphael stops the debate abruptly with the words: "Our task is done: obey; and in that choice, / Thou shalt be blest, and Angels shall rejoyce."

Adam does not rejoice. Left alone after the dazzling spectacle of the angelic host has disappeared, Adam bitterly laments:

> Hard state of life! since Heav'n fore-knows my will,
> Why am I not ty'd up from doing ill?
> Why am I trusted with my self at large,
> When he's more able to sustain the charge?
> Since Angels fell, whose strength was more than mine,
> 'Twould show more grace my frailty to confine.
> Fore-knowing the success [outcome], to leave me free,
> Excuses him, and yet supports not me.
>
> (4.1.113–20)

Bruce King has argued that Dryden was attracted to this theme by the recent controversy between Thomas Hobbes and Bishop

Bramhall.[17] This may well be so, but, as King says, this was a dominant issue throughout the seventeenth century. The controversy between the adherents of Calvinistic predestination and the believers in free will sustained by the sacraments lies at the heart of the tumultuous conflicts in seventeenth-century religion. It was a turmoil that, abetted by financial issues, led to the destruction of the monarchy and the execution of the king. Would it have been wise, then, not fifteen years after the Restoration, to set forth this problem so boldly on the public stage?

However this may be, the problem provides the unifying "moral" of this work, as explained in Dryden's preface to *Troilus and Cressida:*

> The first Rule which *Bossu,* prescribes to the Writer of an Heroic Poem, and which holds too by the same reason in all Dramatic Poetry, is to make the moral of the work; that is, to lay down to your self what that precept of morality shall be, which you would insinuate into the people . . . 'Tis the moral that directs the whole action of the Play to one center . . .[18]

The conflict between Reason and Love produces the "precept of morality" insinuated into the audience. The problem of free will arises from Adam's sense of helplessness before the power of Love; in his sense of his own weakness he would like to think that he lacks freedom of will, that his course is predestined by some "cause" in his created being for which he cannot be held responsible. As Adam says: "I can but chuse what he has first design'd, / For he before that choice, my will confin'd" (4.1.73–4). This debate, visually framed within an elaborate setting of the angelic guards, is the climax and revelation of an issue that runs throughout the poem, from the first scene to the last. Its cause is here immediately enforced in the second half of this very scene, where Adam's Reason is utterly defeated by Eve's determination to garden by herself, and Adam closes the whole double scene by saying:

> One look of hers my resolution breaks;
> Reason it self turns folly when she speaks:
> And aw'd by her whom it was made to sway,
> Flatters her pow'r, and does its own betray.
>
> (4.1.201–4)

In *Paradise Lost* this confession is at once rebuked by Raphael, but Dryden allows the words to stand, emphatically, as the close of this drama's central scene, after which the Temptation scenes quickly follow, as though preordained.

In the opening scene Dryden has prepared the way for the theme of free will by Lucifer's surprisingly detailed view of the workings of the human mind, when he describes the nature of this rumored new creation:

> I heard it; through all Heav'n the rumour ran,
> And much the talk of this intended *Man*:
> Of form Divine; but less in excellence
> Than we; indu'd with Reason lodg'd in Sence:
> The Soul pure Fire, like ours, of equal force;
> But, pent in Flesh, must issue by discourse . . .
> (1.1.144–49)

This stress on Reason is then repeated in the next scene, where Raphael explains: "Right Reason's Law" (2.1.29–30).

A little later, at the outset of act 3, Lucifer himself, in his soliloquy derived from Milton, admits that God had "bounteously bestow'd unenvy'd good / On me: in arbitrary Grace I stood." (3.1.9–10). That phrase "arbitrary Grace" has caused considerable puzzlement, because it might be taken to indicate God's arbitrary power. But Dryden is using the word "arbitrary" in the legal sense of his day: "Relating to, or dependent on, the discretion of an arbiter;" or, in more general usage: "To be decided by one's liking; dependent upon will or pleasure; at the discretion or option of anyone" (*OED*). Lucifer, in short, was created with free will. Later in act 3, when Lucifer derides Gabriel and Ithuriel as "slaves" in base "servitude" to God, Ithuriel replies:

> Freedome is choice of what we will and do:
> Then blame not servants who are freely so.
> (3.3.64–65)

And Gabriel adds:

> Made for his use; yet he has form'd us so
> We, unconstrain'd, what he commands us do.
> So praise we him and serve him freely best:
> Thus thou, by choice, art fall'n, and we are blest.
> (3.3.75–78)

And Adam, as he is about to eat the fruit, declares "Not cozen'd, I; with choice, my life resign" (5.1.69).

So then, despite its touches of levity, Dryden's poem is a basically serious work, a religious poem that explores the central issue of his day. This concern with free will might be taken as a sign of Dryden's movement toward the adoption of Roman Catholicism that he revealed a dozen years later. Some support for such a view may be found in his dedication of "this Poem" to the Duchess of York, consort of James. The fulsome praise of her beauty, which so disgusted Samuel Johnson,[19] may be seen as a screen to cover his loyalty to the Catholic Duke and his Catholic Duchess, well known for her religious devotion and her earlier wish to be a nun. Dryden's praise of her beauty is throughout cast in religious terms that would no doubt please her, but which may also be taken to show Dryden's grasp of Catholic devotion. He says at the outset that he will not talk of her Greatness, but then proceeds to give a glowing account of her "Illustrious Family," concluding with a bold reference to "the hopes of those which You are to produce for the *British* Chronicle." That is, hope for the heir that many English feared could produce a Catholic dynasty; and when that heir appeared King James and his spouse were forced into exile. But Dryden goes on to say that he has "wav'd the Subject of Your Greatness" in favor of the theme of Beauty. Still, he cannot refrain from telling how that Greatness is supported by her marriage to a prince "whose Conduct, Courage, and Success in War, whose Fidelity to His Royal Brother, whose Love for His Country, whose Constancy to His Friends, whose Bounty to His Servants, whose Justice to Merit, whose Inviolable Truth, and whose Magnanimity in all His Actions, seem to have been rewarded by Heaven by the gift of You." Bold words indeed, when the main political issue of the day was worry over "a Popish Successor" to Charles. But Dryden insists he is not concerned with religious or political issues: his theme is Beauty. Viewed from this standpoint, Dryden's dedication might be seen as one of his most artful pieces of rhetoric.[20]

Dryden's exploration of the theme of free will does not lead to any comforting conclusion, though near the close it appears that the play may end in pious platitudes. After Adam and Eve have suffered through the story of their punishment and have witnessed the woes visited upon their progeny, Raphael presents them with a consolatory bit of operatic machinery: "Here a Heaven descends, full of Angels and blessed Spirits, with soft Music, a Song and Chorus."[21]

Adam responds with the words and thoughts of Milton's Adam: "O goodness infinite! whose Heav'nly will / Can so much good produce, from so much ill!" And Eve in turn picks up the thought that Adam expresses in Milton's poem: "Ravish'd, with Joy, I can but half repent / The sin which Heav'n makes happy in th' event."[22] But this momentary response to an impressive spectacle does not represent her deeper feelings, which Dryden now presents in the most powerful speech in the play, his adaptation of Eve's lament. In Milton, it is a soliloquy spoken in a place of solitary retirement:

> O flours,
> That never will in other Climate grow,
> My early visitation, and my last
> At Eev'n, which I bred up with tender hand
> From the first op'ning bud, and gave ye Names,
> Who now shall reare ye to the Sun, or ranke
> Your Tribes, and water from th' ambrosial Fount?
> Thee lastly nuptial Bowre, by mee adornd
> With what to sight or smell was sweet; from thee
> How shall I part, and whither wander down
> Into a lower World, to this obscure
> And wilde, how shall we breath in other Aire
> Less pure, accustomed to immortal Fruits?
>
> (*PL*, 11.273–85)

Adapting this quite freely, with touches all his own, Dryden turns this private lament into a bold piece of public oratory, with a bitter conclusion:

> Farewell, you flow'rs, whose buds, with early care,
> I watch'd, and to the chearful sun did rear:
> Who now shall bind your stems? or, when you fall,
> With fountain streams, your fainting souls recall?

This is pure Dryden, with the realistic touch of binding, and Eve's sensitive feeling that the flowers have an almost human relationship to her. Then she continues:

> A long farewell to thee, my nuptial bow'r,
> Adorn'd with ev'ry fair and fragrant flow'r.
> And last, farewell, farewell my place of birth;
> I go to wander in the lower earth,
> As distant as I can; for, dispossest,
> Farthest from what I once enjoy'd, is best.
>
> (5.4.250–59)

That last line echoes the bitter words of Milton's Satan in Hell, referring to the victorious Deity: "fardest from him is best" (*Paradise Lost,* 1.247). The Satanic echo suggests that Eve is far from reconciled to her fate: the emphasis on "dispossest" shows her deep resentment. Indeed, she has shown herself to be unreconciled throughout this closing scene, where Dryden gives to her lines drawn from Adam's lamentations in Milton.[23] Thus, when Raphael enters to pronounce the dreadful sentence, Dryden's Adam is totally submissive: "I neither can dispute his will, nor dare: / Death will dismiss me from my future care . . ." (5.4.114–15). But Eve bursts out with bitter resentment:

> Why seek you death? consider ere you speak:
> The laws were hard; the pow'r to keep 'em, weak.
> Did we solicite Heav'n to mould our clay?
> From darkness, to produce us to the day?
> Did we concur to life, or chuse to be,
> Was it our will which form'd, or was it he?
> Since 'twas his choice, not ours, which plac'd us here;
> The laws we did not chuse, why should we bear?
>
> (5.4.118–25)

Adam attempts to quell this rebellion by reasserting the doctrine of free will: "Seek not, in vain, our maker to accuse: / Terms were propos'd; pow'r left us to refuse" (5.4.126–27).

But Eve remains unconvinced. After they have viewed the spectacle of "deaths of several sorts," Adam cries out with guilt, but Eve does not conform: "Why is life forc'd on man; who might he choose, / Would not accept, what he, with pain, must lose?" (5.4.183–84). And again, after seeing "yon' mad fools who, for some trivial Right, / For love, or for mistaken honour fight" and "those, more mad, who throw their lives away / In needless wars" (5.4.191–94), Eve bitterly resents the vision:

> Who would the miseries of man foreknow?
> Not knowing; we but share our part of woe:
> Now, we the fate of future Ages bear;
> And, ere their birth, behold our dead appear.
>
> (5.4.200–203)

Her view of death is far more grim than that of Adam, who hopes to die "Like timely fruit, not shaken by the wind, / But ripely dropping from the sapless bough." But Eve grimly anticipates the cruel decay of her sensory life: "Thus, daily changing, with a duller tast / Of less'ning joyes, I, by degrees, would wast" (5.4.215–16, 218–19).

It should come as no surprise, then, that Dryden should at the end give to this heroine the most powerful speech in the play, after which the brief closing words of Raphael offer no consolation. Dryden's Eve has throughout the play brought spontaneous life to the action: wilful, vain, argumentative, sexy, quick in repartee, indulgent in ironic self-pity:

> Th' unhappiest of creation is a wife,
> Made lowest, in the highest rank of life:
> Her fellow's slave; to know and not to chuse:
> Curst with that reason she must never use.
>
> (5.4.58–61)

Dryden has thus created a heroine that is in every way at least "equal" to her mate.[24] A fine actress could make much of this role. One would like to see her presented on the stage with all the vital variety that Adam so angrily has found in her:

> Add, that she's proud, fantastick, apt to change;
> Restless at home; and ever prone to range:
> With shows delighted, and so vain is she,
> She'll meet the Devil; rather than not see.
>
> (5.4. 62–65)

But what does this rebellious heroine have to do with the "moral" that the drama attempts to "insinuate into the people?" Or rather, what is that moral? On an abstract level we are told by the angels that free will exists and that we should beware of misusing that privilege. Yet the main thrust of the drama lies in the rebellious thoughts of both Adam and Eve. Dryden seems to be insinuating that the problem of free will, with its related problem of divine justice, cannot be resolved by Reason, but remains a mystery that only faith in some higher authority can resolve. Ultimately, as we know, Dryden turned to accept that authority.

Notes

1. *The Works of John Dryden*, vol. 12, ed. Vinton A. Dearing (Berkeley and Los Angeles: University of California Press, 1994), 86. Dryden seems to prefer calling his work a "POEM," as the strong capitalization here indicates. But he calls it an "Opera" in the opening sentence of this preface, and the work is of

course announced as an Opera on the title page. For the function of the operatic elements see the essay by Bernard Harris, "'That Soft Seducer, Love,': Dryden's *The State of Innocence and Fall of Man,*" in *Approaches to Paradise Lost,* ed. C. A. Patrides (London: Arnold, 1968), 119–36.

2. "John Dreyden, Esq., Poet Laureate, who very much admires him, went to him to have leave to putt his *Paradise Lost* into a Drame in rythme [i.e., rhyme]. Mr. Milton recieved him civilly, and told him *he would give him leave to tagge his Verses.*" John Aubrey, *Brief Lives,* ed. Oliver Lawson Dick (London: Secker and Warburg, 1950), 203.

3. *Works,* 12:86.

4. T. S. Eliot, *Selected Essays,* new ed. (New York: Harcourt, Brace, 1950), 271.

5. Quotations from *Paradise Lost* are taken from *The Student's Milton,* ed. Frank Allen Patterson (New York: Crofts, 1931). This text is based on the first edition.

6. *Works,* 12:95. Other readers have remarked upon Dryden's reduction of the heroic in Lucifer. See Dustin Griffin, *Regaining Paradise: Milton and the Eighteenth Century* (Cambridge: Cambridge University Press, 1986), 144–47. Also D. W. Jefferson, "Dryden's Style in *The State of Innocence,*" *Essays in Criticism* 32 (1982): 361–68; Jefferson says Dryden's "reductive version of the great rebel has a comic flavour" (364).

7. See his "Dedication of the Æneis," *Works,* 5:276.

8. Jean Gagen, "Anomalies in Eden: Adam and Eve in Dryden's *The State of Innocence,*" in *Milton's Legacy in the Arts,* ed. Albert C. Labriola and Edward Sichi Jr. (University Park: Pennsylvania State University Press, 1988), 135–50.

9. William Kerrigan and Gordon Braden, "Milton's Coy Eve: *Paradise Lost* and Renaissance Love Poetry," *ELH* 53 (1986): 27–51; see esp. p. 45.

10. 2.3.28–31; *PL,* 9.896–97: "O fairest of Creation, last and best / Of all Gods Works." *PL,* 9.547: "A Goddess among Gods." *PL,* 9.732: "Goddess humane." Lines 28–29 do not rhyme; is this a deliberate effect of dissonance?

11. *PL,* 4.313: "Then was not guiltie shame."

12. Samuel Johnson, *Works* (New Haven: Yale University Press, 1968), 8:1030.

13. Ibid., 12:86.

14. See Charles E. Ward, *The Life of John Dryden* (Chapel Hill: University of North Carolina Press, 1961), 105; and James Anderson Winn, *John Dryden and his World* (New Haven: Yale University Press, 1987), 262–64.

15. *Works,* 12:323–24.

16. K. W. Gransden, "Milton, Dryden, and the Comedy of the Fall," *Essays in Criticism* 26 (1976): 116–33.

17. Bruce King, *Dryden's Major Plays* (Edinburgh and London: Oliver and Boyd, 1966), chap. 6.

18. *Works,* 13:234.

19. Samuel Johnson, *Lives of the English Poets,* ed. G. B. Hill (Oxford: Clarendon Press, 1905), 1:359. Johnson sees "a strain of flattery which disgraces genius." But he has the dedication by the right end when he adds: "It is an attempt to mingle earth and heaven, by praising human excellence in the language of religion."

20. *Works,* 12:81–82.

21. Ibid., 12:145.

22. 5.4.226–27; 235–36; *PL,* 12.469–76.

23. See *PL,* 10.743-70.
24. See Jean Gagen's view of Eve in the essay cited above: "Dryden has . . . presented an Eve who is a genuine intellectual and spiritual partner to Adam and who is much more capable of 'careful questioning' and 'sober reflection' than Milton's Eve" (147).

Dryden, Marvell, and the Painful Lesson of Laughter

Annabel Patterson

*A*BSALOM AND ACHITOPHEL IS A MASTERPIECE, AND WAS RECOGNIZED so when it first appeared, in late November 1681. Yet nobody could have anticipated it. Very little in Dryden's previous output was as shrewdly under control in terms of its subject matter, and nothing had earlier indicated that Dryden possessed that mastery of rhythm and the energetic verse paragraph that makes us, as it must have made the reader in 1681, spring to attention:

> In pious times, e'r Priest-craft did begin,
> Before *Polygamy* was made a sin;
> When man, on many, multiply'd his kind,
> E'r one to one, was cursedly, confind:
> When Nature prompted, and no law deny'd
> Promiscuous use of Concubine and Bride;
> Then, *Israel*'s Monarch, after Heaven's own heart,
> His vigorous warmth did, variously, impart
> To Wives and Slaves: And, wide as his Command,
> Scatter'd his Maker's Image through the Land.[1]

This engaging introduction of Charles II as King David of Israel is as vigorous, metrically, as the sexual energy Dryden still attributes to him at the opening, despite the later admission (or claim) by Absalom that this potency is exhausted: "grown in *Bathsheba*'s Embraces old" (l.710). Springy, outrageous, defying convention, the power of this new writing comes not only from the brilliant use of alliteration to pit piety and priestcraft against each other, and from the occasional, surprising polysyllables (polygamy, promiscuous) deployed to embody this counterintuitive ethic, but from the discovery that Dryden had at last learned a fundamental lesson: rhyme is the agent, the sound, the sign, of comedy, *not* of heroic tragedy.

How did Dryden come to learn this lesson? The hard way. His

style had been itself a joke—a joke made in rhymed couplets—for some time. In 1674 Andrew Marvell had concluded his commendatory poem for the new edition of Milton's *Paradise Lost* (licensed 6 July) with four lines marking the difference between Milton's grand blank verse and Dryden's couplets:

> Well mightst thou scorn thy Readers to allure
> With tinkling Rhime, of thy own Sense secure;
> While the *Town-Bays* writes all the time and spells,
> And like a Pack-Horse tires without his Bells.[2]

In April of that year, Dryden had acquired a license for his rhymed and dramatized version of *Paradise Lost*, but the appearance of this poem may well have decided him not to publish *The State of Innocence* for another three years, waiting for Marvell's rudeness to be forgotten.[3]

In the winter of 1675–76, most probably, Rochester wrote his version of contemporary literary criticism, *An Allusion to Horace 10 Sat: 1st Book*, which both begins with, and then returns to, a derogatory account of Dryden's style:

> Well Sir 'tis granted, I said Dryden's Rhymes / Were stollen, unequal, nay dull many times.[4]

When the rhyme word is itself "Rhymes" the matter of meter catches our attention, even though Dryden's subject matter is also under review; and later Rochester turns his attention to the laureate's nonheroic poems, praising Charles Sackville, Lord Buckhurst, for "pointed Satyrs" and Charles Sedley for "songs and verses mannerly Obscene," but declaring that Dryden cannot handle either genre:

> Dryden in vain tryd this nice way of Witt,
> For he to be a tearing Blade thought fitt.
> But when he would be sharp he still was blunt:
> To frisk his frolick fancy hee'd cry Cunt;
> Wou'd give the Ladyes a drye bawdy bobb,
> And thus he gott the name of Poet Squobb.
>
> (71–76)

Worse still (since Rochester at least had the grace to admit that Dryden's "Excellencys more than faults abound," [78]) was the fact that Buckingham's comedy, *The Rehearsal*, had skewered Dryden forever on the name of Bayes, was reissued in 1675 in a revised version. The interlocked worlds of theater, coffeehouse, court and parliament were therefore reminded that the playwright-poet who had thrown in his lot with James, Duke of York had laid himself open to hilarious parody. This is what had become of the impossible choices between love and honor in Dryden's heroic drama: a man struggling to decide which of his boots to pull on first:

> My Legs, the Emblem of my various thought,
> Shew to what sad distraction I am brought.
> . . . .
> Shall I to Honour or to Love give way?
> Go on, cryes Honour; tender Love says, nay:
> Honour, aloud, commands, pluck both Boots on;
> But softer Love does whisper, put on none.
> . . . .
> So does my Honour and my Love together
> Puzzle me so, I can resolve for neither.
> [*Goes out hopping with one Boot on, and the other off.*]
> (3.5.89–104)

It was not surprising, therefore, that in November 1675 (and so he might already have seen a manuscript copy of Rochester's satire) Dryden abandoned rhyme as a heroic meter. The prologue that he wrote for *Aureng-Zebe*, which was published in the spring of 1676, announced his defeat, in part by preempting the criticism he expected for this, the last of his rhymed tragedies:

> Our Author by experience finds it true,
> 'Tis much more hard to please himself than you:
> And out of no feign'd modesty, this day,
> Damns his laborious Trifle of a Play:
> Not that its worse than what before he writ,
> But he has now another taste of Wit;
> And to confess a truth, (though out of time)
> Grows weary of his long-lov'd Mistris, Rhyme.
> (1–8)

What was the "other taste of Wit" that Dryden had now acquired? The answer seems surprisingly simple. Dryden had decided to become a satirist, and to reclaim his much-excoriated meter for a more appropriate purpose. How did he do this? He saturated himself in the satires of the Whig poets, listening to their rhythms, incorporating some of their phrases, turning the genre of parody back upon themselves. The author from whom he learned the most was Andrew Marvell; but to complete his revenge, he would in *Absalom and Achitophel* apply Marvell's satiric style and strategies to Milton's grand matter in *Paradise Lost,* producing a mock-epic of Father-Son relations, and substituting for Milton's Eve the all-too-beautiful Monmouth.

But before we advance to a demonstration of this claim, it is essential to make the point that the battle of the books over style and meter was only the surface layer of a larger struggle for control of the culture. This was the era in which Tory and Whig poets identified themselves by the manner in which they wrote, as well as by the color of the ribbons they wore, the clubs they attended, or the aristocratic patrons they chose. Roughly speaking, the high genres of epic and tragedy were signs of commitment to the Stuart Restoration, whereas satire and parody were the vehicles of the Opposition. This takes us back to Buckingham's *Rehearsal.* In 1974, George McFadden first gave serious attention to the political satire of which that play was the vehicle, claiming that Buckingham's real target was not Dryden, but rather Henry Bennet, Earl of Arlington, who had recently done him an injury;[5] and though McFadden was half-mistaken in that specific claim, he opened our eyes to the possibility that Buckingham's animus was directed at the Restoration government more generally. More recently, N. H. Keeble's essay, "Why Transprose *The Rehearsal,*" reopened the question of why Marvell should, in the two parts of *The Rehearsal Transpros'd,* have appropriated Buckingham's attack on Dryden to a new purpose, the defense of the king's Declaration of Indulgence, announced in March 1672. Keeble's answer, that Buckingham had already established a reputation as an advocate for religious toleration, while undoubtedly true and helpful, diverts our attention from *The Rehearsal* itself and from Dryden's role in it.[6]

I believe that there is more to be known about this matter. How could Buckingham's play be *simultaneously* an attack on Dryden (as their contemporaries quickly accepted as matter of fact) *and* a protest against the way Charles II was running the country? These objectives were more than interwoven in *The Rehearsal*: each entailed the other. The play's performance, and even more its printing, marked the moment when the Restoration war between the theaters took a far more interesting and intellectual turn than mere rivalry between the King's and the Duke's Companies, or the staged exchange of insults between rival playwrights. The turn was to a debate on styles of theater, of performance and representation, to a metacriticism that was, simultaneously, a political battle over what sort of literature, what sort of church, and what sort of state was possible, desirable, or necessary in the 1670s.

The conflation of style and political stance had been the talk of the town in the late 1660s, when Dryden and Waller competed with Opposition satirists for media control over the Second Dutch War; but Dryden himself had recently reignited the issue. When McFadden argued against his role as Buckingham's target, he assumed that it was only Dryden's plays and person, habits of speech and hygiene, that were at issue. He did not consider the role of Dryden's elaborate prefaces and dedications, which combined with the plays themselves to elaborate a political as well as a literary theory. While *The Rehearsal* had been begun in the late 1660s as a spoof on heroic drama generally, and included in its parodic sweep the work of Davenant, Killigrew, Edward Howard, and others, its most immediate provocation and the cause of its updating was Dryden's most recent runaway success, the two-part *Conquest of Granada,* which opened in December 1670. In it, Dryden had not only established himself as the master of the new genre, visually spectacular, emotionally grandiose, and rhetorically overblown. He had also indicated that the role of the poet laureate was going to include the sustained celebration of James, Duke of York, of a bellicose foreign policy, and continuous reminders of just how bad were the bad old days of the Commonwealth.

Set in fifteenth-century Spain, its ostensible topic the reclamation of Granada for the Catholic monarchs Ferdinand and Isabella, the *Conquest* celebrated the obsolete values of personal military heroism and virtuous romantic love. The hypocritical gap between the play and the culture to which it was addressed was remarked upon even by one of its admirers, the wife of John Evelyn, who wrote in a letter to Dr. Bohun: "love is made so pure, and valor so nice, that one would imagine it designed for an / Utopia then our stage. I do not quarrell with the poet, but admire one borne in the / decline of morality should be able to feigne such exact virtue."[7] If this were not target enough for a cynic like Buckingham, Dryden had dedicated the printed text of his play, published in late February 1672, to James, in the same tone of hyperbolic praise for the duke's military achievements that had marked *Annus Mirabilis* in 1667; he had glossed over the naval disasters of the Second Dutch War as he had in that earlier poem, and had, shockingly, indicated that the consequences of Charles's negotiations with Louis XIV would be the Third Dutch War, actually declared in March 1672. As Dryden put it to James in this remarkable dedication, "when our former enemies again provoke us, you will again solicite fate to provide you another Navy to overcome, and another Admiral to be slain. You will, then, lead forth a Nation eager to revenge their past injuries" (11:5). The result will be a bonus for the poet, who in August 1670 had been appointed Historiographer Royal in addition to Poet Laureate: the new war will provide him with "abundant matter to fill the Annals of a glorious Reign," allowing him to "perform the part of a just Historian to my Royal Master" (11:6). Given that Charles had recalled parliament on 4 February 1672, precisely in order to request the funds for the war, the publication of Dryden's dedication in the same month could have been seen as an attempt to influence the parliamentarians to vote the king a war chest. In other words, Dryden had not only preselected James as his hero for the Third Dutch War, about which he was evidently cognizant long before it was declared, but was effectively giving political advice to the nation.

Political advice under the guise of stylistic and generic advice. In the essay, "Of Heroique Playes," that followed the dedication, Dryden created a genealogy for this essentially Restoration genre, by tracing it back to Sir William Davenant and the closing of the theaters during the Commonwealth period. "It being forbidden him in the Rebellious times," wrote Dryden,

> to act Tragedies and Comedies, because they contain'd some matter of Scandal to those good people, who could more easily dispossess their lawful Sovereign than endure a wanton jeast; he was forc'd to turn his thoughts another way: and to introduce the examples of moral vertue, writ in verse, and perform'd in Recitative Musique; (11:9)

that is to say, opera, which was not only a way around the prohibition against theater, but the progenitor of Dryden's operatic style, which is thus presented as inheriting royalist solidarity and resistance techniques, even as it flourishes in the now liberated Restoration culture.

For the second part of the *Conquest,* Dryden inserted another stylistic manifesto in the epilogue, where he cast scorn on the Elizabethan and Jacobean stage as uncultivated in comparison to his own:

> If Love and Honour now are higher rais'd,
> 'Tis not the Poet, but the Age is prais'd.

> Wit's now ariv'd to a more high degree;
> Our native Language more refin'd and free.
> Our Ladies and our men now speak more wit
> In conversation, than those Poets writ.
>
> (21-26)

Immediately challenged for his impudence, Dryden then wrote and published a "Defence of the Epilogue. Or, *An Essay on the* Dramatique Poetry *of the last Age*," in which he explained that the source of this new wit and refinement is, of course, the court and the king:

> His own mis-fortunes and the Nations, afforded him an opportunity, which is rarely allow'd to Sovereign Princes, I mean of travelling, and being conversant in the most polish'd Courts of *Europe:* . . . At his return, he found a Nation lost as much in Barbarism as in Rebellion: and as the excellency of his Nature forgave the one, so the excellency of his manners reform'd the other. . . . Thus, insensibly, our way of living became more free: and the fire of the *English* wit, which was before stifled under a constrain'd melancholy way of breeding, began first to display its force: by mixing the solidity of our Nation, with the air and gayety of our neighbours. (11:216-17)

To translate: Charles has brought back with him from France a powerful medicine, by which the culture became "more free," liberated from the bonds of national seriousness. Unspoken here, though explicit in the dedication to James that preceded both plays in the printed edition, was the knowledge that French influence now pervaded much more than English conversational style; it was contained in the Treaty of Dover of 1670, whereby Charles had agreed with Louis XIV to an alliance that would serve French interests in Europe, in return for massive subsidies that would permit him to bypass parliament when necessary. A secret corollary was Charles's promise to reinstate Roman Catholicism as the English national religion.

We are now in a better position to understand the long genesis of *Absalom and Achitophel,* which would address the disruption in the Duke of York's long wait to become his brother's successor, the political struggle between Whigs and Tories still generally known as the Exclusion Crisis. It should not be forgotten, however, that Dryden *preceded* his masterpiece with another, less ambitious parody, *Mac Flecknoe*. Like Rochester's *Allusion to Horace, Mac Flecknoe* uses literary criticism as a broader cultural critique, which in turn impinges on political values. The poem was written in the summer of 1676, just after Dryden's renunciation of his signature style, and, as Hammond explains, was given a restricted form of scribal publication, mostly in London circles. Dryden's butt is Thomas Shadwell, who had irritated Dryden by attacking heroic tragedy in the Preface to *The Sullen Lovers* and elsewhere, and generally by proclaiming himself the heir to Ben Jonson. Dryden responded by making Shadwell the heir instead to Richard Flecknoe, who had already been identified as the protypical poetaster by Andrew Marvell. Hammond thinks that Marvell could have seen in manuscript Marvell's first attempt at satire: *Fleckno, an English Priest at Rome*;[8] but in fact he need only have heard of its existence, since the title, and Flecknoe's reputation, is all that he borrows. But the Marvell connection remains interesting because of the parody of which there can be no doubt: Dryden's appropriation of the Father-Son relationship in *Paradise Lost*. Looking forward to retirement, Dryden's Flecknoe selects Shadwell as his heir, in language that evokes *specifically* the third book of *Paradise Lost*, when the Son confirms his right to succeed by his sacrificial gesture; but the language *also* evokes the second book of Milton's poem, where Satan "High on a throne of Royal State" (2:1) imitates God in majesty, and Sin, addressing Satan as her father ("Thyself in me thy perfect image viewing") horrifically preempts the redemptive family relationship:

> *Sh*—alone my perfect image bears,
> Mature in dullness from his tender years.
> *Sh*—alone, of all my Sons, is he
> Who stands confirm'd in full stupidity.
> . . . .
> The hoary Prince in Majesty appear'd,
> High on a Throne of his own Labours rear'd.
> At his right hand our young *Ascanius* sate,
> *Rome*'s other hope, and pillar of the State:
> . . . .
> The *Syre* then shook the honours of his head,
> And from his brows damps of oblivion shed
> Full on the filial dullness.[9]

There is no trace of Marvell in this poem, other than the presence of Flecknoe. But it is worth noting that Marvell had probably once more upset Dryden in June of 1676, when he appropriated three lines of Dryden's epilogue to Etherege's *The Man of Mode* to the Whig cause of religious toleration. In *Mr. Smirke, or the Divine in Mode*, Marvell defended Bishop Herbert

Croft, against the scorn of Francis Turner, chaplain to the Duke of York, and made Turner an object of scorn in his turn. In his epilogue to Etherege's play, Dryden had written:

> Yet none Sir *Fopling* him, or him can call;
> He's Knight o' th' Shire, and represents ye all.
> From each he meets, he culls what e're he can,
> Legion's his name, a people in a Man.
>
> (15–18)

Dryden's point was that what Fopling represented was so ubiquitous a form of folly in Restoration London that his local or topical referent could not be established. Marvell's point was that Turner had misunderstood his authority:

> not content with having passed his own Ecclesiastical Censure upon the Author, he forges too in his mind a sentence of the Lords and Commons assembled in Parliament: who, *he believes* and *'tis probable*, would have doom'd the Book to be burnt by the Hang-man. In this he hath medled beyond his Last: . . . But what has he to do . . . with Parliament business? or how can so thin a skull comprehend or divine the results of the Wisdom of the Nation? Unless he can, as in the Epilogue,
>
> > *Legion his name, a People in a Man,*
> > And, instead of Sir Fopling Flutter, he, Mr. Smirke,
> > *Be Knight oth'shire and represent them all.*

It must have embarrassed Dryden in front of the duke, his own patron, to have been made complicit in Turner's humiliation.

From this point onward there are signs that Dryden had Marvell (and Milton) on his mind, or under his skin. Milton was already dead, and by August 1678 Marvell would be so also. But what they had written had still to be defended against, and by that most cunning of military strategies, appropriation. In November 1677 Dryden's poem to Nathaniel Lee on his play, *The Rival Queens, or The Death of Alexander the Great* was published. The poem contains a reference to the Third Dutch War, but concludes with a memory of the Second Dutch War, as rendered an object of satire by one of the notorious *Painter* poems. "Your beauteous Images must be allow'd," wrote Dryden to Lee,

> By all but some vile Poets of the Crowd;
> But how shou'd any Sign-post-dawber know
> The worth of *Titian*, or of *Angelo*?
>
> (49–52

This makes it clear that Dryden remembered the *Second Advice to the Painter*, which advised the realistic poet/painter not to gloss the battle scene with false idealism, but "draw the Battell terribler to show / Then the last judgment was of Angelo" (107–8). He also, apparently, had at least once seen a copy of Marvell's *The last Instructions to the Painter,* where Marvell asks his painter:

> Canst thou paint without Colours? Then 'tis right:
> For so we too without a Fleet can fight.
> Or canst thou dawb a Sign-post, and that ill?
> 'Twill suit our great debauch and little skill.
>
> (5–8)[10]

In a critical culture that now realizes the widespread use of scribal publication during the Restoration, we can allow the possibility of influence and echoes from one text to another when the pre-text has still many years to go before publication.[11] And Dryden would have had very good reasons to acquire a copy of *Last Instructions,* since, as I have argued elsewhere, the poem was in part a riposte to his own performance in *Annus Mirabilis,* whose preface had set out a theory of representation that endorsed, in pictorial terms, the idealization of political events.[12]

In the spring of 1678 Dryden published *All for Love,* dedicated to the Earl of Danby, Charles's chief minister, with a preface attacking the Whig wits, especially Rochester. *All for Love* was his first unrhymed tragedy, and it sent a challenge. "He fights this day unarm'd; without his Rhyme," Dryden wrote in the prologue (1.7), and the epilogue adds: "Nor likes your Wit just as you like his Plays; / He has not yet so much of Mr. *Bays*" (16–17), thereby confronting his earlier humiliation head on. By December 1679, with the furor of the Popish Plot in the background, Dryden was making the politics of the war of the theaters explicit. In his prologue to Nahum Tate's *Loyal General,* he wrote:

> The Plays that take on our Corrupted Stage,
> Methinks resemble the distracted Age;
> Noise, Madness, all unreasonable Things,
> That strike at Sense, as Rebels do at Kings!
> The stile of Forty One our Poets write,
> And you are grown to judge like Forty Eight.
>
> (12–17)

In other words, the theaters are restaging the civil war of the 1640s, and the critics are as cruel as the regicides who condemned Charles I to death.

It might at this point be helpful to pause and review events in the real world. It is striking, for example, to see that Paul Hammond's chronology, preceding his otherwise invaluable edition of Dryden's poetry, gives, with only two exceptions, merely literary events. Those exceptions are the death of Charles II and the invasion of Monmouth, both in 1685. But what happens if we enter here another chronology, one which entwines political and "literary" (or at least published) moments of significance.

1678 January 29: Parliament recalled.
Marvell publishes *An Account of the Growth of Popery and Arbitrary Government*
June 21: *All for Love* advertised (with dedication to Danby) in the *London Gazette*, immediately above L'Estrange's offer of a reward for detection of the author/publisher of the *Account*.
September: Titus Oates gives depositions about Popish Plot
October 17: Sir Edmund Berry Godfrey found murdered
Trials and executions of Catholics
Second Test Act against Catholics.
1679 Monmouth sent into exile in Holland
Third edition of Marvell's *Account* published in folio, over his name, recommended "To the Reading of all English Protestants."
April: Danby sent to the Tower
November 17: Settle's anti-popish pageant
1680 Summer: Monmouth's return and unauthorized progresses
October 15: Mary "Marvell's" dating of Marvell's *Miscellaneous Poems*.
October 21: Parliament recalled
November 11: Exclusion Bill passes Commons, fails to pass the Lords
1681 January 18: Charles dissolves parliament; Narcissus Luttrell dated his copy of Marvell's *Miscellaneous Poems*.
March 21: Oxford Parliament—dissolved on March 28—the last parliament of the reign.
March 24: Shaftesbury passes on to Charles anonymous letter calling for Monmouth's succession to the crown.
April 8. Charles's *Declaration touching the Causes . . . That moved him to dissolve the two last parliaments*.
June: Dryden's *His Majesties Declaration Defended*.
1681 July 1: Fitzharris tried for treason and executed
July 2: Shaftesbury arrested on charge of treason
July ?: Stephen College tried and executed
November: *Absalom and Achitophel*

November 24: Whig jury brings in ignoramus verdict for Shaftesbury
1682 March 16: Dryden's *The Medall.*

Of course there could be many other versions of this time frame that would stress other interactions. That this was a chronology that deeply affected Dryden, however, can be charted by his own reactions. First, as James Winn has remarked, Dryden's dedication of *All for Love* to Danby was not only the most explicitly political writing he had published, it also answers Marvell's conspiratorial version of Restoration history and attacks Shaftesbury and Buckingham, though without naming them.[13] As Winn also observes, though without making the connection to Milton, the metaphors Dryden chooses to promote Danby and denigrate Shaftesbury invoke *Paradise Lost,* the first being miraculously able to bring order out of Chaos ("not only to separate the Jarring Elements, but (if that boldness of expression might be allow'd me) to Create them" [13:4]), the second seducing mankind "into the same Rebellion with him, by telling him he might yet be freer than he was" (13:7). As well as delivering his well-known attack on "that specious Name of a *Republick*" (13:6), Dryden warns the Whig leaders that "they who trouble the Waters first, have seldom the benefit of the Fishing: As they who began the late Rebellion, enjoy'd not the fruit of their undertaking, but were crush'd themselves by the Usurpation of their own Instrument" (13:7). While there was a well-known proverb about fishing in troubled waters, it looks as though Dryden is here alluding also to Marvell's *First Anniversary,* which celebrated in grand metaphors the Cromwellian Instrument of Government of 1654, and ends by presenting Cromwell as "the *Angel* of our Commonweal; / [who] Troubling the Waters, yearly mak'st them Heal" (401–2).

Second, when in June 1681 (just a few months before he produced *Absalom and Achitophel*) Dryden wrote *His Majesties Declaration Defended,* he went so far as to name Marvell as the person who had occupied, for the Whigs, the position he now assumed for the Tories. Fortunately, Marvell was now dead, and the Whigs, Dryden proposes, are scrambling to find a substitute:

> It was generally agreed by the heads of the discontented Party, that this Declaration must be answer'd, and that with all the ingredients of malice which the ablest among them could squeeze into it. Accordingly, upon the first appearance of it in Print, five several Pens of their Cabal were set to work; and the product of each having been

examin'd, a certain person of Quality appears to have carried the majority of Votes, and to be chosen like a new *Matthias,* to succeed in the place of their deceas'd *Judas.* (17:195)

We know that "their deceas'd Judas" is Marvell because later Dryden transfers to the author of the offending *Letter from a Person of Quality* the charge of dullness that Whig and Tory writers had been throwing at each other for the last decade:

After this, why does not some resenting Friend of *Marvel*'s, put up a Petition to the Soveraigns of his party, that his Pension of four hundred pounds *per annum*,[14] may be transferred to some one amongst them, who will not so notoriously betray their cause by dullness and insufficiency? (17:213)

Third—and I am now breaking chronology in order to establish the nature of Dryden's obsession—*The Medall,* which rounds off Dryden's most pugnacious moment, opens with an "Epistle to the Whigs" in which Dryden not only reverts to his metaphor of "Sign-post painting," but links his two great rivals in a league of obliquity. "I have perus'd many of your Papers," Dryden writes (and this is more revealing than perhaps he intended):

and to show you that I have, the third part of your *No-protestant Plot* is much of it stolen, from your dead Authour's Pamphlet call'd, the *Growth of Popery*; as manifestly as *Milton*'s defence of the *English* People, is from *Buchanan, De jure regni apud Scotos.* (2:40)

"Your dead Authour": a most interesting phrase, especially if we now remember that one of the examples of Marvell's authorship that belongs in this context is the sudden appearance of his posthumous *Miscellaneous Poems,* circulating in January 1681, with a strong message on its title page: "by Andrew Marvell, Esq; Late Member of the Honourable House of Commons." Obviously timed to resonate with the debates on Exclusion in the 1680 session, and ironically coinciding with the king's dissolution of parliament in January, Marvell's volume was proof that Whigs could write excellent poetry. Too bad for Dryden that here, once again, was republished Marvell's poem on Milton's *Paradise Lost,* with its stings in the tail on the subject of tinkling rhyme.

There remains the most interesting question as to how many copies of *Miscellaneous Poems* escaped into public hands with the *Horatian Ode* and the *First Anniversary of the Government under O.C.* intact, before those poems and the elegy for Cromwell were cancelled while the volume was still in press. If two such copies survive, there may have been more. The question becomes pertinent again in the light of the fact that Paul Hammond has traced the ghostly presence of the *Horatian Ode* in several phrases in *Absalom and Achitophel*.[15] The most important of these echoes is probably Dryden's defense of the Duke of York's claim to the throne:

> His Brother, though Opprest with Vulgar Spight,
> Yet Dauntless and Secure of Native Right.
>
> (354–55)

This couplet not only echoes, but answers—both metrically and in terms of the turns and counterturns of history—Marvell's description of how Charles I was forced to abandon *his* claim at his execution:

> Nor call'd the Gods with vulgar spight
> To vindicate his helpless Right.
>
> (61–62)

Hammond has argued that Dryden could have seen a copy of the *Horatian Ode* in manuscript when they made contact under the Protectorate; but the timing suggests rather that he might well have been the owner of a not-quite-perfect copy of *Miscellaneous Poems*.[16] But *Absalom and Achitophel* can also be seen as a reply to the most dangerous of Marvell's other poems. When Dryden analyzes the different groups of dissidents in the Restoration state, his third group are those who "thought Kings an useless heavy Load, / Who Cost too much, and did too little Good" (505–6). The allusion is surely to Marvell's *First Anniversary,* where he claims that, in contrast to Cromwell's speed and efficiency, "**heavy** Monarchs make a wide Return, / Longer, and more Malignant then **Saturn**.... Thus (Image-like) an **useless** time they tell ... Nor more contribute to the state of Things, / Then wooden Heads unto the Viols strings" (15, 41–44). And we can better understand Dryden's own appropriation of the rebuilding metaphor so frequent in the revolutionary period if we remember that Marvell had applied it, brilliantly if impresciently, to the Cromwellian Instrument of Government. When Dryden (in his own voice) writes:

> If ancient **Fabricks** nod, and threat to fall,
> To Patch the Flaws, and Buttress up the Wall,

> Thus far 'tis Duty; but here fix the Mark:
> For all beyond it is to touch our Ark.
> To change **Foundations**, cast the **Frame** anew,
> Is work for Rebels who base Ends pursue:
> At once Divine and Humane Laws controul;
> And mend the Parts by ruine of the Whole.
>
> (801–8)

he may even have had in front of him Marvell's over-optimistic metaphor for the revised Cromwellian constitution, with its architectural stresses and strains:

> The Commonwealth then first together came,
> And each one enter'd in the willing **Frame**
> . . . .
> None to be sunk in the **Foundation** bends,
> Each in the House the highest Place contends,
> . . . .
> But the most Equal still sustein the Height,
> And they as **Pillars** keep the Work upright;
> While the resistance of opposed Minds,
> The **Fabrick** as with Arches stronger binds,
> Which on the Basis of a Senate free,
> Knit by the Roofs Protecting **weight** agree.
>
> (75–98)

Indeed, Dryden may also have been answering Marvell directly on the constitutional issue of the respective importance of king and parliament in the English constitution. Where Marvell had asserted that it was the "most Equal," that is, members of the House of Commons, who "as **Pillars** keep the Work upright," and that it was Cromwell as Protector whose weight, pressing downward from the top, locked the whole structure together, Dryden handed over to Charles II the riposte: "Kings are the publick **Pillars** of the State, / Born to sustain and prop the Nations **weight**" (953–54). But it was *The last Instructions to a Painter* (not, of course, included in any copy of *Miscellaneous Poems*) that seems to have given Dryden more than the occasional allusion, however central to his argument. It gave him his inspiration for the structure of *Absalom and Achitophel,* as a set of portraits of good and bad politicians and courtiers. Of the three components of the poem, portraits, speeches and editorial political analysis, it is, as we all know, the major hostile portraits, of Shaftesbury (Achitophel), Buckingham (Zimri), Slingsby Bethel (Shimei), and

Titus Oates (Corah) that make the poem memorable. But how many readers realize that Dryden had been anticipated in this strategy by Marvell's portraits, in the *Instructions*, of those he saw as the villains of the Second Dutch War: of Henry Jermyn, Earl of St. Albans; of Anne Hyde, the first Duchess of York; of Barbara Villiers, Countess of Castlemaine, the king's first *maitresse en titre;* of Henry Turner, Speaker of the House of Commons; and, in the background, the most sinister figure, Clarendon himself, Charles's chief minister? The fact that Dryden's portraits were also broadly, though not specifically, reminiscent of Milton's demonic leaders in Pandemonium, Lucifer, Moloch, Belial, Mammon, and Beelzebub, was also suggested by David's prophecy of division among the Exclusionists: "Their *Belial* with their *Belzebub* will fight" (1016).[17]

We have, thus, in *Absalom and Achitophel,* the fruits of Dryden's bitter retraining in a mode that better fitted his natural talents. The respect that he showed for Milton in the preface to *The State of Innocence* (its title probably an important political pun) now had to give way to head-on collision with Milton's political theory as expressed in *The Tenure of Kings and Magistrates;* but this collision was achieved partly by parody of Milton's Father and Son theology in *Mac Flecknoe,* and partly by appropriating Milton's drama of temptation to the Shaftesbury/Monmouth relationship. If he had ever been friends with Marvell—they had walked together in Cromwell's funeral procession, and their elegies for Cromwell had originally been intended to appear in the same volume—Dryden now saw him as his chief rival in the cultural/political hierarchy. But in order to inoculate his readers against Marvell, he had to sound more like him. Although we have found specific echoes, there was also the fact that Marvell—not always, to be sure—had discovered how extraordinarily neat the pentameter couplet could be, when combined with various kinds of semantic balance. Here are some lines from the *Last Instructions* that anticipate the spring of Dryden's mature satire:

> Gross Bodies, grosser Minds, and grossest Cheats. (179)
> For one had much, the other nought to lose. (226)
> Thick was the Morning, and the *House* was thin,
> The *Speaker* early, when they all fell in. (235–36)
> Had he not built, none of these faults had bin;
> If no Creation, there had been no Sin. (787–88)
> Not so, quoth *Tomkins*; and straight drew his Tongue,
> Trusty as Steel, that always ready hung; (841–42)[18]

> His Fathers Ghost too whisper'd him one Note,
> That who does cut his Purse will cut his Throat. (937–38)

True, the poem has other effective echoes: of Marchamont Needham's *Lachrymae Musarum* (1649), which shows Dryden looking back to civil war satire; and quite surprisingly, of Richard Knolles *Generall Historie of the Turkes* (1621).[19] He also learned from the Tory satirists, particularly those who had previously taken aim at Buckingham.[20] This shows that Dryden went shopping quite far afield for the trenchant line and the memorable phrase. It is also certainly the case that Dryden brought to perfection what Marvell was only on the verge of inventing when he was distracted from verse satire by the challenge of the *Rehearsal Transpros'd*–a fact to which Dryden returned in his portrait of Settle as Doeg in the *Second Part*: "For to write Verse with him is to *Transprose*" (2:75, 1.444).

But something is still missing: a model for that brilliant first opening verse paragraph, the one that must have made every reader of *Absalom and Achitophel* breathe a breath of fresh air when the poem first appeared. There is nothing in *Last Instructions* to match it. But there was, if we give full credit to the culture of scribal publication, another poem subsequently attributed to Marvell, which was evidently circulating during the Popish Plot and Exclusion crises, perhaps with lines added at the end to make it duly topical. This is the simply entitled *An Historicall Poem*, first published in 1689, and included by Legouis among the less firmly attributable satires of Marvell. This is how it begins:

> Of a tall Stature and of sable hue,
> Much like the Son of Kish that lofty Jew,
> Twelve Yeares compleat he suffer'd in Exile
> And kept his Fathers Asses all the while.
> At length by wonderfull impulse of Fate
> The People call him home to helpe the State,
> And what is more they send him Mony too,
> And cloath him all from head to foot anew;
> Nor did he such small favours then disdain
> But in his thirtieth yeare began to Raigne.
> In a slasht doublet then he came to shoare,
> And dubd poore Palmer's wife his Royall Whore.
> (1–12)

Here is the zest, the narrative leap, that Dryden also achieved; and here is the joke. The son of Kish was, of course, not David but

Saul, selected by Samuel to serve the Israelites right for having demanded a king (1 Sam. 8, 9). The sexual bravado of Dryden's opening paragraph can now be seen as acknowledging, but making the biblical best of, the scandal that attends the king's arrival at Dover, his instant acquisition as his premier mistress of Barbara Palmer, soon to be countess of Castlemaine.

Nor did Dryden outgrow his curious infatuation with Marvell, whom he had berated in the Preface to *Religio Laici* as the *second* "Presbyterian Scribler, who sanctify'd Libels and Scurrility to the use of the Good Old Cause," (2:106). And in 1685, when he came to write *Threnodia Augustalis,* a poem as much in praise of the Duke of York as of the just deceased Charles II, Dryden went back to Marvell's Cromwell poems, and wrote his own version of an Horatian ode, with many Marvellian echoes. But that is another story.

Notes

1. *The Works of John Dryden,* ed. H. T. Swedenberg, Jr. et al., 20 vols. (Berkeley and Los Angeles: University of California Press, 1956–); vol. 2, ed. H. T. Swedenberg (1972). Though it offers only a modernized text, Paul Hammond's edition, *The Poems of John Dryden,* 4 vols. (London: Longman, 1995–), in the Longman Annotated series, (hereafter cited as Hammond), has been consulted for its invaluable notes.

2. *On Mr. Milton's Paradise lost,* in *Poems and Letters of Andrew Marvell,* ed. H. M. Margoliouth, rev. Pierre Legouis, 2 vols. (Oxford: Clarendon Press, 1971), 1:139.

3. For another explanation for Dryden's delay in publication, see *Works,* 12:325: "Samuel Simmons, the copyright holder of *Paradise Lost,* may not have allowed Dryden to publish his opera until the epic's second edition (1674) had sold out. One might prefer to suppose that Dryden was willing to wait until Simmons and Milton's family would have had their fair profit of the second edition." Against this high-minded explanation, one might imagine that Dryden's work would have been seen as good advertisement for *Paradise Lost.*

4. *The Works of John Wilmot, Earl of Rochester,* ed. Harold Love (Oxford: Oxford University Press, 1999), 71–74. Dryden retorted in the Preface to *All for Love* (1678), but Love cites J. H. Wilson, "Rochester, Dryden and the Rose-street affair," *Review of English Studies* 15 (1939): 294–301, on the earlier date for the poem's composition.

5. George McFadden, "Political Satire in *The Rehearsal,*" *Yearbook of English Studies* 4 (1974): 120–28.

6. N. H. Keeble, "Why Transprose *The Rehearsal?*" in *Marvell and Liberty,* eds. Warren Chernaik and Martin Dzelzainis (Basingstoke: Macmillan, 1999), 249–68.

7. *Diary and Correspondence of John Evelyn,* eds. William Bray and Henry B. Wheatley (London: Bickers, 1906), 4:56–57.

8. See Hammond, 1:309–10. If Dryden had seen this poem, he would have

learned nothing from it except scorn of Flecknoe, since at that early stage Marvell was attempting to write satire in the crabbed style of Donne.

9. *Works,* 2:54, 57–58, lines 15–18, 106–9, 134–36. Other wicked echoes include an allusion to Milton's Beelzebub as "A Pillar of State," (2:302), and Milton's phrase, "filial obedience," 3:269, which Dryden converts to "filial dullness." Some of these allusions were observed by Michael Wilding, "Allusion and Innuendo in *MacFlecknoe*," *Essays in Criticism* 19 (1969): 355–70.

10. For the *Last Instructions,* see *Poems and Letters* 1:147; for my argument that the *Second* and *Third Advices* were, like the *Last Instructions,* the work of Marvell, see "Lady State's First Two Sittings: Marvell's Satiric Canon," *SEL: Studies in English Literature 1500–1900* 40 (2000): 395–411. Dryden would return to the notion of "signpost painting" in his "Epistle to the Whigs" preceding *The Medall,* a point observed by A. E. Wallace Maurer, *PLL: Papers On Language and Literature* 2 (1966): 298.

11. *Last Instructions* was first published in *The Third Part of the Collection of Poems on Affairs of State, Containing, Esquire Marvel's further Instructions to a Painter* (1689).

12. For the relationship between Dryden's *Annus Mirabilis* and the Painter poems, in which Marvell had the last word, see my *Marvell: The Writer in Public Life* (Harlow, U.K.: Longman, 2000), 89–106.

13. James Winn, *John Dryden and his World* (New Haven: Yale University Press, 1987), 305.

14. There is no evidence that Marvell ever received a pension from the Whig leaders. New evidence has determined that during his last years he was in financial straits.

15. Hammond, 482; and *Notes and Queries* 236 (1988): 172–73.

16. For a more detailed account of the publication of *Miscellaneous Poems,* see my "Miscellaneous Marvell," in *The Political Identity of Andrew Marvell,* ed. Conal Condren and A. D. Cousins (Aldershot, U.K.: Scolar Press, 1990), 188–212. Hammond's suggestions of echoes of *Horatian Ode* in pre-1681 poems by Dryden are not convincing enough to posit that Dryden knew Marvell personally through contact in Thurloe's office.

17. That this was Dryden's intention is confirmed in *The Second Part of Absalom and Achitophel* by the portrait of Ishban, or Sir Robert Clayton, the wealthy London merchant and Whig mayor in 1679–80, of whom we are told that "Mammon has not so engrost him quite, / But *Belial* lays as large a Claim of Spight" (lines 286–87).

18. This couplet may be the origin of Dryden's description of "well hung Balaam," which Hammond glosses as "with large genitals," adding that "the meaning 'fluent of tongue' preferred by some editors is irrelevant here."

19. Hammond, 473, 475.

20. See the extensive parallels adduced by Hammond, 494–95; but note that Dryden also turns back against Shadwell his satire on Killigrew, which gave him his effective closing rhyme: buffoon.

Dryden and Swift

Ian Higgins

THE TERCENTENARY CELEBRATION OF JOHN DRYDEN WOULD NOT have pleased Jonathan Swift. This essay will look at why Swift did not like Dryden.

There is no hard evidence that Dryden ever noticed Swift, whose literary career was just beginning when Dryden died. Swift, however, knew Dryden's work. Echoes of Dryden have been detected throughout Swift's poetry and prose, from his earliest Pindaric odes to the epitaph on his tomb.[1] Swift's familiarity with Dryden's work bred parody and the great repository of hostile Swiftian parodies of Dryden is *A Tale of a Tub To which is added The Battle of the Books and the Mechanical Operation of the Spirit,* published in 1704, four years after Dryden's death. Swift's satiric volume is, in part, a belated reply to Dryden's *The Hind and the Panther* (1687) and to writings by other Roman Catholic partisans such as the polemicist Abraham Woodhead with whom the convert Dryden was closely linked in contemporary Tory satire. Thomas Brown in *The Late Converts Exposed* (1690) depicts Dryden attacking Martin Luther (called 'Little Martin') and being converted from Protestantism by reading Woodhead's *Considerations Concerning the Spirit of Martin Luther, and the Original of the Reformation* (1687).[2] Contemporary pamphlet attacks on Dryden may have prompted Swift to take aim at Woodhead's *Spirit of Martin Luther* in *A Tale of a Tub.* The particular characterization of Martin in *A Tale of a Tub* as meek and moderate is explicable as Swift's polemical response to the treatment of Martin Luther by Woodhead and Dryden and is informed by Francis Atterbury's defence of Martin Luther's spirit of moderation in a paper war of 1687–88.[3] The religious satire of the *Tale* responds to the Roman Catholic–Dissenting alliance of 1687–88 and to James II's policy of prerogative toleration, which Dryden was seen to support.

The *Tale of a Tub* volume is also reactionary satire on what

Swift regarded as contemporary literary decadence. Dryden is pilloried as one of the "Modernist" authors personally responsible for the self-indulgence and decline in the contemporary state of letters. The modernist style with which Dryden is identified is pathologically confessional and digressive. Authorial affectation of politeness is the imposture of a hackney writer. A typical Dryden production is disfigured by the liminal mediations between author, patron, and reader: self-promoting title pages, dedications, prefaces, and introductions. As the putative hack author of the *Tale* puts it in his "Digression in the Modern Kind,"

> *Prefaces, Epistles, Advertisements, Introductions, Prolegomena's, Apparatus's, To-the-Reader's.* This Expedient was admirable at first; Our Great *Dryden* has long carried it as far as it would go, and with incredible Success. He has often said to me in Confidence, that the World would have never suspected him to be so great a Poet, if he had not assured them so frequently in his Prefaces, that it was impossible they could either doubt or forget it.[4]

For the "Preface" in *A Tale of a Tub,* Swift parodies a phrase ("the Precepts of the *Porch*") from Dryden's preliminary "Discourse concerning the Original and Progress of Satire" (1693) and refers to the modernist paraphernalia of paratexts as keeping the "impatient Reader" in "Attendance at the *Porch*."[5] Dryden's prefaces are the dodges of a poet who appears in *A Tale of a Tub* as an effigy of modern hubris.

Swift's satire is directed at both Dryden the author and the critic, appropriating material from contemporary publications attacking Dryden. The cultural standard in Dryden ridicule was "Mr. Bayes" in the Duke of Buckingham's *The Rehearsal*. The character is a satiric original for the hack author of *A Tale of a Tub*. When "Mr. Bayes" in Buckingham's play has "any thing to invent," he explains, "I never trouble my head about it." He consults his "book of *Drama Common places*." Swift's hack author in the *Tale* explains the method of the modern writer: "what tho' his *Head* be empty, provided his *Common-place-Book* be full."[6] In the "Discourse of Satire," Dryden denied he was *The Rehearsal's* "*Bays*" and he rounded on his lampooners: "let me be thought by Posterity, what those Authors wou'd be thought, if any Memory of them, or of their Writings cou'd endure so long, as to another Age" (*Works,* 4:9). Dryden's sentence on the ephemerality of his enemies seems to echo phrases from the Authorized Version of the Bible, for example from Psalms 9:6: "their memorial is perished with them," or Psalms 109:13: "Let his posterity be cut off ... let their name be blotted out," or Ecclesiastes 9:5: "the memory of them is forgotten," or Deuteronomy 32:26: "the remembrance of them to cease from among men." Swift sought to expose Dryden as profane. In the "Dedication to Prince Posterity" in the *Tale*, the hack author cannot find the writings of his contemporaries: "I enquired after them among Readers and Booksellers, but I enquired in vain, the *Memorial of them was lost among Men, their Place was no more to be found*" (*Tale*, 34–35). Swift's parody of Dryden, however, was itself accused of profanity, as Swift complains in the "Apology" for the *Tale* (*Tale*, 7, 18). In attempting to expose Dryden, Swift had only exposed himself to censure.

The ridicule of Dryden in contemporary pamphlet attacks on *The Hind and the Panther* is incorporated into the texture of Swift's satire. Thomas Brown's *The Late Converts Exposed*, for example, had mocked Dryden's use of the quotation from Virgil in the epigraph on the title page of *The Hind and the Panther* (*"Antiquam exquirite matrem"* [Seek your ancient mother]), portraying the convert as an obsessed genealogist. Here is Brown's *"Bays"* on a passage from *"Troilus* and *Cressid"*: "Pray Gentlemen did you ever hear of a certain Noble *Grecian* call'd *Ajax*? ... Now this *Ajax*, you must know, was *Hector*'s Cousin-german, and I'le acquaint you how the Kindred came in. *Hesione, Priam*'s Aunt, no I mistake I gad, *Hesione, Priam*'s Sister." *"Bays"* is interrupted and entreated to set aside the genealogy. He then tells the story "without the Pedigree and all that" of how Hector was unwilling to strike at the kinsman Ajax. *"Bays"* the genealogist is sure he does not have "any Protestant Blood." Later in the dialogue he congratulates himself on his "stock of patience" to hear out a "tedious harangue ... full as troublesome as an *Irish* Genealogy." *"Bays"* compares the trouble of reckoning up the sects and subdivisions of the Protestant religion to running the gauntlet "through a Genealogy Chapter in the *Chronicles*." Swift is reanimating contemporary caricature when Dryden seeks out his ancient relation Virgil in *The Battle of the Books*: "*Dryden* in a long Harangue soothed up the good *Antient*, called him *Father*, and by a large deduction of Genealogies, made it plainly appear, that they were nearly related."[7] Matthew Prior's and Charles Montague's parody *The Hind and the Panther Transvers'd to the Story of The Country Mouse and the City-Mouse* (1687) has Dryden praising *Reynard the Fox* as the source for the name of the Wolf (*"Isgrim"*) in *The Hind and the Panther*: "there is as good *Morality*, and as sound *Precepts*, in the *delectable History of Rey-*

nard the Fox, as in any Book I know, except *Seneca.*" In *A Tale of a Tub,* the hack author declares "the History of *Reynard* the *Fox*" "to be a compleat Body of Civil Knowledge, and the *Revelation,* or rather the *Apocalyps* of all State-*Arcana.*" It heads a list of over-hyped Grub-Street productions including chapbooks and *The Hind and the Panther.*[8]

Swift's satire targets Dryden's presumption as a critic. The "Discourse Concerning . . . Satire," for example, is refunctioned in *A Tale of a Tub* as the model for hackney production. Swift's volume mimics Dryden's example. Both works have a dedication to a Williamite grandee. Alluding to the story in Herodotus 8.123–24 of Themistocles being awarded first place after receiving everyone's vote for second place, Dryden in his dedication to the Earl of Dorset says that all English writers give the first place to Dorset: "The most Vain, and the most Ambitious of our Age have not dar'd to assume so much, as the Competitours of *Themistocles:* They have yielded the first place, without dispute; and have been arrogantly content, to be esteem'd as second to your Lordship" (*Works,* 4:5). Swift's "Bookseller's Dedication to Lord Somers" says everybody allows second place to Somers while claiming first place for themselves (*Tale,* 24). There is in both works an appeal to posterity, authorial disavowal of satire, complaint about prefaces and digressions in the midst of a digression, and complaint about the multitude of scribblers who pester the world. In short, the *Tale* displays Swift's unfriendly reading of one of Dryden's major critical texts.

Swift and Dryden were related. They were second cousins, once removed. (Swift's paternal grandfather, Thomas Swift, had married Elizabeth Dryden, the daughter of Nicholas Dryden. A brother of Swift's great-grandfather Nicholas Dryden was John Dryden's grandfather.)[9] Swift almost brings himself to acknowledge this familial relation when he deals with his family skeletons in his autobiographical fragment "Family of Swift."[10] Swift mentions his second cousin once removed, in a parenthesis, in an aside about an uncle who has an odd first name. This uncle, "Dryden Swift," was given Swift's paternal grandmother's maiden name: "Mr Dryden Swift (called so after the name of his mother, who was a near relation to Mr Dryden the Poet)" (*Prose Writings,* 5:191). Quarantined within a parenthesis, this is the only reference in the autobiography to his famous cousin.[11] Elsewhere, however, Swift called Dryden his (rather than his grandmother's) "near relation." The well-known instance is in a letter to Thomas

Beach of 12 April 1735 describing Dryden's corrupt poetic practice. The reference to his second cousin once removed as a "near relation" seems calculated to enhance, in this literary-critical letter, the sense of Swift's objectivity in matters of literary criticism. Beach must expect a candid account of his own poem, which he has submitted to Swift for comment. After all, Swift has not let even his relation to Dryden affect his critical judgment of that poet. Swift wrote to Thomas Beach:

> I read your poem several times, and showed it to three or four judicious friends, who all approved it, but agreed with me, that it wanted some corrections; upon which I took a number of lines, which are in all two hundred and ninety-nine, the odd number being occasioned by what they call a triplet, which was a vicious way of rhyming, wherewith Dryden abounded, and was imitated by all the bad versifiers in Charles the Second's reign. Dryden, though my near relation, is one I have often blamed as well as pitied. He was poor, and in great haste to finish his plays, because by them he chiefly supported his family, and this made him so very uncorrect; he likewise brought-in the Alexandrine verse at the end of his triplets. I was so angry at these corruptions, that about twenty-four years ago I banished them all by one triplet, with the Alexandrine, upon a very ridiculous subject.[12]

In an explanatory note to the triplet at the end of *A Description of a City Shower,* the poem to which he refers, Swift announces that Dryden's innovation has been abolished from the canon of English poetry: "These triplets . . . were brought in by Dryden, and other poets in the reign of Charles II. They were the mere effect of haste, idleness, and want of money; and have been wholly avoided by the best poets, since these verses were written."[13] Not "wholly avoided," however. Swift used triplets and continued to do so even after he had abolished them. They can be found in at least fifteen of his poems and he uses them for the kind of emphatic effect Dryden achieves with them.

To digress for a moment. Swift's denigration of Dryden's triplets extended to Dryden's parentheses. The rhetorical use of round brackets was a favorite device of Swift's for satiric intensification. Dryden often uses parentheses in conjunction with his triplets. John Lennard's wonderful book on parentheses in English printed verse, which includes a photograph of a natural parenthesis (the crescent moon), has illustrated just how brilliant Dryden could be with the figure. As Lennard shows, in *The Hind and the Panther* (which Swift had other reasons to hate) the heroic couplets swell into triplets, this swelling is sometimes marked by round brackets as well as by the conventional curly brackets or braces. Dryden uses round brackets to keep his triplets within bounds, to mark the closure of a triplet or to encase the following couplet.[14] He achieves visual puns on the page. In part 1 of *The Hind and the Panther* the Anglican church is reminded of its past loyalty to the crown:

> Nor will I meanly tax her constancy,
> That int'rest or obligement made the tye,
> (Bound to the fate of murdr'd Monarchy:)
> (Before the sounding Ax so falls the Vine,
> Whose tender branches round the Poplar twine.)
>
> (436–40)

Round brackets bind the line: "(Bound to the fate of murdr'd Monarchy:)" and tie it to its triplet. Round brackets wrap around the lines about the vine twining round the poplar.[15] In part 3 of *The Hind and the Panther,* James II requires the persecuting Anglican church's submission to the sovereign will in religious matters. The king's supremacy is pointed by a parenthesis; the tolerationist policy epitomized in a triplet:

> The *Lyon,* studious of our common good,
> Desires, (and Kings desires are ill withstood,)
> To join our Nations in a lasting love;
> The barrs betwixt are easie to remove,
> For sanguinary laws were never made above.
>
> (675–79)

Swift hated the tolerationist policy and its triplet-ridden poem advancing arbitrary power in parenthesis. In the letter to Beach of 1735, Swift commented on James II and may even distantly recall Dryden's phrase ("Kings desires") for James's prerogative toleration. Correcting Beach's description of James II as a tyrant, Swift wrote that James II "was a weak bigoted Papist, desirous like all Kings of absolute power, but not properly a tyrant" (*Correspondence,* 4:321). For Swift in 1735, it was the Hanoverian monarchs who were tyrants (*Correspondence,* 4:336–37, 381). In a poem of 1733 Swift parodies Dryden's parentheses. They are to be disregarded as superfluous filling like his bloated prefaces:

> Read all the prefaces of Dryden,
> For these our critics much confide in,

> (Though merely writ at first for filling
> To raise the volume's price, a shilling.)
> (*On Poetry: A Rhapsody*, 267–70;
> *Poems*, 529)

Whereas Dryden is at pains to bind his triplets, Swift's satiric triplets suggest overflow, the content straining at the braces. In an early unfinished poem entitled "On the Burning of Whitehall in 1698" (*Poems*, 80–81), Swift gives a satiric history of English courts. When he gets to Charles II's reign the heroic couplets suddenly engorge into a triplet:

> When sauntering Charles returned, a fulsome crew
> Of parasites, buffoons, he with him drew;
> Nay worse than these fill the polluted hall,
> Bawds, pimps and pandars the detested squall
> Of riots, fancied rapes, the devil and all.
> (17–21)

The poem's only other triplet deals with William III's court. Heroic couplets cannot contain the seething corruption at that court:

> Projectors, peculates the palace hold,
> Patriots exchanging liberty for gold,
> Monsters unknown to this blessed land of old.
> (36–38)

The well-known triplet trashing Dryden at the end of *A Description of a City Shower* achieves brilliant mimetic effect, suggesting overflowing gutters and flooded sewer:

> Sweepings from butchers' stalls, dung, guts, and blood,
> Drowned puppies, stinking sprats, all drenched in mud,
> Dead cats and turnip-tops come tumbling down the flood.
> (*Poems*, 114)

The final alexandrine, as Irvin Ehrenpreis and others have noted, echoes one from Dryden's translation of the *Georgics* (1.418): "And cakes of rustling Ice come rolling down the Flood" (*Works*, 5:169). Swift's mock-georgic, urban pastoral poem as a whole has been shown to echo lines from Dryden's translations of Virgil's *Georgics* and *Aeneid*.[16] The rural prospects and agricultural produce in Dryden's translation of the *Georgics* are past their use-by date in Swift's poem.

To return from this digression to Swift's relations. What Swift valorizes in his family background, I think, explains the withering contempt with which Swift treats Dryden, especially Dryden's claim to be a sufferer for loyalty and religion. In the "Discourse Concerning . . . Satire," Dryden writes that he was "encourag'd only with fair Words, by King *Charles* II, my little Sallary ill paid, and no prospect of a future Subsistance . . . since this Revolution . . . I have patiently suffer'd the Ruin of my small Fortune, and the loss of that poor Subsistance which I had from two Kings, whom I had serv'd more Faithfully than Profitably to my self." Later in the "Discourse" he says "I have . . . suffer'd in silence, and possess'd my Soul in quiet" (*Works,* 4:23, 59–60). In the "Dedication of the Pastorals" (1697), Dryden writes: "What I now offer to your Lordship, is the wretched remainder of a sickly Age, worn out with Study, and oppress'd by Fortune: without other support than the Constancy and Patience of a Christian" (*Works,* 5:3). Swift's satiric parody of this in the "Introduction" of *A Tale of a Tub* is explicitly explained in the "Apology": Dryden and others *"who having spent their Lives in Faction, and Apostacies, and all manner of Vice, pretended to be Sufferers for Loyalty and Religion. So* Dryden *tells us in one of his Prefaces of his Merits and Suffering, thanks God that he* possesses his Soul in Patience: *In other Places he talks at the same Rate"* (*Tale,* 7, 70).

In Swift's account of his family the honorific "sufferer for loyalty and religion" applies to his paternal grandfather, Thomas Swift, a royalist vicar whom Swift venerated "for his extraordinary Services and zeal, and persecutions in the royal cause" and commemorated with a monument (*Prose Writings,* 5:190; 334).[17] Here was a genuine sufferer for the House of Stuart and true religion (embodied, for Swift, in the Laudian Church of England). Swift writes in "Family of Swift": "This Thomas was much distinguished by his courage, as well as his loyalty to K. Charles the Ist, and the Sufferings he underwent for that Prince, more than any person of his condition in England." Swift instances "what he acted, and what hardships he underwent for the Person and cause of that blessed Martyred Prince" (*Prose Writings,* 5:188–89). Swift identified with his grandfather's cause. In "A Sermon upon the Martyrdom of K. Charles I," Swift describes Charles I as "that excellent King and blessed Martyr . . . who rather chose to die on a scaffold than betray the religion and liberties of his people" (*Prose Writings,* 9:219). Swift's famous declaration of his own commitment to liberty in *Verses on the Death of Dr Swift,*

D. S. P. D. ("Fair LIBERTY was all his cry; / For her he stood prepared to die") echoes a passage in John Denham's royalist poem *Coopers Hill* alluding to the trial and martyrdom of Charles I ("Fair liberty pursu'd, and meant a Prey / To lawless power, here turn'd, and stood at bay").[18] Dryden complains about not profiting from his loyalty. Swift celebrates his grandfather who in wartime gave all the gold he had to his king. The hack author of *A Tale of a Tub,* explicitly modeled on Dryden, was in "the Service of six and thirty Factions" (*Tale,* 70). Swift's loyal grandfather "was plundred by the round-heads six and thirty times." Swift narrates how his grandfather "engaged his small estate, and gatherd all the money he could get, quilted it in his waistcoat, got off to a town held for the King." When asked by the town's royalist governor "what he could do for his Majesty," Thomas Swift "said he would give the King his Coat." He also gave his waistcoat with three hundred broad pieces of gold in the lining (*Prose Writings,* 5:189). Whereas Swift's loyal grandfather suffered for King Charles, his cousin Dryden wrote a poem for Cromwell: "Heroique Stanza's, Consecrated to the Glorious Memory of his most Serene and Renowned Highnesse Oliver Late Lord Protector of this Common-Wealth." "Renowned" would become a Swiftian epithet for Dryden. Dryden wrote "Heroique Stanzas"; Thomas Swift performed heroics against the usurper. Swift reports with relish how his grandfather single-handedly managed to kill two hundred rebel cavalry with iron spikes. Deprived under the parliament, the Cavalier vicar's preferments "were given to a fanatical Saint, who scrupled not however to conform upon the Restoration, and lived many years, I think till after the Revolution." Unlike Dryden, Thomas Swift and his family got nothing at all from Charles II: "Mr Swifts merit dyed with himself" two years before the Restoration (*Prose Writings,* 5:188–90).

The satiric depiction of Dryden in Swift's *The Battle of the Books* evokes Civil War history. Though a "private Trooper," Dryden pretends to the chief Command of the Horse of the Rebel Modern army against the Ancients. Dryden and the republican poet George Wither who had fought for the parliament are paired (*Tale,* 226, 235).[19] In the *Battle,* Dryden's advance toward Virgil, an Ancient cavalier, is marked by the "loud Clashing of his Armor." Virgil does not recognize him. The Modern stranger obscured by his heavy armor of "rusty Iron" wishes to parley with the Ancient cavalier:

> lifting up the Vizard of his Helmet, a Face hardly appeared from within, which after a pause, was known for that of the renowned *Dry-*

den ... the Helmet was nine times too large for the Head, which appeared Situate far in the hinder Part, even like the Lady in a Lobster. (*Tale*, 246-47)

Dryden's pretension to be the English Virgil is being punctured, but Dryden, as Hermann Real has noticed, is imaged as a member of a famous (and hard-core republican) regiment of horse in Cromwell's New Model Army—one of Arthur Haselrig's Lobsters.[20] In his *History of the Rebellion,* Clarendon described Haselrig's regiment of horse: the men "were so prodigiously armed that they were called by the other side *the regiment of lobsters,* because of their bright iron shells with which they were covered."[21] There are other literary and epic analogues for this description of Dryden,[22] but Dryden is certainly being discredited as a Cromwellian. The author who charged the Anglican clergy with rebellion in a notorious parenthesis in the "Dedication of the Æneis" (*Works*, 5:278) is pilloried as ridiculous and a rebel. Swift did not keep a copy of Dryden's *Virgil* in his library, but he did keep an annotated school edition of Virgil that had belonged to his royalist grandfather.[23]

In *A Tale of a Tub*, Dryden is recognized as a celebrity, but the future for his *Virgil* is insecure:

> There is now actually in being, a certain Poet called *John Dryden,* whose Translation of *Virgil* was lately printed in a large Folio, well bound, and if diligent search were made, for ought I know, is yet to be seen. (*Tale*, 36)

The folio first edition of Dryden's *Virgil,* the editors of the California *Dryden* explain: "was sold unbound, and constituted a sort of kit complete with assembly instructions, a set of *Directions to the Binders how to place the Several Parts of this Book.*"[24] *A Tale of a Tub* is presumed unbound by its putative author. It is presented in sections, but the hack author leaves the reader free to assemble the text without instructions. At the end of section 7, "A Digression in Praise of Digressions," Swift's hack author informs readers:

> I have chosen for [this Digression] as proper a Place as I could readily find. If the judicious Reader can assign a fitter, I do here empower him to remove it into any other Corner he pleases. (*Tale*, 149)

Swift's parody of Dryden unbound has anticipated modern British experimental fiction. B. S. Johnson's famous "book in a box,"

The Unfortunates, published in 1969, presented its twenty-seven sections unbound with the following direction: "If readers prefer not to accept the random order in which they receive the novel, then they may re-arrange the sections into any other random order before reading."[25]

Swift's hostile parodies of Dryden might be seen as so many instalments in a project to decanonize the "Great Dryden." The anticlerical Whig and critic, John Dennis, wrote in 1715 of a *"Conspiracy against the Reputation of Mr.* Dryden." The publisher Jacob Tonson was aware of "the Attempt to lessen the Reputation of Mr. *Dryden."* The current attempt, incredibly, according to Dennis, seemed to be proposing Alexander Pope as Great Dryden's canonical replacement. For Dennis this was an appalling instance of how High Church Jacobitism can pervert even one's literary judgment. "Good God!" wrote Dennis, "was there ever any Nation in which (I will not say a false Taste, for we never had a true one, but in which) a wrong Sense and a fatal Delusion so generally prevail'd!" Too many now prefer

> "Fury and Madness to Moderation, . . . Slavery to Liberty, Idolatry to Religion, the Duke of *O*[*rmond*] to the D[uke] of *M*[*arlborough*], the empty Pretender to the Royal *George* our only rightful King, and the little Mr. *Pope* to the illustrious Mr. *Dryden*."[26]

It was the case that some prominent High Church extremists were involved in the denigration of Dryden. Luke Milbourne was one. His Thirtieth of January sermons collected in *The Royal Martyr Lamented* preach passive obedience and absolute nonresistance to lawful kings and approve the assassination of usurping tyrants.[27] His literary-critical production of 1698, *Notes on Dryden's Virgil,* attacks Dryden for republicanism, anticlericalism, and for associating the Anglican clergy with rebellion against Stuart monarchy. Milbourne answers Dryden with the familiar High Church imputation that it was the Papists and Dissenters who agreed in rebellious political principle.[28] Another prominent Dryden critic was the Jacobite cleric and pamphleteer Jeremy Collier. This future nonjuring bishop had been deprived in 1690, arrested in 1689 and 1692, and outlawed for publicly absolving Sir William Parkyns and Sir John Friend who had been condemned for their part in the Jacobite assassination plot against King William III. Collier anathematizes Dryden in his *A Short View of the Immorality, and Profaneness of the English Stage* (1698). Swift's *A Project for the Advancement of Religion, and the Reformation of Manners* (1709) shows that he shared Collier's assessment of the corruptions of the stage (*Prose Writings,* 2:56). Collier admired the "*Lacedemonians,* who were remarkable for the Wisdom of their *Laws,* the Sobriety of their *Manners,* and their Breeding of brave Men. This *Government* would not endure the *Stage* in any Form, nor under any Regulation."[29] Ancient Sparta is one of the models for the utopia of the Houyhnhnms in part 4 of *Gulliver's Travels* and Houyhnhnm poetry resembles Spartan poetry.[30] There is no mention of plays or the stage in Houyhnhnmland.

For Swift, libertine Restoration comedy was the stuff of nightmare. In his "Holyhead Journal, 1727" Swift records a dream he had that ended with the libertine Lord Bolingbroke in Swift's pulpit preaching a sermon: "I did not like his quoting Mr. Wycherly by name, and his Plays" (*Prose Writings,* 5:205–6). After this, Swift woke. Swift anticipated Collier's attack on the stage, though he idiosyncratically joined in the contemporary promotion of his friend William Congreve as Dryden's successor.[31] In his poem, "To Mr. Congreve," written in late 1693, Swift refers to Dryden by his caricature nickname as "Mr. Bays" and looks to Congreve to "reform the stage" with his "poetic mine" of "cleaner ore." Stealing a coinage trope current in Dryden's recently-published "Discourse Concerning . . . Satire," Swift says he can tell Congreve's bullion from all the "counterfeit," "base coin," "current like copper" (*Poems,* 67–73; *Works,* 4:10). Swift expressed a desire to have this poem printed with Congreve's next play. In fact, it was Dryden's poem "To my Dear Friend Mr. Congreve" that was published with *The Double Dealer* in 1694. Congreve, of course, sided with Dryden. He too had been attacked by Collier and would publish a refutation of Collier's view of the stage.[32]

Swift's *A Tale of a Tub* is surely the supreme literary example of a High Church assault on Dryden, the animus fueled by Swift's family memory. For the High Churchman, *The Hind and the Panther* was Dryden's unforgivable work: a cultural artifact of the Catholic-Dissenting alliance and poetic declaration for liberty of conscience. Dryden's "To the Reader" welcomes James II's gracious "Declaration for Liberty of Conscience" (*Works,* 3:121, 119). The poem proper pays moving tribute to Pope Innocent XI's and to the king's relief of Protestants. James II's coreligionists and the Dissenters are now protected from the persecuting Anglican parliament:

> the Sheep and harmless Hind
> Were never of the persecuting kind.
> Such pity now the pious Pastor shows,
> Such mercy from the *British Lyon* flows,
> That both provide protection for their foes.
> (part 1, lines 286–90)

"Liberty of conscience, under the present acceptation," wrote Swift in one of his "Thoughts on Religion," "produces revolutions, or at least convulsions and disturbances in a state" (*Prose Writings*, 9:263). *A Tale of a Tub* presents the events of 1687–89 as a design by Catholic Peter and Dissenter Jack to dispossess Anglican Martin, with the unhappy result that James II's toleration is perpetuated under William III. Jack is still at large and in fashion in Court and City (*Tale*, 204–5).

The Hind and the Panther is explicitly ridiculed in the *Tale*. It is listed as a chapbook. Celebrated by the *Tale*'s hack author as the mystical "Master-piece of a famous Writer now living," the poem is the epitome of Roman Catholic dunces: "intended for a compleat Abstract of sixteen thousand Schoolmen from *Scotus* to *Bellarmin*." The sequel to *The Hind and the Panther* is a popular love ballad about fair Rosamond and Tommy Pots: "TOMMY POTTS. Another Piece supposed by the same Hand, by way of Supplement to the former" (*Tale*, 69). The jeering satire recalls that Dryden had written an epilogue in 1692 to a stage version of the fair Rosamond legend.[33] Swift's satire rewrites Dryden's formulation of central Roman Catholic claims in *The Hind and the Panther*. For example, in Dryden's poem the undivided Catholic Church alone defeats heresy:

> Thus she, and none but she, th' insulting rage
> Of Hereticks oppos'd from age to age:
> Still when the Gyant-brood invades her throne
> She stoops from heav'n, and meets 'em half way down,
> And with paternal thunder vindicates her crown.
> (part 2, lines 533–537)

In Swift's version the future Protestant brothers are smiting heretics too: the *Tale*'s three brothers "travelled thro' several Countries, encountred a reasonable Quantity of Gyants, and slew certain Dragons" (*Tale*, 74). In *The Hind and the Panther* the "dying Saviour's" "will" is only rightly interpreted by the Roman Catholic Hind (*Works*, 3:150; part 2, lines 376–77).[34] In the *Tale*, Roman Catholic Peter is a modern literary critic performing self-serving confidence tricks on his brothers in his interpretations of the "Will." Peter sometimes seems to recall the ridiculous Dryden of contemporary satire. For instance, pontifical Peter in section 2 of the *Tale* and "Mr. *Bays*" in Thomas Brown's *The Reasons of Mr. Bays Changing his Religion* both prevail on the subject of "Shoulder-knots."[35]

A Tale of a Tub was well received by the High Churchmen Francis Atterbury and Francis Gastrell. Gastrell was probably the "polite" author whose approval Swift is pleased to cite in the first paragraph of the "Apology" later affixed to *A Tale of a Tub* (*Tale*, 3). Swift later became friendly with both men. In the Ancients and Moderns controversy, and importantly, in an earlier campaign against the partisans of Rome in 1687–88, the literary and religious satire of the *Tale* aligns itself with the Oxford High Church party. *The Hind and the Panther* and Abraham Woodhead's *Considerations Concerning the Spirit of Martin Luther*, posthumously published in Oxford in 1687 under license from James II, represented the Reformer as violent, profane, and wanton. Martin Luther is represented as destitute in the virtues of the Holy Spirit such as temperance and meekness, and is identified with the Islamic Antichrist. Dryden's "jolly *Luther*" interprets Scripture by the Koran (*Works,* 3:134; part 1, lines 380–81). The impiety of the slandering Anglican Panther in Dryden's poem derives from Luther:

> The patience of the *Hind* did almost fail,
> For well she mark'd the malice of the tale:
> Which Ribbald art their church to *Luther* owes,
> In malice it began, by malice grows
>   (*Works,* 3:180; part 3, lines 639–42)

Atterbury's *An Answer to Some Considerations on the Spirit of Martin Luther* (1687) represented Luther as meek, mild, and moderate, proceeding calmly in the work of reformation in his "mild Scholastic way." If there is a "*Flaw*" in the body of Luther's doctrine, the Reformer's "*Crowd of Virtues*" needs also to be recognized. Atterbury's apologia for Luther against Woodhead glances at *The Hind and the Panther* as the companion poem to Woodhead's *Considerations*. In my view, this particular polemical controversy influenced the characterization of Martin in the *Tale*. Martin, indeed, is so pious that he would deliver a soporific "admirable Lecture of Morality." Swift's grave, patient, and unexceptional moderate alludes to Atterbury's Anglican answer and is, indeed, a droll revival of a High Church hit from a paper war involving Dryden.[36]

Of course, since the eighteenth century it has been supposed that Swift nursed a personal grudge against Dryden. The hearsay story is perhaps too good to be true, but it is well known and needs to be noted here. Maurice Johnson pointed out that the account of a personal grudge seems to have first appeared in print in Theophilus Cibber's *Lives of the Poets of Great Britain and Ireland* (1753), half a century after Dryden's death and eight years after Swift's. The story's source is anonymous but Cibber says it is "authentic information":

> When Swift was a young man, and not so well acquainted with the world as he afterwards became, he wrote some Pindaric Odes . . . As Mr. Dryden was Swift's kinsman, these odes were shewn to him for his approbation, who said to him with an unreserved freedom, and in the candour of a friend, "Cousin Swift, turn your thoughts some other way, for nature has never formed you for a Pindaric poet."[37]

Samuel Johnson's aesthetically pleasing version is more famous and more humiliating for Swift:

> I have been told that Dryden, having perused these verses, said, "Cousin Swift, you will never be a poet"; and that this denunciation was the motive of Swift's perpetual malevolence to Dryden.

Although Johnson recognized Dryden's "Malevolence to the clergy," he chose to explain Swift's "malevolence" to Dryden as personal not ideological in motivation.[38]

But Dryden's animus against priests (a line from *Absalom and Achitophel*: "For Priests of all Religions are the same" was one of Collier's exhibits) does explain why a Jacobite such as Dryden could be defended by John Dennis, an anticlerical Whig, and attacked by Jeremy Collier, a Jacobite cleric. Dryden's anticlericalism, Roman Catholic conversion and partisanship, and support for liberty of conscience by edict undoubtedly provoked Swift as a High Church priest. The apostate cousin's pretension to be a sufferer for loyalty and religion affronted Swift's family memory of clerical suffering for true religion and Stuart loyalty. Dryden's Jacobitism was not the reason, as is sometimes supposed, for Swift's dislike of him. Indeed, in private, Swift could express Jacobite views. Swift, for example, regarded William III as a usurper and, like Dryden, praised Viscount Dundee, the Jacobite resistance hero (*Prose Writings*, 5:288–90). Rather, Dryden's apparent Erastianism in supporting rulers (whether Cromwell or James II) against the rights, powers, and privileges of the Church of England was probably the crime, sufficient in Swift's eyes, to have "Dryden the Poet" placed in a parenthesis.

NOTES

1. On Swift and Dryden, see Maurice Johnson, "A Literary Chestnut: Dryden's 'Cousin Swift,'" *PMLA* 67 (1952): 1024–34; John R. Moore and Maurice Johnson, "Dryden's 'Cousin Swift,'" *PMLA* 68 (1953): 1232–40; David Novarr, "Swift's Relation with Dryden, and Gulliver's *Annus Mirabilis*," *English Studies* 47 (1966): 341–54; J. V. Luce, "A Note on the Composition of Swift's Epitaph," *Hermathena* 104 (1967): 78–81.

2. [Thomas Brown], *The Late Converts Exposed: or the Reasons of Mr. Bays's Changing his Religion. Considered in a Dialogue. Part the Second* (London, 1690; reprinted in *Mr. Bays and his Religion, 1688–1690,* [New York: Garland, 1974]), 8, 28–29; Anne Barbeau Gardiner, "Islam as Antichrist in the Writings of Abraham Woodhead, Spokesman for Restoration Catholics," *Restoration* 15 (Fall 1991): 91.

3. [Abraham Woodhead], *Two Discourses. The First, Concerning the Spirit of Martin Luther, and the Original of the Reformation. The Second, Concerning the Celibacy of the Clergy* (Oxford, 1687); [Francis Atterbury], *An Answer to Some Considerations on the Spirit of Martin Luther and the Original of the Reformation; Lately Printed at Oxford* (Oxford, 1687).

4. Jonathan Swift, *A Tale of a Tub To which is added The Battle of the Books and the Mechanical Operation of the Spirit,* ed. A. C. Guthkelch and D. Nichol Smith, 2d ed. (Oxford: Clarendon Press, 1958), 131 (hereafter *Tale*).

5. *The Works of John Dryden,* ed. H. T. Swedenberg, Jr. et al., 20 vols. (Berkeley and Los Angeles: University of California Press, 1956–), 4:81; *Tale,* 54. On "paratexts," see Gérard Genette, *Paratexts: Thresholds of Interpretation,* trans. Jane E. Lewin (Cambridge: Cambridge University Press, 1997).

6. George Villiers, Duke of Buckingham, *The Rehearsal,* ed. D. E. L. Crane (Durham: University of Durham, 1976), 5–6; act I, scene 1, lines 129–31, 84–85; *Tale,* 148, 209. See Hugh Ormsby-Lennon, "Commonplace Swift," in *Reading Swift: Papers from The Third Münster Symposium on Jonathan Swift,* ed. Hermann J. Real and Helgard Stöver-Leidig (München: Wilhelm Fink, 1998), 37.

7. *The Late Converts Exposed,* 2–4, 17, 22; *Tale,* 247.

8. *Dryden: The Critical Heritage,* ed. James Kinsley and Helen Kinsley (London: Routledge & Kegan Paul, 1971), 171–72. The allusion is to *The Hind and the Panther,* part 1, line 449, (*Works,* 3:136); *Tale,* 67–69.

9. Irvin Ehrenpreis, *Swift: The Man, His Works and the Age,* 3 vols. (London: Methuen, 1962–83), 1:3–7 and Appendices A–C, 267–74; James Anderson Winn, *John Dryden and His World* (New Haven: Yale University Press, 1987), "Dryden Genealogy," insert between pages 12 and 13.

10. *The Prose Writings of Jonathan Swift,* ed. Herbert Davis and others, 16 vols. (Oxford: Basil Blackwell, 1939–74), 5:187–95.

11. *"Bays"* refers to "the Parenthesis of my Life" in Thomas Brown's *The*

Reasons of Mr. Bays Changing his Religion, (London, 1688; reprint in *Mr. Bays and his Religion, 1688–1690,* New York: Garland, 1974), 1.

12. *The Correspondence of Jonathan Swift,* ed. Harold Williams, 5 vols. (Oxford: Clarendon Press, 1963–65), 4:320–21. Swift's assertion here of his "near relation" to Dryden may ironically recall the mocking passage in the earlier *Battle of the Books* where Dryden spuriously claims he is "nearly related" to Virgil.

13. *Jonathan Swift: The Complete Poems,* ed. Pat Rogers (Harmondsworth: Penguin, 1983), 642 (hereafter *Poems*). The note appeared in the 1735 edition of Swift's *Works*.

14. John Lennard, *But I Digress: The Exploitation of Parentheses in English Printed Verse* (Oxford: Clarendon Press, 1991), 97–98.

15. *The Hind and the Panther,* part 1, lines 436–40 (*Works,* 3:135); Lennard, 98. Fine examples of the use of triplets and the visual effect of curly brackets to complement the sense of a passage occur in *The State of Innocence, and Fall of Man: An Opera,* 3.1.60–65; 4.2.11–13 (*Works,* 12:115, 129). Dryden defends his use of triplet rhymes and the alexandrine in his "Dedication of the Æneis," *Works,* 5:322, 331.

16. For the echoes, see Ehrenpreis, *Swift,* 2:384–87.

17. See Hermann J. Real, "The Dean's Grandfather, Thomas Swift (1595–1658): Forgotten Evidence," *Swift Studies* 8 (1993): 84–93.

18. *Verses on the Death of Dr Swift,* lines 351–52; *Poems,* 494; John Denham, *Coopers Hill,* lines 325–26; *Expans'd Hieroglyphicks: A Critical Edition of Sir John Denham's Coopers Hill,* ed. Brendan O Hehir (Berkeley and Los Angeles: University of California Press, 1969), 159, see also 251.

19. A familiar pairing in pamphlet attacks on Dryden. See Martin Clifford, *Notes upon Mr. Dryden's Poems in Four Letters* (1687), in *Dryden: The Critical Heritage,* 184, and Luke Milbourne, *Notes on Dryden's Virgil* (London, 1698; reprint, New York: Garland, 1974), 27.

20. Hermann J. Real, "'The Renowned *Dryden*' as the Lady in a Lobster," *Swift Studies* 5 (1990): 112.

21. Edward Hyde, Earl of Clarendon, *The History of the Rebellion and Civil Wars in England Begun in the Year 1641,* ed. W. Dunn Macray, 6 vols. (Oxford: Clarendon Press, 1888), 3:89; Charles Firth and Godfrey Davies, *The Regimental History of Cromwell's Army,* 2 vols. (Oxford: Clarendon Press, 1940), 1:81.

22. See Real, "'The Renowned Dryden,'" 112 (for Shadwell's *Sullen Lovers*), and Claude Rawson, *Satire and Sentiment 1660–1830: Stress Points in the English Augustan Tradition,* new edition (New Haven: Yale University Press, 2000), 95 (for Camoens's *Lusiads*).

23. For this book in Swift's library, see Real, "The Dean's Grandfather," 92.

24. *Works,* 5:vii (italics reversed); Robert Phiddian, *Swift's Parody* (Cambridge: Cambridge University Press, 1995), 128.

25. B. S. Johnson, *The Unfortunates,* intro. Jonathan Coe (London: Picador, 1999), "Note" on the inside of the box.

26. *Dryden: The Critical Heritage,* 257–58. See also John Dennis, *The Stage Defended . . . Occasion'd by Mr. Law's late Pamphlet against Stage-Entertainments* (London, 1726; reprint with introduction by Arthur Freeman, New York: Garland, 1973), vi–vii, 4, 16, 28, 32–34.

27. Luke Milbourne, *The Royal Martyr Lamented, In Fourteen Sermons, Preach'd on the Thirtieth of January. Wherein the Rights of Monarchy are occasionally asserted . . .* (London, [1724]), see especially sermon 8, *The Traytors Reward* (1714).

28. Luke Milbourne, *Notes on Dryden's Virgil,* 8–9 and passim.

29. Jeremy Collier, *A Short View of the Immorality, and Profaneness of the English Stage, Together With the Sense of Antiquity upon this Argument* (London, 1698), 240.

30. William H. Halewood, "Plutarch in Houyhnhnmland: A Neglected Source for Gulliver's Fourth Voyage," *Philological Quarterly* 44 (April 1965): 185–94; Jonathan Swift, *Gulliver's Travels,* ed. Paul Turner (Oxford: Oxford University Press, 1994), "Explanatory Notes," 364.

31. On this episode in cultural history, see Brean S. Hammond, *Professional Imaginative Writing in England, 1670–1740: 'Hackney for Bread'* (Oxford: Clarendon Press, 1997), 206–9.

32. *Poems,* 611–12 (notes); Winn, *John Dryden,* 497–98.

33. See Frank H. Ellis, "Notes on *A Tale of a Tub,*" *Swift Studies* 1 (1986), 10.

34. See also Anne Barbeau Gardiner, "A Witty French Preacher in the English Court, Dryden, and the Great Debate on the Real Presence, 1661–1688," *ELH* 65 (1998): 605–6.

35. *Tale,* 82–85; Brown, *The Reasons of Mr. Bays Changing his Religion,* 8.

36. Atterbury, *An Answer,* 7, 68, 42–43. For further discussion of Swift's allusion to this paper war, see my *Swift's Politics: A Study in Disaffection* (Cambridge: Cambridge University Press, 1994), 133–43.

37. *The Lives of the Poets of Great-Britain and Ireland. By Mr. Cibber, and other Hands,* 5 vols. (London, 1753), 5:97–98. Quoted in Johnson, "A Literary Chestnut," 1025.

38. Samuel Johnson, *Lives of the English Poets,* ed. G. B. Hill, 3 vols. (Oxford: Clarendon Press, 1905), 3:7–8, 1:404.

Plotting Parallel Lives: Pope's "A Parallel of the Characters of Mr. Dryden and Mr. Pope"

VALERIE RUMBOLD

IN THE APPENDICES TO *THE DUNCIAD VARIORUM* OF 1729 AND *THE Dunciad in Four Books* of 1743, Pope presented what he called "A Parallel of the Characters of Mr. Dryden and Mr. Pope [or, on facing pages, "of Mr. Pope and Mr. Dryden"]. As drawn by certain of their Contemporaries."[1] The "Parallel" consists entirely of hostile quotations about the two writers, arranged thematically by accusation, and laid out in parallel across each opening, thus offering a typographical image of the comparability that Pope is concerned to assert between himself and his great predecessor. In effect, the appendix asserts the fulfillment of the prophecy the young Pope had made in the *Essay on Criticism*:

> *Pride, Malice, Folly,* against *Dryden* rose,
> In various Shapes of *Parsons, Criticks, Beaus*;
> But *Sense* surviv'd, when *merry Jests* were past;
> For rising Merit will *buoy up* at last.
> Might he return, and bless once more our Eyes,
> New *Blackmores* and new *Milbourns* must arise;
> Nay shou'd great *Homer* lift his awful Head,
> *Zoilus* again would start up from the Dead.[2]

As early as his late teens, Pope was testing the identity of a *Dryden redivivus* for a possible fit to his own aspirations. Even the amused citing of two of the more risible of Dryden's detractors, memorably paired as targets at the close of Dryden's Preface to *Fables* (one of the young Pope's favorite books), seems a confidently dismissive measuring in advance of the risks of becoming that new Dryden.[3]

Pope later bound together a collection of the pamphlets published against him, and copied into it a text from the Book of Job: "Behold it is my desire that mine Adversary had written a Book. Surely I would take it on my Shoulder, and bind it as a crown unto me."⁴ In fashioning extracts from such pamphlets into the matching columns of abuse that form his "Parallel," Pope seems to have done exactly that, transforming their intended obloquy—and the pain it caused him—into a very specific "crown," a triumphant proclamation of his succession from Dryden.[5] Job, despite the uncharitable suspicions of observers, does not deserve the misery he endures, and is in the end vindicated by God. He can thus be read as a type of innocent suffering, a prefiguring of Christ: the "crown" becomes a type of the crown of thorns, aligning the poet's indignation at the subversion of traditional hierarchies of value with the suffering of the God whose authority had once guaranteed them.

The deployment of Dryden and his antagonists in Pope's "Parallel" constitutes a highly self-conscious positioning of his own career on Pope's part, and one strategically integrated into the work that would arguably constitute, in its final 1743 form as *The Dunciad in Four Books,* his most complex and wide-ranging engagement with the cultural challenges of his time. The "Parallel" focuses a range of questions, not only about the significance that Pope found in Dryden, but also about how readers today—separated by three centuries from Dryden, and by two from the celebrated comparison made by Johnson in *Lives of the Poets*—make sense of the connections and contrasts between the two writers.[6] At the most superficial level, Dryden and Pope make an obvious pair: both seem very English figures who never traveled abroad; both excelled in their use of the heroic couplet; both are celebrated for satire and for translation; both mounted major subscription projects; both became subtle and effective spokesmen for political opposition; both hoped to write an epic but were unable to do so; and both were Roman Catholics (though, in Dryden's case, only in later life). But, as the latter point begins to suggest, such parallels are dangerously bland, erasing difference and difficulty. Pope's own "Parallel," founded on the experience of media attack that had prompted his rueful yet proud quotation from Job, suggests a more personal, painful, and ambitious reading on his part, rendering shared obloquy as a crown of thorns that stands in for the compromised and diverted laurel.

By designing himself a role as Dryden's successor, Pope was responding to a major topic in Dryden's own work. As a boy, Pope read in the Preface to *Fables* of the "Lineal Descents and Clans" of writers—an image that may have seemed to offer the young aspirant an encouragingly familial rather than agonistic context for seeking his own place in literary tradition.[7] In *Mac Flecknoe* he recognized a mock-epic rendition of the theme of succession that was to become the foundation of his *Dunciad*s; and in Dryden's "To My Dear Friend Mr. Congreve," written after the Revolution of 1688, he found a potent model for ridiculing officially sanctioned but arguably spurious lines of succession: by declaring, near the beginning of the *Dunciad*s, that "Dunce the second reigns like Dunce the first," he recalled Dryden's "For *Tom* the Second reigns like *Tom* the First" (48), making even more specific, shortly after the coronation of George II, the contemptuous linkage between literary and regal succession.[8]

Pope's "Parallel" is better understood as a claim to succession from Dryden than as a substantive allusion to Plutarch's *Parallel Lives*: the material is all, apart from the section headings, taken verbatim from other writers, and there is no explicit evaluative comment.[9] However, the inevitable recollection of Plutarch does serve as a reminder of a tendency in Pope to judge the past from the assumption that moral and aesthetic values are directly comparable over time.[10] Pope's loyalty to the anti-Bentley party in the affair of the supposed Epistles of Phalaris set him on a course of determined opposition to the historicism of Bentley and Theobald; and although he recognized on occasion (notably in relation to Shakespeare) that the prevailing conditions of a particular time and milieu had to be taken into account in estimating the achievement of writers of the past, he tended nonetheless to base his judgments on his own universalizing standards of morality and aesthetics.[11] In relation to Shakespeare, for instance, contextual factors figure more as an excuse for alleged faults than as an invitation to conceive of Shakespeare's art as intrinsically different from the art of the present.[12] Comparable attitudes emerge in his attitude to Dryden; and Dryden's favorite metaphor of succession was useful to him because, while it referred to political structures and rituals of crucial importance to both poets, it allowed both for similarity to and difference from the authorizing father: the heir is authenticated by likeness to the father, but can justify his place in the succession by recognizing the shortcomings of his inheritance and developing it appropriately.[13] Pope's "Parallel" can certainly be read, if the reader is so disposed, in terms of a Plutarchan comparison of moral absolutes across different lifetimes (though the differences may seem minor in comparison to Plutarch's contrasted Greeks and Romans), but the making of the "Parallel" is primarily a rhetorical move, as, at the height of a much-controverted career, Pope focuses through the point-by-point account of his and Dryden's sufferings at the hands of their critics a long-meditated claim to be seen as Dryden's heir.

The habit of structuring literary debate around parallels and comparisons between past and present writers presented Pope with two kinds of problem. The first was inflation of modern achievement, as manifested by the public appointment of risible laureates, and by private collusion in self-satisfied puffery. In the *Imitations of Horace* 2.2, Pope indicts a whole repertory of facile compliment, as poetasters connive in mutual identification with great predecessors:

> allow me *Dryden*'s strains,
> And you shall rise up *Otway* for your pains.[14]

Pope also represents himself in the *Epistle to Dr. Arbuthnot* as the object of a particularly crass variant on such parallels. Flatterers who compliment him on looking like famous writers focus irrelevant and unwelcome attention on his "Person," where he is forced to recognize "All that disgrac'd my Betters, met in me."[15]

The second problem that Pope sees in the use of parallels is the temptation to minimize one kind of achievement in an attempt to promote another. He discussed this with Joseph Spence, probably in 1728, the year before he first published his "Parallel" between himself and Dryden:

> In speaking of comparisons upon an absurd and unnatural footing, he [Pope] mentioned Virgil and Homer, Corneille and Racine, [and] the little ivory statue of Polyclitus and the Colossus.
> "Magis pares, quam similes?" [suggested Spence].
> Aye, that's it, in one word.[16]

The Latin tag quoted by Spence, "equal rather than alike," comes from a remark cited by Quintilian. Quintilian was considering whether Roman historians had equaled the Greeks, and had concluded not only that Sallust was the equal of Thucydides and Livy of Herodotus, but also that, within the narrower sphere of purely Roman achievement, Livy had equaled Sallust: "For it seems to me that Servilius Novianus put it very well when he said that they were equal rather than alike."[17] Quintilian's discussion of Roman and Greek historians thus adumbrates Pope's concern with drawing parallels and connections both among modern contemporaries and between modern and ancient culture, as demonstrated in the passage earlier quoted from the *Essay on Criticism*

ing in the light of this belief, Pope simply could not see any evidence for Dryden's belief that "the verses Jonson made on Shakespeare's death had something of satire at the bottom."[24] Despite this and other remarks by Dryden suggesting struggle as the necessary condition of literary inheritance—often in the context of the need for innovation rather than futile attempts at repetition—Pope may also have been encouraged in his optimistic appraisal of writerly inheritance by another strain in Dryden, a characteristically relaxed lack of defensiveness in linking himself with literary forebears, allied with a markedly provisional mapping of lineages in relation to specific literary opportunities.[25]

In dealing with Dryden in the early *Essay on Criticism,* Pope invariably introduces him in the context of a parallel that places him in relation to the wider literary heritage; but these are never freighted with evaluative commentary of the sort that might drive a wedge between writers of reputation (as in the Homer/Virgil parallels of which Pope later expressed disapproval to Spence). There is the parallel between Dryden and Homer quoted above; there is a compliment to *Alexander's Feast,* declaring that "what *Timotheus* was, is *Dryden* now"; and there is the lament that the English language is so transient a medium that "such as *Chaucer* is, shall *Dryden* be."[26] There is also the indiscriminate faultfinding of the "bookful Blockhead":

> All Books he reads, and all he reads assails,
> From *Dryden*'s *Fables* down to *Durfey*'s *Tales.*[27]

This last is an ironic rendition of the kind of kinship through shared opprobrium that Pope was later to claim with Dryden—although in this case, with the much ridiculed Durfey as partner, the pairing works very much to Dryden's advantage. But even in this most explicitly evaluative of the parallels, the single potentially negative phrase "down to" gives only the slightest adverse turn. Pope seems sufficiently comfortable with Dryden to be unconcerned with ranking him, and not even particularly interested in using his achievement to lambaste less distinguished moderns.

In relation to the construction of his own career, Pope had very early focused on Dryden as his significant predecessor, testifying that as a youth he "learned versification wholly from Dryden's works."[28] As a young man, he delighted in cultivating older men who had been "great *Dryden*'s friends before"; and cemented his introduction to Wycherley by writing to say how much he had appreciated hearing Wycherley talk about Dryden, adding "Had been born early enough, I must have known and lov'd him."[29] Indeed, he presented himself, in *To Arbuthnot,* as encouraged to publish by Dryden's friends, whose welcome with "open arms" takes on the character of a corporate adoption, enfolding the young man into the circle as "one Poet more": it is as if they are enacting by proxy a paternal recognition that only death had prevented. The importance of this scene in Pope's apology for his career suggests that these men fill so important a gap that it is vital to name them for the sake of their connection to Dryden, even though Pope must have been well aware by this time of how far he had excelled the achievement of most of them.[30]

However, the role of Dryden's heir was not uncontested, and Addison posed a particular problem. (Erskine-Hill calls Pope "a political as well as poetic heir" to Dryden, but Addison "a poetic heir but not a political one."[31]) Pope's sense of being obstructed by Addison was not, however, just a matter of different political and cultural agendas, or asymmetries of status, age, and privilege. Among Pope's recollections to Spence about the wits he had known in youth there are two that suggest, obliquely and in apparently trivial contexts, that Addison had become associated with a quite literal shutting off of the space vacated by Dryden:

> It was Dryden who made Will's Coffee-House the great resort for the wits of his time. After his death Addison transferred it to Button's, who had been a servant of his.[32]
>
> Addison passed each day alike, and much in the manner that Dryden did. Dryden employed his mornings in writing, dined *en famille,* and then went to Will's—only he came home earlier a' nights.[33]

Pope soon realized that his chronic poor health made this routine of the literary man-about-town unsustainable, and he settled into a routine that guaranteed more quiet and more time at home—which, in line with the laws against Papists, was out at Binfield or, later, out at Twickenham, neither within easy reach of coffee-house society. As time went on, Pope ostentatiously distanced himself, rejecting coffeehouse urbanity in favor of idealized suburban detachment.[34] In 1743 he explained to Spence, "Addison usually studied all the morning, then met his party at Button's, dined there, and stayed five or six hours—and sometimes far into the night. I was of the company for about a year, but found it too much for me. It hurt my health, and so I quitted it."[35] This, however, was not the only reason, for at about this time he had also come to suspect that Addison had attempted to sabotage his

Homer translation by encouraging Ambrose Philips's rival version; and Pope had, probably in 1715 or 1716, brought matters to a head by sending Addison a draft of the satire that was later to become the character of Atticus in the *Epistle to Dr. Arbuthnot*.[36] As finally placed in the poem, it sets Addison adrift from the group in which he might otherwise have been included, the early encouragers of Pope's talent who had been "great *Dryden's* friends before."[37] They constitute a group worthy to be remembered by their real names, men who by embracing Pope have provided for the future of poetry. Atticus, instead, is a satirical "character" marooned in defensive sterility among inferiors not worth naming: his fear of any "brother near the throne" makes him perversely concerned to contain talent rather than to nurture it.

Vindicating his claim to be Dryden's heir had thus been a long-term theme in Pope's self-construction, and the "Parallel" published as part of the *Dunciad Variorum* in 1729 and again as part of the *Dunciad in Four Books* in 1743 reflected deeply meditated strategies. In particular, it focused an argument about his relation to Dryden that had been developed piece by piece in the *Dunciad*s themselves, perhaps most obviously in their prose commentaries. While the verse, with its dense mosaic of reminiscence from Dryden, is relatively familiar, the commentaries are generally less so (partly because editions have so often omitted or abbreviated them, or interspersed them with material by later editors or from other versions of the text). It is therefore worth detailing Pope's deployment of Dryden in the commentary to his final and fullest *Dunciad: The Dunciad in Four Books* of 1743.

There is a clear pattern in this commentary of associating Dryden's career with Pope's, coupled with an insistent pressure toward notions of parallel and succession. In introducing Blackmore, for example, the note comments, "This gentleman in his first works abused the character of Mr. Dryden; and in his last, of Mr. Pope."[38] (The note also pursues the theme of parallel characters by glancing with typically subtle misrepresentation at Charles Gildon's consideration of whether Blackmore had equalled Homer: in contrast, Pope had in *Peri Bathous* declared him "the Father of the Bathos, and indeed the Homer of it").[39] Crucial too is the figure of Luke Milbourne, whom Pope introduces as "the fairest of Critics; who, when he wrote against Mr. Dryden's Virgil, did him justice in printing at the same time his own translations of him, which were intolerable."[40] Pope then proceeds to compare him to the critics who have attacked the

Dunciads, and drops in a cross-reference to the evidence collected in the "Parallel": "His manner of writing has a great resemblance with that of the Gentlemen of the Dunciad against our author, as will be seen in the Parallel of Mr. Dryden and him. Append."[41]

This note is prompted by the episode in which the clergyman Jonathan Smedley reports his initiation into the mysteries of clerical duncery, having been escorted by the mud-nymphs to a part of the underworld reserved for versifying clergy, where

> Milbourn chief, deputed by the rest,
> Gave him the cassock, surcingle, and vest.
> "Receive (he said) these robes which once were mine,
> Dulness is sacred in a sound divine."[42]

The words attributed to Milbourne are shrewdly focused on the two writers' shared clerical status and on the zeal for the privileges of their order, which had fueled Milbourne's intemperate attack on Dryden's Virgil.[43] In the commentary, however, the motif of succession is highlighted by Pope's citation of the passage from Virgil's *Eclogues* in which the poet Gallus receives from the legendary bard Linus the pipes the Muses had formerly given to Hesiod.[44] The annotation constructs a complex intertextual vista converging on a striking absence: we are directed to a primal site of poetic succession, but within the poem there is no context in which the succession from Dryden can actually be enacted.

Pope might be thought to have early, and perhaps rashly, "used up" the Virgilian theme of succession, when he imitated another Virgilian gift of pipes in the "summer" of his *Pastorals*. There Spenser rather than Dryden had been the target predecessor:

> That Flute is mine which *Colin*'s tuneful breath
> Inspir'd when living, and bequeath'd in Death;
> He said; *Alexis,* take this Pipe, the same
> That taught the Groves my *Rosalinda*'s Name . . .[45]

Pope's early desire to identify himself as Spenser's heir had been brought into question by the crude, derivative, but effectively puffed Whig *Pastorals* of Addison's protégé Philips. (His revenge, an ironic review in the *Guardian* of his own and Philips's pastorals which affected to admire Philips's rusticity while deploring Pope's failure to put realistically crude language into the mouths of his peasants, still seemed important enough to him in 1743 to be included as appendix 5 to *The Dunciad in Four Books.*) Pope thought of Spenser again when starting work on the *Dunciads,* and planned an epigraph from the *Faerie Queene* (1.1.23) in which the Redcross knight fighting Error's offspring is like a shepherd swatting the "combrous gnattes" that irritate him with their "feeble stings."[46] Indeed he may have been thinking of this simile in relation to Dryden and his critics, and by analogy to his own prospects, as early as 1704, when he told Wycherley that "those Scriblers who attack'd him in his latter times, were only like Gnats in a Summer's evening, which are never very troublesome but in the finest and the most glorious Season; (for his fire, like the Sun's, shin'd clearest towards its setting)."[47] But the epigraph was finally dropped: Pope apparently decided it was too long, and Spence surmised that "clownish hands" may have been a problem (uncomfortably reminiscent of Philips's deliberately "clownish" pastoral, it may also have seemed too obvious a gift to Pope's enemies).[48] In the *Dunciad*s as published, it is Dryden, not Spenser, who is the significant target, marked out by allusion to Virgil's account of the handing of Hesiod's pipes to Gallus. Yet the passage is deployed parodically, and in relation to Milbourne. It seems that the closest Pope can now come to framing his relation to Dryden through this hallowed Virgilian motif is to say, in effect, that his enemies are the successors to Dryden's enemies.

This oblique claim is also instanced in the introduction of Settle:

> All as the vest, appear'd the wearer's frame,
> Old in new state, another yet the same.
> Bland and familiar as in life, begun
> Thus the great Father to the greater Son.[49]

By making Settle address his "son" Bays, alias Cibber, Pope again parodically shadows the absent scene of succession between Dryden and himself. The note elaborates: "Elkanah Settle was once a Writer in vogue, as well as Cibber, both for Dramatic Poetry and Politics. . . . These are comfortable opinions! and no wonder some authors indulge them."[50]

Apart from such explicit allusions to poetic succession, the prose apparatus is continually busy in elaborating a more general pattern of association between Pope and Dryden. In the prefatory critical anthology gathered by Scriblerus under the title "Testimonies of Authors" we read:

> The illiterate among our own countrymen may learn to judge from Dryden's Virgil of the most perfect Epic performance. And those

parts of Homer which have been published already by Mr. Pope, give us reason to think that the Iliad will appear in English with as little disadvantage to that immortal poem.[51]

The fact that the commentator here is Addison is crucial, given his preemptive role in blocking the Dryden succession, aggravated by Pope's conviction that he had deliberately undermined his Homer subscription. Pope in fact works hard in the *Dunciad*s to discredit accusations against Addison that he actually believed. His presentation of Addison is calculatedly respectful, enabling Pope to foreground his pious care for the reputation of a good writer and early benefactor, while averting any danger to his own reputation from publicizing the breach between them, still less from casting himself in the role of attacker.

Others had made comparisons between Pope and Dryden that were intended to disparage Pope by comparison, and in "Testimonies of Authors" he delights in subverting their arguments. Oldmixon, for example, is cited as having sneered at the *Essay on Criticism*: "If any more curious reader has discovered in it something *new* which is not in Dryden's prefaces, dedications, and his essay on dramatic poetry, not to mention the French critics, I should be very glad to have the benefit of the discovery."[52] Oldmixon's charge of derivativeness is turned against him, his belief in originality implicitly dismissed as modern shallowness, as Pope highlights his enemy's testimony to the respected, classically based yet up-to-date sources through which his critical learning had been filtered. Dennis and Gildon are also shown making a would-be negative comparison with Dryden, as Pope inserts a sly parenthesis into an allusion to *The Rehearsal*:

> Mr. DENNIS and Mr. GILDON,
> in the most furious of all their works . . . do in concert confess, "That some men of *good understanding* value him for his rhymes." And . . . "That he has got, like Mr. Bays in the Rehearsal, (that is, like Mr. Dryden) a notable knack at rhyming, and writing smooth verse."[53]

Quoting selectively, and making a strategically blunt identification between Mr. Bays and Dryden that undermines the dismissive tone of the original, Pope has the pleasure of citing his enemies as claiming for him a level of technical achievement on a level with that of his admired predecessor.

The commentary on particular passages of the verse of *The Dunciad in Four Books* also uses Dryden strategically to claim precedents for controversial aspects of Pope's practice. Pope attempts to justify the scatalogical fantasies of book 2 by the familiar device of a double parallel not only with Homer and Virgil, but also with Dryden: "Mr. Dryden in *Mack-Fleckno,* has not scrupled to mention the *Morning Toast* at which the fishes bite in the Thames, *Pissing Alley, Reliques of the Bum, etc.*"[54] He also counters the allegation that he has unfairly mocked the poverty of writers by citing Juvenal's account of the poverty of Codrus, where the translation quoted is Dryden's and is credited as such, so that Dryden's name immediately precedes the ostentatious incredulity of Pope's exclamation that "Mr. Concanen . . . assures us that 'Juvenal never satyrized the poverty of Codrus.'"[55]

Thus, by the time the reader of *The Dunciad in Four Books* reaches Pope's formal "Parallel" in appendix 8, the themes of parallel and succession linking Pope and Dryden are already thoroughly established. Dryden, as predecessor, occupies the left-hand page of the opening, perhaps suggesting that the reader should start there, then look across to make comparisons with Pope. The right-hand page, however, is the page where readers expect to find beginnings, and it may be that the reader's eye will be, by habit, drawn there first, and will then look back from Pope to Dryden. This would subvert, though subtly, the ostensibly respectful priority given to Dryden, and might arguably supplement the emphasis on Pope's career insinuated by the markedly larger number of authors and works cited against him (in comparison with the relatively few though admittedly intemperate publications repeatedly cited against Dryden). For each poet, however, the headings are nearly always identical, beginning with "His POLITICS, RELIGION, MORALS." On the Pope page, critics who despise his Roman Catholic faith and political stance are cited, and a list is given of the establishment figures he has allegedly attacked. A brief citation under the heading "Mr. POPE only a Versifier" then serves as preamble to three sections of attacks on his Homer project: "Mr. POPE's HOMER," "Mr. POPE understood no Greek," and "Mr. POPE trick'd his Subscribers." The final section, "Names bestow'd on Mr. POPE," cites abuse of him under the subheadings of "APE," "ASS," "FROG," "COWARD," "KNAVE," "FOOL," and "A THING." Each section, even down to the identical names in the final list, is paralleled for Dryden (with Virgil substituted for Homer as appropriate).

Pope does manage to find a remarkably detailed symmetry in the charges—and without, in Dryden's case, searching the archives much beyond the remarkably copious Milbourne. The religion Pope shared with Dryden in his later years prompted accusations that both held the Bible in contempt, and abrogated to themselves a poetic infallibility on the papal model (though Pope's unfortunate surname made this an even more obvious gibe); and the lists of the great and supposedly good abused in *Absalom and Achitophel* and in Pope's works chime remarkably closely—a match that Pope emphasizes by setting the key terms in capitals. The condescending praise of the two poets' technical mastery also suggests that the two men suffered under the same perverse failure of appreciation. Both are further accused of taking one of the greatest authors of antiquity and perverting him, and of rendering epic in unsuitably smooth verse.

However, when Pope comes to the question of classical competence, an area in which his lack of standard schooling made him particularly vulnerable, he deftly uses the fact that Dryden had translated mainly from Latin while he himself had translated mainly from Greek to vary their respective headings, so that "Mr. POPE understood no Greek" is paralleled with "Mr. DRYDEN understood no Greek *nor Latin*" (my emphasis), an accusation amply illustrated by Milbourne's obligingly comprehensive denunciations of Dryden's classical attainments. Pope's basic problem was that as a Roman Catholic he had been excluded from standard education, and was instead trained by family priests and, briefly, at small and illegal Catholic schools; Dryden, on the other hand, had attended Westminster School under the celebrated Dr. Busby. Latin, however, was very much the dominant language in the English school curriculum, and for Dryden to be accused of incompetence in that language is damaging indeed, more damaging than simply to be accused, as Pope is in the parallel section, of incompetence in Greek.[56] The apparently slight addition of "nor Latin" effectively shifts attention away from the frequently alleged consequences of Pope's exclusion from standard schooling.

A subtler misdirection characterizes the heading that alleges that each man "trick'd his Subscribers." All Milbourne means by this is that Dryden's translation was so poor that taking money for it amounted to daylight robbery; but in relation to Pope's subscriptions the heading seems designed, by leveling his situation with Dryden's, to screen out embarrassing attacks on his evasions over precisely how much of his *Odyssey* he had translated himself. Maynard Mack concludes of this episode that "The deception had cast a shadow on his reputation that was real and had given enemies an opening for attacks that would not readily be closed"; and the "Testimonies of Authors" prefaced to *The Dunciad in Four Books* is still engaged in attempting to face down the accusations.[57] The closest Pope's quotations against himself come to any accusations of dishonesty attaching to his career in subscription publishing is the more readily refuted charge that "Pope has been concerned in Jobs, and hired out his Name to Booksellers."

Pope's final topic is "Names bestow'd," a list of terms of abuse. Here, however, although the coincidence of the names "APE," "FROG," and "A THING" is exact, the effect is vastly different: for Dryden to be called "A crafty Ape drest up in a gaudy gown," or "Poet Squab," "an ugly, croaking kind of Vermin," or even "so little a Thing as Mr. Dryden" is to see himself figuratively reduced and humiliated; but in Pope's case a term like "Squab" is a disconcertingly literal fit for his hunched four-foot-six body. In relation to Dryden these insults seem no more than the kind of ritual abuse that a great writer has to expect; but in relation to Pope, because the identical terms can be read so much more literally, they highlight both the cruelty of his attackers, and the sheer quality of a triumph achieved against the physical odds.[58] Also, the very fact that such language can be displayed as having been applied to Dryden de-emphasizes the peculiarities of a body that Pope's enemies had always kept painfully in the public eye.

By ending with the topic of deformity, the "Parallel" in fact highlights one of the most obvious differences between Pope and Dryden. Pope joined to the political disability of being heir to a family barred from owning land the personal disability that led him to dismiss any possibility of marriage and heirs of his own. Dryden, in contrast, was heir to family property, able-bodied, unexceptionable in appearance, a husband, and a father of sons.[59] Pope lacked any such live connection to patriarchal values, even as he lacked any monarch or potential monarch capable of focusing those values.

In effect, as Pope's decision to conclude with the topic of physical deformity reminds us, it is impossible to make sense of Pope's desire to link himself to Dryden without a concept of difference as well as similarity. (Dryden, after all, had been quite comfortable with the traditional equation of physical and moral deformity when, in *Absalom and Achitophel,* he set the grotesque bodies of the rebels in contrast with the sacred body of the king.[60]) One very pressing set of differences that Pope was concerned to imply was a variety of ways in which he felt he had improved on Dryden's inheritance. This could have been intrinsically problematic in the light of Pope's allegiance to the Ancient party in the quarrel of the Ancients and the Moderns: he was skeptical both about modern claims to have outdone ancient achievements, and about the historicism of a Bentley or Theobald that would qualify the supposed universality of those achievements. His strategy was therefore to imply that the real direction of progress was toward a more thoroughly classicizing correctness, as he argues in *To Augustus*:

> Britain to soft refinements less a foe,
> Wit grew polite, and Numbers learn'd to flow.
> Waller was smooth; but Dryden taught to join
> The varying verse, the full resounding line,
> The long majestic march, and energy divine.[61]

And later:

> But Otway fail'd to polish or refine,
> And fluent Shakespear scarce effac'd a line.
> Ev'n copious Dryden, wanted, or forgot,
> The last and greatest Art, the Art to Blot.[62]

If Dryden is identified with energy, variety, and majesty, he is also given the perhaps slightly compromising epithet "copious," associated with the oratorical flow admired by the older, still primarily oral culture from which Pope, with his meticulously corrected editions and strict supervision of the printing process, was helping to distance the art of poetry. And although the final comment may seem at first sight more raillery than criticism, since wanting "the Art to Blot" levels Dryden with Shakespeare, Pope declares in the commentary to *The Dunciad in Four Books*: "It was a ridiculous praise which the Players gave to Shakespear, 'that he never blotted a line.' Ben Johnson honestly wished he had blotted a thousand...."[63] That Dryden could be represented as lacking this "Art" gave Pope an opening. Moreover, since Dryden himself had written in the Preface to *Fables* of the impertinence of seeking to excuse slapdash work, and since it was one of his friends, William Walsh, who told Pope that "we never had any one great poet that was correct" and "desired me to make that my study and aim," it was almost as if Dryden himself had lent his sanction.[64] Indeed, Dryden had, later in the Preface to *Fables*, said of his modernization of Chaucer's text that "another poet, in another age, may take the same liberty with my writings"; and he had prefaced the comment with a declaration of kinship with

Chaucer that put a collegial rather than combative gloss on the sense of superiority implicit in the notion of belonging to an age that could improve on past masters: "I found I had a soul congenial to his, and that I had been conversant in the same studies."[65]

On the other hand, Pope was acutely conscious of areas in which he might be vulnerable to adverse comparison with Dryden. In 1736, Spence recorded Pope making a somewhat defensive comparison of their speed as translators: "I began translating the *Iliad* in my twenty-fifth year, and it took up that and five years more to finish it. Mr. Dryden, though they always talk of his being hurried so much, was as long in translating Virgil."[66] Then, as if realizing he had been unfair, he added, "Indeed, he wrote plays and other things in the same period." Uneasiness also seems to have characterized his feeling about another project in which he might have been seen as trying to parallel his great predecessor: "Many people would like my ode on music better if Dryden had never written on that subject. It was at the request of Mr. Steele that I wrote mine, and not with any thought of rivalling that great man, whose memory I do and have always reverenced."[67] Yet it appears that the ode had originally been composed in 1708, however much it may have been revised to meet Steele's request for words to be set to music in 1711, suggesting that the urge to emulation had played its part in the choice of form and subject, if not in the actual decision to make the poem public.[68]

Pope was less cautious in asserting that he had improved on Dryden's versification, although he was careful to cite in Dryden's defense the haste in which he worked.[69] In effect, this was a more respectful version of Rochester's line of criticism, that "Five hundred Verses every morning writt / Proves you no more a Poet than a Witt"; and in his own career Pope certainly adopted the scrupulousness that Rochester goes on to recommend:

> To write what may securely stand the Test
> Of being well read over thrice at least,
> Compare each Phrase, Examine every line,
> Weigh every word, and every thought refine.[70]

The problem here was one of money and rank: Rochester's advice to "scorn all applause the Vile Rout can bestow / And be content to pleas those few who know" was useless to a poet of the minor gentry who, in the absence of reliable patronage, found his best hope of long-term financial support in the playhouse; but Pope contrived to take Rochester's fastidiousness as his watchword.

He told Spence: "After I had got acquainted with the town I resolved never to write anything for the stage . . . from seeing how much everybody that did write for the stage was obliged to subject themselves to the players and the town."[71] He followed up this resolution with an exceptionally shrewd management of the new opportunities for profit in the rapidly commercializing market for literature, and was able to make enough money to render himself independent.[72] In this, his handling of the *Iliad* translation was crucial; and his remarks to Spence show how interested he was in the financial detail of Dryden's Virgil project, and how conscious he was of Dryden's Virgil as the significant watershed in the development of subscription projects.[73] His ambivalence toward the modernizing forces that facilitated his independence through subscription translation is well known, but one positive effect of his acumen in managing his intellectual property was that from the culturally novel position of a writer made independent by the fruits of his own labor, he could plan his projects so that he never had to expose rushed work to public scrutiny. Samuel Johnson, himself so conscious of the pressures on a professional writer, highlighted the fact that "his effusions were always voluntary," an achievement only possible because of that independence.[74] It also made feasible the committed craftsmanship repeatedly emphasized in Johnson's *Life:* Pope habitually "retouched every part with indefatigable diligence," again something only practicable for a writer who set his own deadlines.[75] Though Johnson ultimately ranked Pope slightly below Dryden, his description of Pope's genius as "always endeavouring more than it can do" significantly concedes a kind of sublimity to a career marked by painstaking professionalism.[76]

The same independence that enabled Pope to avoid Dryden's haste also exempted him from the pressure to servile conformity whose influence on Dryden he lamented, whether this meant flattering the great, or pandering to the tastes of "a lewd, or unbelieving Court."[77] Again, Johnson recognized that "very few poets have ever aspired" to make themselves morally independent in this way: "Pope never set genius to sale: he never flattered those whom he did not love, or praised those whom he did not esteem."[78] Dryden, though a gentleman born, cultivated aristocrats because he needed patrons who could pay, whereas Pope, a tradesman's son, relished being able, as Warburton reported, to "fling off Lords by dozens."[79] Pope could attack Hervey and Lady Mary Wortley Montagu as Dryden could never have attacked Rochester, and could even note to Spence that Dryden himself was "not a very genteel man," and "was intimate with none but poetical men."[80] In an early poem to Henry Cromwell (one of "great Dryden's friends before"), Pope had also risked a joke about Dryden's lack of politeness:

> He had some Fancy, and cou'd write;
> Was very learn'd, but not polite—[81]

Although, as Brean Hammond has argued, Pope was to take violent exception to the Whiggish cult of politeness in its high Addisonian form (and although, as the *Dunciads* and other works declare, he was to make radical play of a politeness of form that rendered only more questionable his coarseness of content), this anecdote shows how valuable an opportunity the shift in social tone seemed to offer to a young writer in the first decades of the eighteenth century.[82] Again, Dryden himself may have seemed to ease the way for an improving generation when in the Preface to *Fables* he expressed regret for former work in which he had been less careful to avoid "anything which shocks religion or good manners."[83]

Despite the real continuities that persisted across the century boundary at which Dryden died, Pope and Dryden were formed in worlds half a century apart, and even some things that they had in common played very different roles in their lives. Dryden, for example, converted to Roman Catholicism at a time when English Catholics enjoyed a short-lived ascendancy, whereas Pope was born into it at a time of low-key but persistent persecution. For Dryden, James Winn argues, it was a real conclusion to a real spiritual journey; whereas for Pope, whatever his faith may have been to him in private, in public and among his friends it seems to have figured as an inherited awkwardness that he defended out of scruple to the parents who had taught it to him; and after some difficult early maneuvering with fellow Catholics who objected to his criticisms of their Church, he seems in later life to have somewhat reduced the intensity of his involvement in Catholic circles.[84] While church apologetics was a central concern for Dryden, Pope liked to play down the importance of choosing a particular church, and emphasize instead the basic beliefs shared by all Christians; and he clung to a determinedly catholic reading of the "Catholic" in "Roman Catholic" as defense for his own practice amongst his Anglican friends.[85] His discussions with Spence about the unfinished "opus magnum" suggest that religious considerations would have been decidedly peripheral to it, and

Roman Catholicism even more so; in fact, his comments have about them a distinctly anti-metaphysical thrust that seems more of the time than of his Church, which he told Spence with lofty skepticism he would not now leave to take up a new set of errors elsewhere.[86] Such differences of attitude may well reflect differences of temper, but they surely also reflect the changing contexts of lifetimes separated by half a century.

On the other hand, Pope as satirist still had an enormous amount in common with Dryden. Winn suggests that the Rose Alley attack, "intended to discourage Dryden's satiric pen," actually "unleashed the true powers of the century's greatest satirist"; and a similar point might be made of Pope's response to attack, though in Pope's case, the response extended as far as deliberate provocation designed to elicit more attacks and justify more revenge.[87] Like Dryden, Pope also felt the awkwardness, as a Christian, of lampooning his enemies; but the evidence suggests that he gave way far more readily to the temptation to do so.[88] Winn several times remarks Dryden's reluctance to respond in kind to attacks (his slowness, for example, in publishing *Mac Flecknoe*); but Pope played out his whole career in the new world of the marketplace, where controversy was part of his strategy. A similar point might be made about the publication of his letters, a move that for Pope formed part of a self-construction prompted by the now unstoppable dynamics of attack and counterattack he had helped to foster.[89] The fact that because of this we now have so many of Pope's letters, whereas we have so few of Dryden's, is another sign of how deeply the cultural landscape was changing.

Where political satire is concerned, as Howard Erskine-Hill has argued, Pope "deploys a poetry of obliquity and innuendo which he inherited from the last twelve years of Dryden."[90] Rose Zimbardo has claimed, moreover, that the later Dryden played a decisive role in shifting satire from a Renaissance focus on the snarling play of rhetorical personae to a modernizing focus on a speaker judiciously assessing the world around him; and although her argument for this line of development leads to a rather stolid and monolithic Pope, she offers an interesting context for Erskine-Hill's perception that from the 1729 *Dunciad Variorum* onward Pope "blends with his more personal tones a national and oratorical manner" as he becomes "one of the strongest voices to articulate a nation-wide campaign of opposition to Britain under the Hanoverian establishment."[91] It is certainly this manner, further weighted with Warburtonian religious scruple, that assumes control over the closing stages of the four-book

Dunciad—even though the *Dunciad* project could never have come into existence without the more playful Scriblerian Pope of earlier days.

Pope certainly learned from Dryden how a despised artisan of the world of letters (Shadwell or Theobald or Cibber) could be used as a stand-in for the unnameable "Great"; and in using Theobald and Cibber to strike beyond Walpole at the king, Pope audaciously extended the range of the technique.[92] More deviously, in contrast with Dryden's hope of dedicating his Virgil to a restored James II, and his refusal to dedicate it to William III, Pope evolved a stance of obliquity that allowed him to have Walpole actually present the *Dunciad* to George II, and to frame *To Augustus* as an ostensible compliment to the same monarch.[93] Like Dryden, Pope continued to exercise his skepticism about the direction of political developments even when things seemed to be going his way: in *The Hind and the Panther* Dryden had made plain the dangers he saw in James's promotion of Catholicism, and Pope abstained quite markedly from enthusing about any potential hope that the Patriot movement might have seemed to offer. Indeed, his refusal in the *Dunciad*s to treat the Patriots as any kind of positive to Walpole's negative is resounding.[94]

What does, in the end, seem to distinguish Dryden most from Pope in later life is Dryden's much-acclaimed hope and flexibility, the confidence he expresses in the Preface to the *Fables* of being "as vigorous as ever in the Faculties of my Soul."[95] Many readers have responded warmly to Dryden's undiminished capacity in old age to engage creatively and positively with adverse change; and it is easy to connect this disposition with the sense of excitement at new possibilities that Paul Hammond has discerned in Dryden's reappraisal of the classical heritage, and with his lifelong sense that to attempt to repeat the past or lament its absence is not only futile, but also perverse.[96] Pope, coming later on the scene, took up the Ancient cause as it had been embraced by his older mentors during the Phalaris affair (and older mentors were a very marked feature of a childhood spent with elderly parents among neighbors, several of whom had retired to Binfield on account of age or the religious penalties attached to being Roman Catholics or Quakers). For Pope, in this respect, a turn to the classics was less obviously an engagement with the potential of the new. It seems indeed that though Pope was a teenager at the dawn of a new century, he had far less of a sense than Dryden at the Restoration of living in a new age; for while Dryden had lived through the execution of Charles I, the Restoration, and the Revolution of 1688, and found his ideology repeatedly challenged, moving while an Anglican away from the Puritanism of his upbringing, and finally leaving the Church of England for the Church of Rome, Pope was born to quieter times and less obvious calls for imaginative rethinking of heritage and ideology. He made a lifelong commitment to the religion in which he was born and spent his maturity in settled opposition to entrenched Whig government. His quest to be the first "correct" English poet, though from one point of view a challenging commitment to carry forward a tradition inherited from Dryden, may also have constituted an inhibition against Dryden's "copious" flow of experimental, sometimes contradictory engagements with his world. (It certainly militated against the taste for romance that Zwicker and Erskine-Hill identify as a factor in the relaxed and magnanimous view of historical change that Dryden was able to achieve after the Revolution.[97])

Indeed, the emphasis on free associative play that marks the opening of the Preface to *Fables,* with its account of one selection leading to another until "I have built a House where I intended but a Lodge," is indicative of a deep temperamental disparity between the two men.[98] There is no equivalent in Pope, for example, for the range and fertility of Dryden's miscellaneous prose.[99] To have left so much of his best work shaped by such peripheral or contingent contexts would have irked Pope, who characteristically strove for polish and consolidation, conceiving his career in terms of large-scale, carefully managed projects. From the *Works* of 1717, through the Homer translations and his edition of his correspondence, to the authorized edition of his poetry planned with William Warburton in his last years, he exercised a detailed and strategic control over the way his work appeared before the public. Rather than leaving his two mock epics in their first form and moving on (as Dryden did with *Mac Flecknoe* and *Absalom and Achitophel*), he repeatedly reworked them, producing texts of vastly more impressive form and scope. On the other hand, no one seems much to regret his failure to wrest such poems as the *Essay on Man,* the *Epistles* to Bathurst and Burlington, and parts of what are now the *Dunciad*s into a systematic "Opus Magnum."[100] However vital to the full realization of his poetry, significant in terms of publishing history, or comprehensible in view of the derision aimed at his physical body, Pope's drive to appear before the public in print icons of elegance, coherence, and comprehensiveness was not an unmixed good, any more than Dryden's willingness to let things go and move on was an unmixed good. (Johnson had no compunction in suggesting that, in comparison to Pope, "Dryden never desired to apply all the judgement that he had," and "never attempted to make that better which was already good, nor often to mend what he must have known to be faulty."[101]) Pope's attitude, however, ruled out the apparently casual discoveries, the openness to experiment, and the commitment to process that have been so lavishly admired in Dryden. Such praise of Dryden often seems the more diminishing to Pope from its tendency to take on a biographical as well as aesthetic dimension: Greg Clingham celebrates the attitudes of the later Dryden as a sign of deep psychological security; while Cedric Reverand, who reads the *Fables* as "celebrating the changing world instead of denouncing the change in *his* world," makes an explicit contrast with the fall of the curtain that constitutes Pope's final word in *The Dunciad in Four Books*.[102]

It seems clear that one thing Pope could not inherit from Dryden, still less improve upon, was this openness and flexibility. Ironically, Pope's very desire to affiliate himself to Dryden, with the backward-looking orientation toward the wits of the last age that it entailed, may have limited his room for maneuver. Though he proved a master of exploitation of the new commercial opportunities in literature, it is characteristic that he used his profits to present himself not as a novel instance of what talent could achieve in a changing marketplace, but as a gentleman poet on an older model, aloof from any necessity of seeking profit.[103] Although he congratulated himself on escaping the need "to please a lewd or unbelieving court," the price of that freedom was his long-term exclusion from any kind of rapport with a government apparently permanently skewed to Whig and commercial pressures, and one that had made obsolete the whole structure of myth and expectation within which poets had traditionally hoped to influence the social order. Although the Patriot movement might have been seen as offering, through Frederic Prince of Wales, precisely the restoration of a poet's traditional authority in speaking to and for the monarch that he, unlike Dryden, had never experienced, Pope effectively declined to become laureate-in-waiting.[104] Perhaps part of his reluctance represented an underlying recognition that things had indeed moved on, and that the role of independent poet in the marketplace was not one that in the end he wanted to gamble on a movement about whose leaders he remained deeply skeptical. But so deeply does Pope seem to have become acculturated to Walpole's dominance—and so weakened by the accumulating consequences of the spinal tuberculosis that would soon kill him—that when Walpole finally fell from power in 1742, there was apparently no question of substantially revising the myth of the *Dunciads;* and *The Dunciad in Four Books* came out in 1743 with very little changed by Walpole's going. It did not help either that Pope was now collaborating so closely with his newly authorized editor and literary heir William Warburton, whose concern to refocus the final *Dunciad* around his own dogmatic religious orthodoxy would hardly have encouraged any radical rethinking of the *Dunciads*' engagement with the politics of the day.

Thus the times that had initially brought Pope opportunities for, in his view, progressing beyond Dryden probably also helped, ultimately, to bound his options, leaving him unable either to revive the ancient role of the poet speaking to and for the prince, or to relax wholeheartedly into the modern flow of individuality, diversity, and commercialization. After Pope there would be no serious bid to take on his mantle: his literary heir (an expression here to be taken only in the most literal sense) was the commentator, controversialist, and bishop William Warburton. (This accounts for the piquant fact that that, as its subtitle reveals, Donald Nichol's invaluable *Pope's Literary Legacy* is concerned not, as the casual browser might have assumed, with Pope's influence on younger poets, but with Warburton's letters to his bookseller.[105]) This lack of a poetic heir may have been related not only to the perception that Pope had been so overwhelmingly accomplished as to be inimitable, but also to some kind of sense that it was no longer appropriate for a talented and well-placed young man to form himself in a career mould that was in effect an adaptation of late Renaissance models. In particular, Pope's strategy for surmounting the divide between pre- and post-commercial writing could not be repeated (there was, after all, no further epic poet to be translated who commanded either the prestige or the market appeal of Virgil or Homer). Pope had in fact lamented to Spence in 1735 that the last age had been the best for poetry, and that "the young ones seem to have no emulation among them."[106] We can surely assume here that these "young ones" are men, and men of conventional background and education at that: it is symptomatic of what was changing that one talented writer who *was* going through a strenuous course of Popeian emulation at the time of Pope's death, but whom he had never met nor been likely to meet, was the Northamptonshire kitchen maid Mary Leapor.[107]

Very shortly before he died, Pope made a somewhat uncharacteristically historicist remark to Spence: "Facts in ancient history are not very instructive now; the principles of acting vary so often and so greatly. The actions of a great man were quite different even in Scipio's and Julius Caesar's times."[108] For Pope, although the tone of such an isolated remark is admittedly hard to judge, this seems an unwelcome perception: it certainly runs counter to many of the working assumptions of his creative life. Three hundred years on, in an age less uncomfortable with historicist specificity, Pope's gestures toward parallelism with Dryden ironically underline the force of cultural difference. Dynastic imagery, drawing on but not limited to notions of resemblance, not only provides a better model for the relation of selection, adaptation, and development that links Pope to the great writer he never properly met, but also commends itself as imagery rooted in concerns that both writers shared, however differently those concerns were inflected in the context of the particular politics of their respective times. In the end, however, whatever the rhetorical force of Pope's "Parallel of the Characters of Mr. Pope and Mr. Dryden" in staking Pope's claims for the significance of his career, it remains the case for each of them that, as Pope had made Settle cry out in acclaiming Tibbald (and something like what Dryden had said in translating the ancient epigram on Plutarch), "None but Thy self can be thy parallel."[109]

Notes

1. *The Dunciad in Four Books (1743)*, ed. Valerie Rumbold (Harlow: Longman, 1999), appendix 8, 390–95. All references to *The Dunciad in Four Books* are to this edition. References to other *Dunciad*s and all other poems by Pope are to *The Twickenham Edition of the Poems of Alexander Pope,* ed. John Butt et al., 11 vols. (London: Methuen, 1939–69).

2. *Essay on Criticism*, 458–65.

3. Preface to *Fables*, in *The Poems of John Dryden*, ed. James Kinsley, 4 vols. (Oxford: Clarendon Press, 1958), 4:1461.

4. Job 31.35–36, written by Pope into a bound collection of pamphlets, British Library C.116.b.1–4; transcribed in J. V. Guerinot, *Pamphlet Attacks on Alexander Pope, 1711–1744* (New York: New York University Press, 1969), p. li.

5. Pope claimed not to have been much upset by attacks on him (Joseph Spence, *Observations, Anecdotes, and Characters of Books and Men,* 2 vols. [Oxford: Clarendon Press, 1966], no. 100). Jonathan Richardson, however, who saw "his features writhen with anguish" while reading one of Cibber's pamphlets, noted how bitterly this contradicted his claim that "These things are my diversion" (Samuel Johnson, *Lives of the English Poets,* ed. George Birkbeck Hill, 3 vols. [Oxford: Clarendon Press, 1905], 3:188).

6. Johnson, *Lives*, 3:220–23.

7. Preface to *Fables*, 4:1445.
8. *Works of John Dryden,* ed. H. T. Swedenberg et al., 20 vols. (Berkeley and Los Angeles: University of California Press, 1956–); James Anderson Winn, *John Dryden and His World* (New Haven: Yale University Press, 1987), 461; *The Dunciad in Four Books,* 98, 1.6; Erskine-Hill, *Poetry of Opposition and Revolution: Dryden to Wordsworth* (Oxford: Clarendon Press, 1996), 31–32, 101.
9. Johnson's celebrated comparison of Dryden and Pope is, by contrast, a structured discursive exercise more readily comparable to the Plutarchan model: Johnson himself calls it a "parallel" (*Lives,* 3:223).
10. For the historical assumptions underlying Plutarch's *Parallel Lives,* see D. A. Russell, *Plutarch* (London: Duckworth, 1972), 102–3; Tim Duff, *Plutarch's "Lives": Exploring Virtue and Vice* (Oxford: Clarendon Press, 1999), 52–3, 248–52, 288–91.
11. For Phalaris, see Joseph M. Levine, *The Battle of the Books: History and Literature in the Augustan Age* (Ithaca: Cornell University Press, 1991), chapter 2. For Pope's opposition to Bentley and Theobald, see *The Dunciad in Four Books,* 3–4, 7–9 (introduction).
12. The Preface of the Editor to *The Works of Shakespear,* in *The Prose Works of Alexander Pope,* vol. 2, ed. Rosemary Cowler (Oxford: Blackwell, 1986), 14–17.
13. For an extended example of Pope's projection of current notions of politeness into previous reigns, framed by a comparison with classical precedent, see Spence, no. 539.
14. Imitations of Horace, 2.2.145–46.
15. *An Epistle to Dr. Arbuthnot,* lines 115–24.
16. Spence, no. 549.
17. The Latin text reads "Nam mihi egregie dixisse videtur Servilius Novianus, pares eos magis quam similes" (*Quintilian,* ed. and trans. H. E. Butler, 4 vols., Loeb Classical Library 124–27 (Cambridge: Harvard University Press, 1920–22), 4:10.1.101–7).
18. Twickenham ed., 7:15. See also *Selected Prose of Alexander Pope,* ed. Paul Hammond (Cambridge: Cambridge University Press, 1987), 97–101.
19. Spence, no. 57 and appendix pp. 611–12. Mack suggests, from Pope's later quotation of a simile used by Dryden "in conversation," that although he probably knew this "from report," it is possible he had actually "heard him holding forth" (Mack, *Life,* 836, note on 89). He later told Wycherley, "I was not so happy as to know him; *Virgilium tantum vidi*" (*Correspondence,* 1:2).
20. Johnson would later comment, "Who does not wish that Dryden could have known the value of the homage that was paid him, and foreseen the greatness of his young admirer?" (*Lives,* 3:87).
21. *Prose, 1668–1691,* 283–87.
22. Preface to Plutarch, 288.
23. The Preface of the Editor to *The Works of Shakespear,* 18–20; Spence, no. 54.
24. Spence, no. 67.
25. For a subtle exploration of these issues in relation to Roman writers, see Paul Hammond, *Dryden and the Traces of Classical Rome* (Oxford: Clarendon Press, 1999), especially chapter 1. Jennifer Brady suggests that "Dryden presents influence as a paradox of fluid, discovered affinities" ("Dryden and Negotiations of Literary Succession and Precession," in *Literary Transmission and Authority: Dryden and Other Writers,* ed. Earl Miner (Cambridge: Cambridge

University Press, 1993), 27–54, (31–33). Winn, *John Dryden,* 331, discusses the balance of judicious appraisal with proper respect in his references to literary predecessors.

26. *Essay on Criticism,* lines 383, 483.
27. Ibid., lines 616–7.
28. Spence, no. 55.
29. The "friends" of Dryden are listed in *An Epistle to Dr. Arbuthnot,* lines 135–42. For the letter to Wycherley, see Pope, *Correspondence,* 1:2.
30. The passage also allows him an allusion to Rochester's listing in "An Allusion to Horace" (*The Works of John Wilmot Earl of Rochester,* ed. Harold Love (Oxford: Clarendon Press, 1999), lines 120–24).
31. Erskine-Hill, *Opposition and Revolution,* 3.
32. Spence, no. 68.
33. Spence, no. 182.
34. For the classic treatment of this theme, see Maynard Mack, *The Garden and the City: Retirement and Politics in the Later Poetry of Pope* (Toronto: University of Toronto Press, 1969).
35. Spence, no. 181.
36. Spence, nos. 160–68; *An Epistle to Dr. Arbuthnot,* lines 197–214.
37. *An Epistle to Dr. Arbuthnot,* lines 135–42.
38. *Dunciad in Four Books,* 187–88; note on 2.268.
39. *Peri Bathous,* in *Prose Works,* 2:196.
40. *Dunciad in Four Books,* 202–3; note on 2.349.
41. i.e., in the appendices.
42. *Dunciad in Four Books,* 202–3, 2.349–52.
43. For Milbourne's resentment of Dryden's association of the clergy with rebellion, see Winn, *John Dryden,* 499.
44. *Virgil,* ed. and trans. H. R. Fairclough, 2 vols., Loeb Classical Library 194 (Cambridge, Mass.: Harvard University Press, 1937), *Eclogues* 6.64–71.
45. "Summer," lines 39–42, imitating Virgil, *Eclogues* 2.36–38 (Alexis tells of the pipes given him by Damoetas).
46. Spence, no. 420.
47. Pope, *Correspondence,* 1:2.
48. Spence, no. 420.
49. *Dunciad in Four Books,* 227, 3.39–42.
50. Ibid., 226, note on 3.37.
51. Ibid., 51.
52. Ibid., 46.
53. *Dunciad in Four Books,* 64.
54. Ibid., 158, note on 2.75.
55. Ibid., 168–69, note on 2.144.
56. Pope, however, told Spence that his first tutor, the family priest, had started him on both languages together (Spence, nos. 14–15). Johnson commented that for a variety of reasons, in which he included "irregular education," "it is not very likely that he overflowed with Greek" (*Lives,* 3:113).
57. Mack, *Life,* 412–17; *Dunciad in Four Books,* "Testimonies of Authors," 52–53.
58. This is not to overlook Dryden's complaint in old age of being "a Cripple in my Limbs" (Preface to *Fables,* 1446), which Winn suggests may have been a long-term result of the Rose Alley attack (Winn, *John Dryden,* 325), rather to differentiate it from Pope's condition, which, though not congenital, involved a

85. Witness his response to Atterbury's suggestion that he might convert to Anglicanism following the death of his father (*Correspondence*, 1:453–54).

86. Spence, no. 630.

87. Winn, *John Dryden*, 327. For Pope's deliberate provocation of the victims of the *Dunciads*, see *Dunciad in Four Books*, 6 (introduction), 26, 363–64 (editorial commentary on appendices).

88. For Dryden's unease, see Winn, *John Dryden*, 460. For his refusal to answer attacks, see also 236, 261, 293, 428. For Pope's memory of his father's biblically based scruple that "It was a Sin to call our Neighbour Fool," see *An Epistle to Dr. Arbuthnot*, line 383.

89. *Correspondence*, 1:xi–xviii.

90. Erskine-Hill, *Opposition and Revolution*, 59.

91. Rose A. Zimbardo, *At Zero Point: Discourse, Culture, and Satire in Restoration England* (Lexington: University Press of Kentucky, 1998), 59–60, 68, 141–55; Erskine-Hill, *Opposition and Revolution*, 59.

92. For Shadwell as standing for Rochester in *Mac Flecknoe* and in the Dedication to *All for Love*, see Winn, *John Dryden*, 289, 307–8.

93. Erskine-Hill, *Opposition and Revolution*, 39–40; *Dunciad in Four Books*, 95, 97, note on 1.1.

94. Christine Gerrard, *The Patriot Opposition to Walpole: Politics, Poetry, and National Myth, 1725–1742* (Oxford: Clarendon Press, 1994), chapter 4.

95. Preface to the *Fables*, 1446.

96. Paul Hammond, *Dryden and the Traces of Classical Rome*, especially 31–32.

97. Steven N. Zwicker, *Politics and Language in Dryden's Poetry: The Arts of Disguise* (Princeton: Princeton University Press, 1984), 175; Erskine-Hill, *Opposition and Revolution*, 53.

98. Preface to *Fables*, 4:1444–45.

99. In connection with their respective choices of format and context, see Johnson's contrast between their prose styles (*Lives*, 3:222).

100. See Miriam Leranbaum, *Alexander Pope's "Opus Magnum," 1729–1744* (Oxford: Clarendon Press, 1977).

101. *Lives*, 3:220.

102. Greg Clingham, "Another and the same: Johnson's Dryden," in *Literary Transmission and Authority: Dryden and Other Writers*, ed. Earl Miner, 121–59 (133, 138–42); Cedric D. Reverand, *Dryden's Final Poetic Mode: The* Fables (Philadelphia: University of Pennsylavania Press, 1988), 218.

103. See Brean Hammond, *Pope*, Harvester New Readings (Brighton, U.K.: Harvester Wheatsheaf, 1986), particularly chapter 3.

104. See his account to Spence of how closely Charles II had collaborated with Dryden (Spence, no. 66).

105. Donald W. Nichol, ed., *Pope's Literary Legacy: The Book-Trade Correspondence of William Warburton and John Knapton* (Oxford: Oxford Bibliographical Society, 1992).

106. Spence, no. 485.

107. For women poets responding to Pope, see Claudia Thomas, *Alexander Pope and his Eighteenth-Century Women Readers* (Carbondale: Southern Illinois University Press, 1994).

108. Spence, no. 579.

109. *Dunciad Variorum*, 3.272 and commentary.

Dryden's *Hamlet*:
The Unwritten Masterpiece

BARBARA EVERETT

DRYDEN OF COURSE NEITHER WROTE NOR ADAPTED A *HAMLET*. There may be something dour about contributing to a celebration of this kind a word as to what our subject didn't do. But sometimes negatives, or questions, can say as much as positives. And Dryden is perhaps an odder, a more involved figure than might be surmised from his enormous productivity—from his energy, his directness, his mass and variety of achievement. This first of our great professional poets may have understood very fully the oxymoron in that phrase, "professional poet"; may have known, even beyond the withdrawals of his own temperament, how many silences went into being so formidably articulate. Biographers don't forget the history of himself that the poet was to have given John Aubrey, but that he never gave.

The Restoration poet adapted Shakespeare, out of confidence and from a sense of necessity. I have chosen *Hamlet* as a point of comparison between them—a comparison, after all, provoked by Dryden himself—for a reason best given by anecdote. A very long while ago I found myself in the stalls enjoying Shakespeare's play. At the interval one of the two ladies in front of me turned to the other and said, with deep if philosophical sadness, "Don't tell me, May. I don't want to know. But he isn't going to come through, is he?" I think Shakespeare would have been delighted. This is not the only way to define a classic—by the power to hold and move two sensitive and intelligent if not particularly literate persons, three hundred and fifty years after first publication. But it is one way: and, though that was certainly a more innocent phase of our culture, I was glad to see a warning in a recent *Radio Times* that *Romeo and Juliet* contains violence and "drug abuse."

I use *Hamlet* as a case, as *the* case, of the power to be taken seriously (while not forgetting that Shakespeare is also characterized by *Henry VI* and *King John* and *Timon* and *Cymbeline*). If Dryden died three hundred years ago, then a tercentenary feels like the right moment to ask what his *Hamlet* is, or what it is that we now recommend him for. The interest of the question is increased, though also complicated, by the fact that the writer's public esteem has surely never been so low. Perhaps the few readers of poetry who still exist need a kind of intensity of verse that Dryden never cared to supply—perhaps his great virtue was to relieve his readers of that intensity. Whatever the explanation, and though this is by no means the only or best definition of a good readership, I have to acknowledge after decades of teaching that only the rarest of able pupils has agreed to try Dryden, or indeed (it sometimes seems) heard of him. It is true that these rarities have gone on to join the still flourishing and admirable world of Dryden scholarship. But it remains equally true that *Hamlet* has had a life beyond scholarship.

An obvious place to begin would be among the plays themselves. Dryden's output, of rising thirty dramas, was nearly as extensive and various as Shakespeare's own. They filled the first half of his career, and he was still writing for the theater at the beginning of his last decade. Even if the poet himself came to hate his work for the stage, this enormous labor can hardly be just dismissed. And in fact the quandary is in itself interesting. The plays represent in the simplest way that utilitarianism governing post-Restoration arts, and coloring in different forms all Dryden's career. He wrote (necessarily) for money, for a political party, or for an audience.

There are scholars who are happy to extend his success in the theater into the present moment. Deference used to go to *All for Love*. Mark van Doren called it "the maturest of the tragedies," its style "virtually impeccable"—but his general critique of the plays is always disaffected: a judgment that matters, given that his eighty-year-old study of Dryden remains that unusual thing, a more or less perfect critical book, deeply learned, fine in analysis and marvelously written (no wonder Eliot liked it). The preference has moved now to *Amphitryon*, called by Earl Miner "his greatest comedy and one of the greatest comedies in English." More recently, Howard Erskine-Hill, pursuing a political theme, sees the writer as doing a "particularly brilliant thing" in *Amphitryon*; and Michael Cordner three times reiterates the word "masterpiece" when introducing his edition of the play.

There is an appealing American proverb: "If you're so smart, why ain't you rich?" It seems to throw light on the difficult case of Dryden. The fact is that during the past century productions of Dryden's plays have been few and far between. Directors and *dramaturgs* in our major theaters, always desperately hunting for new plays and in themselves neither illiterate nor inexperienced, have clearly done what my directorial or theater-minded students have done, when invited to go away and read *Marriage A-la-Mode* or *Sir Martin Mar-all* or *Don Sebastian* or *Amphitryon*. They have nodded, said "Interesting," and gone away to direct Congreve or Otway or Vanbrugh or Etherege or Wycherley or Southerne or Behn, sometimes with dazzling success.

Dryden's plays lack the dramatic pace and rhythm that come only from a belief in the significance of human action, and his characters have no character. But again and again stylistic confidence and point will make these things seem not to matter. There are the lovers in *Marriage A-la-Mode* who "when they came to possession, have sigh'd and cri'd to themselves, Is this all?"—a brutalism modern in its economy. Or there is this grace note from *The Rival Ladies*:

> I think and think on things impossible,
> Yet love to wander in that Golden maze ...

—a note almost Racinian. But the fact is that Dryden disliked Racine. What we have here is what his plays often give us, imitation Racine and pastiche drama: something flawlessly achieved from outside without any sympathetic or original life from within. This has been much better said before, and by a great critic: "He could more easily fill the ear with some splendid novelty than awaken those ideas that slumber in the heart"—Samuel Johnson, who in a page or two of unanswerable analysis clarifies the reasons why a poet whom he both loved and respected could not conceal "the difficulty which he found in exhibiting the genuine operations of the heart." The key word is "genuine." Probably all Drydenians tolerantly accept that the heroic dramas are, in their exposition of love and honor, farcical, pure Cecil B. de Mille (though *Aureng-Zebe*, too, or *The Conquest of Granada,* it would be good to see just once, for the fun of it).

This speciousness or fine hollowness always touches the rest of the plays. Their steady assurance and their real intelligence can prove persuasive for those who don't much like the theater: but on stage, they would die the death. Since criticism is pointless without honesty, I will admit that *Amphitryon* strikes me, with all its momentary stylishness, as inept and unstructured. It startlingly wastes its peculiar but haunting source story, which it renders above all heartless, therefore weightless. By "heartless" I don't mean simply "cold" or "cruel." It is to be noted that Johnson, unlike Earl Miner, does not simply contrast "intellect" and "feeling." He is saying something much subtler and truer with his "ideas that slumber in the heart." Real thinking and real feeling are indivisible in great dramatists, or even good minor ones.

For reasons partly social or sociological, the theater of Dryden's time operated at a great distance from whatever we mean by "reality." Though the work of a mind at once shrewd and large, Dryden's plays have a kind of false purchase on human experience in general. This is a point I shall return to. But they also lack—as, indeed, his poems often do too—social actuality in a quite limited sense. We don't turn to Dryden for anything like the vision of the common life of his time that makes Pepys, say (so much less of an artist in considerable ways) all the same survive so much more widely through his diary. Probably Dryden's whole dramatic canon contains nothing seen with the clarity of that old muff of his wife's that Pepys borrowed when the fashion moved to men; or those London pigeons, unwilling to leave their nests in the Great Fire and falling to the ground, their wings burned; or Pepys himself, walking home reading by the light his man carried. These are small things. But *Hamlet*, after all, begins with "not a mouse stirring."

If we find the plays lifeless, where then do we look for Dryden's *Hamlet*, the focal and representative work that can still command our attention? Van Doren, who is as solidly appreciative as he is sharply critical, loves much in the poet, but at one point decides that "on the whole it may be said that Dryden's Odes . . . seem the most indestructible portions of his verse." Of all his judgments, this most reminds us that van Doren's *Dryden* was first published in 1920. Certainly *Alexander's Feast* was uproariously welcomed in the eighteenth century. And the odes remain marvelous pieces of baroque performance art. But it is hard to know how at this moment they can be praised in language less external.

For van Doren, then, the odes. Anthologizing Dryden, W. H. Auden remarked appreciatively that left to himself he would have filled his whole book with prologues and epilogues. Or again, Keith Walker, in his Oxford Poetry Library selection, confines himself almost entirely (after *MacFlecknoe*, parts of *Absalom and Achitophel*, "To the Memory of Mr. Oldham," "St. Cecilia's Day," the "Lady's Song") to translations and *Fables*. All these preferences are understandable, have something to be said for them.

Modern opinion in general agrees with Walker in a stress on the late work, and on translation or adaptation in particular—though there is division of taste here too. Walker does not include the twenty-ninth ode of the third book of Horace ("Happy the Man . . .") chosen by H. A. Mason to write on as an example of the poet-translator at his most genuinely inspired.

Critics do and should differ, where an art is alive to them. But there may be something exceptional in Dryden's case. He is plainly one of the most uneven of all our major poets, with a variability both in apparent temperament or character and in actual literary performance. It's at moments hard to believe that the same man effected the beautiful poise of the critical prose and the gross flat-footedness of the heroic drama. These are changes that perhaps depend on the new implications of professionalism, of literature pursued as labor. It took an extraordinary mix of qualities to make a writer succeed in the second half of the century of revolution. Dryden's whole literary being—the ambition, the vulgarity, the intelligence, the marvelous maturing musical skill, the reflectiveness, the humor, the brutality, the staying power—all together provoke the quotation of Walt Whitman's protest, "Do I contradict myself? Very well, I contradict myself. / I am large, I contain multitudes."

Contemporaries of the poet picked up something of this self-contradiction, reflected in the fact that Dryden was, though a silent withdrawn man, very decidedly loved and hated: sweetly commemorated by Congreve, beaten up verbally and physically by the Duke of Buckingham and others. When the poet Rochester wanted to malign his ex-friend, he spoke of "a rarity that I cannot but be fond of, as one would be of a hog that could fiddle, or a singing owl." This is a mean remark that off-loads on to the rival and greater poet Rochester's own feeling for the paradoxical, the metaphysical; but there is something in it that has the ring of truth as well as of wit. All Dryden's portraits except that by Kneller (which shows a fine fastidious face that doesn't want to be painted) are of singing owls, hogs that fiddle.

Interestingly, Dryden himself made rather the same point in a late letter. Socially, he seems to have fused (as many poets do) the morbidly modest—Congreve's description suggests this—with the downright arrogant (van Doren: "He looked down not only upon other controversialists but even upon the events which he was to treat"). This is evidently true of the poems, though their writer sounds trustworthy when he explains himself as one who is more ready to speak fiercely than ingratiatingly. It is easy, comparably, to envisage Dryden as not very agreeable socially, silent and almost surly in company, yet in private relations capable of the peculiar charm that touches the sentence he wrote in a letter to Mrs. Seward, not long before his death: "I am still drudgeing on: always a poet, and never a good one." This is the singing owl in person; all Dryden's great yet elusive quality as a writer is momentarily compounded in this tough, depressed, and comic sentence.

Precisely the same qualities give extraordinary character to the six best-known lines he ever wrote:

> All, all, of a piece throughout;
> Thy Chase had a Beast in View;
> Thy Wars brought nothing about;
> Thy Lovers were all untrue.
> 'Tis well an Old Age is out,
> And time to begin a New.

I happened the other day to reopen Iris Murdoch's first published novel, *Under the Net,* and was faintly surprised to find Dryden's lines inscribed as epigraph, perhaps not exactly appositely; but their appearance there is a reminder how widely they reached, in the wake of Modernism and Eliot's essay on the poet, through another period heavy with the sense of something finishing. But the lines are of course only a fragment of *The Secular Masque,* written in the poet's last year, as almost his last poem. They are not in themselves a *Hamlet,* only perhaps suggestive—in their quality as in their regret—of the *Hamlet* that Dryden never quite wrote, the local intensity of art that wasn't quite his game. And, as his letter to Mrs. Seward shows, there were moments when he felt it.

"All, all, of a piece" is not exactly satire. The potency of the stanza comes from the brisk ache of idealism refuted. Dryden's idealism is surely, despite the late Catholicism, in practice more literary than political or ecclesiastical. His hunger for order was that of an artist who achieved in words what he did not find in matters of state. Even the Catholicism might be understood less as devotion or policy than a gesture of desperation at the inoperancy of his earlier quasi-political maneuvers: his Jacobitism a withdrawal, not an advance into the actual. With all his penetrating shrewdness, Dryden's idealism is tired, it is the nostalgia that can beautify the plays (and his best writing outside the plays tends to the elegiac, "Mr. Oldham" being a case in point). The elegance, even the sterile elegance that gilds *All for Love,* is a salute to that uncouth, almost Caliban-like power of high dreaming open to the Shakespeare of *Antony and Cleopatra* but closed to civilized men now—a nostalgia, and a closure, that explain the lifelessness of Dryden's "masterpieces" in the theater. The magnificent presence of the poet's stance is really just a supportive limitation of experience, and it can't compare to that haunted and perspectived grasp on the moment ("the bell then beating one") that characterizes every performance of *Hamlet*. This is one of the reasons why, as any history of drama tells us, the English theater started to die for two centuries in the year of Dryden's own death.

The anxieties of time and history, in the newly self-conscious if self-confident Restoration culture, trouble Dryden's verse throughout. The extremely fine "To My Dear Friend Mr. Congreve," which is, like "Mr. Oldham," another of the poet's strictly social or fragmentary *Hamlet*s, is about being "always a poet, and never a good one"—about being always caught, by the powers of a high conceptual intelligence, between the admired or imagined idealisms of the past and the enforced, responsible realities of the present. "Theirs," he says warmly yet placingly of Shakespeare's generation, "was the Gyant Race, before the Flood." This is the unsafe strategy of cultures that, like his and our own, suffer degrees of change so great and so sudden as to enforce a securing of balance, a defining of the viewer's point of vantage. It is our place to be superior, our calling to miss something. Intense regret at being belated in history, at having failed somehow, touches Dryden's easy conversational lines. The result is a trenchant monosyllabic lucidity that turns some corner and becomes wholly poetry. The lines to "My Dear Friend Mr. Congreve" can linger in the mind, seeming to mean much more than they should. "The second Temple was not like the First," and more bitterly, "*Tom* the Second reigns like *Tom* the First"—the very plainness here incises what an ironic imagination sees.

Dryden's *Hamlet* does not consist in any given work. But it does consist, perhaps, in the understanding, that grew as he grew older, that his *Hamlet* wasn't going to be written, that it couldn't be. To say this is to run the risk of paradox. The point seems worth making explicitly, because not (so far as I know) stated elsewhere: scholarly criticism may not always be ready enough to see advance in the arts as dependent on the embrace of difficulty. In fact, in the form of an idea about Dryden's long-proposed heroic poem, an altogether opposite sense of the poet has been voiced. Paul Hammond's *John Dryden: A Literary Life* (1991) lucidly affirms that Dryden could most certainly have realized his early hope to "make the world some part of amends for many ill plays by an heroic poem." Hammond goes on:

> The writing of an heroic poem was thwarted, however, not by any lack of abilities on Dryden's part, but by his failure to find patronage. What might easily have been the crowning glory of Restoration culture never materialised. Though Dryden always remained loyal to his ungrateful master [i.e., Charles II] he was to devote much of his writing to the absurdities and tyrannies of those who wield power.

This last sentence may be true, but it does reduce a satirical artist's main motive to self-interest. Hammond is surely damaging Dryden in his attempt to excuse, to reassure. The main drift of his case I can't help disagreeing with, even when it is translated into Howard Erskine-Hill's contention that Dryden did in fact write his epic: Milton and Dryden, he says, each "produced an epic poem, Dryden's *Æneis* being a sufficiently independent version of its original." But it seems from the letter to Mrs. Seward that Dryden's *Æneis* wasn't "sufficiently independent" for *him*.

Hammond's and Erskine-Hill's wish to unsimplify, to invent some alternative world in which Dryden could have written or actually did write his epic, is not without interest. And Erskine-Hill's pairing of Milton and Dryden similarly happens to make the point of the extreme incompatibilities within late seventeenth-century culture which it was necessary to live through and, more, to contain, in order to be a Restoration writer: Milton and Bunyan, Bunyan and Rochester, Rochester and Marvell, Marvell and Pepys. These juxtapositions reflect the changes and instabilities of the culture itself. Someone born under Elizabeth might, just possibly, have lived into Anne's reign. The Restoration writer looks back to Donne and forward to Defoe. There is a gulf between (say) Marvell's "green" poems and his political verses, and some of the first may be contemporary with the second. An artist may or must (like Hamlet) look back and forward, "before and after," as Dryden himself does in "To Mr. Congreve": "Well then; the promis'd hour is come at last."

This new and hard historical attainment of balance, after so much change, has its technical effects. One of Dryden's great achievements was to settle terms on which poetry could survive in the Augustan world: and those terms included a partial rejection of the more lyrical and private stanzaic modes for the establishment of couplet forms, meters of strong closure that defeat chaos with balance and control. But it is vital, too, that Dryden does so much in that "other harmony of prose," coming near to inventing the method of modern prose and the substance of literary criticism as it was recognizable until some fifty years ago. His prose is what most sixteenth-century prose wasn't: a civilized talking, a high and agreeable social utility of conversation. It matters that the *Essay of Dramatic Poesy* is a conversation, an unresolved chime of debating voices, sustained against the distant thunder of guns downriver.

Something comparable may be said about the means by which Dryden began to make his poetic breakthrough, in the theatrical prologues and epilogues. These colloquial addresses, which Auden admired so much, helped the later poet to discover his 1930s verse style as (similarly) an open conversation. In Dryden's hands, Nell Gwynn, who has just died in the role of St. Catherine, bounces back into her own life to speak the Epilogue to *Tyrannick Love*:

> Hold, are you mad? You damn'd confounded Dog,
> I am to rise, and speak the Epilogue.
> I come, kind Gentlemen, strange news to tell ye,
> I am the Ghost of poor departed *Nelly* . . .
> O Poet, damn'd dull Poet, who could prove
> So senseless! to make *Nelly* dye for Love.

This is more than Audenesque modernist: it is positively postmodernist, in its nerve, its irresponsible knowingness about the lack of stability in aesthetic illusion, its full mix of finesse and brutality, of vulgarity and advanced expertise. Surviving as an artist after the Restoration was a complex business, though oddly recognizable. If we talk of Dryden's obvious maturing as a writer through the 1660s and 1670s, of his emergence as himself in the 1680s and 1690s, then what we mean is that the poet learns an art of survival.

Philip Larkin once told an interviewer that there is one significant fact about poets that all interviewers ought to know. Poets, he said, don't write what they want to write; they write what they must. Dryden's career has its strange features, because it shows him meeting conditions—psychological, social, cultural, and political—that have made poetry, and especially any form of heroic poetry, peculiarly difficult. The 1690s, for instance, possess few outstanding works of imaginative literature: the best Restoration comedies, Dryden's last poems (mostly translations and adaptations), and what is in some ways the most brilliant of all these works, Swift's as yet unpublished *Tale of a Tub,* which could be said characteristically to raise the whole question of what imagination is, and whether it actually has any value. The answer to that second question isn't at all a simple yes.

Dryden wrote to Kneller of "Thy genius, bounded by the times, like mine." By "the times," he probably didn't refer only to the course of history. He is alluding to Kneller's own work as a painter, an artist limited to fabrication, to colored objects. He is phrasing that uncertain involvement he has himself, of mixed love and hatred, with materiality, earthiness, mundanity; and he is all but saying that for the conscious and rational person, life is a physical instant, a now, or what Rochester called "this live-long minute." In the world of the minute, epic cannot survive, and the heroic and the tragic are lost with it, converted into that spectacularly flash medium, heroic drama. The Preface to *Religio Laici* makes plain how little a poet who in a sense loved the higher form and style could now write it: "The Florid, Elevated and Figurative way is for the passions . . . either greater than the Life, or less . . . A Man is to be cheated into Passion, but to be reason'd into Truth." We are back with the period's false distinction between "passion" and "truth," so different from Johnson's "ideas that slumber in the heart." And yet Dryden's position is more clearly understood from the fact that Johnson must surely have been remembering Dryden's own *aperçu* of the artist, in more self-forgetting mood, "moving the sleeping images of things towards the light." In his more fully public self, Dryden—the distinguished dramatic critic—can sound as if he understands *Hamlet* considerably less well than my neighbors in the stalls.

The honest attempt to serve public functions can bring to all of Dryden's work these stultifications, these dead ends. *All for Love,* once so much praised by scholars, is certainly pretty: but its tragedy, like its heroics, approximates to the lifeless—which is to say the passionless, the immaterial, the unembodied. It would be easy to guess from this work, not perhaps absolutely accurately, that its maker, like many poets, cared for few human beings outside himself, and failed to understand them, except for women, whom he disliked. *All for Love* has no notion of the depth and breadth of human pain, of the experienced loss and betrayal and destruction that form (paradoxically) the inexhaustible life of Shakespeare's tragedies. *All for Love* is, by contrast, an impertinent masterpiece of the lifeless, a fine study of cessation, of blankness, of breathlessness:

> Five thousand *Romans* with their faces upward,
> Lye breathless on the Plain . . .
> . . . .
> The World stands before me
> Like a black Desart, at th' approach of night:
> I'll lay me down, and stray no farther on.

Its fourth act is full of echoes, not of the Roman source play, but of Iago-speech: because *Othello,* Shakespeare's most Restoration drama, gives Iago that dangerous dialect that severs passion and reason. There is something similar in the way in which the more dramatic and heroic *Don Sebastian* handles action by negation, by canceling out: as in the decidedly peculiar effect with which Dorax will be killed by secret poison and then cured by secret poison; or Sebastian and Almeyda will manage brother-and-sister love, *and* a conjugal night of bliss, *and* eternal separation, *and* a shared spiritual life of honor. Whether or not Don Sebastian resembles William III is hard to argue about, where the political life and the active life are all a canceling out. As Dorax sharply says:

> My Master? By what title,
> Because I happen'd to be born where he
> Happen'd to be a King?

Take reason out of passion, take God out of history, put Hobbes into the theater, and tragedy and the heroic become impossible, a world of "happening." Certain very strong minds writing in the later seventeenth century are able to hold on to heroic traces of the culture they were born into. Part of the experience of reading through *Paradise Lost* is to feel the century change in it, to watch Satan's corrupt if once Shakespearean heroics mutate steadily toward the gray light of the quotidian that fills the last two books. There is something comparable in the way that extremely different master, Bunyan, gives the first book of his *Pilgrim's Progress* to male warriors, their heroic crossing of the river one of the great sequences in literature, and the second book to a small group of women, through whose chattering voices we can almost hear the comedies of the time. The ending of the second book, full of compassion for the frightened and weak and depressed, is no less fine than the first, but a great contrast too. In 1691, in his preface to

William Walsh's *Dialogue,* Dryden wrote of "this Age, and . . . this time particularly, wherein I find more Heroines than Heroes"— and there is room in this quiet jibe for Bunyan.

There are moreover other great nonliterary geniuses who (like Milton and Bunyan) found ways of shaping their ideals around needs of the moment. Christopher Wren built his churches around congregations ("In our reformed religion it would seem vain to make a Parish Church larger than that all who are present can both hear and see"), and Purcell comparably trained his music into an art of function, moving from the ecclesiastical into the operatic.

Dryden, probably less of an absolute genius than Wren or Purcell, and probably less sure of himself than Milton and Bunyan, all the same works his way forward through change and uncertainty. The pure Drydenian voice develops first in those theaters half hated by the poet, and the prologues and epilogues leap into life like Nelly herself; and there is a style curiously Drydenian in this irritated learning, this "still drudgeing on." The poet is making a language that will last into the age of, say, Swift ("Cousin Swift, you will never be a poet"), or, say, Defoe: the new master of a form that will all but replace poetry for a century, as *Robinson Crusoe* in its extreme shipwrecked mundanity throws away every heroic convention that has preceded it. Robinson was born the year after Dryden, 1632. If there is, in the age of Defoe, any way forward for real poets, then it is owed to the writer who looked "to begin a new."

In the Dedication to the *Georgics,* Dryden recommends "not him who never knew a Court, but him who forsakes it because he knows it." This Miltonic echo is a good analogy to Dryden's own remaking of the heroic as the satirical mock-heroic. Poets' satire is on the whole beneficent, it has warmth: the warmth audible in another dedication, that to the *Examen Poeticum:* "Homer forms and equips those ungodly man-killers, whom we poets, when we flatter them, call Heroes: a race of men who can never enjoy quiet in themselves, 'till they have taken it from all the world." His own heroes, Almanzor and Aurengzebe, are in this line—ungodly man-killers, roarers, and slaves of passion, unrefined in the fires of irony: and so less revivable now than Nelly herself. And yet Dryden is not random when he observes in the *Original and Progress of Satire* that satire is "undoubtedly a Species" of "Heroique Poetry it selfe."

I am hoping to suggest the literary conditions of a paradox. If Dryden could have written, or indeed did write, some kind of heroic poem, then the result does not depend on the pay of Charles or the work of Virgil. It derives from his own sense of what was possible and impossible for himself in his own time (the Dedication to *Don Sebastian*: "A wise man will never attempt an impossibility . . ."). But wisdom may have as much of the imaginative in it as of the prudent. The German Symbolist poet Christian Morgenstern wrote a poem about an architect who would go out at night and collect up the spaces between the palings of council fences: from these spaces he built his castle in Spain. Dryden's heroic poems are mock-heroic; his only *Hamlet* the knowledge of what he couldn't write.

Among the public satires, *Absalom and Achitophel* is usually reckoned Dryden's chief poem. Vivid and magnificent it certainly is, a triumph in itself. But it is perhaps not quite humanly large enough to fill its own scale. There is an element in the treatment of Achitophel's son, "that unfeather'd, two Leg'd thing," "born a shapeless Lump, like Anarchy," that illustrates Johnson's sober charge against the poet whose art he loved—that he lacked "nature." It isn't the cruelty that is especially worrying here, but an inanity or unreason. A marvelous story, both ancient and contemporary, is being sacrificed to political pattern-making.

Oddly much for a man who writes for his social audience, and who generalizes wonderfully, Dryden's principles were those of a poet's poet: he hated artlessness, formlessness, disorderliness. At some level these are standards too private for the public task Dryden is taking on himself, or which the functionalist and professional artist of the time found himself pursuing. Hence the suffusion in Dryden's work of tones too hollow for the private artist and too personal for the public man. Too large a human subject can leave him lacking something. For this reason, *Mac Flecknoe*, written some years before *Absalom and Achitophel* though published after it, can claim to be the most perfectly original of his poems. Though public in its impersonality, it seems private in that there is an animation in its insults that gives an intimate and even inward tone. Johnson remarked reflectively that "Dryden and Settle had both placed their happiness in the claps of multitudes." Long before he was politically out of favor, the man who felt himself to be "always a poet, and never a good one" is living with Grub Street around the next corner. This is perhaps why the shadow of Shadwell (to whom the poet laureateship would pass, a decade later, when it was taken from Dryden) has a power beyond caricature:

> S[hadwell] alone, of all my Sons, is he
> Who stands confirm'd in full stupidity.
> The rest to some faint meaning make pretence,
> But S[hadwell] never deviates into sense.

Released into poetry as a primary mode, irony gives to "sense" lights and shadows, heights and depths it didn't have before: even makes it a secret back door into self-knowing. The fading Renaissance panoplies of myth blow about the poem's Grub Street like the newspapers in Eliot's Tube station corridors. If we laugh and yet feel a certain awe at Shadwell, it is because Dryden catches in him the mundanity of all time, held in a *locus classicus* of history, a century of revolution. If epics die, Shadwell is not the only dullard. The poem finds a genuine mystery in the lapses and failures of civilization, as if we only perceive the supernatural through what is boring in the natural, or the metaphysical through what is mad in the physical. Dryden takes up his position "Amidst this monument of vanished minds": and such writing is neither heroic nor burlesque, neither for nor against, neither political nor aesthetic. This is heroic writing that despairs of itself and laughs at itself; it is satire that for the first time in English takes on not Juvenalian power nor Horatian civility but something softer and wilder, and if one wants, more English. This is satire as dream ("His rising Fogs prevail upon the day," "Thoughtless as Monarch Oakes, that shade the plain," "And lambent dullness plaid around his face")—satire as longing, as true poetry.

David Nichol Smith said: "He could not have given us our greatest epic; but he is our greatest satirist." Pope, who offers some strong competition, must have learned from Dryden the interaction of these two ideas. The gift in the older poet that provokes this word "great" is the understanding that satire, the art of drudging on, is in itself a hard, odd poetry too.

Mac Flecknoe is still not Dryden's *Hamlet*. Its intensely individual character, its seminal quality, unfit it for any function more simply classic. It is, in a word, too strange a poem, too brilliantly inhuman, with its litter of letters, its dead gods and dunces, its jokes and dirty ceremonies; all its furious brooding on the artlessness of art. Dryden really was what Auden called him, "the greatest occasional poet in English," a master of the publicly discursive and privately argumentative, and of all social and conversational kinds of verse: in a sense *Mac Flecknoe* is a lament for a world made up of occasion, of mere happening.

But a reader may also find Dryden "occasional" in a different way: able to survive with peculiar strength and character through the sudden intensities and mockeries of lines that can occur anywhere, early and late in his work ("Whilst the deep Secrets beyond practice goe," from the *Heroique Stanzas*, or, from *The Hind and the Panther*, "All wou'd be happy at the cheapest rate"). My own favorite line from Dryden is that kindest and most unbeatable of insults from *Mac Flecknoe*, "Trust Nature, do not labour to be dull." Dryden hardly seems to have trusted nature in his life, labored all his days in his literary profession, and very possibly died thinking himself a dull dog. The work he left is dense with such entirely Drydenian moments, all glittering fragments of his *Hamlet*, the masterpiece that was never written.

Frontispiece to *Marriage A-la-Mode,* from *The Dramatick Works of John Dryden, Esq.* (Tonson, London, 1735). By permission of the Yale University Libraries.

Appendix
The Yale Production of *Marriage A-la-Mode*

From the program for the production of Marriage A-la-Mode *at the Beinecke Rare Book and Manuscript Library, Yale University, October 5, 6, 7, and 8, 2000, directed by Murray Biggs:*

Dryden's Lineage
Eugene M. Waith

Dryden's comments on John Fletcher in his *Essay of Dramatick Poesie* come close to defining the sort of comedy Dryden was writing in *Marriage A-la-Mode*. He famously praised Fletcher and his collaborator, Francis Beaumont, for their imitation of "the conversation of gentlemen . . . whose wilde debaucheries and quickness of wit in repartees no poet before them could paint as they have done." And Neander, Dryden's spokesman in this Platonic dialogue, claims that "the greatest pleasure of the Audience is a chase of wit kept up on both sides and swiftly manag'd. And this our forefathers, if not we, have had in Fletcher's plays to a much higher degree of perfection than the *French* Poets can, reasonably, hope to reach." Palamede and Rhodophil are clearly quick-witted, if not wildly debauched, gentlemen of this Fletcherian cast, given the manners and language of Dryden's time.

Combined with this witty sort of comedy, which Dryden thought the best kind, is the heroic plot, so reminiscent of the lost and recovered royal children of Shakespeare's late romances and clearly derivative of Fletcherian tragicomedy, with its exploitation of highly emotional situations. In *Marriage A-la-Mode* the heroic and witty plots seem almost to rub off on each other, each partially commenting on the other. If Palmyra and Amalthea are not as silly as Melantha's attempts to imitate them, neither, perhaps, should we take them as seriously as they take themselves.

French Connections
Vincent Giroud

Dryden's title makes it clear that the play is about fashion, and equally clear (*Marriage A-la-Mode*, rather than "Fashionable Wedding") that it is about French fashion; and in this respect it is largely Melantha's play.

Fashion of any kind is based on the imitation of models and Melantha's real-life models are the so-called Précieuses who, in the 1650s, following the French civil war known as the Fronde, in which women played a prominent part, attempted to create a new code of civility regulating relations between the sexes. In literature, this movement found expression in the long neo-chivalrous romances of Madeleine de Scudéry, *Clélie* and *Artamène ou le Grand Cyrus,* which were both quickly translated into English: they are no doubt among the ones "drained," or rather *épuisés,* by Melantha, and by Dryden as well, since Cyrus is one of the apparent sources for the "serious" part of *Marriage A-la-Mode.* The Préciosité's influence can also be felt in the plays of Racine, the late work of Corneille, the libretti Quinault wrote for Lully, and Mme de Sévigné's letters. Molière's first stage success, *Les Précieuses ridicules* (1659), made his audience laugh at Cathos and Madelon, the daughters of a down-to-earth bourgeois who hopelessly ape the manners and language of their aristocratic models; but Célimène, the witty and coquettish heroine of *Le Misanthrope,* is also a Précieuse of sorts, and not at all ridiculous (nor is, closer to our time, the Roxane of *Cyrano de Bergerac*).

Melantha, as an aspiring Précieuse, may have her literary models in Cathos and her sister, but as a social climber she is also related to another Molière character, the hero of *Le Bourgeois gentilhomme,* obsessive imitator of aristocrats who make fun of him. The play triumphed in Paris in November 1670 and was still performed when *Marriage A-la-Mode* was written and staged: the songs "Ah, qu'il fait beau dans ces bocages" and "Vois, ma Climène," which Palamede and Melantha sing in act 5, both come from it, while Melantha's hilarious French lesson in act 3 was probably inspired by Monsieur Jourdain's initiation to linguistics.

These borrowings testify to Molière's popularity in England during the Restoration, usually through adaptation, from Medbourne's 1670 version of *Tartuffe,* Shadwell's *Miser* (1672), and Otway's *Cheats of Scapin* (1677), to Wycherley's *Country Wife* (1683), based on *L'école des femmes,* and Congreve's *Plain-Dealer* (1691), partly inspired by *Le Misanthrope.*

There is, of course, an added dimension to Melantha since, being "Sicilian" (i.e. English), she is a sort of fifth column unto herself as she tries to import into her reluctant island an imperialistic foreign culture: foreign manners, foreign literature, foreign vocabulary, hence all those French words which gave Dryden's printers—and have given his editors since—so much trouble. Melantha's insistence on peppering her speech with French idioms can be seen as an anticipation of the francophone Russian aristocrats of *War and Peace* or, in reverse and less extreme fashion, the anglophilia of Mme Swann in *A la recherche du temps perdu*. But Melantha's extremism is what makes her, anachronistically, such an endearing heroine to a modern audience. Her camp posturings, especially in male dress ("I'll sacrifice my life for French poetry") also anticipate the decadent aesthetes of the 1880s: by a felicitous coincidence, her fiancé à la mode, Palamded, it may be recalled, is the namesake of Baron de Charlus.

Staging *Marriage A-la-Mode*

MURRAY BIGGS

I CLAIM NO EXPERTISE IN THE STAGING OF DRYDEN, OR FOR THAT matter any of his contemporaries. I have taught the drama of the period once, and played Pinchwife in a production of *The Country Wife*. But until *Marriage A-la-Mode*, I had never directed a Restoration play. I came to it rather like Rhodophil leaping boldly ashore onto terra incognita.

When I announced *Marriage A-la-Mode* on the Yale campus, I was not exactly besieged by students wishing to audition for it. For modern actors, everything begins with character; and the first things that both my cast and I had to come to terms with was the disconcerting simplicity of most of Dryden's people: relative, that is, to what we are used to, say, in the mature Shakespeare, or in the modern theater of psychological realism. Only two of Dryden's characters—Polydamas and Amalthea—can, I think, be said to shift or develop in the way that contemporary actors like them to.

It is often, and wisely, said that 50 percent of a director's task lies in the casting. I might add that the other 50, at least with a play of this period, lies in the editing. And here another simply practical consideration enters in. Long experience has convinced me that, with few exceptions, no student production should run for more than two-and-a-half hours, including intermission. To ensure that limit on Dryden's play, I cut it by almost 20 percent. Inevitably, many Drydenians in our audience will have missed cherished lines, even some lines, perhaps, that the most expert would deem critically indispensable. Of course, any editing is a dangerously creative exercise: trimming even the odd lines can re-shape a character, a scene, or even the import of the whole play.

I did not consciously aim to change the play fundamentally; but to thin it only, and to stay true both to its careful structure and to what I understood its spirit to be. I resisted the temptation, for example, to cut more of the Palmyra-Leonidas exchanges than I actually did, feeling that my two actors could sustain enough of that hothouse verse without reducing their characters to the absurdity with which they are likely to be regarded by us sophisticated moderns. Much of Dryden's prologue, on the other hand, struck me as unspeakable, or at least as a too-alienating beginning for an uninitiated twenty-first-century audience. This problem was solved when my English Department colleague John Hollander sent me a modern version of the prologue written by a Columbia undergraduate for a Barnard College performance of the play fifty years ago. I was only a few lines into it when I realized that only one person could have penned this new prologue, even then: and that, of course, was Hollander himself.[1]

The most conspicuous of my cuts were probably those that abbreviated Dryden's account of Charles II's England, especially in act 3, scene 1, where Doralice goes on about court, city, and country. But there was one narrative change that came about, again, through contingency, and that had to do with Argaleon's role at the end of the masquerade, where Dryden has him use his disguise, which resembles Leonidas's, to learn of the young lovers' planned tryst:

Palmyra (to Argaleon): Leonidas, what means this quick return?
Argaleon (aside): O heav'n! 'tis what I fear'd.
Palmyra: Is ought of moment happen'd since you went?
Argaleon: No, Madam, but I understood not fully Your last commands
Palmyra: And yet you answer'd to 'em. Retire; you are too indiscreet a lover. I'll meet you where I promised.

This exchange was omitted simply because I needed the actor of Argaleon as a singer in the same scene, and he could hardly do both. The cut involved patching in some lines to cover the gap, and to provide a transition neglected by the playwright. I should add that we also corrected Dryden's misquotation of *Macbeth*, on the grounds that it seemed more probably his mistake than Palamede's.

The allusion to *Macbeth* recalls an earlier production of *Marriage A-la-Mode* at Yale, "adapted and presented by students" in early May 1935, in the courtyard of one of the residential colleges. All the actors were male. The students' edition was handsomely published, as the first of a projected series of "college comedies"; this text, far more radically reduced than our own, ends, amazingly, with *Macbeth*'s final cry: a choice that surely confirms the modern suspicion that the Bard was more deferentially received then than now, as if that pre-World War II audience had to be sent home from the Shakespeare imitation with the reassurance of the real thing ringing louder in their ears. That Yale production also corrects Dryden's quotation of *Macbeth*'s last line, but (as it happens) incorrectly. There are a few other rewritings; but of particular interest to a director are some detailed stage directions, and a tantalizingly cryptic footnote to Doralice's line to her husband in 5.1: "Then I have found my account in raising your jealousy, Oh 'tis the most delicate sharp sauce to a cloyed stomach." The footnote advises us that "at this point a celebrated incident occurred, which upset Mr. Sweet as Rhodophil, but amused his audience vastly." It turns out that Eugene Waith, Emeritus Professor of English at Yale, was sitting in the courtyard of Saybrook College for this performance, and he unlocks the mysterious incident following the mention of that "cloyed stomach." "Some of the actors were quite drunk," he recalls, and the reminder of stomachs tipped Rhodophil over the edge. He had to betake himself to the nearest bush, and throw up.

But the most intriguing feature of the New Haven edition of Dryden's play is its critical preamble: first a foreword by R. G. H., who (as Harold Love has suggested) is Roswell Gray Ham. Ham's biography of Otway and Lee had been published in 1931, and in 1935 he was a professor of English at Yale. (He went on to become president of Mount Holyoke College). His foreword describes Dryden's play as "modern to its fingertips, [speaking] without shame and with infinite wit a language that may be understood by the youth of today. It calls perhaps for a few excisions, but those in deference rather to taste than to morals." There follows a longer introduction by the play's editor, "W. A. A.," identified by Eugene Waith as William Appleton Aiken, then a graduate student resident in Saybrook College. Aiken develops the notion that the play "present[s] a gay and elaborate discussion of certain problems which may confront, at any time and in any place, those who have perhaps too rashly entered into that state called matrimony. In this respect the play is primarily designed as a bit of worldly advice to a lovelorn generation." The writer goes on to cite alternative, up-to-date solutions to those perennial problems: the advice of Marie Stopes, for example, mother of modern birth control; or (for the "cynically inclined"), Noel Coward's *Design for Living* (which had been seen for the first time in New York just two years earlier, and which is built round a love triangle); and finally, if "you would solve your problems in a different manner—well, there is always Andre Gide." All this is about the comic plot. The "secondary plot," "a pastoral romance in blank verse" (though not all that blank, if you remember), in the opinion of W. A. A. "retard[s] the action [and] obscure[s] the main purpose of the play." At Yale in 1935, at least, the solution seemed obvious. An "amputation was . . . performed and the entire secondary plot discarded. The limb thereby lost was never missed."

The language of Dryden's play proved alien to almost all my undergraduate actors, bright, attentive, and willing though they all were. The verse came somewhat more easily than the prose, no doubt because of its echoes of a Shakespeare that many students were already somewhat familiar with. The relentless couplets in the Leonidas-Palmyra duologues create a potentially disconcerting effect, since their Shakespearean originals (Florizel-Perdita, for example, in *The Winter's Tale*) are versified much more freely, in the usual manner of late Shakespeare. More surprising was the difficulty that most of my actors had with the comic prose, which is not nearly as easy to deliver as it looks: while the vocabulary is relatively easy (relative, again, to Shakespeare), the syntax is often not. Actors have to dig out those antitheses and double antitheses with every bit as much address as in Shakespeare; and there are more general problems of identifying the words that really key the meaning. At rehearsal, for example, one might have heard Palamede declaim thus, in response to Rhodophil's lament that his mistress's beauty is not enough to redeem her one "unpardonable" fault: "O friend, this is not an age to be critical in **beauty.** When we had good store of handsome **women,** and but few chapmen, you might have been more curious in your **choice**; but now the price is enhanc'd upon us, and all mankind set up for **mistresses** . . ." (Note an actor's characteristic tendency to stress the last word of a unit.) But the speaker's meaning is, I believe, more accurately rendered like this: "O friend, this is not an age to be critical in **beauty.** When we had **good** store of handsome women, and but few chapmen, you might have been more curious in your choice; but now the price is **enhanc'd** upon us, and **all mankind** set up for mistresses . . ." Despite my best efforts, not all these verbal roads were made smooth (in either prose or verse).

A slightly different problem emerged in the playing of Melantha. How good is her French? She is, so far as I can tell, completely literate in it as far as it goes. She seems to understand what all her French words mean, and to place them correctly. The fun had therefore to come from her mispronouncing them, which was easy enough to achieve, since the actress herself was happily innocent of the language, and was willing enough to stay so. She was also helped by contrast with Philotis and Palamede, both played by actors with naturally plausible French accents. All in all, these attentions to the verbal behaviors of the text claimed an unusually large share of rehearsal time.

Last, a word about the performance site. The Beinecke Rare Book and Manuscript Library at Yale proved a fortunate choice. Spectacular Restoration costumes played brilliantly against the largely gray translucent marble panels forming the outer wall of Gordon Bunshaft's noble building (1963). Opposite that backdrop stood the vivid reminder of a seventeenth-century gentleman's library—if on a rather grander scale; so that one might conceivably have half-imagined a performance of Dryden's play in his own time in one of the county houses he so affects to despise.

    1. Prologue
    (John Hollander)

(Spoken by Mr. Robert Laguardia as Hermogenes)

    Dear me! How dull and delicate we've grown
    Since the rough days when first this play was done:
    We play at work, and labor at our play;
    Our women's hair looks golden past its day;
    While our poor infants would be grey at birth
    Could they but know how little gold is worth.
    But rather than refer to tiresome lists
    I'd turn instead to all our dramatists
    Who weep and posture to themselves, and show it,
    Each writing like a sick Romantic poet,
    While poets write for stages in their souls,
    Poor verses, like their hose, all full of holes.
    Some poet once swore wit was clear enough
    Although the lines that bore the thought were rough,
    But modern wits might think in mis-spelled Greek,
    For all the thoughts that peek through their technique,
    Which they can't phrase, but make poor actors speak.
    Now in the play that we're to do tonight
    I do a smallish part, and have no right

To stand here, cursing weeds, while waving flowers,
For Dryden's age was quite as mad as ours;
But Theatre, freed from Puritanic rule,
Like a young lady raised in Convent School
Who came to dwell in Hewitt Hall instead,
Lived so gaily, that it might be said,
"She ran loose, old confinements all disrupted
And lived a while, before she was corrupted."
But here's enough . . . unless the play soon start,
This prologue'll be longer than my part.

Marriage A-la-Mode: Director's Initial Notes to Actors

Amalthea: A potentially tragic character who must not come across as maudlin or melodramatic. She bears a double burden (knowledge that her brother is a heel; unrequited love), yet the fact that she keeps both griefs hidden suggests an active inner life. But though perceptive and cautious, she is not just an observer either. We should feel deeply for her without her setting herself up as a martyr; in fact such a stance would alienate us. Overall, an attractive and sympathetic character, who deserves much better than we see her get.

Argaleon: The role should not be played too heavily. He is a snob and a political climber, but that does not mean his love for Palmyra cannot be genuine: she is the woman he has been waiting for, the only one good enough for him. He is all pride and passion, though much of the time that has to be bottled up. Not much of a sense of humor, and what there is is sarcastic. Think of a Spanish grandee whose view of the world comes from entirely above his ruff collar.

Artemis: She is a somewhat shadowy figure, who becomes most interesting if played as a smart and watchful courtier, who gives very little away. She is not sinister (quite the opposite); rather, she keeps her place and gets along with everyone through her gracious personality and diplomatic skill. She knows how much she can say, to whom, and when: everyone's natural confidante, who is a more powerful influence than the size of her role suggests; a kind of ballast in court politics and gossip.

Doralice: This is a particularly interesting character, because she has not quite lost her innocence. She is sophisticated, witty, and knows how to take care of herself, indeed is a match for anyone in society; yet she has not become seriously cynical. She is cool but not corrupt, vivacious and good-natured. Her inner assurance must be matched by physical poise. She teases the audience as well as Palamede: we may never be quite sure of what for her is "diversion" and what is seriously possible by way of amorous intrigue. Either way, she is capable of genuine affection and loyalty.

Eubulus: He is the surprise character of the play, held back until act 4, when he provides a second engine to the serious plot, just when it needs accelerating to the finish. Hermogenes immediately defers to him as his political and domestic superior; in fact, Eubulus takes over his role as the rightful heir's right-hand man. Though he has few lines, every one rings of the country's imminent emergency.

Hermogenes: The danger here is turning him into a caricature of the older man. Because of his narrative and moral importance, he must be played straight, with the full energy of his convictions up front. Whenever he speaks, we should feel the moral weight of the play behind him. Even his lie is told with moral justification, and an authority that we are not invited to question. He stands for integrity, courage, and the "natural" virtues of rural living: a model guardian to Leonidas and Palmyra.

Leonidas: He is the straight arrow of the piece, but his righteousness must sit easily and naturally on him, like all true-born nobility. He should contain no hint of stiffness, priggishness, or pomposity. He is earnest but not heavy; devoted to Palmyra but not sappily so; an impulsive creature, whose impulses are naturally—indeed almost unconsciously—right.

Melantha: The challenge is to find the balances to her obvious pretentiousness: she has some genuine knowledge of French (though her accent can still be atrocious); she is able to function at court (no mere upstart would get by); she should not seem a totally absurd idol for Rhodophil. Her French words and phrases must be "chosen" and isolated. The main thing, of course, is to have fun with her; she can hardly be too extravagant.

Rhodophil: He comes in second every time, both as lover and as courtier (Argaleon is the King's favorite). He needs to convey disillusionment with the "banes" of matrimony against the temptations of "forbidden" love (however unrealized). But at the same time he is captain of the king's guard, so he needs a strong military bearing and demeanor; perhaps it is this responsibility that impedes his romantic dreams.

Palamede: Clearly, he is the lecher of the piece, but the emphasis should be on witty (though serious, indeed calculated) flirtation, not blatant lust (except once or twice). The rivalry with

Rhodophil, like the coming-on to Doralice, should come across as an enjoyable game, so that the prevailing tone remains comic. There may be a serious sexual agenda under the banter, but the persona should remain bright, fast-moving, and attractive.

Palmyra: She is obviously the straight woman, the ingénue. At the same time, we should not feel that her integrity is conventional or inherited. She has been impeccably brought up, but in circumstances that have developed courage and independence of mind. Although not a natural rebel, she is willing and able to stand up for what she knows or believes is right, without seeming priggish or petulant. There is more to her than her "type" suggests: a fully-formed, three-dimensional character whom anyone would respect and admire.

Philotis (and Beliza): Although the two characters are generically akin, they need to be distinguished beyond the apron-change (perhaps one of them could be Irish). The main thing to keep in mind is that ladies' maids in this period (at least as they appear in the plays) were all "in-the-know." They were smart; potentially manipulative (though usually to comic effect); had often earned, through daily knowledge of their mistresses, the right to answer back; and were pert, even cheeky, with outsiders, especially to their ladies' would-be suitors, whom they were always ready to appropriate for themselves. They flatter or deny at will, usually in their own interests: worldly-wise (even mercenary), energetic, and engaging.

Polydamas: Although he is one of the two villains, he must not be played too simply so. Since the text shows him troubled by moral doubts, he needs to develop an inner life, which might be revealed to the audience by outbursts of anger, as if their very "irrationality" gave away the fact that this man is not quite as confident in his position as the position itself would normally allow a king to be. Still, authority comes to him naturally, and when he is on stage he must always command the space. Physique and voice should convey the sense of someone who deserves power, if not monarchy. This usurper is a natural leader, who commands respect, but is also capable of family love. An interestingly complex character.

Notes on Contributors

SUSANNAH MORTON BRAUND is Professor of Classics at Yale University. She has edited the satires of Juvenal and her books include *Roman Satirists and their Masks* (1996), *The Passions in Roman Thought and Literature* (1997), and *Latin Literature* (2002).

HOWARD ERSKINE-HILL is Professor of Literary History at Cambridge University. His books include *The Social Milieu of Alexander Pope* (1975), *The Augustan Idea in English Literature* (1983), *Poetry and the Realm of Politics* (1996), and *Poetry of Opposition and Revolution* (1996).

BARBARA EVERETT has held University posts and College Fellowships at Newnham College, Cambridge, and Somerville College, Oxford. Two collections of her essays are *Poets in Their Time: Essays on English Poetry from Donne to Larkin* (1986) and *Young Hamlet: Essays on Shakespeare's Tragedies* (1989). She has edited *All's Well That Ends Well* and *Antony and Cleopatra*. Recent publications include essays on Shakespeare's poems and sonnets and on modern Anglo-American poetry.

PAUL HAMMOND is Professor of Seventeenth-Century English Literature at the University of Leeds. He is co-editor with David Hopkins of the Longman Annotated English Poets edition of Dryden (1995-), and of *John Dryden: Tercentenary Essays* (2000). His monographs include *John Dryden: A Literary Life* (1991), *Love between Men in English Literature* (1995), and *Figuring Sex between Men from Shakespeare to Rochester* (2002).

IAN HIGGINS is a senior lecturer in English literature at The Australian National University in Canberra. He is the author of *Swift's Politics: A Study in Disaffection* (1994) and of several articles on Swift and Jacobite authors. He is a general editor of the Cambridge Edition of the Works of Jonathan Swift, in preparation.

EMRYS JONES is Goldsmiths' Professor of English at New College, Oxford. Among his publications are *Scenic Form in Shakespeare* (1971, 1985) and *The Origins of Shakespeare* (1977), and he has written on More, Jonson, Dryden, Pope, Johnson, and Byron. He has edited the *Poems* of Henry Howard, Earl of Surrey, *Antony and Cleopatra*, and *The New Oxford Book of Sixteenth-Century Verse*.

HAROLD LOVE is a Professor in the School of Literary, Visual and Performance Studies at Monash University, Melbourne. He has edited the complete works of Thomas Southerne (with R. J. Jordan) and of Rochester, as well as publishing widely on the interactions of written, oral and printed media in seventeenth-century England. His most recent book is *Attributing Authorship: An Introduction* (2002).

LAWRENCE MANLEY, Professor of English at Yale University, is the author of *Convention: 1500–1700* (1980) and *Literature and Culture in Early Modern London* (1995). He is currently writing a book on Strange's Men.

LOUIS MARTZ was Sterling Professor Emeritus of English at Yale University. His books included *The Poetry of Meditation*, *The Paradise Within: Studies in Vaughan, Traherne, and Milton* (1964), *Poet of Exile: a Study of Milton's Poetry* (1980, 1986) and *Many Gods and Many Voices: the Role of the Prophet in English and American Modernism* (1998). He edited H.D.'s *Collected Poems, 1912–1944* and the Yale edition of *The Complete Works of St. Thomas More*.

MAXIMILLIAN E. NOVAK is Professor Emeritus in the English Department at UCLA. The editor of two volumes in the recently completed California Edition of the Works of John Dryden, he also participated in several others. He has written widely on the literature of the Restoration, and his biography of Daniel Defoe was published in 2001.

ANNABEL PATTERSON is Sterling Professor of English at Yale University and the author, most recently, of *Nobody's Perfect: A New Whig Interpretation of History*.

CLAUDE RAWSON is Maynard Mack Professor of English at Yale University. His most recent books are *Satire and Sentiment*

1660–1830 (1994) and *God, Gulliver, & Genocide: Barbarism and the European Imagination, 1492–1945* (2001).

VALERIE RUMBOLD is Senior Lecturer in English at the University of Birmingham. She is author of *Women's Place in Pope's World* (1989) and editor of *Alexander Pope: The Dunciad in Four Books (1743)* (1999). She is currently one of the editors preparing the Longman Annotated English Poets edition of the poetry of Pope, and will be contributing a volume to the Cambridge Edition of the Works of Jonathan Swift.

AARON SANTESSO is Assistant Professor of English at the University of Nevada. He has published on Dryden, Pope, Hogarth, Defoe, and Delarivier Manley. He is currently working on a study of poetic education in seventeenth-century English public schools.

DAVID WOMERSLEY is Thomas Warton Professor of English Literature at the University of Oxford. He is editor of the three-volume edition of *The Decline and Fall of the Roman Empire* (2000), and *English Literature: Milton to Blake* (2000). His publications include *The Transformation of the Decline and Fall of the Roman Empire* (1998), and *Gibbon and the Watchmen of the Holy City: the Historian and his Reputation, 1776–1815* (2002).

STEVEN ZWICKER is Stanley Elkin Professor of Humanities at Washington University, St. Louis. He has written on Marvell, Milton, and Dryden and, more broadly, on the intersections of literary and political culture in early modern England. He has edited, with David Bywaters, a new *Selected Poems of John Dryden* and is preparing a *Companion to John Dryden* and for Blackwell's *Critical Biographies* series, *The Life of John Dryden*.

Index

Adams, J. N., 156n
Addison, Joseph, 241–42, 245
Aeschylus, 171–72
Aiken, William Appleton, 286
Alsop, Vincent, 25
Anderson, William S., 133, 137n, 157n
Aristotle, 170–71
Ashcraft, Richard, 19
Atterbury, Francis, 217, 230
Aubrey, John, 196n, 263
Auden, W. H., 56, 266, 276

Bailey, Cyril, 140
Baldwin, T. W., 175n
Beach, Thomas, 220–21
Beaumont, Francis, 162
Behn, Aphra, 265
Beljame, Alexandre, 86–87, 97
Bennet, Henry, Earl of Arlington, 201
Bentley, Richard, 237, 249
Bethel, Slingsby, 29, 212
Betterton, Thomas, 59
Biggs, Murray, 61
Blackmore, Richard, 239, 242
Bohun, Edward, 103n, 202
Boileau, Nicolas, 96, 178
Bolingbroke, Henry St. John, 228
Bourdieu, Pierre, 21
Boutell, Elizabeth, 45
Braden, Gordon, 185
Brady, Jennifer, 259n
Bramhall, John Bishop, 189–90
Braund, Susanna, 156n
Bredvold, Louis, 68
Brower, Reuben, 122n
Brown, Thomas, 217, 219, 230
Buckhurst. *See* Sackville, Charles, Lord Buckhurst (later Earl of Dorset)
Buckingham. *See* Villiers, George, Duke of Buckingham

Bunyan, John, 270, 273, 274
Burke, Edmund, 72–73
Busby, Dr., 127, 247
Butler, Martin, 34n
Butler, Samuel, 43
Bywaters, David, 64, 122

Caldwell, Tanya, 122n
Callot, Jacques, 92
Capel, Arthur, 73
Carafa, Giuseppe, 92
Care, Henry, 88
Carnochan, W. B., 155n
Casaubon, Isaac, 128
Cato, 63
Cavendish, Margaret, Duchess of Newcastle, 166, 174
Character of a Coffee House, 27
Charles I, 37, 88, 207, 254
Charles II, 15, 32, 56, 61, 65, 67, 72, 82–83n, 98, 99, 198, 203, 224
Chaucer, Geoffrey, 121, 173, 240
Cibber, Colley, 179n, 244, 254
Cibber, Theophilus, 231
Cicero, 63, 99
Civil War, 98, 167
Clarendon. *See* Hyde, Edward, Earl of Clarendon
Clark, Jonathan, 82n
Clarke, Samuel, 103n
Clingham, Greg, 256
Clayton, Thomas, 18
Coffee-Houses Vindicated, 28
College, Stephen, 208
Collier, Jeremy, 227–28, 231
Condell, Henry, 159–60, 161, 166, 168
Congreve, William, 100, 228, 265, 267
Cooper, Anthony Ashley, Earl of Shaftesbury, 16, 29, 65, 83n, 88, 91, 94, 99, 208–9, 212
Cordner, Michael, 264

295

INDEX

Corneille, Pierre, 53, 102n, 238, 282
Cotterill, Anne, 122n
Coward, Noel, 286–87
Croft, Herbert Bishop, 205–6
Cromwell, Oliver, 87, 91, 92, 209, 213, 225, 226
Crouch, Nathaniel, 103n
Crowne, John, 36

Danby. *See* Osborne, Thomas, Earl of Danby
Davenant, William, 86, 101n, 202, 203
Dearing, Vinton, 69–70, 75, 180
Defoe, Daniel, 270, 274
DeKrey, Gary, 19, 34n, 35n
De Laune, Thomas, 18, 26
Denham, John, 225
Dennis, John, 227, 231, 233n, 245
Derrida, Jacques, 167
Descartes, René, 185
Deutsch, Helen, 261n
DeVries, Jan, 18
Digges, Leonard, 162, 167
Dillon, Wentworth, Earl of Roscommon, 165–66
Donne, John, 216n, 270
Dorset. *See* Sackville, Charles, Lord Buckhurst (later Earl of Dorset)
Dover, Treaty of, 204
Drummond, William, 176n
Dryden, John
—Poems: *Absalom and Achitophel*, 28, 65, 68, 94, 99, 111, 114, 198, 231, 248, 255, 266, 275; *Alexander's Feast*, 101, 240, 266; *Annus Mirabilis*, 31, 109, 111, 158, 202, 207; *Astrea Redux*, 109; *Britannia Rediviva*, 109; *Eleonora*, 109; "Epilogue to *All for Love*," 207; "Epilogue to *The Duke of Guise*," 95; "Epilogue (To the King and Queen . . .)," 41; "Epilogue to *The Loyal Brother*," 24; "Epilogue to *Marriage A-la-Mode*," 36; "Epilogue to Sir Martin Mar-all," 50n; "Epilogue to *Tyrannick Love*," 271; *Fables*, 101, 105n, 109; *Heroique Stanza's*, 225, 277; *Hind and the Panther, The*, 32, 59, 61, 109, 111, 217, 254, 277; *Mac Flecknoe*, 24, 170, 204, 237, 253, 255, 266, 275–77; *Medall, The*, 16, 30, 94–95, 99, 101, 209, 210; "Prologue to *Albumanzar Revived*," 96; "Prologue to *All for Love*," 207; "Prologue to Aureng Zebe," 178n; "Prologue to the Duchess on her return from Scotland," 104n; "Prologue to *The Duke of Guise*," 25; "Prologue and Epilogue to the University of Oxford," 50n; "Prologue to *The Loyal General*," 24, 207; "Prologue to *Marriage A-la-Mode*," 36; "Prologue to *The Rival Ladies*," 40; "Prologue to *The Spanish Fryar*," 71; "Prologue to *The Tempest*," 170; "Prologue to *The Wild Gallant*," 23; *Religio Laici*, 55, 99; *Satires of Juvenal and Persius*, 43, 123; —, "De Rerum Natura," 139; —, "Sixth Satyr of Juvenal," 144; *Threnodia Augustalis*, 109, 215; "To Her Grace the Duchess of Ormonde," 121; "To the Memory of Mr. Oldham," 111, 121, 266, 268; "To My Dear Friend Mr. Congreve," 177n, 228, 237, 269, 270; "To My Honour'd Kinsman, John Driden," 90; "To My Honored Friend, Sir Robert Howard . . . ," 163, 168; "To Nathaniel Lee . . . ," 206; "To the Pious Memory of . . . Anne Killigrew," 59; "To Sir Godfrey Kneller," 105n, 174, 272; "Translation of the Latter Part of the third Book of Lucretius," 55–56, 166; *Works of Virgil*, 109, 223, 243, 250–51, 270
—Prose: "Argument of the First Satyr," 43; "Argument of the Sixth Satyr," 144–45; "Dedication to the *Aeneis*," 115, 226, 233n; "Dedication to *All for Love*," 207, 209; "Dedication to *Annus Mirabilis*," 15; "Dedication to *The Assignation*," 23; "Dedication to *Aureng-Zebe*," 56; "Dedication to *The Conquest of Granada*," 202–3; "Dedication to *Discourse . . . of Satire*," 220; "Dedication to *Don Sebastian*," 275; "Dedication to *The Duke of Guise*," 87; "Dedication to *Examen*

Poeticum," 274; "Dedication to *Georgics,*" 274; "Dedication to *The Rival Ladies,*" 165; "Dedication to *The Spanish Fryar,*" 70, 74;"Dedication to *The State of Innocence,*" 192; "Defence of the Epilogue. Or, an Essay on the Dramatique Poetry of the; Last Age," 204; *Discourse concerning the Original and Progress of Satire,* 32–33, 218,; 220, 224, 274; "Epistle to the Whigs," 28, 210; *Essay of Dramatick Poesie,* 158, 164, 271, 281; *His Majesties Declaration Defended,* 209–10; *History of the League,* 88–89, 94, 247; "Of Heroique Plays," 203; "Preface to *Absalom and Achitophel,*" 71; "Preface to *All for Love,*" 24, 169; "Preface to *Annus Mirabilis,*" 110, 114, 122 n; "Preface to *A Dialogue Concerning Women,*" 156 n; "Preface to *Fables,*" 109, 118, 173–74, 235, 236, 249, 260 n; "Preface to *Ovid's Epistles,*" 173; "Preface to *Religio Laici,*" 111, 215, 272; "Preface to *Plutarch's Lives,*" 239; "Preface to *Second Miscellany,*" 143–44; "Preface to *Sylvae,*" 111–12; "Preface to *The State of Innocence,* 171, 213; "Preface to *The Sullen Lovers,*" 205; "Preface to *Troilus and Cressida,*" 170, 190; "Preface to Walsh's *Dialogue,*" 156, 274; "To the Reader" (*The Hind and the Panther*), 228; "Vindication of *The Duke of Guise,*" 97
–Drama: *Albion and Albanius,* 87, 98; *All for Love,* 52, 54, 100, 172, 207, 264, 269, 272–73; *Amphytrion,* 58–59, 91, 100, 264, 265–66; *Aureng-Zebe,* 54–56, 172, 200, 265; *Cleomenes,* 58, 60; *Conquest of Granada,* 52–53, 202, 265*; Don Sebastian,* 53, 56–58, 62, 95–96, 97–98, 265, 273; *Duke of Guise,* 98; *Indian Emperour, The,* 172; *King Arthur,* 59, 61, 98, 99, 100, 104 n; *Love Triumphant,* 58, 59–60, 86; *Marriage A-la-Mode,* 23, 42, 61, 90, 265, 281; *Rival Ladies, The,* 265; *Secular Masque, The,* 268; *Sir Martin Mar-all,* 265; *Spanish Fryar,* 65, 94; *State of Innocence, The,* 180 , 199; *Tempest, The* (with Davenant), 88, 93; *Troilus and Cressida,* 96, 171;
Duckett, Lionel, 73
D'Urfey, Thomas, 21, 24, 93, 101, 104, 240

Ehrenpreis, Irvin, 223, 233 n
Eliot, T. S., 125, 181, 264, 268, 276
Ellis, Frank, 234 n
Epicurus, 168–69
Erskine-Hill, Howard, 253, 255, 264, 270
Etherege, George, 265; *Man of Mode, The,* 38, 205
Evelyn, John, 21
Evelyn, Mary, 52, 102 n, 202
Exclusion Crisis, 17, 19, 24, 70, 82, 208, 214

Fairfax, Thomas, 119
Fight Club, 89
Fitzharris, Edward, 208
Flecknoe, Richard, 164, 170, 205
Fletcher, John, 159, 172, 281
Foxon, David, 261 n
Frederic, Prince of Wales, 256
Friend, John, 227
Fronde, The, 92, 281–82
Frost, William, 137
Fujimura, Thomas, 122 n
Fuller, Thomas, 20, 164

Gagen, Jean, 185, 197 n
Gardiner, Anne Barbeau, 234 n
Gastrell, Francis, 230
Genette, Gérard, 232
George II, 237, 254
Gifford, William, 137
Gildersleeve, B. L., 129
Gildon, Charles, 179 n, 245
Giraffi, Alessandro, 92, 93
Glorious Revolution, 113
Godfrey, Edmund Berry, 208
Godfrey of Bouillon, 119
Godolphin, Sidney, 43
Gould, Robert, 22, 68, 178 n
Grandsen, K. W., 189
Graunt, John, 17
Great Fire, 37, 266

Griffin, Dustin, 196n
Grimes, Sarah, 138n
Guffey, George, 63, 93

Haley, David, 103n, 104–5n
Haley, K. H. D., 35n
Ham, Roswell Gray, 286
Hammond, Brean, 234n, 252, 262n
Hammond, Paul, 15, 56, 62, 122n, 139, 175n, 176n, 205, 208, 211, 216n, 254, 259n, 270
Harris, Bernard, 196n
Harris, Tim, 19
Harth, Philip, 64n, 68, 81n, 89, 95, 96, 103n
Hartsock, Mildred, 91
Haselrig, Arthur, 226
Hastings, Theophilus, Earl of Huntingdon, 72
Haughton, Lord. *See* Holles, John, Lord Haughton
Heidegger, Martin, 167
Heminge, John, 159–60, 161, 166, 168
Henderson, J. G., 124, 126–27, 136, 137n
Herodotus, 220, 238
Hervey, John Baron, 251
Higgins, Ian, 234
Higgons, Bevill, 179n
Hobbes, Thomas, 86, 89, 189
Hollander, John, 285
Holles, John, Lord Haughton, 74
Homer, 119–20, 121, 123, 153, 173, 239, 240, 242
Hooley, D. M., 124, 126, 129, 137
Hopkins, David, 62, 139, 173, 178n
Horace, 20, 21, 62, 123–25, 136, 170
Howard, Edward, 202
Howe, John, 26, 32
Howell, James, 93
Hume, Robert, 68, 81n, 97, 103n
Huntingdon. *See* Hastings, Theophilus, Earl of Huntingdon
Hyde, Anne, Duchess of York, 192, 213
Hyde, Edward, Earl of Clarendon, 213, 226

Interregnum, 167

James II, 56, 58, 60–61, 87, 91, 94, 97, 103n, 192, 200, 217, 222, 228–29, 230, 254

Jefferson, D. W., 196n
Jensen, James, 166, 176–77n
Jermyn, Henry, Earl of St. Albans, 213
Johnson, B. S.: "The Unfortunates," 226–27
Johnson, Maurice, 231, 232n
Johnson, Samuel, 134, 188, 192, 196n, 231, 236, 251, 259n, 265, 266, 275
Johnson, W. R., 156n
Jonson, Ben, 159, 167, 168, 170, 239–40; *Catiline*, 46; *Epicoene*, 124; "To the memory of my beloved, the author Mr. William Shakespeare," 160–62
Juvenal, 21, 120, 123, 127, 134, 139, 246

Keeble, N. H., 201
Kenyon, J. P., 49n
Kéroualle, Louise de, Duchess of Portsmouth, 47, 100
Kerrigan, William, 185
Killigrew, Thomas, 92, 202
King, Bruce, 189–90
Kinsley, James, 61
Kneller, Godfrey, 267, 272
Knolles, Richard, 214
Kramer, David, 122n

Larkin, Philip, 271
Lawrence, D. H., 89
Leapor, Mary, 257
Lee, Guy, 129
Lee, Nathaniel, 206; *Duke of Guise, The*, 89; "Epilogue" to *Theodosius*, 48
Legouis, Pierre, 214
Lennard, John, 221–22
Leranbaum, Miriam, 262n
Letter from a Person of Quality, 210
Levine, Joseph, 259n
Lewis, C. S., 175n
Livy, 238
Lobb, Stephen, 25, 26
Locke, John, 99, 104n
Longinus, 171–72, 178n
Louis XIV, 56, 89, 100, 202, 204
Love, Harold, 286
Lovejoy, Arthur, 175n
Lucan, 124, 128

INDEX 299

Luce, J. V., 232n
Lucretius, 59, 123, 125, 135, 139, 166
Lully, Jean-Baptiste, 282
Luther, Martin, 217, 230
Luttrell, Narcissus, 208

Mack, Maynard, 247, 259n, 260n
Maimbourg, Louis, 88–89, 94, 247
Malone, Edmund, 86
Manley, Lawrence, 36
Marshall, William, 70
Martial, 21
Martindale, Charles, 136
Marvell, Andrew, 88, 199, 270; *Account of the Growth of Popery and Arbitrary Government, An*, 208; *First Anniversary*, 209–11; *Fleckno, an English Priest at Rome*, 205; *Historicall Poem, An*, 214; *Horatian Ode*, 210–11; *last Instructions to the Painter, The* 207, 212; *Miscellaneous Poems*, 210; *Mr. Smrike, or the Divine in Mode*, 205–6; *Rehearsal Transpros'd. The*, 214
Mary II, 24, 59, 131
Masaniello, 92, 97
Mason, H. A., 267
Maurer, A. E. Wallace, 216n
McCabe, Richard, 84n
McFadden, George, 201
McLaverty, James, 261n
Meres, Francis, 165, 173
Milbourne, Luke, 227, 239
Milhous, Judith, 68, 81n
Milton, John, 16, 32, 119–20, 163–64, 171, 180, 199, 205, 206, 270, 274; *L'Allegro*, 163; *Paradise Lost*, 22, 163, 180, 199, 205, 209, 210, 213, 273; *Tenure of Kings and Magistrates, The*, 213
Miner, Earl, 20, 264, 266
Molière, 282
Molyneux, William, 104n
Monmouth. *See* Scott, James, Duke of Monmouth
Montaigne, Michel de, 63
Montagu, Mary Wortley, 251
Montague, Charles, 219–20
Moore, John R., 232n
Morgenstern, Christian, 275
Mouffe, Chantal, 102n

Mulgrave. *See* Sheffield, John, Earl of Mulgrave (later Duke of Buckingham)
Murdoch, Iris, 268

Needham, Marchamont, 214
Newman, Richard, 101n
Nichol, Donald, 257
Nicholson, Marjorie, 261n
Nisbet, R. G. M., 123, 128–29
North, Roger, 88, 98, 102
Novak, Maximillian, 35
Novarr, David, 232

Oates, Titus, 208, 213
Oldham, John, 21, 51n
Oldmixon, John, 245
Orsmby-Lennon, Hugh, 232n
Osborne, Thomas, Earl of Danby, 207, 209
Otway, Thomas, 36, 249, 265
Ovid, 110–11, 121, 123, 173, 174
Owen, John, 26
Owen, Susan, 69, 70
Oxford Parliament, 208

Pacuvius, 128
Palmer, Barbara, 215
Park, Robert, 18
Parker, Bishop, 88
Parkyns, William, 227
Patterson, Annabel, 216n
Payne, Henry Nevil, 88, 96
Pecora, Vincent, 104n
Penn, William, 26, 27
Pepys, Samuel 23, 266, 270
Persius, 123
Peterson, R. G., 122, 137n
Petty, William, 17
Phalaris Affair, 237
Philips, Ambrose, 242–44
Plato, 63, 168
Player, Sir Thomas, 27
Plutarch, 237
Pocock, J. G. A., 104n
Pope, 136, 227, 235, 276; *Dunciad, The*, 125, 235; *Epistle to Arbuthnot*, 238, 241–42; *Epistle to Bathhurst*, 135, 255; *Epistle to Burlington*, 255; "Epistle to Henry Cromwell, Esq., An," 252; *Essay on Criticism*, 178n,

235, 238–40; *Essay on Man*, 255; *Imitations of Horace*, 136, 179, 238; "Parallel of the Characters of Mr. Dryden and Mr. Pope," 235; *Peri Bathous*, 242; "Preface to the *Iliad*," 239; "To Augustus," 249
Popish Plot, 68, 70, 103n, 207, 214
Portsmouth. *See* Kéroualle, Louise de, Duchess of Portsmouth
Pound, Ezra, 126
Poussin, Nicolas, 177n
Prior, Matthew, 219–20
Proust, Marcel, 283
Purcell, Henry, 274

Quinault, Philippe, 282
Quintilian, 172, 238–39

Racine, Jean, 238, 265, 282
Radcliffe, Alexander, 34n
Ranters, 25
Rapin, 96, 265
Rawls, John, 101–2n
Rawson, Claude, 233n
Real, Hermann, 226, 233n
Remarques on the Conversations of the Town, 27
Reverand, Cedric, 256
Richardson, Jonathan, 258n
Ricks, Christopher, 178n
Rochester, 41, 199–200, 207, 267, 270, 272; "Against Reason and Mankind," 46; "An Allusion to Horace," 23–24, 43, 199–200, 204, 250–51; "Artemzia to Chloe," 39, 43; "The Maimed Debauchee," 46; "A Pastoral Dialogue between Alexis and Strephon," 47; "Song," 47; "Timon," 42
Roper, Alan, 95
Roscommon. *See* Dillon, Wentworth, Earl of Roscommon
Rousseau, George, 261n
Roworth, Wendy Wassyng, 103n
Rumbold, Valerie, 261n
Rye House Plot, 82n, 88, 91, 99
Ryswick, Treaty of, 98, 101

Sacheverel, William, 73
Sackville, Charles, Lord Buckhurst (later Earl of Dorset), 24, 43, 199, 220
Salingar, Leo, 175n
Sallust, 238
Scott, James, Duke of Monmouth, 76–77, 201, 208
Scott, Jonathan, 19, 82n
Scott, Walter, 61, 65, 87
Schmitt, Carl, 90, 99, 102n
Scudéry, Madeleine de, 282
Second Advice to the Painter, 207
Second Dutch War, 202, 206, 213n
Second Test Act, 208
Sedley, Charles, 23, 24, 42, 199
Seneca, 99
Settle, Elkanah, 214, 244, 258, 275
Sévigné, Madame de, 282
Seward, Mrs., 268
Shadwell, Thomas, 24, 36, 43, 165, 205, 254, 275
Shaftesbury. *See* Cooper, Anthony Ashley, Earl of Shaftesbury
Shakespeare, William, 52, 54, 78–79, 158, 237, 239–40, 249, 263, 281; *Antony and Cleopatra*, 54, 78–79, 172, 269; *Cymbeline*, 264; *Hamlet*, 263; *Henry V*, 79; *Henry VI*, 264; *Julius Caesar*, 171; *King John*, 264; *King Lear*, 61, 78; *Macbeth*, 131, 286; *Othello*, 188, 273; *Romeo and Juliet*, 263; *Tempest, The*, 58; *Timon of Athens*, 264; *Troilus and Cressida*, 96; *Winter's Tale, The*, 160, 166–67, 287
Sheffield, John, Earl of Mulgrave (later Duke of Buckingham), 22
Sidney, Algernon, 72, 73
Simmel, Georg, 20, 22
Simonsuuri, Kirsti, 178n
Skelton, John, 125
Smedley, Jonathan, 243
Smith, David Nichol, 177n, 276
Smith, Warren, 156n
Southerne, Thomas, 40, 265
Sowerby, Robin, 178n
Spaddo, Micco, 92
Spence, Joseph, 238, 259n
Spencer, John, 21
Spenser, Edmund, 243, 244
Steele, Richard, 250
Sterne, Lawrence, 97

Stevens, Wallace, 66–67, 75, 80
Sullivan, J. P., 123, 126, 127, 128
Swift, Jonathan, 217, 274; "Battle of the Books," 116–17, 225–26; "Description of a City Shower," 221, 223; *Gulliver's Travels*, 228; "Holyhead Journal, 1727," 228; "On the Burning of Whitehall in 1698," 223; "On Poetry: A Rhapsody," 222–23; *Project for the Advancement of Religion, A*, 227–28; *Tale of a Tub*, 116, 217, 272; "To Congreve," 228; *Verses on the Death of Dr. Swift*, 224–25
Swift, Thomas, 220, 224

"Tatham, John, 175 n
Tate, Nahum, 176 n
Temple, William, 65–66
Theobald, Lewis, 237, 249, 254, 258
Third Dutch War, 203, 206
Thomas, Claudia, 262 n
Thomlinson, Charles, 123
Thormählen, Marianne, 45
Thucydides, 238
"To Mr. Dryden, on his Excellent Translation of Virgil," 133
Tolstoy, Leo, 282
Tonson, Jacob, 227
Turner, Francis, 206
Turner, Henry, 213
Turner, James G., 35 n
Tyrrell, James, 99, 104 n

Vanbrugh, John, 265
Van Doren, Mark, 264, 266, 267
Villers, Barbara, 213
Villiers, George, Duke of Buckingham, 199–200; *Rehearsal, The*, 23, 29, 36, 53, 199, 218, 245, 267
Virgil, 62, 109, 123, 169, 173, 219, 239, 243, 244

Waith, Eugene, 286
Walker, Keith, 139, 266–67
Wallace, John, 98
Waller, Edmund, 165, 202
Walpole, Robert, 254, 257
Walsh, William, 249
Walters, Lucy, 76
Walzer, Michael, 25
Warburton, William, 251, 255, 257
Ward, Charles, 196 n
Ward, Patience, 27
Warren, John, 162–63
Waterhouse, Edward, 18
Webster, John, 177 n
Whitman, Walt, 267
Whyman, Susan, 39
William III, 60, 61, 97, 98, 100, 118, 122 n, 128, 131, 227, 229, 231, 254
Williams, Raymond, 175 n
Willman, Robert, 82 n
Winkler, Martin, 155–56 n
Winn, James, 23, 59, 62, 68, 156 n, 196 n, 209, 252, 253, 260 n, 261 n, 262 n
Winnington, Francis, 73
Winterbottom, William, 91
Wither, George, 225
Woodhead, Abraham, 217, 230
Wooley, Hannah, 39, 45
Word for the City, A, 17
Wren, Christopher, 274
Wyatt, Thomas, 132
Wycherley, William, 43, 240–41, 228, 244; *Country Wife, The*, 39, 40, 265

York, Duchess of. *See* Hyde, Anne, Duchess of York

Zimbardo, Rose, 253
Žižek, Slavoj, 89
Zwicker, Steven, 122, 255